Alienation and Nature in Environmental Philosophy

Many environmental scientists, scholars and activists characterize our situation as one of alienation from nature, but this notion can easily seem meaningless or irrational. In this book, Simon Hailwood critically analyses the idea of alienation from nature and argues that it can be a useful notion when understood pluralistically. He distinguishes different senses of alienation from nature pertaining to different environmental contexts and concerns, and draws upon a range of philosophical and environmental ideas and themes including pragmatism, eco-phenomenology, climate change, ecological justice, Marxism and critical theory. His novel perspective shows that different environmental concerns – both anthropocentric and nonanthropocentric – can dovetail, rather than compete, with each other, and that our alienation from nature need not be something to be regretted or overcome. His book will interest a broad readership in environmental philosophy and ethics, political philosophy, geography and environmental studies.

SIMON HAILWOOD is Senior Lecturer in Philosophy at the University of Liverpool. He is the author of *Exploring Nozick: Beyond Anarchy, State and Utopia* (1996) and *How to be a Green Liberal: Nature, Value and Liberal Philosophy* (2004). He is also Managing Editor of the journal *Environmental Values*.

Alienation and Nature in Environmental Philosophy

Simon Hailwood
University of Liverpool

CAMBRIDGE
UNIVERSITY PRESS

University Printing House, Cambridge CB2 8BS, United Kingdom

Cambridge University Press is part of the University of Cambridge.

It furthers the University's mission by disseminating knowledge in the pursuit of education, learning and research at the highest international levels of excellence.

www.cambridge.org
Information on this title: www.cambridge.org/9781107081963

© Simon Hailwood 2015

This publication is in copyright. Subject to statutory exception and to the provisions of relevant collective licensing agreements, no reproduction of any part may take place without the written permission of Cambridge University Press.

First published 2015

A catalogue record for this publication is available from the British Library

Library of Congress Cataloguing in Publication data
Hailwood, Simon A.
Alienation and nature in environmental philosophy / Simon Hailwood, University of Liverpool.
    pages   cm
Includes bibliographical references and index.
ISBN 978-1-107-08196-3 (hardback)
1. Human ecology–Philosophy.   2. Environmental sciences–Philosophy.
3. Human beings–Effect of environment on–Philosophy.   4. Alienation
(Philosophy)   I. Title.
GF21.H345 2015
304.201–dc23
2015005649

ISBN 978-1-107-08196-3 Hardback

Cambridge University Press has no responsibility for the persistence or accuracy of URLs for external or third-party internet websites referred to in this publication, and does not guarantee that any content on such websites is, or will remain, accurate or appropriate.

For Jan and Verity

Contents

	Acknowledgements	*page* viii
	Introduction	1
1	Alienations and natures	16
2	Pragmatists and sea squirts	49
3	Landscape	86
4	Nonhuman nature: estrangement	124
5	Nonhuman nature: alienation	155
6	Estrangement from the natural world	185
7	Entailments and entanglements	223
8	Concluding remarks	248
	References	253
	Index	262

Acknowledgements

I have given talks on topics covered in this book at universities in Dortmund, Edinburgh, Essen, Lampeter, Lancaster, Manchester, Münster, Newport, Oxford, Reading and Reykjavik. I am grateful to the participants in the various workshops, conferences and seminars involved for their comments. I was greatly helped in developing the ideas in this book by discussions at workshops in Liverpool and Germany on the 'New Thinking on Alienation' research networking project that I organized with the assistance of Professors Logi Gunnarsson and Michael Quante (Arts and Humanities Research Council, AH/H013030/1, 2010–11). I am grateful also to colleagues at Liverpool for their helpful comments on my works in progress. I cannot remember now exactly who said what, where and when but I would like to thank the following in particular for their constructive comments and discussion in one or more of the contexts I have mentioned: Chris Bartley, Isis Brook, Gideon Calder, Clare Carlisle, Stephen Clark, Andrew Dobson, Tim Henning, Daniel Hill, Catriona McKinnon, Thomas Schramme, Kate Soper, Piers Stephens, Alison Stone, Steven Vogel, Daniel Whistler and Marcel Wissenburg.

I owe special thanks to my colleague Professor Gillian Howie, who passed away in 2013 after a long struggle with cancer. Gill was inspirational in many ways. In relation to this book she convinced me to take more seriously than I had been doing the insights of Hegel and Marx. Had she seen the final result I am sure she would still think I fail to take them sufficiently seriously. I deeply regret the end of that discussion and miss her kind and critical presence. I owe special thanks also to Logi Gunnarsson for the discussions we have had since he was a colleague at Liverpool several years ago. A central argument of this book is that, contrary to popular opinion, alienation from nature can be a 'good thing', something to be welcomed to some extent in some ways and in some contexts. The initial impetus for this thought was discussion in the light of institutional developments that we could not avoid and could not wholly condemn, yet could not fully identify with either. We thought it not obvious that the resulting state of alienation, if such it was, should be considered something one *ought* to seek to overcome, insofar as one could. The next thought was that perhaps this notion of a condition of alienation that, while not unqualifiedly positive, is not something one ought to overcome (or maybe something one ought not to overcome) could be generalized to apply to areas of ongoing philosophical interest to us. In terms of my own interests, for example, it might characterize certain conceptions of the relation between citizen and state. And it might bring out aspects of our relation to nature 'as other', a topic I had been working on for a while. I am not sure that I would have followed up this line of thought had it not been for Logi's interest in and encouragement of it.

My thanks also to Hilary Gaskin and Rosemary Crawley at Cambridge University Press for their kind and patient assistance, and to Andrew Dobson and an anonymous reviewer who read and commented helpfully on the highly imperfect draft manuscript. I must also thank my family – especially my wife, Jan – for their loving support during the writing of this book, not least because I think it was an alienating experience for them at times, and not always in a particularly good way.

It is usual at this point to say that none of the above bears any responsibility for what follows. And of course none of them would agree with all of it; some will disagree with most – if not all – of it. So I hereby absolve them. Having said that, they did at least encourage me to some extent. It is for the reader to decide whether they were right to do so.

In various parts of the book I expand upon previously published material. Chapter 2 includes material from 'Landscape, Nature and Neopragmatism' published in *Environmental Ethics* (29 February 2007, pp. 131–49), and Chapter 3 includes material from my review of Peter Cannavò's book *The Working Landscape*, published in *Organization and Environment* (22 February 2009, pp. 262–5). With the permission of Taylor & Francis Ltd, Chapter 5 draws upon 'Disowning the Weather', *Critical Review of International Social and Political Philosophy* (14 February 2011, pp. 215–34), and the Introduction and Chapters 2–6 include material from 'Alienations and Natures' published in *Environmental Politics* (21 June 2012, pp. 882–900). With the permission of Springer Science + Business Media, Chapters 6 and 7 include material from 'Nature, Estrangement and "the Flesh"', *Ethical Theory and Moral Practice* (17 January 2014, pp. 71–85).

Introduction

0.1 Environmental crisis and alienation from nature

The claim that we are in some deeply unfortunate way 'alienated from nature' is an old one, going back at least to Rousseau. It is a claim that continues to resonate in the context of our current environmental woes. We live in a time of anthropogenic mass extinction, serious climate change, ecosystem destruction, large-scale soil erosion and ocean acidification. Many believe that such matters, together with serious environmental injustice and the steady depletion of nonrenewable resources, constitute an environmental crisis that shows there is something seriously amiss with our relationship to nature. And many think that what is seriously amiss is that we are, or have become, alienated from nature.

References to an environmental *crisis* might seem overdramatic; perhaps even mere hyperbole designed to empower environmental organizations, parties and scientists, much as talk of *economic* crises serves to further empower certain other interest groups. Certainly, crisis-talk can be dangerous and should not be engaged in lightly.[1] On the other hand, if we bear in mind the ordinary meaning of a crisis as a time of great difficulty calling urgently for important and difficult decisions, then references to a current environmental crisis seem undeniably justified. The scale of problems such as those just mentioned make environmental crisis-talk reasonable whether we look at the situation anthropocentrically, taking into account only human interests, or nonanthropocentrically, taking account of nonhuman interests or the plight of nature 'for its own sake' too. It is a further issue, of course, whether talk of our *alienation from nature* is also reasonable or helpful. Invoking the idea of such alienation suggests that something fairly fundamental has gone awry; something calling for radical critique and remedies. At least in this respect it chimes with references to a crisis: we are confronted not just

---

[1] See Smith (2011) for an interesting analysis of the dangers inherent in convincing the powerful that we are in an environmental crisis situation.

2   Introduction

by another set of problems to be solved by standard techniques, but an environmental crisis that will be resolved only if we overcome our alienation from nature.

Unsurprisingly then this theme is present especially in the more radical perspectives within environmental philosophy, including deep ecology, eco-feminism and bioregionalism, which relate environmentally problematic forms of thought and action directly to wider social and political problems. Presumably most radical of all is the 'primitivist' perspective of writers such as John Zerzan who argue that the environmental crisis was inevitably set in train once our distant ancestors left behind their hunter-gatherer life in the wilderness, took to agriculture and settled in communities with increasingly complex divisions of labour and hierarchical social structures. For our own good, as well as the good of nature, we need to re-acquire as much as we can the closeness to nature enjoyed by humanity before the intervention of civilization (Zerzan 1994).

Not all talk of alienation from nature has quite such radical intent of course. In wider culture too the claim that we are unfortunately alienated from nature is present in some popular nature writing,[2] in the stances of environmental movements and organizations and in some of the pronouncements of naturalists and commentators on environmental issues. For example, the widely respected British broadcaster and naturalist Sir David Attenborough has warned that modern urban living has left people dangerously 'out of touch with nature' (*The Guardian* 2011). Consider also that the idea behind so-called Nature Deficit Disorder (NDD) is that various maladies of the modern world, including depression, diabetes and attention deficit disorders, are the result of an indoors way of life in urbanized environments with minimal interaction with nature. For this reason such problems and disorders are sometimes said to be the 'cost of our alienation from nature' (Louv 2010). The cure is supposed to involve more interaction with nature, although not necessarily to the extent of dismantling civilization along with the biomedical technologies and institutions required to diagnose the disorders in the first place.

Indeed something like this is what people often seem to have in mind when they talk of alienation from nature: modern urban living, industry and technology, and associated behaviour and intellectual trends have made us think, feel and act in ways that make sense only if we are not really part of a wider nature.[3] For example, in a recent book the

[2] Sometimes the theme is completely explicit, as in the poet Melanie Challenger's book *On Extinction: How We Became Estranged from Nature* (Challenger 2011).

[3] It is sometimes added, without going the extra, primitivist mile, that pre-industrial, agricultural society had a 'closer' awareness and appreciation of wider natural processes. See, for example, Challenger (2011).

Environmental crisis and alienation from nature

environmental activist and former director of Friends of the Earth Tony Juniper discusses various ways in which we depend on nature and yet fail to take account of this economically and politically (Juniper 2013). Political and economic short-termism very often holds sway regardless of the long-term damage done to the natural systems on which economic, political and all other social systems depend (Juniper 2013, ch. 11). Much mainstream economic thinking discounts as 'externalities' ecological damage and the degrading of natural systems despite the evidence and warnings of the consequences of this. Much economic discourse and decision-making then proceeds irrationally *as if* nature was an indefinitely self-replenishing storehouse of resources we visit to take things back for profitable employment within our own entirely separate little human world (Juniper 2013, e.g., 278f).

Juniper also discusses the version of the view that we are somehow 'cut off' from nature involved in claims about NDD. Sometimes these are underwritten by an application of the evolutionary psychological concept of 'environment of evolutionary adaptedness'. This refers to the environmental context in which a particular species acquired its adaptive features. The idea is that, like other species, we flourish best in environments that are significantly similar to the natural conditions in which we evolved and so to which our senses and capacities are best adapted (e.g., Juniper 2013, pp. 254ff). In our case this was a savannah environment. Thus, according to the 'biophilia hypothesis', we are predisposed to prefer and flourish best in the company of certain kinds of flora and fauna; in particular, according to the 'savannah hypothesis', those significantly similar to the savannahs of East Africa.[4] Not that we should seek to fully recreate the conditions of the savannah, but it is bound to make us ill when we have little or no access to suitable 'green space' or insufficient contact with certain kinds of plants and nonhuman animals. And the illnesses associated with NDD are bad not only for the individuals suffering them. The sufferers often need time off work and the standard medical treatments are very expensive. Lack of provision of adequate 'contact with nature' is therefore *economically* irrational (Juniper 2013, ch. 10).

That our environmental problems are wrapped up in some way with our alienation from nature seems like an important claim then, one we should take notice of. But what does it mean? How exactly should we understand the idea of alienation from nature? There are plenty of

---

[4] See, for example, Kellert and Wilson (1993). The idea that human well-being is best served by an environment significantly similar to that in which we originally evolved is contestable of course. See Joye and De Block (2011) for a review of empirical and conceptual problems with the biophilia and savannah hypotheses.

4 Introduction

descriptions of our environmental situation as involving various deeply problematic political, ethical, psychological and social elements. But there has not been much focus on the idea of alienation from nature itself. There has not been much discussion of what is really added to our picture of the problems by saying they are a matter of our 'alienation from nature', rather than simply ignorance, short-sightedness, greed, injustice, laziness and unhealthy indoor sedentary lifestyles, for example. Why not just say the environmental crisis is a function of these common or garden defects and frailties, albeit amplified to unprecedented proportions by massive increases in human population and economic development? The situation is bad enough described in those terms, it might be added, without the portentous talk of alienation from nature. What does such talk contribute beyond some occasional extra rhetorical leverage in the struggle to embed environmental issues more deeply within the public imagination? In this book I discuss what 'alienation from nature' should mean. I aim to clarify and explore the notion as one that is indeed helpful in the context of our complex, multifaceted environmental crisis.

0.2   Pleistocene or Anthropocene?

At the outset, however, it is perhaps unsurprising that little attention has been given to the meaning of 'alienation from nature'. A little thought quickly reveals such apparently serious problems with the idea that it can easily seem better to leave it alone as a piece of hazy and misleading rhetoric, or just to drop it altogether. Some of these problems turn on reducing our environmental predicaments to a condition of alienation from nature to be overcome in favour of a difficult to specify 'oneness' with it. There are dangers here of naive romanticism and irrational nostalgia, and of 'anti-progressive' references to 'natural essences', harmonies and blueprints of human moral order outside human history, with which we ought to be in touch. Dangers also arise from the way alienation has been shaped as a critical social and political concept by Hegel and Marx and the traditions of thought they have inspired. These seem vulnerable to environmental critique insofar as they either equate overcoming alienation from nature with assimilation and mastery of it, or eliminate consideration of nature by focusing entirely on the alienation of humanity from itself and from the products of its labour.

Pushed to do some work of its own then, the idea of overcoming pernicious alienation from nature can quickly suggest pictures of us as either somehow submerging ourselves within nature or submerging nature within us; assimilating it to the humanized artefactual world we are busily making. Neither picture seems very plausible or attractive. The

Pleistocene or Anthropocene?

former is compounded by apparently irrational mythologizing of previous conditions of harmony or closeness held out as conditions we need to retrieve. Again, primitivism is the starkest and most dramatic version of this. We should give up our technology, civilization, even agriculture, and 'return to the Pleistocene'. We should retrieve the closeness to nature that was lived out by humanity in Palaeolithic hunter-gatherer mode, a closeness from which we fell:

Before agriculture was midwifed in the Middle East, humans were in the wilderness. We had no concept of 'wilderness' because everything was wilderness and we were a part of it. But with irrigation ditches, crop surpluses, and permanent villages, we *became apart from the natural world* ... Between the wilderness that created us and the civilization created by us grew an *ever-widening rift*.[5]

Obviously, seeking to close up this rift by dismantling civilization is a project with limited appeal, and presumably retaining the original edenic closeness to nature was not a decisive consideration for our distant ancestors either. Nor is it very plausible to suppose that late Pleistocene humanity lived in a close harmony with nature, if that means something like 'refrained altogether from widespread ecological impact or unsustainably destructive practices'.[6]

In an interesting – and ironic – contrast to the proposal that we *return to the Pleistocene* is the increasingly popular suggestion that we should now take ourselves to be living in a new and unprecedented era. This idea has not yet been adopted formally by the scientific community, but is gaining ground among environmental scientists.[7] The claim is that the scale of human impact on the Earth, especially since the Industrial Revolution, is so great and the reshaping of Earth systems so profound and long lasting that it justifies declaring the end of the (now) previous geological era (the Holocene, which succeeded the Pleistocene at the end of the last Ice Age some 10,000–15,000 years ago) and the start of a new one: the Anthropocene (or 'new human') era.[8] Whether

---

[5] Dave Foreman, founder of the Earth First! movement, quoted by William Cronon in his influential critique of the idea of 'pure wilderness' (Cronon 1995, p. 83, emphasis added). I return to the importance of not equating nature with pure wilderness at several places in this book.

[6] For example, although the extent to which the wave of megafauna extinctions in the late Pleistocene were anthropogenic is a matter of controversy, human predation is generally believed to have been a significant causal factor.

[7] See for example, ecologist Erle Ellis (2011) and geologist Jan Zalasiewicz (Zalasiewicz et al. 2011), and the other papers in issue 369 of the *Philosophical Transaction of the Royal Society A*, a special issue devoted to this topic.

[8] The current Anthropocene discourse was initiated mainly by the atmospheric chemist Paul Crutzen (e.g., Crutzen 2002), winner of a Nobel Prize in 1995 for his research on the ozone layer, and well known also for his work on the likely 'nuclear winter' outcome of nuclear warfare.

6   Introduction

this revision of geological eras and the naming of the present one after our own particular species are scientifically respectable is a matter for scientific debate and consideration of the data in the light of the criteria usually employed to decide such matters.[9] My point is that talk of overcoming alienation from nature in *this* context suggests a picture of achieving oneness through yet more thorough but *better controlled* impacts on the Earth. Here we might envisage large-scale climate and geo-engineering projects and the comprehensive use of genetic modification (GM) and nanotechnologies. The more the Earth's systems function as a set of interlocking technologies smoothly operating to better deliver a sustainable environment for humanity, the 'closer' we will be to this new anthropogenic 'nature' of the Anthropocene. In this picture the environmental crisis is one of *uncontrolled* impact, not excessive impact. And overcoming alienation in favour of oneness as a response to *this* crisis looks to be a purely anthropocentric matter of establishing a new kind of environmental harmony through mastery of nature and assimilating the resulting 'nature' to human artefact and technology. This seems no less fantastical or more attractive than returning to the Pleistocene.

0.3   Humans and beavers

Further problems with talk of alienation from nature and its overcoming are conceptual difficulties turning on the idea of *nature*. One difficulty is the apparent nonsensicality of such talk given that we are simply one evolved species among others and so, like them, entirely a part of a natural world that we cannot leave. That 'nature' encompasses us too, such that we are inescapably a part of a wider natural world, is generally agreed by those who talk and worry about alienation from nature. But then no matter how artificial, civilized and technological we make our lives and surroundings, everything we are, do and produce is just as much a part of nature, just as 'natural' in that sense, as is anything else, including anything else we could be, do and produce. What then could count as *alienation from nature*? I am sitting indoors in front of a computer typing these words rather than walking through the woods with the wind in my hair. But the interior of my house, my computer and these words are no less part of the overall natural world than are the woods, the wind and my hair. I am just as closely and inescapably in touch with nature here as I would be there. Nuclear power stations might be problematic

---

[9] See Zalasiewicz et al. (2011) for a discussion of the stratigraphical issues involved in distinguishing and dating geological periods.

in various different ways, but why think they involve our being alienated from nature, any more than the construction of dams by beavers involves *their* being alienated from nature?

Steven Vogel makes this point as part of a forceful argument against Andrew Biro's explanation of the 'fact of humanity's alienation' in terms of 'human beings' self-conscious transformation of their natural environment' (Biro 2005; Vogel 2011, pp. 188f). Unlike purely instinctual animals, we can 'deny our instincts'; stand back from them and use our cognitive and physical abilities to do something other than what they dictate. In this sense we can 'break from the dictates of nature', and so have history and culture (Biro 2005, p. 30). Here then is an account of what the idea of alienation from nature amounts to in itself. For Biro it consists in a self-conscious transformative stance towards nature, focused on moulding it and using it for non-instinctual purposes. In this case the movement from a 'purely instinctive' mode of interaction with nature to a self-conscious one is inherently alienating. It involves the repression of 'inner nature' (spontaneous instincts) and the purposive transformation of our surroundings, or 'external nature'. Biro locates the root of this understanding of alienation from nature in Rousseau's contrast between the strong and independent 'natural man' whose needs are satisfied in a 'state of nature', a situation without civilization and government, and the vain, weak, fearful, dependent and servile 'civilized man', who is subject to a multitude of unsatisfiable artificial needs under conditions of social inequality.

The influence of Rousseau's view is detectable across a range of (therefore more or less romantic) environmental and political thought, including primitivism of course. For Rousseau, however, there is no question of our going back to, or retrieving, a pre-civilized, fully 'natural' way of life: contrary to Voltaire's jibe he did not advocate a human 'return to the forest to walk on all fours'. Rather the move from state of nature to civilization is made inevitable by human Reason, particularly the capacity for comparative thought or reflection on difference. Reason enables us to form the idea of inequality and to distinguish between human subject and natural object. It also allows us to reflect upon and 'deny' our instincts and to *labour* in the sense of self-consciously transforming our environment (Biro 2005, pp. 59ff).

The problem Vogel raises with this is that, even if we accept that our status as cultural, historical and labouring beings turns crucially on our capacity to 'deny our instincts', it is difficult to see why *that* should constitute our alienation *from nature*, given that our self-consciousness, transformative activities and their results all occur within nature too. However repressed our spontaneous instincts, however relentless our toil

8   Introduction

and wonderful or appalling the results, this would still all be going on *within* nature, no less than would minimum repression and toil to produce minimum environmental transformation.

This point also tells against the other claims mentioned above. For example, it might seem plausible that, when out of sight and out of mind in urban cultures with little contact with them, nature's ecological relations are more easily discounted, and that therefore something like NDD and ecologically irrational political and economic short-termism are mutually reinforcing (compare Juniper 2013, e.g., pp. 264f). But notice that however plausible or implausible they are in other terms, such claims cannot establish that we are alienated from nature in the sense of somehow *not or no longer really being part of the natural world*. If the savannah hypothesis is true and we wish to invoke the idea of alienation to summarize our plight in being cut off from savannah-like conditions, why not just say that we are alienated *from the savannah*?

Thus it is not only *unclear* what is added to charges of ignorance or false beliefs about our location in nature, perhaps accompanied by ecologically irrational and destructive decision-making and technology, by saying that they amount to 'alienation from nature'. Given that the conditions constituted by these problems occur within nature, no less than would conditions in which they are absent, it seems entirely mysterious what *could be* added meaningfully by saying they amount to alienation from nature. By definition, both sets of conditions are equally 'natural' in this sense. If a beaver displays ignorance and ecologically unfortunate behaviour by building a dam in an unsuitable location, oblivious to its unsustainability there, and disregarding the damaging flood it causes, is it alienated from nature? If it survives the situation and proceeds to find a more suitable location where it builds a better, more sustainable dam less destructive of the surrounding habitat, has it now overcome its previous state of alienation from nature?

The issue cannot be escaped by arguing that such questions don't arise for beavers because, unlike us, they are not self-conscious rational agents. This difference justifies withholding responsibility and blameworthiness with respect to beavers, but why should that affect the situation with respect to our alienation from nature? As Vogel points out, to insist that it does – that certain ways of exercising, or failing to exercise, rational agency are not only blameworthy but *alienate us from nature* – seems to presuppose the dualist idea that our rational agency, at least when exercised in certain problematical ways, somehow puts us outside nature (Vogel 2011, pp. 188f). Otherwise, like the beaver's dam-building skills, it is just another evolved trait that remains within nature, however badly exercised.

Don't give up on the idea

Of course *we* shouldn't be so stupid or greedy as to build homes on flood plains disregarding the known flood risks. But if such appraisals are to be couched in terms of alienation from nature then this must involve some other sense of 'nature', given that we, our greed and stupidity and their consequences are part of nature in the sense of the natural world. The other candidate that initially presents itself as in keeping with the appraisal is 'nonhuman nature': our environmentally problematic attitudes and behaviour involve our alienation from *nonhuman nature*. This sets up the dualism just mentioned, however; a dualism between us, or the rational, self-consciously transformative side of us, and the nature from which we are said to be alienated. And it makes the alienation rationally inescapable by definition. These consequences raise further problems (Vogel 2011, pp. 188f).

One is that if we are alienated from nature by definition then references to our alienation from nature are trivial and lacking in critical purchase. We cannot be anything *but* alienated from nature defined as the *non*human, or in opposition to rational agency. Yet alienation is a critical concept, one usually used to appraise a condition more or less radically as one to be avoided or overcome. There is no room for this critical work if by definition we must be alienated from that which we are alienated. *Any* course of action we choose to adopt will involve our alienation from nature. Whether I spend my life indoors sitting in front of a computer screen dealing with emails or outside in the woods closely observing the web of ecological interdependencies around me, I am still alienated from a nonhuman nature defined in contrast to me. A further problem here is that the dualism imposed by defining alienation from nature like this is inconsistent with the naturalistic hypothesis that we, and all of our attributes and abilities, are no less part of nature than is the case with any other naturally evolved species. This thought pushes us back to the previous sense of nature as the natural world encompassing us and all of our doings. But, as we have just seen, when we run 'nature' in that sense our alienation from it seems to become impossible by definition.

0.4   Don't give up on the idea

It looks like a mistake then to talk of alienation from nature as a condition to be overcome over and above the moral, political, economic, educational, health-related and whatever other more common or garden failings we might associate with the environmental crisis. Once we focus on the idea to ask what it adds to our picture of the situation it too easily suggests unattractive and impossible dreams of returning to some imagined past close harmony with nature or of engineering a new

10 Introduction

harmony through God-like domination of the Earth's systems. Further reflection suggests that even if such pictures, or variations on them, were more plausible and attractive it would be difficult to see them as really about us overcoming our alienation from nature. As Vogel's argument brings out, attempting to see them like that seems to mire us in conceptual confusions as we oscillate between different senses of nature. It does not appear helpful to talk of our being alienated from nature in either of these senses of nature. In one sense the alienation is inescapable by definition and so trivial; in the other sense it seems impossible, also by definition, to see how we could be alienated from it in any meaningful way. Vogel concludes from these that we should drop talk of 'alienation from nature' and worry instead about our alienation from '*something like nature*': from the environment always already produced by human labour (Vogel 2011). Such alienation is non-trivial, only too possible and yet may be escaped, at least in principle.

I think the appearances are misleading, however, and that it would be a mistake to drop talk of alienation *from nature*. I aim to show that it can be a helpful notion with which to illuminate our problematic environmental situation. I am taking it that the problems I have mentioned do not entirely demolish the suspicion that alienation from nature is somehow part of the picture of the environmental crisis, as a crisis involving serious deficiencies in our relation with our surroundings that call for a relatively radical critical response. Problems with the idea of alienation from nature serve to amplify the sense of crisis as an *inchoate* sense of a difficult situation requiring difficult important steps. But what steps? We need to deal with our alienation from nature. Yes, but what is *that*, and what could 'dealing with it' possibly and plausibly amount to? I take it that a satisfactory account of alienation from nature addresses these questions. It starts with an inchoate sense of a complex environmental crisis as having something important to do with alienation from nature and clarifies what this is and what it is (or would be) to deal with it.

0.5   Main claim and overall argument

My main claim in this book then is that – notwithstanding problems such as those raised above – talk of alienation from nature can be justified, useful and important. The idea can help us to think through our environmental situation when understood in a certain pluralistic way. It is unhelpful, I think, to view alienation and nature, and so alienation from nature, as single things or conditions to be understood in one particular way in the terms of one tradition. Thus the required pluralism comes in two forms.

First, a satisfactory account needs to draw upon and modify intellectual tools – ideas, arguments, theories – from a range of traditions in environmental and wider philosophy, encompassing anthropocentric and nonanthropocentric perspectives on our situation. Second, the account needs to be pluralist also in distinguishing different senses of alienation and different senses of nature, corresponding to different environmental contexts. Several of these different senses of alienation and nature can be mapped onto each other to produce different interrelated senses of alienation from nature, *some of which are to be viewed positively, as something to be accepted or even encouraged, rather than avoided or overcome.* Put in the form of an overall argument, my reasons for claiming that alienation from nature is a useful and important notion when understood in this pluralistic way are as follows:

1. The different senses of alienation from nature involved entail each other, in that concern for one rationally requires concern for the others (at least in our actual environmental crisis situation).

   Therefore,

2. The pluralistic approach enables us to see important relationships between different senses of alienation from nature.
3. The different senses of alienation from nature encompass or 'capture' different specific environmental concerns, including both anthropocentric (for example, instrumental and constructionist) concerns and nonanthropocentric concerns (for example, respect for nonhuman nature and a wish to resist the 'domination of nature').

   Therefore,

4. Under the description of the associated senses of alienation from nature these environmental concerns entail each other: in our actual environmental situation concern for one rationally requires concern for the others.

   Therefore,

5. The pluralistic approach allows us to see important relations between different specific environmental concerns. Particularly important are relations of entailment rather than zero-sum opposition between various anthropocentric and nonanthropocentric concerns. Dealing with the environmental crisis requires progress on all the fronts

12   Introduction

encompassed by the pluralist account of alienation from nature, not some entirely at the expense of the others.

0.6   What is to come

In the following two chapters I provide some explanation of the terms of this overall argument and discuss the kind of environmental philosophy it exemplifies. Because it presupposes that we are in an environmental crisis that somehow involves our alienation from nature, and because alienation is a critical concept, I take my argument to be an exercise in critical environmental philosophy. I discuss the implications of this for its status as 'applied philosophy'. The main notions encompassed by the argument are alienation and nature of course. I introduce in general terms the different senses of these employed in my overall argument. For alienation they are: *estrangement, reification* and *property alienation*. For nature they are the senses already touched upon above: *nonhuman nature, the natural world* and *humanized nature,* or *the landscape produced by human labour.* Chapter 1 also includes a preliminary sketch of relations between the different senses of alienation from nature produced by mapping some of these ideas of alienation onto each other.

That different senses of alienation are interrelated is an idea familiar to the Marxian tradition. Theorists inspired by critical traditions informed by Marxism will worry that my talk of nonhuman nature and the natural world itself reifies social constructions and ignores the ideological role played by the abstraction 'nature'. In Chapter 1 I seek to allay this partly by rejecting some defective senses of alienation from nature as involving reification and partly with reference to the implications of the fuzzy indeterminacy of the distinction between humanized landscape and nonhuman nature, which has to be a matter of degree.

Chapter 2 continues to discuss constructionist concerns in light of the type of environmental philosophy my argument exemplifies. I start from a practical problem (the environmental crisis) and view theories and ideas as adjustable tools to deal with such problems, rather than devices to deliver fixed certainties. I emphasize matters of degree over strict dichotomies and, as I have said, I adopt a pluralist approach. All this suggests a strong affinity with pragmatism; an affinity I am happy to accept and emphasize. Thus in Chapter 2 I discuss how what Dewey called the 'quest for certainty' can function as a philosophical motivation for the excessively strong constructionism about nature exemplified by Steven Vogel's position.

What is to come 13

Yet pragmatism can also bring constructionist pressures apparently strong enough to threaten central elements of my account, including the contrast between landscape and nonhuman nature and the importance of sustaining a substantial measure of nonanthropocentrism with regard to the latter. I consider these issues in the light of Richard Rorty's neo-pragmatism and Ben Minteer's environmental pragmatism. I argue that pragmatism is itself an intellectual tool that can be shaped to fit and help clarify the shape of the problem, even when, as in the case of the environmental crisis, this involves some commitment to nonanthropocentrism. In Chapter 2 I show how this can be done with my overall argument about alienation from nature in mind.

Chapters 3 to 6 consider some important ways in which the senses of alienation play out in the different contexts of landscape, nonhuman nature and the natural world. These chapters speak mostly to premise three of the arguments as set out above: the different senses of alienation from nature encompass or 'capture' different specific environmental concerns, including both anthropocentric concerns and nonanthropocentric concerns.

Chapter 3 focuses on the landscape and ways in which the three senses of alienation work in this anthropocentric environmental context. I show how they may be related to ideas of justice, especially recognitional justice, and thereby address matters of climate justice and environmental justice generally. Relations of injustice thickened by the mediating role of landscapes into relations of *environmental* injustice constitute an unacceptable form of estrangement between persons. However, there may be deeply problematic estrangement constituted not so much by unjust relations between persons as by the lack (or serious deterioration) of important relations between persons and landscapes. People may fail to find themselves 'at home' in the world they are making, for example by failing to acknowledge and take responsibility for their role in making it. This is a matter not only of reification of landscape but of a pernicious kind of estrangement from it as reified. I discuss this in relation to climate change and in the light of some themes from Hegel, who usefully brings together ideas of being at home, recognition, responsibility and realization of personhood.

The default position here is that estrangement, including in the form of unjust property alienation, is to be avoided or overcome. However, I also consider environmentally problematic 'crises' of place, and a form of estrangement contrasted with the idea of making ourselves at home through the 'practice of place'. Given a plurality of different places and of different interpretations of places, one cannot expect to be equally at home in all of them, in all humanized landscapes. So I argue that a

14   Introduction

degree of estrangement from landscapes is required by the just recognition of human difference.

Chapter 4 moves the discussion into the nonanthropocentric territory encompassed by my account. The focus is nonhuman nature and especially our estrangement from it. The main claim of this chapter is that accepting and living with some such estrangement is a way of expressing 'respect for nature' and resisting the 'domination of nature'. This move, along with emphasizing matters of degree, defuses the charges of triviality and critical inefficacy laid against the idea of alienation from nature in this sense.

I discuss this move in relation to the Marxian tradition and to the early Frankfurt School critique of the 'domination of nature' and of Marx as caught up in the domination agenda. I also discuss my position in relation to more mainstream environmental philosophies, including the extension of respect in the form of recognitional justice to the nonhuman. Different forms of 'moral extensionism' are more or less helpful in unpacking the content of living with some estrangement from the nonhuman. I discuss the complex issues of sameness and difference involved here in the light of Val Plumwood's analysis of problems with the contrasting positions of environmental philosophers Arne Naess and Peter Reed. I argue that it is helpful to approach the tricky issues of sameness and difference in our dealings with (the rest of) nature through ideas of estrangement from nonhuman nature and the natural world.

Chapter 5 maintains the focus on nonhuman nature but this time considers alienation in the sense related to property or ownership. Living with some estrangement from nonhuman nature entails some alienation *of* nonhuman nature. By 'alienation of nonhuman nature' I mean a rejection of the assumption that nonhuman nature should enter into considerations of ownership and property rights *only* as something to be owned for the sake of human interests. Traditional political philosophy has tended to run this assumption in the background of its accounts of property. This and what it means to reject it are the topics of this chapter. Although I touch on other thinkers, including Locke, I illustrate the issues mainly with reference to Hegel's derivation of private property rights and its place within his philosophical system. I also discuss the issues in Marxian terms to show how my argument applies to that tradition too. The problem is not specifically private property as such but the terms of the derivation of the concept of property that is operating (whether private, collective or common). A critical perspective on our environmental situation should say that it requires us to not only 'take ownership' of the world we are making (landscapes) but also disown (alienate) nonhuman nature in the sense of rejecting purely anthropocentric assumptions in

What is to come 15

our thinking on property. In this way the theme of property alienation speaks to environmental concerns pertaining both to the humanized landscape and to nonhuman nature.

Chapter 6 focuses on the wider context of the natural world, especially with regards to estrangement. To get around the objection that 'alienation from nature' is unintelligible given that we remain part of the natural world whatever we do, I suggest we understand the estrangement in terms of 'misperception'. I distinguish two pertinent senses of this. In one – cognitive – sense it means false beliefs or lack of knowledge about ecological realities. This might be part of the picture but is insufficient given that the account of estrangement is to help articulate a critical environmental perspective that speaks of more than mere ignorance. I suggest that some of the insights of eco-phenomenology are helpful here and that we understand the estranging misperception in more praxis-oriented and phenomenologically 'primordial' terms. In Chapter 6 then I draw upon Merleau-Ponty's account of perception, especially his later notion of 'flesh', to develop an account of estrangement from the natural world as *inadequate participation* within it. This closely connects the idea of estrangement with environmental concerns about our being 'cut off' from the 'more than human' natural world in a way that involves instrumentalization and domination.

Chapter 7 brings things together by focusing on relations between the different ideas of alienation from nature and associated environmental concerns. It is in this chapter that I try to make good on the relational claims in my overall argument: the pluralistic approach allows us to see important relations between different specific environmental issues encompassed by the ideas of alienation. For example, estrangement from the natural world cannot be overcome without regard to problematic estrangement, reification and alienation in humanized landscapes. I also argue that given the intertwining of human and nonhuman within the overall natural world the converse is equally true. Thus I argue that viewed in terms of different senses of alienation from nature, the more anthropocentric concerns of environmental justice, NDD and crises of place cannot be addressed properly without also addressing the more nonanthropocentric concerns of domination and instrumentalization of nature. I illustrate these claims with a (wary and critical) discussion of Tony Juniper's *What Has Nature Ever Done for Us?* I then finish the book with a short chapter briefly summarizing some of the main points to take away from my argument.

1 Alienations and natures

1.1 Types of alienation from nature and their main relations

In this chapter and the next I discuss the kind of environmental philosophy exemplified by the overall argument of this book. I will also discuss in more detail and defend the main terms of the argument: the senses of alienation from nature it draws upon, the relations between them and the environmental concerns they capture. It will be helpful to say a little more about these at the outset.

My aim is not to provide a comprehensive survey of actual and possible senses of 'alienation', 'nature', 'alienation from nature' or 'environmental alienation'. Although I will argue against some possible ways of understanding alienation from nature, my aim is not to legislate on the only proper meanings of these terms. I use some traditional and central senses to try to indicate some helpful ways of understanding 'alienation from nature' and the relations between them, and to suggest that it should be understood as a plurality of conditions, some of which we should and some of which we should not seek to overcome.

As I have said, the senses of 'alienation' I consider are: first, *estrangement*, in the sense of a state of being separated or cut off from something. Second is *alienation*, in the sense in which the notion concerns property – a renunciation of ownership. Third, *reification*, in the sense of the reduction of humanity, human processes and products to merely given 'things'. The main senses of 'nature' I consider indicate three main contexts of environmental concern: first, *the natural world*, the encompassing sense of nature, in which it is wider than humanity and of which humanity is a part but not the whole. Second, *nonhuman nature*, the natural world insofar as it is not human or has not been shaped and interpreted by humanity for human-oriented ends. Third, *the humanized environment*, or what I shall call 'landscape': the natural world insofar as it *has* been so shaped.

Put together these different ideas of alienation and nature produce various helpful and interrelated senses of alienation from nature.

Some environmental concerns captured through estrangement 17

Concern for alienation from nature in one sense rationally requires concern for it in the other senses. Their main relations seem to me to be as follows. Estrangement from the natural world and the humanized landscape should be overcome in general *without* seeking the elimination of all estrangement from nonhuman nature: overcoming estrangement from the natural world *entails* endorsing some estrangement from nonhuman nature. Consequently, overcoming alienation from nature in the sense of estrangement from the overall natural world cannot be equated with becoming fully at home in the world. Similarly, a critique of alienation in the sense of alienation of property within the humanized landscape should leave space for the *encouragement* of some such alienation with respect to nonhuman nature and the natural world. Although an attempt to overcome estrangement from the natural world cannot ignore reification, estrangement and alienation within (from or of) the landscape, nor can it seek to eliminate estrangement and alienation with respect to nonhuman nature. And a concern to avoid reification of humanity should not remove nonhuman nature and the natural world from consideration. A concern with alienation and estrangement, whether with respect to landscape, nonhuman nature or natural world, and whether or not the concern is for their overcoming actually presupposes some limitation of the scope of the idea of reification.

1.2 Some environmental concerns captured through estrangement

Presented in such abstract and compressed terms these claims are not as meaningful or helpful as they might be. Their expansion and defence is the work of later chapters. For the time being consider briefly the idea of estrangement: the state of being separated or cut off from something. The precise meaning of this must vary of course, depending on whether it concerns the humanized landscape, the natural world or nonhuman nature. Our estrangement from nonhuman nature is a matter of our being confronted with the 'otherness' of the nonhuman. We are 'separate' or 'distanced' from it in the sense that *insofar as it is a nonhuman world*, it is not an embodiment of human will; it is not set up to serve human interests or ideals. This is a form of estrangement from nature I am suggesting we need to live with to some extent.

We have seen that it can seem to be a trivial definitional matter, however, to speak of estrangement from nature in these terms. Thus Vogel argues that if we define nature as nonhuman nature and say that our alienation from it consists merely in its being nonhuman then, by definition, we are alienated from nature whatever we do (Vogel 2011, p. 188).

18   Alienations and natures

In Chapter 4 I shall argue that this is not at all trivial once one thinks in terms of matters of degree and drops the assumption that alienation as estrangement is always to be overcome as much as possible. Living with some estrangement from nonhuman nature, rather than seeking always to overcome it, then becomes equivalent to resisting what some call the 'domination' or 'mastery' of nature. Available ways of filling this out include theories of ecological justice and other nonanthropocentric environmental approaches concerned to avoid excessive anthropogenic destruction of nonhuman nature. Viewed in the light of (endorsing and living with some) estrangement from nonhuman nature, these in turn entail some positive endorsement of alienation of nonhuman nature in the sense of alienation concerning ownership; the topic of Chapter 5.

The idea of estrangement from the overall natural world is different. It runs straight into the thought that given we always remain within nature in this sense we can never be genuinely estranged – cut off, set apart or distanced – from it. In Chapter 6 I consider two versions of the idea of estrangement from the overall natural world that seem to get around this problem. One involves a lack of awareness of humanity's embeddedness within and dependence upon a wider natural world, as if that wider world either did not exist or we were somehow *ecologically* separate from it. I am not suggesting we should live with such a condition. However, this picture of estrangement makes it consist simply in ignorance about, or disregard of, our ecological relations. Although it seems right to keep ecological ignorance and irrationality as part of the picture, there are at least two problems with leaving it at that.

One is that because it is obvious that ignorance of our ecological embeddedness in wider nature doesn't put us outside nature, it remains unclear why we should say such ignorance constitutes *estrangement from nature*. True, estrangement and ignorance are closely related in certain theological doctrines and philosophical theories. For example, it has been said that to be ignorant of God is to be estranged from Him.[1] For Hegel, ignorance of the ultimate unity of the highest stage of thought (absolute spirit) and objective reality constitutes a form of estrangement. For the Marxist, reification of social labour products as naturally given (ignorance as to their social origin) either constitutes or generates estrangement. But these accounts either focus on the humanized landscape (labour products) or tend to reduce nature to humanized landscape (the unity of Spirit and Nature within Absolute Idealism), or concern our relationship

---

[1] As Paul tells the Ephesians (4:17–18): 'This I say therefore, and testify in the Lord, that ye henceforth walk not as other Gentiles walk, in the vanity of their mind. Having the understanding darkened, being alienated from the life of God through the ignorance that is in them, because of the blindness of their heart.'

Some environmental concerns captured through estrangement   19

to the supernatural (God). I touch on the Marxian position below and return to it in the following chapters. I discuss the Hegelian picture in Chapters 3 and 5. However, we do not usually take ignorance of facts or relations discovered, or discoverable, by natural science as in itself a state of estrangement, even if the ignorance concerns matters of fundamental pressing importance. The ignorance might be extremely unfortunate, as when we are in the dark about diseases, but calling it a state of estrangement without further qualification or discussion seems to be superfluous. We do sometimes talk of people being 'strangers to the truth', but by that we mean that they lie, not that they are ignorant. Although I shall make use of the idea, especially in Chapter 7, it is something of a stretch to refer to ecological ignorance as a matter of estrangement.

A further problem with taking estrangement from wider nature to be constituted *only* by ecological ignorance is that it makes overcoming the estrangement consist simply in acquiring and acting upon scientific knowledge, regardless of the context and aims of the acquisition and action. While replacing ignorance with knowledge is no doubt always good in some sense, it is also problematic when the knowledge is pursued in the light of a purely instrumental 'dominating' approach to nature that reduces nature to landscape materials. So in Chapter 6 I draw upon phenomenological considerations, centred on Merleau-Ponty's account of our perceptual being in the 'flesh of the world' to suggest a second sense of estrangement from the natural world. This time the estrangement consists in a less than ideal *participation* in the 'more than human' perceptual world. The 'flesh' account points to a way of understanding the overall natural world as a set of fundamental relations that one is always already involved in, where these are not just causal relations. We are familiar with the idea of a less than ideal participation in ongoing social relations. I argue that something analogous might be the case with respect to the natural world. I am not suggesting that we positively endorse estrangement from the natural world in this sense either. Indeed, the kind of environmental concerns captured by the idea of *endorsing* some estrangement from *nonhuman nature* (respect for nature, ecological justice, resisting domination) coincide with those captured by the idea of *overcoming* estrangement from the *natural world*. That said, the aim of completely overcoming personal estrangement from the natural world understood in this way runs into problems that highlight the need for a pluralistic approach involving different senses of alienation from nature. I discuss this in Chapter 7.

Nor, apart from one important qualification concerning human difference, am I suggesting we live with estrangement from the humanized environment or landscape. Estrangement in this context is perhaps a

20 Alienations and natures

more familiar idea. It involves a lack of homeliness; a lack of identification with humanized surroundings, including fellow humans and our shared social surroundings. It captures concerns for such 'breakdowns in the practice of place' as the phenomenon of 'sprawl', as well as concerns for distributive and recognitional justice, including of course with regard to environmental goods and bads, such as the consequences of anthropogenic climate change. I discuss these issues in Chapter 3.

1.3 Anthropocentric and nonanthropocentric

Again the relations involved in the bigger overall picture are of crucial importance. The humanized landscape is *within* the natural world, not set apart from it. So, for example, overcoming estrangement from the natural world requires the practice of place to be pursued in full appreciation of humanity's embeddedness within and engagement with a wider more than human reality. To be efficacious the practice informed by this awareness has to be a self and collectively controlled practice, whose environmental manifestation is of responsible will rather than estranged homelessness. Overcoming estrangement from the humanized world requires perception of that world as the homely embodiment of human will in order to ground stable identity and responsibility. Precisely because of that it requires progress in appreciating and participating adequately in the wider, more than human reality in which it is embedded. Otherwise it will be only accidentally sustainable and free from the radical loss of control following ecological catastrophe. Consequently, overcoming estrangement from the humanized world and the natural world rely upon each other as part of a project to overcome pernicious forms of estrangement from nature. At least they do so in our actual, precarious environmental situation. Nevertheless, if I'm right, that same project requires qualifying the quest to be fully at 'home in the world' in that it requires some estrangement and alienation from and of the nonhuman.

Again, my overall argument for a pluralistic understanding of alienation from nature is that it allows us to see such relations between environmental concerns, most importantly between those that are anthropocentric and those that are nonanthropocentric. The nonanthropocentric concerns include those already mentioned as encompassed by the ideas of overcoming estrangement from that natural world and *endorsing* some estrangement from (and alienation of) nonhuman nature. To endorse such nonanthropocentrism is not to deny the following, presumably inescapable, ways of 'being anthropocentric':

1. Perspectival anthropocentrism – whatever nonanthropocentric respect for nature is going on, it is *us* who are doing the respecting, from *our* point of view, and in the light of *our* own present understanding of the world, and what it contains, an understanding revisable by *us*;
2. the recognition that many natural items are also of crucial instrumental importance to humanity and so have to be 'brought within the landscape' (we must overcome estrangement from nonhuman nature to some extent and to some extent retain ownership of nature for the sake of human interests);
3. acceptable value judgements, including nonanthropocentric value judgements, have to be intelligible in the light of other present human values. Thus the account of alienation from nature I am defending is constructed through an engagement with – a series of partial endorsements of and distancing from – more familiar positions in political and environmental thought.

But for the nonanthropocentric elements of the overall picture to survive and for the relations between them and the anthropocentric elements to be visible, it is necessary to see that anthropocentrism is not inescapable in all of its possible senses. In particular it is necessary to avoid a purely 'anthropocentric instrumental' view of nature or the natural world as 'just our world', there merely to serve our interests. This is an important point that goes to the kind of environmental philosophy involved in the argument of this book.

1.4 Critical environmental philosophy and applied philosophy

It seems to me reasonable to expect an affinity between a *critical* environmental philosophy, activated by a sense of crisis, and a view of theories, concepts and intellectual products generally as more or less useful tools for coping with the world. The environmental crisis suggests we are not coping too well and might not have quite the right intellectual tools. It is unsurprising then that much philosophizing about the environment at least partly takes the form of examining philosophical assumptions, moves and concepts as more or less useful tools for coping with the world as environment. Neil Evernden, for example, follows Schumacher in talking of such intellectual products as inherited 'societal maps' that are more or less useful guides to negotiating the world. Evernden views the 'Cartesian' map, which divides things as either self-conscious, rational and active subjects (us) and a realm of objects as 'mere things' to be acted upon, as particularly unhelpful for guiding our relations with the rest of

22 Alienations and natures

nature (Evernden 1993, pp. 26, 35). He also warns against identifying such maps with reality itself so as to view their revision as unthinkable, when they have simply been helpful in some particular way or context (Evernden 1993, pp. 25ff, 36f, 53f).

Another example is Mary Midgley's discussion of environmental issues in the light of her conception of philosophy as akin to plumbing in its focus on problems with the unnoticed background or subterranean aspects of practical life and its troubles. Not faulty pipes, taps or drains, of course, but troublesome conceptual schemes, models and metaphors that need to be 'dug up' and adjusted or replaced (Midgley 1996b). Val Plumwood's general eco-feminist critique of the pernicious dualisms pervading traditional Western thought has this orientation (Plumwood 1993); as do Lynn White's infamous critique of Judaeo Christian theology (White 1967) and the deep ecology critique of philosophical atomism. Consider also Mick Smith's recent critique of 'ecological sovereignty in all its many disguises'. He intends this critique as an exercise in 'radical ecology': the rejection of 'human dominion over the natural world' (Smith 2011, p. xi). For Smith ecological sovereignty exemplifies Giorgio Agamben's idea of the '"anthropological machine" – the historically variable but constantly recurring manufacture of metaphysical distinctions to separate and elevate the properly human from the less-than-fully-human and the natural world' (Smith 2011, p. xii). Examples of environmental philosophy in this mode can be multiplied and many of them might be interpreted as critiques of ways of living and thinking that have alienated us from nature.

Such criticisms of the intellectual tools bequeathed to us for dealing with the world as environment don't invent themselves out of thin air, of course. They must draw upon and adapt already available ideas in the very acts of diagnosing erroneous tendencies and suggesting improvements. So, for example, a deep ecologist may draw upon certain kinds of metaphysical holism or phenomenological considerations to articulate alternatives to, as well as diagnose and reject, what she takes to be the pernicious grip of atomistic patterns of thought. A social ecologist may draw upon anarchist ideas to diagnose and counter hierarchical, statist ways of thinking taken to reproduce ecologically disastrous political structures and action. A primitivist calling for a 'return' to a prehistoric form of human life supposedly more 'in harmony' with nature might be influenced by Rousseau's conception of the state of nature and contrast between 'natural' and 'civilized' living. And so on. Such proposals may themselves be criticized as more or less helpful, of course, as well as in terms of coherence and intelligibility; and I shall be discussing and criticizing some of them below and in later chapters. For example, the strongly holist orientation of deep ecology suggests a view of alienation from nature only as something to be overcome as much as possible. As I have said already, I think it will be helpful to abandon this assumption.

While they don't arise from someplace uninformed by existing philosophical traditions, it should be clear also that these critical approaches do not conform happily to a conception of 'applied philosophy' as the literal application of given philosophical theories, concepts and arguments to problematic 'issues' with currency in practical public life. In environmental terms these issues include climate change, mass extinction, preservation of 'natural resources' for the sake of future generations and so on as components of the environmental crisis. Thus one might have thought that the thing to do is to take such an issue and apply an already formulated philosophical approach to it; an approach given as already more or less fully worked out. Mass extinction, for example – is that bad? What should we do? Well, what does utilitarianism or Kantianism say we should do? Rather than this, the approach I have in mind treats the philosophical tradition itself with critical caution, in the light of the environmental crisis. If a strong contrast is called for at all here between the 'given' and that to which the given is 'applied', then it is that crisis that is given and, as it were, applied to philosophy at least as much as the other way around. The environmental crisis is taken as evidence that something has gone seriously wrong with humanity's relation with its surroundings (i.e., everything else) and with traditional assumptions and ways of thinking, or not thinking, about 'the environment'. This model of environmental philosophy then involves a critical examination of the philosophical tradition in the light of the environmental crisis.

Of course, as Midgley points out, it should be acknowledged that the great thinkers who have shaped our philosophical traditions have been concerned with practical matters and not just 'pure' philosophy completely divorced from all practice. Except for relatively brief phases of its history, it is hardly plausible to view philosophy's relationship to wider practice entirely on the model of a cadre of 'true philosophers' doing 'basic' or 'pure' work that is then handed down in abstract form to the more junior department of application, where philosophy deigns to touch the world.[2] I am interested here in the entanglement of philosophy and practical affairs in the relatively strong sense of *starting from* a fairly specific practical problem thrown up by contemporary life – the 'environmental crisis' – with the main point of philosophical reflection being to help clarify it, get a handle on it. This I think points to a close affinity between critical environmental philosophy and philosophical

---

[2] Midgley (1996b, ch. 3). See also, for example, Callicott (2002).

24   Alienations and natures

pragmatism. Because it has an important bearing on my own argument I discuss this in some detail in the next chapter.

It is important to keep in mind that the starting problem is not simply a set of 'neutral' facts about our environmental situation to which philosophy is to be applied. It is that our environmental situation constitutes a crisis. I am taking it that we have an inchoate sense that it represents a serious failure in our dealings with our surroundings, including our nonhuman surroundings, and that this has something to do with our alienation from nature. The problematic starting point is already evaluative then and, as my mention of 'anthropocentric instrumentalism' has already begun to unpack, it is evaluative in a way already inclined to be critical of traditional mainstream ways of thinking and not thinking about nature.

Obviously, it is a question begging in a certain way to have this as the starting point. I am not starting off by first *proving* that we are in a crisis representing a failure in our dealings with our surroundings that renders many traditional, especially anthropocentric, views of nature suspect. I am taking this for granted and asking how talk of alienation from nature should be interpreted if it is to help articulate, clarify and understand that sense of crisis and that suspicion. Someone who thinks there is no such problem and is already committed to a *purely* anthropocentric instrumentalist outlook will find this project pointless in much the same way as a moral philosophical project about pernicious interpersonal alienation is likely to strike a convinced egoist prepared to consider alternatives only if he is first shown a knockdown argument against his current position.[3]

1.5   Property alienation

An important bastion of anthropocentric instrumentalism is located within traditional philosophical accounts of property. These do tend to imply that the world is just there to be possessed by humanity for human interests. The concept of property is a central mediator of human/nonhuman as well as inter-human relations in political contexts. If its focus is purely anthropocentric then this is a major obstacle in the way of political thought's ability to 'look outside' the humanized landscape to consider impacts on anything other than human interests.

Thus the traditional understanding of property, the cluster of concepts and assumptions associated with ownership, is an intellectual device

[3] See Nolt (2013) for a useful discussion of the parallels between egoism and anthropocentrism ('egoism writ large – the egoism of the human species').

that requires attention to prevent it from functioning in environmentally problematic ways. Otherwise it risks being what, in an echo of the anthropological machine idea, Plumwood calls a 'meta-level hoist' that has become 'stuck above ground level' (Plumwood 2006, p. 124). These are concepts that 'elevate' us above and away from the rest of nature and that can get 'stuck' in ways that focus attention on the humanized landscape as the only thing to be considered. They can even lend a spurious plausibility to scepticism about nature. I return to this issue below. Interestingly, some philosophical tools designed with the intention of improving the wider environmental situation also seem to stick in problematic ways.[4] I argue that one way of attending to the 'design faults' in such 'pieces of philosophical technology' (Plumwood 2006, p. 124) is via a pluralistic understanding of alienation, shaped such as to be encouraged in certain senses and ways.

For example, Raymond Williams (1990, p. 33) tells us that in its sense of a renunciation of ownership (the holding of rights, estates, money), or the transfer of ownership from one person to another, the notion of 'alienation' came into English usage in the fifteenth century. Such *property-alienation* was not originally viewed as necessarily bad, but in its dominant uses the term acquired the negative connotations associated with improper, for example involuntary, loss of possession or transfers of ownership. 'Alienation of property' thus often suggests a regrettable loss of entitlements, as in cases of outright theft or deprivation of (what one took to be) a rightful inheritance or just reward by fraud or other arbitrary and unjustified manipulation of legal and other social relationships. A way of addressing the anthropocentric instrumentalism of traditional philosophical theories of property is to reject such connotations when alienation in this (ownership-related) sense is viewed in relation to nonhuman nature and the natural world. Alienation *of* nature, in the sense of a renunciation of a purely anthropocentrically oriented assumption of ownership over the world, is something to be encouraged. This is the main topic of Chapter 5.

1.6   Estrangement is not always to be overcome: Biro and Evernden

This emphasis on the thought that in some of its senses alienation from nature should be viewed positively is a key element in the position

---

[4] I have mentioned already that some of the doctrines associated with deep ecology seem less than ideal as tools for dealing with the environmental crisis: very strong forms of holism and versions of the idea of 'identification with nature' risk eclipsing the otherness of nonhuman nature. I return to this in Chapter 4.

26   Alienations and natures

I develop. I don't just mean that a state of alienation might be endorsed as a necessary stage in some larger process of self-realization or movement towards final unity. I mean that it should be endorsed more positively in its own right, for example as a condition to be lived with on a more ongoing basis. This suggestion may seem strange, for we are used to seeing alienation mentioned in a wholly negative light, as a pure loss; something to be avoided, overcome or at least as absent under ideal conditions, in favour of a self- – or socially – possessed unified wholeness.

Consider estrangement. The understanding of alienation in political, and perhaps most philosophical, contexts has been shaped most profoundly by the work of Marx, adapting that of Hegel. But it is worth remembering that talk of alienation long preceded Marx or Hegel (or indeed Rousseau). Thus Williams reports that one of the main senses of the English word 'alienation' dates back to the fourteenth century and refers to an act or state of *estrangement* (Williams 1990, p. 33). Examples include being cut off from God, or suffering a breakdown in political or other central social relationships. Indeed it could be that one is estranged in all these ways at once.[5]

Alienation in this sense of *estrangement* then certainly tends to be seen as in some sense bad, or to be regretted; as involving a separation, cutting off or distancing between things that should not be separated, cut off or distanced, at least not in the ways envisaged. This includes when the estrangement is held to be from something referred to as 'nature': the environmental crisis won't be solved until we overcome such estrangement. But in fact, despite the general trend to the contrary, there are some environmental philosophies that, without strongly emphasizing the point or giving it the more positive gloss I shall be giving it, do suggest it can be something we need to live with rather than seek to overcome entirely.[6] It will help to set the scene for my own position if I sketch a couple of examples of such accounts here; those of Andrew Biro (2005) and Neil Evernden (1993).

We saw in the Introduction that Biro explains the 'fact of humanity's alienation' in terms of 'human beings' self-conscious transformation of

---

[5] Such a condition of multiple estrangements and its overcoming is suggested in this passage from Chapter 2 of Paul's *Epistle to the Ephesians*: 'Remember that ye were without Christ, being aliens from the commonwealth of Israel, and strangers from the covenant of promise, having no hope, and without God in the world: But now in Christ Jesus ye who sometimes were far off are made nigh by the blood of Christ ... Now therefore ye are no more strangers and foreigners, but fellow citizens with the saints, and of the household of God' (quoted by Mészáros 2005, p. 28).
[6] Mick Smith has recently endorsed a form of estrangement from nature in something like the positive way that I do; but he makes the point only in a passing note (Smith 2011, p. 230 n. 15).

their natural environment', and that he traces the root of this understanding to Rousseau's account of the move from state of nature to civilized society. Biro emphasizes that Rousseau's state of nature is a dynamic, historical context, not a static scenario abruptly left in a single radical moment of alienation. Such key developments as the splitting of subject and object and the creation of private property, and with that the foundation of political authority and divisions of labour, are not 'originary moments setting previously static conditions into motion', but depend on 'already evolved conditions' (Biro 2005, p. 177). For Biro this suggests a picture of humanity's alienation from nature as itself a dynamic historical process, a picture that allows us to think in terms of more or less intense forms and moments of alienation from nature and of the 'civilized ills' associated with it.

Rousseau's own prescriptions in *The Social Contract* for ameliorating our situation through a higher form of freedom and the moral employment of our rational will be notoriously problematic.[7] Biro particularly emphasizes another problem with Rousseau's thinking, one that occurs in *Discourse on the Origins of Inequality*. In that work, Rousseau tends (like Adam Smith) to conflate the ideas of division of labour and 'exchange' (commercial relations). This obscures an important distinction between an inevitable element of alienation from nature (brought by a division of labour) and what is necessitated in terms of such alienation only when the division of labour takes the particular form of *exchange* (Biro 2005, p. 177).

Biro takes this theme of alienation from nature as the inevitable self-conscious transformation of nature that is both necessary for civilization and a dynamic, historical process with moments that go beyond what is necessary, and pursues it through the twists and turns of Marx's views and those of the Frankfurt School. This adds dialectical materialist complexity to the picture in which notions of 'natural man' and 'state of nature' become ideological and mythical. But most significant for us here is the combination of Marx and Freud expressed in Marcuse's distinction between basic and surplus repression. Biro adapts this distinction into one between *basic and surplus alienation from nature* (Biro 2005, p. 168). Freud believed that the application of the 'reality principle' to repress, and so 'alienate' us from, our 'spontaneous inner nature' is necessary for human civilization. According to Marcuse, however, Freud did not differentiate the reality principle as a self and socially imposed discipline necessary for civilization as such from the merely 'bourgeois performance principle'. The relentless toil and repression of spontaneous instinct

---

[7] For example, in his recourse to the Lawgiver and to Civic Religion.

28   Alienations and natures

and creativity dictated by that performance principle is *not* necessary to civilization as such. It is not *basic* in that sense, but necessary only to civilization at a certain stage of development: it is the *surplus* repression required for the generation of surplus value by capitalism.

Similarly, Biro suggests, 'basic alienation' is that alienation from nature necessary for recognizably human life: *some* self-conscious transformation of nature is necessary. *Surplus* alienation, on the other hand, is alienation from nature necessitated only 'by particular forms of social organisation' (Biro 2005, p. 168); it is the excess instrumentalization and mastery of human and 'external' nature dictated by capitalism. But we can hardly envisage ourselves ever being in the position of no longer 'denying' our instincts and of refraining altogether from self-consciously transforming our surroundings. Even if the surplus-imposing conditions are overcome, *basic* alienation remains ineliminable and this degree of alienation from nature is *endorsed* as a condition of civilization (or of recognizably human life).

Evernden, by contrast, draws on biology and existential phenomenology in his influential portrayal of humanity as a 'naturally alien' species whose members do not mature into an inflexible concrete form fitted to a specific ecological 'place' (Evernden 1993, ch. 5). It seems that part of what is involved in some cases of rapid evolution and speciation, such as the relatively abrupt development of our own species, is 'paedomorphosis' and 'neoteny': a slowed or arrested development of individuals who are able to breed despite retaining characteristically juvenile features into adulthood.

The significance of these factors in the evolutionary process generally and in the evolution of our species specifically (the fact that while we share physiological features with other primates we share more with other primate infants than with other primate adults, for example) is a matter of ongoing controversy within developmental biology. Evernden argues that 'if the conjecture of neotenic development in humans is correct' then it is reasonable to suppose that 'characteristically juvenile' behavioural and psychological dispositions might also be retained into adulthood (Evernden 1993, pp. 115ff). Such dispositions of 'youthfulness' (or their analogues) are observable across vertebrate species (Evernden 1993, pp. 116ff)[8] and include: a 'want of direction' (there not yet being a direct adaptation to environment); a movement-oriented, non-passivity with respect to surroundings and a 'shyly' ambivalent to-and-fro between inside and outside the 'home' (immediate proximity to parents) that

---

[8] Here Evernden draws mainly on the work of biologist F.J.J. Buytendijk, especially as interpreted by Marjorie Grene.

fades with maturity. The main point here is that 'youthful' organisms are not (yet) locked into a specific environmental situation. And, given that we are neotenic organisms,

> it is not at all surprising that the qualities which describe youthfulness in other species also apply to a creature which owes its very form to a slowed or arrested development. We are just what a perpetually youthful being should be: indeterminate, always in motion, ambivalent, obsessed with the "how" of the world and uncommitted to an environmental context. (Evernden 1993, p. 117)

Biologically speaking, then, there is a sense in which we can be said to be 'homeless' creatures. Precisely because it is biologically intelligible and evolutionarily explicable, this 'alien' status is *within* nature, not a matter of transcending nature (Evernden 1993, p. 118). Still, as ecologically 'homeless' and 'uncommitted', we don't find ourselves maturing in ways 'already dedicated to a specific slot within nature'. This means we must '*construct*' a home, and (within indeterminate limits) *decide* how to differentiate it from the rest of nature; how to understand and enact our relation to the nonhuman (Evernden 1993, pp. 118ff). Our decisions, understandings and actions in this area are not always as sensible as they might be, hence the environmental crisis.

For Evernden the environmental crisis involves two main elements. First, at least since the Early Modern period of European civilization we have been refining and following the 'Cartesian' map mentioned above: an 'objective' view of nature as inert matter against which we differentiate ourselves as rational subjects for whom the nonhuman is a mere resource (e.g., Evernden 1993, p. 128). The issue here is not simply Cartesian mind/body dualism as a metaphysical dualism of distinct substances. The division between active subjects and inert objects to be manipulated by those subjects is frequently condemned by critical environmental philosophers. It is not confined to Descartes' own metaphysical dualism (although that might be the metaphysical picture most consistent with it). Evernden's second element of the environmental crisis is a tendency to view the world so constructed 'inauthentically' as unquestionable, the inescapable *given* truth about the world and our place within it (e.g., Evernden 1993, pp. 120f). Even those who worry about the situation and who would want to reject its anthropocentric instrumental associations – 'environmentalists' and 'ecologists' – are following this map when they think of the 'natural environment' as an object for us to do something to, in contrast to the human subject.

In Chapter 6 I return to phenomenological considerations relating to the subject/object distinction and its role in an idea of estrangement

30   Alienations and natures

from the natural world. Here I want to emphasize that one implication of Evernden's account is that we cannot overcome our 'natural alien' status. If we are natural aliens in his sense then this is presumably inescapable. It is just a matter of how things are with us given our particular natural history. Even if we agreed that we could and should cope with our situation in less ecologically disastrous ways by abandoning our 'inauthentic Cartesianism', and we succeeded in doing this, our natural alien status would still be left intact.[9] Still, although our being natural aliens makes it easy for us to fall into ecologically destructive patterns, *that* isn't inescapable and different forms of culture may relieve the destructive symptoms of ecological exoticism and placelessness more or less successfully (Evernden 1993, p. 123). We need to acknowledge our natural alien status and recognize that we certainly cannot overcome it, or do anything other than intensify those symptoms, by treating the deeply questionable *construction* of ourselves as 'masters of objects' as the unquestionable truth about our place in the world.

This matter of our 'construction' of ourselves and nature is very important and I return to it below and in the next chapter. It seems to me that both Biro and Evernden point to parts of the story of our alienation from nature, but that there is more to it as a story involving interrelated elements of constructionism, anthropocentrism, nonanthropocentrism, overcoming and – more emphatically – not overcoming.

Rousseau's account of our being cut off from 'original nature' by 'artificial civilization' is an account of alienation as estrangement. While regarding any return to a natural state as impossible and any serious attempt to achieve it as bound to bring disaster given our corrupt conditioning by society, he does lament the loss of a 'natural innocence' and paint a vivid contrast between that and the weak, vain, servile and dissatisfied condition of civilized man (Biro 2005, pp. 60ff). Biro's contrast between basic and surplus alienation from nature also concerns alienation as estrangement and implies a default negative view of estrangement from nature.

---

[9] As Vogel objects to Biro's account: we remain within nature whatever we do, so how can any of this count as 'alienation from nature'? Because Evernden doesn't quite claim that it does count as alienation from nature, this is not strictly an objection to his account. However, he, or we, might say that it is our way of dealing with this status that alienates us from nature: our natural alien status is not inherently such as to alienate us *from* nature, but our ways of coping with it can be. Thus perhaps such alienation is a matter of the traps we can fall into when considering (or ignoring) our relationship to an encompassing nature, the sorts of mistakes Evernden associates with Cartesianism, rather than something necessarily accompanying either human transformative agency as such or lack of specific ecological niche. This might take a number of different forms, for example, a tendency to *view* humanity, or the 'highest' element of humanity, as *apart from*, rather than a *part of* nature, as when we understand ourselves as something like Platonic or Cartesian souls (cf. Evernden 1993, pp. 44f). I develop such a line of thought further in Chapter 6.

Reification 31

Although endorsed to the extent it is necessary for civilization, the basic/
surplus contrast suggests that ideally there should be *this much* estrangement from nature (i.e., the basic amount) and no more: it is good only
insofar as it is necessary. As I have said, I question the negative connotation of estrangement from *nonhuman* nature more emphatically than
this, while keeping the default negative view of estrangement from the
natural world. Where *nonhuman* nature is concerned the basic/surplus
contrast is better thought of in relation to *overcoming* estrangement: some
overcoming estrangement from nonhuman nature is required but more
than that (the 'surplus') is problematic and may be criticized as such. To
borrow Evernden's terms, as ecologically placeless natural aliens we are
estranged from nonhuman nature. In making our own place in the world
we construct landscapes in which ideally we should be (largely) at home.
But we shouldn't try to pursue this project with the aim of eliminating
all estrangement from our surroundings because *that* would require the
elimination of nonhuman nature.

1.7 Reification

It is no accident that the single term 'alienation' has been used to refer
to both estrangement and property alienation. They can come very
closely related within an overall package. For example, in Rousseau's
story, the invention of private property is a key moment of estrangement
from nature, and a great boost to the ills he associates with it. Given the
existence of property, the hopes and expectations of ownership, then
the being cut off, separated or distanced involved in estrangement, and
the deprivation or loss of possession involved in property alienation, can
produce and intensify each other. In fact we might think of property
alienation as a special case of estrangement. Even so it is useful to distinguish them in order to consider the relationships between different
kinds and ways of understanding each and how these relate to the third
sense of alienation I am interested in.

Williams points out that Hegel and Marx introduced variations of
alienation as estrangement (*entfremdung*), by relating it to notions of
property-alienation that highlight the idea of 'externalization' (*entäußerung*) (Williams 1990, pp. 34f). Thus Martin Milligan translates
Marx's use of *entfremden* in the *1844 Manuscripts* as 'estrange', reserving
'alienate' for Marx's use of *entäussern* in that text. This, he explains in his
translator's notes, is because 'alienate' is the only English word that, very
similarly to *entäussern*, brings together such ideas as 'selling' and 'exter-
nalizing'; 'losing something that remains over-against one'; 'as a result
of one's own action' and 'a simultaneous transfer and renunciation of

32   Alienations and natures

ownership' (Marx 2007, p. 11). *Entfremden*, on the other hand, corresponds closely to 'alienate' in only one sense of the English word (where we speak of people 'feeling alienated', for example), without any necessary connotation of transfer of ownership. Estrangement, as opposed to (property) alienation, is therefore a better translation of *entfremdung* as opposed to *entäußerung*.

From now on when the context makes it clear that I am referring to that specific type of alienation, I shall use the word 'alienation' to refer to property alienation. However, Marx also uses the term *Vergegenständlichung*, sometimes translated as 'alienation' but more often as 'reification', to refer to the mistake of taking human social processes and products as merely given 'things' (Williams 1990, pp. 34f). This – the reification of humanity, human processes and products, as 'mere things' – is my third sense of alienation. I do not suggest that we view this positively.

For the Marxian tradition, estrangement and reification are multifaceted, interrelated affairs produced when the social labour process itself is mediated by the definitive institution of capitalism: private property. Private property necessitates alienation. Workers must *alienate their labour* by selling it. This both presupposes and determines the treatment of their productive capacities as mere commodities *to be sold* (commodification). And it is a situation that conditions workers' 'essential life activity' (labour) as a mere means to survival rather than an expression and affirmation of their rich humanity. Because this is a general feature of their social conditions, and not the isolated situation of an unfortunate minority, they *must* alienate their labour and toil in competition with other workers. The conditions and machinery of production are produced and reproduced by their labour. Yet they have no ownership of this machinery and these conditions; they and their labour being more or less replaceable thing-like parts of the machinery. Nor, as workers, do they own the other products of their labour: the goods it is profitable to capital to have them create. The alienation of labour therefore estranges the workers from themselves, each other and from the social and material environment of capitalist society.

This environment then appears to them in a reified form as a set of things 'confronting them as a hostile and alien power', rather than a homely expression of their own creative humanity, for which they would be willing and able to take responsibility.[10] It is the environmental

---

[10] Obviously this is not meant to be a statement, not even a very compressed statement, of historical materialism as such, or of Marx's analysis of capitalism. It is meant to indicate the basic Marxian picture of the relationship between alienation, estrangement and reification. See Mészáros (2005) for a thorough discussion of the role of alienation in Marx's thinking as a whole.

Reification

33

situation Vogel mainly has in mind (and refers to as alienation) when, as we saw in the Introduction, he argues that talk of 'alienation from nature' should be replaced by talk of 'alienation from something like nature': from the world produced by human labour. That is, the humanized environment or landscape. He is right of course that our needs to recognize the world we are making as one that we are making, and to take responsibility for it and exercise some control over it, are crucially important elements of our environmental situation.

But then from this point of view my whole approach in this book seems vulnerable to an important objection: my employment of such notions as nonhuman nature and the natural world ignores the ideological role such notions play when presented as *ahistorical abstractions* rather than in historical and mediated terms. The ideas of nonhuman nature and the natural world featured in my argument seem simply to be posited, like the reified 'abstract man' of moral philosophy rejected by Marx, as unmediated external constraints on the historical unfolding of the humanized landscape produced by human labour.[11] In reality we encounter the world in concrete forms always already mediated by particular productive relations characterizing a specific stage within that unfolding. Don't I ignore this, for example, when I claim that we should endorse some alienation of nonhuman nature? This seems simply to posit a reified abstraction – nonhuman nature – as something ahistorically to be 'respected' alongside, and as an attempted partial constraint over, the equally abstract ahistorical 'possessive individual' within traditional justifications of private property. Such a manoeuvre will do no more about the concrete reality of alienation, estrangement and reification than did Adam Smith's appeal to 'moral sentiments' as a qualification of the 'propensity to truck and barter' within his account of abstract 'human nature'.

My position need not be interpreted like this. My overall argument, remember, turns on entailment relations between alienation, reification and estrangement with respect to different senses of nature. These ideas and the ideas of nature involved are not just posited and juxtaposed in the abstract – they are internally related, especially so in the light of our concrete environmental situation. I do want to say that nonhuman nature 'as such' is 'outside history' simply in virtue of its landscape-independence. But it is not obvious why this should be inconsistent with emphasizing

[11] In the next chapter I discuss a similar pragmatist argument: references to 'nature' as an external ahistorical constraint (for example, as intrinsically valuable) or source of authority over of us, to which we are supposed to kowtow, are both inconsistent with a mature humanism and serve as 'conversation-stoppers' to short-circuit deliberation in favour of fixing in place a nonanthropocentric worldview.

34   Alienations and natures

that it is encountered, *even as nonhuman nature*, in particular forms mediated by historically specific forms of production. Thus we might agree that from the materialist standpoint, or the standpoint of productive labour, nonhuman nature *must* appear in the particular, concrete forms of those physical, chemical, topographical, biological features relevant to specific labour processes and the science that accompanies these processes. That does not mean that what appears can only be fully humanized (i.e., cannot be nonhuman *at all*).

In Chapter 4 I consider these matters in the light of Ted Benton's 'ecoregulatory' conception of labour: any labour process has always to accommodate to something nonhuman. But the form that takes, and the extent to which it can be accommodated to, manipulated or transformed depends on the particular socio-technological organization involved as much as on 'purely given nature' (Benton 1992, p. 58). There is no need to deny that 'natural limits' to productive activity are relative to particular historical situations rather than being a simple function of ahistorical nature. The question is whether we can set our own limits ourselves and Benton's main point is that once technological change overcomes a particular 'limit', new features of nonhuman nature always come into focus as conditions to be accommodated to. The idea of overcoming *all* such limits is delusional, if not incoherent.

1.8   (Not) 'following nature'

Moreover, my position has no place for models of ideal human arrangements built into nonhuman nature that would enable a conception of estrangement consisting in our failure to 'live in accordance with' such models, or to 'follow nature' in that sense. Strands of bioregionalist and eco-anarchist thought can be read like this: large-scale, hierarchical statist forms of political organization depart from 'the natural order of things', the spontaneous self-organization of nature, which neither has nor requires formalized coercive power relations.[12]

John Stuart Mill provided the classic objection to such claims. The idea of following (or living in accordance with) nature is absurd whether

---

[12] The most influential bioregionalist work is probably Kirkpatrick Sale's (1985) *Dwellers in the Land: The Bioregionalist Vision*. Because Sale's own bioregionalist vision is not a particularly egalitarian one it is unclear whether he should be counted as an anarchist. The slogan that we ought to 'live in accordance with nature', where this is taken to require a form of anarchist society, was coined by Zeno of Citium, the founder of Stoicism. For discussion of the influence of this Stoic theme on anarchist thought see, for example, Woodcock (1977, pp. 17ff) and Belsey (1994). For more discussion of it in the light of the arguments of Mill I am about to sketch, see Hailwood (2004, especially ch. 3).

(Not) 'following nature' 35

nature is understood in terms of the regularities of the overall natural world, or in terms of the nonhuman. In the former terms, because we always remain within the course of nature in this sense we can't do anything but 'follow' it (Mill 1904, p. 12). With regards to the idea of following *nonhuman* nature, Mill points out that nature in this sense is often characterized by the merciless infliction of suffering, death and destruction; things for which we should be justly condemned were we to emulate them ourselves (Mill 1904, p. 16). The selection of those aspects to follow (the absence of formal hierarchical political institutions in other primate species, say) must then be on grounds other than the supposition that they are 'natural' in the sense of occurring within nonhuman nature.[13]

This is not necessarily to refute such theories as bioregionalism and eco-anarchism. It is just to reject the 'following nature' argument for them. In Evernden's terms, we must construct our own home within the natural world with no naturally given map to follow. It would be inauthentic to suppose any blueprint for human homemaking is *supplied to us* by nonhuman nature, if only we would pay attention properly. We make the map, albeit in the light of our experience and conception of what nonhuman nature is like and what it is doing.[14]

Nor is this to deny that our awareness of nonhuman processes should inform our view of how best to organize ourselves. The distinguished environmental philosopher Holmes Rolston (1979) suggests this involves a sense of 'following nature' that avoids Mill's objections. To observe how intimately wrapped up with nonhuman processes we are within the complex interactions of the natural world is to receive from nature a lesson

[13] I should emphasize that to endorse Mill's arguments against following nature is not to endorse the excessively bad press nonhuman nature receives in the article on nature where he mounts these arguments. There rational human action *always improves* rather than follows nature, which – as nonhuman nature – is 'replete' with terrible things. This suggests a 'Cartesian' view of nonhuman nature as a collection of objects to be corralled into an order in accordance with human preferences. It also suggests a false opposition: nonhuman nature is either something to be followed (if not worshipped) as our moral authority, or something to be brought under our moral control. I return to this issue in the next chapter. I should also emphasize that Mill's views on nonhuman nature are quite different when he is not engaged in a polemic against the idea of 'following nature'. He is much 'greener' for example when explaining the merits of a stationary economy and population in his *Principles of Political Economy* (Book IV, Ch. VI, Sec. 2), where he is a stern critic of the unqualified mastery of nature.

[14] This denial of natural blueprints seems to be an implication of Evernden's position in *Natural Alien* consistently followed through. There are times, however, when he points in the opposite direction. As Smith points out, Evernden does at times seem to celebrate the ecologically embedded and 'placeful' form of nonhuman life, as if this is something we ought to try to emulate, such that we should 'aspire to some cultural imitation of a life of "embodied limits"' (Evernden 1993, p. 154; Smith 2011, pp. 112f).

36   Alienations and natures

about our situation that we had better heed, both for our own sake and for nature's (Rolston, 1979, pp. 14ff). Rolston is surely correct to underline the importance of awareness of our location within and dependence upon an overall more than human nature.[15] But 'taking nature into account' by deciding what to do in the light of attention to our embeddedness within the complex processes of the natural world is not a matter of *following nature*. It is at least unhelpful to refer to it that way because it cannot be a matter of our wondering what to do, deciding to do whatever nonhuman nature is doing, and then doing *that*. There must be an assessment of what it is doing and how it relates to human aspirations and ideals that are not themselves simply read off nonhuman occurrences. This seems to be the force of Mill's argument against following nonhuman nature.[16] For me it is important to note that to take our 'true ideals' to be supplied by nonhuman nature is to ignore its otherness (or seek to overcome the estrangement it involves). It is also a case of *reification*: the taking of human products as naturally given things to which we have to accommodate ourselves, rather than potentially revisable human creations for which we should take responsibility.

Similar considerations apply to another sense of nature in terms of which 'following nature' might be understood and, via that, a notion of estrangement as failure to follow it. This is 'natural essence', the essential nature of something, as in 'human nature'; a blueprint built-in to us, as it were, rather than in wider or nonhuman nature. For example, we might think in Aristotelian terms, with the estranging 'failure to follow' a matter of failing to realize our potential for flourishing as the distinct kind of beings we are: rational animals. This would also be a failure to play our proper role in the overall natural world understood as a teleological system of final causes. The failure to follow nature in this sense then is a failure to fulfil our 'natural purpose', a dereliction with regard to our natural

---

[15] I return to this point in more detail in Chapters 6 and 7.

[16] Rolston does admit that 'nature provides us no guidance in our inter-human affairs' (Rolston 1979, p. 26). Yet it seems to me that he fails to appreciate the force of Mill's argument with respect to other senses of 'following nature' he believes escape what he takes to be its overly narrow scope. For example, he posits an 'axiological' sense of following nature. When we value natural wildness, he says, this seems to be a value we discover rather than invent, and it can form the organizing principle of a pursuit – of certain kinds of delightful activities and experiences – with ramifications for one's whole way of life, including that of seeing one's life in the wider context of a nature we have not made. In following this pursuit we are 'following nature' (Rolston 1979, pp. 13ff). I certainly don't object to following the pursuit that is valuing nature in this way, but I don't see how it is (nonhuman) *nature* that is being *followed*, rather than a decision that is being followed; a decision one has made to pursue a certain kind of value attached to a certain aspect of nature that one has discovered; as opposed to a decision to pursue some other kind of value, attached to some other aspect of nature.

(Not) 'following nature'   37

'station and its duties'. If all things true to their essential natures move towards their perfect realization, the natural world itself being the overall system of such realization, then in failing to do well by our own human essence we also fail to be true to overall nature and are out of step with its other component beings. This then is an indirect way of unpacking what it is to (fail to) follow nature in the sense of the natural world and nonhuman nature, as well as specifically human nature, and so a way of drawing attention to a potential condition of multiple estrangements from nature.

The picture need not be so metaphysical. We might prefer, say, Adam Smith's more 'naturalistic' account of humanity's 'propensity to truck, barter and exchange'. Social conditions that thwart this propensity might then be viewed as an 'unnatural' departure (estrangement) from our essential human nature. Put just like this the claim does not have the wider connotations concerning nonhuman nature and the natural world. But these can be added through understandings of evolutionary processes as inherently competitive, perhaps driven ultimately by the egoistic imperatives of 'selfish genes'. Social relations not characterized by competition between self-interested individuals out for personal profit might then start to seem 'unnatural', and to estrange us from the wider processes that have shaped us and are expressed within our (therefore thwarted) essential nature. Or not: perhaps we should follow Kropotkin and interpret natural selection as expressing more the advantages of 'mutual aid' over individual competition. We might be tempted also to add evolutionary psychological content to the picture through such ideas as the biophilia and savannah hypotheses: we fail to flourish in accordance with our essential nature when we live in surroundings and circumstances far removed from our species' environment of evolutionary adaptedness.

I think it would be better to admit that evolutionary processes are too complex and ambiguous for us to derive any such clear normative imperatives to follow in order to realize our essential selves. Mill's argument that the selection of natural processes to emulate reflects prior evaluative commitments also applies to the selection of components of human nature as 'essential' in any such normatively charged way. From the Marxian point of view, such accounts of human nature are hopelessly ahistorical and ideological, of course. They are reflections of particular historical circumstances reified into fixed natural givens.[17] I have mentioned some possible

---

[17] There is a weaker and historical form of essential human nature involved in the Marxian idea of the human 'species being' – our potential for creative cooperative labour. Humanity is estranged from this by class society in general and by the alienation of labour at the heart of capitalist society in particular. But this seems *too* weak and historicized a form of essentialism with which to generate notions of failing to live in accordance with nature. If capitalism and other class societies are necessary precursors to a form of society in which the estrangement is overcome then it would be misleading to

38   Alienations and natures

ways of understanding estrangement in terms of failing to live in accordance with, or to follow, nature in one sense or another, only to put them aside. Partly because of the dangers of reification involved, I can't see how such notions can be made to work in a helpful way. Moreover, and this is an issue to which I return in the next chapter, essentialism in general is inconsistent with the pragmatist spirit of my approach.

The position I am advocating tries to use ideas of 'alienation from nature' to capture environmental concerns, including nonanthropocentric concerns. To do this it makes use of general ideas of nature: humanized nature (landscape), nonhuman nature and natural world. But it does not make use of 'fixed' ahistorical ideas of intrinsic value or 'natural' blueprints of human moral behaviour. As far as nonhuman nature is concerned it is a matter of us relaxing our crushing grip now, in these socio-technological conditions, in this situation of environmental crisis, by accepting some estrangement from it and some alienation of a presumed anthropocentrically oriented ownership over it. Reifying the result of human agency is to be avoided, of course, but so is letting this *idea* of reification run wild, as it were, so as to eliminate the idea of the 'naturally given' altogether, along with the forms of estrangement and alienation I am suggesting are qualified goods. Both kinds of avoidance seem essential for a theory in this area to do what Biro suggests is required of it. Rather than remaining trapped in the

familiar antinomical binary: either nature is something to be passionately defended against capitalist depredations, or [reified] 'nature' can always be revealed as an ideological mask for oppressive social relations ... what seems to be required ... is a way of talking about nature that avoids both uncritical acceptance and paralysing scepticism – in other words, something that will allow us to talk about both nature and 'nature' at once. [This] obviously requires that we not champion one pole at the expense of the other, but ... also eschew any effort at dialectical sublation that would consume both perspectives in order to generate a greater whole. (Biro 2005, pp. 8–9)

1.9   Constructionism

Yet the issue of the 'social construction of nature' has been widely debated in the environmental philosophy literature.[18] It is not only Marxists who

view estrangement from species being as an 'unnatural' failure to live in accordance with our essential nature.

[18] A good sample includes: Evernden (1992), Soper (1995), Soulé and Lease (1995), Rolston (1997), Peterson (1999), Benton (2001), Vogel (2002), Crist (2004), Baxter (2005, ch. 2), Evanoff (2005).

Constructionism 39

will wonder whether one can really talk about ideas of nonhuman nature and natural world as I have been doing without being guilty of simply describing abstract relations between reified social constructions. If they really encompass nothing more than human constructions then taking them at face value as pertaining to a given nonhuman reality reifies the results of human agency. This would be to risk pernicious estrangement from our humanized surroundings and undermine our ability to take responsibility for and control over the world we are making. A critical environmental philosophy must be at least partly about this.

But it can't be *only* about this. If we grant the ubiquitous social construction of thought then the question of what socially constructed thoughts it is best to have still remains, and it seems that we have very strong conceptual and pragmatic grounds for thinking 'nonhuman nature' and the 'natural world' are not merely human constructions. For example, they seem to be required in order for us to apply the concepts of human responsibility and anthropogenic causation. If it is important to say that *humans* made this, caused that, are responsible for such and such, then we need to run the idea of at least some occurrences as *not* of our doing, despite the difficulties of telling what is what in many cases. The alternative looks like a world where everything is always good and nothing bad. Without contrasting exemplars of badness (or at least of less goodness), talk of things being good would be a meaningless superfluity. Taking responsibility for the environment that humanity is making thus appears to presuppose that we retain some grip on the idea of parts of the environment as not of our making.

This is too quick, however. The constructionist is not committed to the view that everything is always as good as it can be. She might argue that although everything is a human social construction, what is constructed – our socio-economic and material environment – could be much better than it is. Indeed, it could be better in terms of overcoming pernicious estrangement and taking collective control over and responsibility for what is made. A serious obstacle to this, she might continue, is talk of 'nature' as if it were something not made by humanity. Thus there is still a point to asserting that 'natural things' are social constructions – no more than products of human physical and intellectual labour – even though *everything* is a social construction. The point is that many fail to accept this truth and their failure is an obstacle to a much-needed improvement in our situation.

I think this line of thought is mistaken and I return to it in the next chapter where I discuss the issues in terms of Richard Rorty's neopragmatism. I will shortly say some more about the ideas of nature involved in my argument, starting with the idea of humanized nature or landscape,

40   Alienations and natures

and in doing so consider more pressures towards constructionist nature scepticism. Before that I want to emphasize briefly the prima facie absurdity of the claim that nonhuman nature is 'nothing more than a social construction'.

When they invite us to pause and consider just how much of our surroundings is the product of human labour, strongly constructionist writers (such as Vogel) recommend a very important exercise. But it is hardly an exercise that establishes everything in our surroundings as entirely reducible to human constructions. For example, on the relatively crude, empirically immediate level of looking out of the window, I have to report that my view of the spectacle of human ingenuity and embodiment of social labour that was Liverpool during the year 2008 when it was the European Capital of Culture was for a time partially obscured by a large splat of bird droppings. Clearly that environmental occurrence was influenced in many ways by human activity and so was not a 'pure natural given'. At the very least it could not have been on my window if there had been no window. And no doubt there were many anthropogenic elements in the sequence of events resulting in the bird being near to my window at that point. But absent some convincing story involving, say, a robot bird, or fake bird droppings stuck on my window by pranksters, it seems absurd to say the droppings themselves, as opposed to our concept of bird droppings and evaluation of them in terms of aesthetics and hygiene, was a social construction, *no less than the window on which they were deposited*. I shall return to this example of nonhuman nature's awkward and annoying intrusions when I discuss estrangement and alienation with regard to nonhuman nature in Chapters 4 and 5.

Dealing adequately with our needs to recognize and take responsibility for the world we are making as aspects of our environmental situation requires us to take care when distinguishing humanity and the rest of nature. Constructionism does usefully highlight the way our environments are culture/nature hybrids, and that this has to be taken account of when drawing distinctions between humanity and (nonhuman) nature. But such matters as the historical conditioning of concepts of nature do not show that there is no nature (it is '*just* a social construction'). They show that the humanity (or culture)/nature distinction has to be drawn carefully. This is where the idea of humanized nature as 'landscape' comes in.

1.10   Landscape

As I have said, I take a landscape to be a portion of the natural world insofar as it is physically modified by human activity and/or interpreted for human oriented ends; moulded and used, or viewed as malleable and

Landscape
41

useful, for the sake of human-centred interests and needs. A landscape is not just scenery; it is a physical and intellectual *construction*. And land-scap*ing* is the ongoing historical process through which humanity phys-ically shapes its environment, fills it with symbolic meaning, historical and aesthetic significance, and so makes itself something of a home in the larger natural world.[19] Towns, cities, conurbations are landscapes. So, for example, is the English countryside the product of millennia of shaping, building, uprooting, planting, cultivation and, in the process, the injec-tion of shifting, sometimes contested, cultural, historical, aesthetic sig-nificance. Calling such portions of the Earth's surface 'landscapes' does not depart far from the standard meaning of the term, but I want to stretch that meaning a little and apply the term to any discernible item assigned a symbolic significance within a culture. Such items needn't be physically close at hand. Thus I want to say, for example, that insofar as the sun, moon and stars are assigned particular (say religious) roles within the symbolic economy of a culture, they are assimilated within that culture's landscape.

It is important to emphasize the active, practical side here and not think of landscape simply as a static thing, much less a *given* thing. Landscaping is something we *do* – do within the natural world and do to and with nonhuman nature. Having been born into landscapes we are always already involved in their reproduction. There are two basic senses of landscaping as activity here: physical (transformation of nature by human activity) and intellectual (the attachment of anthropocentric sig-nificance and meaning to it). When unqualified it is the latter *intellectual* landscaping I referred to earlier as 'anthropocentric instrumentalism'. I take it to encompass not just the crudely use-oriented instrumentalism involved in viewing items simply as resources for economic exploitation, although presumably this is a particularly important form in the context of the environmental crisis.

It also includes interpretations of the sun, moon and stars, *insofar as* the interpretations are focused on the supposed role of such objects *within* human life; their religious role for example: signs from God or them-selves gods to be propitiated, or anxiously consulted portents of human

---

[19] The notion of 'landscape' as a kind of nature/culture hybrid is hardly new of course, especially to geographers. Val Plumwood, who has concerns about the concept, ascribes its classic statement to the German geographer Carl Sauer in the 1920s (Plumwood 2006, p. 121). There is no space here to discuss the notion of landscape in the geograph-ical literature, although I consider Plumwood's concerns below. The idea of landscape is also central to many debates in environmental aesthetics: I was first led to appreciate the importance of the idea by reading Holmes Rolston's (1995) article 'Does Aesthetic Appreciation of Landscape Need to be Science Based?'. I hope it will be clear, however, that I am not confining it here to specifically aesthetic matters.

42   Alienations and natures

destiny, and so on. *Insofar as* a 'wilderness region' is viewed as a site *for* our spiritual renewal, survivalist adventure or opportunity for intense aesthetic experience, it is being landscaped to that extent, however physically 'untouched by human hands' it is. By contrast, nonhuman nature is 'other' in that it is the natural world insofar as it is *not* landscaped, physically or intellectually. Our understanding of nonhuman nature as other is the understanding we have of it insofar as it is not coloured by anthropocentric instrumentalism. Can we ever have such an understanding? It can seem that we have to say no, especially if we view our concepts and theories as tools for helping us in various ways. This is another matter I shall discuss in the next chapter. But consider that the 'indifference' towards us of nonhuman nature which consists in its lack of provision of models of human life for us to follow is an aspect of its otherness. We do not *have to* qualify nature's otherness in this respect and co-opt nonhuman processes as external sources and underwriters of our plans. Nor are nonhuman items simply given to us with 'presented to humanity for your landscaping purposes only' stamped upon them by a nonhuman authority.

Although physical and intellectual aspects of landscaping are distinguishable, they are not entirely distinct. Possibilities of further action, modifications and interpretations are conditioned by those already in place. So, for example, Marx was referring to landscape in this sense when in *The German Ideology* he wrote of the 'sensual world' that it

> is not a given thing direct from all eternity, remaining ever the same, but the product of industry and the state of society … the result of the activity of a whole succession of generations, each standing on the shoulders of the preceding one … (the result of) social development, industry and commercial intercourse. (McLellan 2000, p. 190)

In landscaping we interact with nature and each other to create and transform the 'material conditions' of human life and culture and so recreate ourselves. This also seems to me to be the sense in such claims as that at the end of this quotation from Gary Lease:

> Most observers agree that aboriginal groups have over long periods of occupancy altered contemporary ecosystems in a concrete way by the use of fire, selective harvesting, selective planting, and similar economic activities. Indeed, social critics have argued, based on ecological evidence, that South and Central American Indians have 'constructed' the rainforest. *This means, of course, that humans and nature exist in a dialectical relationship, each imagining the other.* (Lease 1995, p. 10, emphasis added)

It is the rainforest as *landscape* that is 'constructed' here and with which the constructors have a dialectical relationship: they construct it through

Natural world and nonhuman nature 43

their activities and interpretations, and it in turn shapes their lives and constrains their imaginations. Similarly for all landscapes.

It complicates things, of course, that the concept of nature itself is given various interpretations and ideological uses as part of this process. We have already seen some of these. Indeed, a concern to counter the ideological consequences of failing to recognize the origin in human agency of much of our surroundings – and so of reifying them as 'natural' – can motivate scepticism about nature. For example, in recent decades the concern to recognize relations of production and the results of social labour as precisely social products, not 'natural givens', has been extended and expressed in terms of a 'postcolonial' critique of the way that indigenous peoples' contribution to the production of landscapes is ignored when these are viewed falsely as 'pristine wilderness', in the sense that it is untouched by humanity.

Historically there has been a tendency to view the absence of traces of specifically Western civilization as signalling the absence of a human role in the production of environments. Environmental injustices involved in the Lockean take on *'terra nullius'* unmixed with the labour of the 'industrious and rational' can be perpetuated by talk of 'wilderness' (Plumwood 2006, pp. 134ff). Arguments such as those concerning the 'construction' of the rainforest referred to by Lease above are meant to recover and affirm the role of indigenous human labour excluded by the idea of wilderness as *terra nullius* deployed to prepare the ground for colonial appropriation. Similarly, Kate Soper points to the downplaying in importance of rural labour in references to the English countryside as 'nature', as if that landscape wasn't the product of millennia of hard work by the labouring classes (Soper 1995). Still, not everything is the result of human agency, and acknowledging the presence and environmental contribution of indigenous people hardly requires blanket nature scepticism. Both human and nonhuman contributions should be recognized.

For there is no necessary incompatibility between recognizing denied forms of human agency and natural agency provided we make some simple but important distinctions between different senses and concepts of wilderness and nature. (Plumwood 2006, p. 135)

1.11   Natural world and nonhuman nature

The point for me is not to deny either that conceptions of nature are constructions, or the frequently made claim that there is no more contested and ideological concept than nature.[20] It is that they may be

---

[20] See, for example, Williams (1980, pp. 83ff; 1990, pp. 219ff).

44   Alienations and natures

assessed in terms of how helpful they are with regard to coping with the larger environmental crisis. Again, in assuming that there is something seriously amiss with our surroundings, including our imposition on the nonhuman, this perspective is definitely not 'value free'. In this sense it too reflects an ideological choice, rather than a neutral position from which to point out the ideological status of other positions. Of the many senses of nature around, we can helpfully distinguish and employ some basic usages of the term equivalent to particularly pertinent environmental contexts.[21]

As I have said already, one of these is nature in the sense of the *natural world*; i.e., *everything*, or at least everything subject to the empirical regularities often referred to, sometimes perhaps unfortunately, as 'laws of nature'.[22] In one form or another (for example in the guise of 'cosmos') this all-encompassing, overarching sense of nature is an ancient one. This is not to say that the notion of a single unitary nature has been always in clear focus since ancient times.[23] But the idea of the natural world in this sense is available to *us*, and its most significant definitive aspect for us is precisely that it encompasses more than the human; it includes, but also goes beyond, humanity, our actions and the results of our actions.

Nature in this sense of a natural world that includes us therefore also encompasses what is meant by nature in another sense: the *nonhuman* part of the natural world is also often referred to just as 'nature'. Indeed C.S. Lewis reports that another of the most ancient roots of the term, one required by the needs of 'man as a practical being', refers to that which has not been altered or sustained by human activity. He is worth quoting at length on this idea:

---

[21] Good resources for doing so, in addition to Williams' work, include Mill (1904), Soper (1995) and the section on nature in C.S. Lewis' *Studies in Words* (1967 pp. 24–74).

[22] The phenomenological understanding of the 'more than human' natural world I discuss in Chapter 6 does not define it in terms of empirical regularities.

[23] For example, Père Chenu (1997) compellingly portrays the emergence in twelfth-century Christendom of the idea of nature as a single unity of which humanity (or at least the human body) is a part; a development inspired partly by acquaintance with such ancient texts as Plato's *Timaeus*, but also by new theological trends and technological innovations. Chenu notes how various versions of this concept of nature as a single, ordered whole whose regular interconnections we might try to learn, and indeed control, were to be worked out in detail over subsequent centuries. They increasingly occupied theological attention in the twelfth century, displacing a previous fascination with singular events of a disconnected, marvelous or miraculous character. Part of the subsequent working out set in train then was the contrast between the natural and supernatural worlds. In fact, and despite the difficulties posed by the place in nature of human consciousness, what *we* generally contrast with nature in this overall sense is the supernatural and not the human or artificial (Rolston 1995).

Natural world and nonhuman nature

This, as it is one of the oldest, is one of the hardiest senses of *nature* or *natural*. The nature of anything, its original, innate character, its spontaneous behaviour, can be contrasted with what it is made to be or do by some external agency. A yew-tree is *natural* before the topiarist has carved it; water is forced upwards against its *nature*; raw vegetables are *au naturel*. The *natural* here is the Given. This distinction between the uninterfered with and the interfered with will not probably recommend itself to philosophers. It may be held to enshrine a very primitive, an almost magical and animistic, conception of causality. For of course in the real world everything is continuously 'interfered with' by everything else; total mutual interference (Kant's 'thorough-going reciprocity') is of the essence of *nature* ... [in the overarching sense of the natural word]. What keeps the contrast alive, however, is the daily experience of men as practical, not speculative, beings. The antithesis between unreclaimed land and the cleared, drained, fenced, ploughed, sown, and weeded field – between the broken and unbroken horse – between the fish as caught and the fish opened, cleaned and fried – is forced upon us every day. That is why *nature* as 'the given', the thing we start from, the thing we have not yet 'done anything about', is such a persistent sense. *We* here, of course, means man. If ants had a language they would, no doubt, call their anthill an artefact and describe the brick wall in its neighbourhood as a *natural* object. *Nature* in fact would be for them all that is not 'ant-made'. Just so, for us, *nature* is all that is not man-made; the *natural* state of anything is its state when not modified by man. This is one source of the antithesis (philosophically so scandalous) between *nature* and Man. We, as agents, as interferers, inevitably stand all over against all other things; they are raw material to be exploited or difficulties to be overcome. This is also a fruitful source of favourable and unfavourable overtones. When we deplore the human interferences, then the *nature* which they have altered is of course the unspoiled, the uncorrupted; when we approve them, it is the raw, the unimproved, the savage. Inevitably this contrast is represented in all the languages we have had to consider. (Lewis 1967, pp. 45–6, emphases in original)

'Nature' in this sense then refers to those parts of the natural world that we have not brought about and are not responsible for in that sense; parts of the natural world with an origin and existence independent of humanity. To pre-empt some of the argument of the next chapter, I think that this sense of nature, and the required contrast with humanized landscape, necessarily involve 'primitive' or 'magical' conceptions of causality, and other such 'philosophical scandals' only from a standpoint that seeks to transcend the everyday human, no less than the everyday ant, perspective, so as to see everything as 'really' and continuously implicated in everything else. There is no need to interpret the distinction involved as setting up an unacceptable 'antithesis between nature and Man' if this means an absolute dichotomy between humanity on the one hand and, on the other hand, a purely nonhuman realm taken to be the only possible ultimately real referent of the term 'nature'.

46   Alienations and natures

It is difficult to see why the distinction between humanity and non-human nature must be scandalous, as opposed to *required*, by a more practically oriented critical environmental philosophy. The required distinction refers to a contrast *within* the natural world, a contrast significant not least because it is a matter of degree, rather than something like a dualism between utterly distinct substances whose interaction could only be magical. From this perspective the concepts of natural world (of which we are a part continuous with the rest) and nonhuman nature are not *rivals* in a philosophical contest to fix the ultimate truth about the place of things. Although they can require careful adjustment both seem to be important tools for grappling with our environmental situation.

1.12   The importance of matters of degree

The matter of degree – the element of 'insofar as' – in the contrasting and companion ideas of landscape and nonhuman nature is crucial to their functioning as helpful tools. The line between the humanized landscape and nonhuman nature is fuzzy, moveable and porous; more like an intertwining than a line, much less a radical discontinuity. That nonhuman nature admits of degrees makes it unlike nature in the overall sense of natural world: the human impact on – the 'humanization' of – the natural world can be more or less thoroughgoing; presumably without altering at all the fact that it is the natural world. However, that *nonhuman* nature is a matter of degree seems a deceptively simple matter of 'common sense' and, as we saw Lewis hint just now, this can make the idea seem philosophically disreputable. But it seems to me to be crucially important for any adequate understanding of the humanity/nature relation. Even if the natural world is, as it were, 'constant', how much nonhuman nature there is depends on human effort and ingenuity or stupidity. I am giving this practical 'commonsensical' point more philosophical gloss with the ideas of landscape, including intellectual landscape, and the otherness of nonhuman nature. This serves to detach the idea of nonhuman nature from the traditional anthropocentric instrumentalist associations Lewis mentions ('raw material to be exploited or difficulties to be overcome'). We may distinguish more or less anthropocentric instrumental ways of understanding and interpreting 'nature'; i.e., ways of understanding it that tend more or less to reduce it to landscape or to landscaping material. The extent to which nature's *otherness* is qualified depends on the human-environment-building or *landscaping* that is going on, whether physical or intellectual.

It is an issue of course whether the inevitably fuzzy and flexible distinction between landscape and 'wider' landscape-independent nature,

The importance of matters of degree 47

which throws up many ambiguities, is tenable. A main theme of the next chapter is the importance to my overall argument of giving constructionism its due without this involving the nature scepticism of radical constructionism: 'there is no such thing as nature; it's just a social construction'.

Plumwood worries that the concept of landscape itself risks denying or hiding the contribution of nonhuman agency in the production of our surroundings (Plumwood 2006, e.g., pp. 119ff). It might function as another stuck elevator concept that either removes nature from consideration altogether, or traps us within anthropocentric instrumentalism. This worry might be well-founded when the concept of landscape operating is that of a 'cultural landscape', in which everything we encounter is equally and without qualification designated a 'mere' social construction. But it is not a necessary consequence of using the concept once matters of degree are emphasized. Just as relatively landscaped items need not be nearby, so relative otherness is not shoved far away and out of view on the other side of a great divide. *Insofar as* our surroundings are landscaped then they are the product of human agency; *insofar as* they are not then they represent a nonhuman contribution. Human contributions and nonhuman contributions are intertwined and this is made not only possible but inevitable given that human and nonhuman are continuous parts of the overall natural world, rather than utterly distinct orders of being. These issues are intimately related to both positive and negative forms of estrangement and I return to them in Chapters 4 and 6, and in Chapter 7, where I focus on the relations between the different senses of alienation from nature.

The matters of degree involved in these ideas are important also in heading off another source of scepticism about nature. A strict dichotomy between humanity (or culture) and nature requires us to think that an environment is either a purely nonhuman wilderness or a purely human artefact.[24] For example, in the past couple of decades there has been a tendency to talk of the 'end of nature' on the grounds that there seems to be no place on the surface of the Earth that is free from some degree of anthropogenic impact.[25] This tendency is mistaken precisely because landscaping is a matter of degree, and never complete. We may distinguish environments involving more or less thoroughgoing landscaping, as in Robert Goodin's comparison of Los Angeles with the English countryside (Goodin 1992, pp. 50ff). Thus the moon has been affected by human activity through

[24] William Cronon (1995) emphasizes this point in his critique of the idea of wilderness. See also Plumwood (2006, p. 138).
[25] Bill McKibben's *The End of Nature* (1990) is perhaps the most influential work in this regard.

48   Alienations and natures

the famous exploits of astronauts as well as the ultra-high-frequency (UHF) radiation from human communication technology, but presumably less so than the portion of the Earth's land surface that is Merseyside (however tempted one might be at times to apply the concept 'state of nature' there).

A strict dichotomy between humanity and pure nature combined with the thought that there is no pure nature utterly untouched by humanity can produce a strange kind of idealism; one whose slogan is not so much 'to be is to be perceived' but 'to be is to be produced or affected by humanity'. It seems not so much that people think that the tree falling in the forest makes no sound if there is no one there to hear it, but that the tree cannot be falling in the first place unless someone contributed to making it fall (and given that they did, there are no grounds for calling this a 'natural event' in any sense or to any extent). The scale and scope of human impacts on terrestrial nature is indeed immense and intensifying. The very idea that we are in a crisis situation trades on this fact. Yet landscape is a matter of degree and if we don't acknowledge differences of degrees of influence and independence then we are required to believe, for example, that objects many light years away are themselves (not just our concepts of them) no less constructed and so anthropogenic than is, say, downtown Manhattan. Distant planets too have been subjected to anthropogenic impacts in the form of high frequency transmissions radiating out into space at the speed of light for decades.

As Plumwood says: 'It may be reasonable, in the present context, to doubt that there is any part of the earth that has not felt human influence, but to doubt that the world itself has elements of independence is an indicator of the need for therapy, philosophical (Wittgenstein) or personal, depending on the kind of doubt it is.'[26]

---

[26] (Plumwood 2006, p. 135). Paul Keeling (2008) has also pointed out in later Wittgensteinian terms that this sense of nature – nonhuman nature – simply reflects one of its rule bound uses and is in no need of metaphysical justification. This is not to say that one should just be content with dictionary definitions or take nature in this (or any) sense and all of its common employments, associations and contrasts entirely at face value. For example, nonhuman nature is often also referred to as the 'natural world', misleadingly so in the context of my argument because 'natural world' suggests the (overall) sense of nature, which encompasses ourselves and our doings. Notice that it can be misleading also to call all and only things outside nonhuman nature (i.e., *within* the realm of things *we* have brought about) 'artificial'. A strict distinction between nonhuman nature and *the artificial* is objectionable because it excludes the possibility of nonhuman artifice by definition.

2 Pragmatists and sea squirts

2.1 Elements of pragmatism

I said in the previous chapter that I take my overall argument to illustrate an affinity between a critical environmental philosophy activated by a sense of environmental crisis and philosophical pragmatism. It will help to clarify my overall argument further if I defend this claimed affinity and explain its significance. This is the topic of this chapter. 'Pragmatism' can mean different things to different people. I am taking it here to have the following five main interrelated elements.

First is an emphasis on matters of degree rather than strict dichotomies and boundaries. We have seen the importance of this for the distinction between landscape and nonhuman nature. It is important also to my claims about endorsing *some* estrangement and alienation with respect to nonhuman nature. To *some extent* overcoming estrangement from the nonhuman and taking ownership for the sake of human interests must also be endorsed, of course. Some degree of this must be 'basic' in Biro's sense.

The second element is taking an occurrent problem, given in the sense of thrown up by practical life, as the starting point of inquiry. As I have said, I am interested here in the entanglement of philosophy and practical affairs in the relatively strong sense of *starting from* a fairly specific practical problem thrown up by contemporary life – the environmental crisis. The contrast here is with starting from a 'traditional philosophical problem' (what is knowledge or value 'as such', say) on the assumption that reflection on such problems should be the main focus of specifically philosophical work. Insofar as philosophers start from practical problems then they are being pragmatists *in this respect*. Even Descartes' work is not completely opposed to pragmatism in this respect. Indeed, what Evernden calls 'Cartesian' and some consider to be a core feature of an agenda of mastery or domination of nature (the view of nonhuman nature as a composed of 'mere things' to be manipulated), might be better termed 'Baconian' than Cartesian. Descartes was caught up in an

50 Pragmatists and sea squirts

already existing programme, which always was and remains a practical programme.

It should be acknowledged also that philosophers generally look critically at the philosophical tradition (at least at rival positions and schools in the tradition). Again, however, I am thinking of this as a more specifically pragmatist thing to do when the critical work starts from a particular occurrent practical problem, what John Dewey calls a 'problem situation'. For example, *insofar as* early modern philosophers sought to get the Aristotelian picture out of the way in order to release the Baconian programme as a practical programme, then they were being pragmatists *in this respect*. Granted that much previous philosophy has been significantly pragmatist in criticizing traditional thought for the sake of practical concerns though, it is still a question *for us* whether to philosophize in 'traditional problem' mode. We might consider the 'problem of knowledge', for example, as a matter of debating the plausibility of rival theories of knowledge 'as such' independently of any practical situation that encompasses non-philosophers as well as philosophers, and in which knowledge is an actual problem. Insofar as we do then this is a substantive sense in which we are *not* being pragmatist.

This does not mean that my argument is an exercise in 'environmental pragmatism' in the sense of an attempt to arrive at common ground in environmental policy terms by bracketing disputed philosophical conceptions of nature and value (for example, strongly anthropocentric versus strongly nonanthropocentric conceptions). Matters of policy are in question but so are background pictures of the world and the general orientations[1] they involve, and the latter are more the focus here. Nor then is it a 'pragmatic' exercise in the sense of an attempt to discover 'what will work politically' or how to appeal to democratic electorates to achieve short term 'green' political success. The given practical problem is not that of how to get green parties elected or how to achieve support for better environmental policies (although these are problems of course). It is the environmental crisis. Again, I am taking it that we have an inchoate sense of a serious failure in our dealings with our surroundings, and that this has something to do with our being 'alienated from nature'. The issue is how best to shape the idea of alienation from nature to help clarify this sense and understand the situation better.[2]

---

[1] What William James refers to in *A Pluralistic Universe* as 'visions' (James 1977, e.g., pp. 14f).

[2] Although this pragmatic point is more than the rather vacuous 'having something to do with practical affairs', it is still about *philosophy* as starting from a practical problem: here that of clarifying the environmental crisis and how 'alienation from nature' might be helpful in this task. In and of itself this will not *solve* the crisis of course – it is hardly sensible

The quest for certainty   51

The third pragmatist element then is a view of theories and concepts
as adjustable tools for assisting with problems, rather than devices for
depicting fixed truths (which in the ethical case can be taken as the given
to be 'applied' to the question at issue). An important question for me
is whether a pragmatic-'instrumental'-view of concepts and theories as
tools is itself inevitably bound up with anthropocentric instrumentalism. This is why I say only that my overall argument illustrates an affinity with philosophical pragmatism. I would say it is a straightforward
exercise in philosophical pragmatism except that this suggests a picture
of pragmatism as a given, already fully worked out philosophical theory to be applied to the problem. But versions of pragmatism can also
require some adjustment in order to grip adequately the apparent shape
of the problem and assist in its clarification without themselves imposing
anthropocentric instrumentalism. I argue this below through an examination of Richard Rorty's neopragmatism and Ben Minteer's environmental pragmatism.

In examining theories and concepts as more or less adequate tools
we need to be open to taking from different traditions what seems helpful, while rejecting what doesn't seem helpful. This brings a substantial
degree of pluralism to the issue of how best to understand alienation
from nature. I also emphasized the importance of this, the fourth element
of pragmatism, in the previous chapter and introduction. The pluralism
applies in terms of engaging with a plurality of contexts ('environmental reality' is understood pluralistically rather than monistically as The
Environment or Nature), as well as in terms of a willingness to consider
theories and concepts from a range of philosophical traditions as potentially useful adjustable tools. Thus 'nature' isn't the name of just one
thing, to be understood in one particular way taken to be the final truth
about the matter; there are different serviceable senses of nature that
usefully bring different environmental contexts into focus. Similarly for
'alienation' and so for 'alienation from nature'.

2.2   The quest for certainty

The notion of intellectual tools for coping with the world brings with
it a suspicion of things fixed in place by thought as an obstacle to the
forward-looking progressive improvement in the human situation
that theorizing should be seeking. This suspicion is accompanied by
a rejection of what John Dewey called the 'quest for certainty' as an

---

to expect to *end* the environmental crisis through philosophical reflection, much less a
particular exercise of it.

52   Pragmatists and sea squirts

intellectual motive for strict dichotomizing and the erection of Absolutes and Necessities (Dewey 1929). This is the fifth element of pragmatism I want to emphasize.

Of course, reflection motivated by the quest for certainty can produce inspiring pictures of great beauty and intellectual ingenuity. It can also provide a mental peace to individuals of a cast of mind troubled by contingency and an absence of secure foundations. Yet Richard Bernstein suggests a further problem with the Cartesian picture in his description of this cast of mind as one of 'Cartesian Anxiety': 'Descartes' search for a foundation or Archimedean point is more than a device to solve metaphysical and epistemological problems. It is the quest for some fixed point; some stable rock upon which we can secure our lives against the vicissitudes that constantly threaten us' (Bernstein 2010, p. 53). But a trend of thought that in principle seeks its own perfect completion, and so resting place in a fixed state of security, cannot be ideal from the practical point of view, which requires thought to remain flexible, adaptable and in active play. Consider also Midgley's analogy between the flow of water and the 'flow of ideas':

Useful and familiar though water is, it is not really tame stuff. It is life-giving and it is wild. Floods and storms have appalling force; seas can drown people, rivers carve out valleys. Then, too, rivers produce fertile plains and forests. Water works at the heart of life, and it works there by constant movement, continually responding to what goes on around it. Thought, too, ought to be conceived dynamically, as something that we do, and must constantly keep doing. The static model shown us by Descartes, of final proofs to be shown by science, proofs that will settle everything, is one more model that has very grave limitations. (Midgley 1996b, p. 12)

My point is not that many environmental philosophers state an explicit commitment to finding certainty and fixed foundations. Still, explicitly rejecting such a quest is important because it can be a *background* source of excessively radical constructionism about nature in environmental philosophy. On the other hand, environmental philosophy sometimes presents itself *as if* it is the search for a fixed point – often the intrinsic value of nature – that will provide a new nonanthropocentric ethical foundation capable of trumping other considerations in advance. I discuss both of these issues below. As I have said, an important feature of my overall argument is an attempt to give weight to both anthropocentric (including decidedly constructionist) considerations and nonanthropocentric considerations (including 'respect for nature'). Both sides need to remain in play in a relation of mutual implication and accommodation, and having a quest for certainty or utterly secure foundations running in the background is a serious philosophical obstacle to this.

2.3 The sea squirt danger

In order to form a useful understanding of alienation from nature, then, I am suggesting we should follow the call associated most particularly with the pragmatist tradition to 'unstiffen' philosophy; drop the preoccupation with attaining certainty, along with the implied search for a secure mental stillness, an intellectually attained and guaranteed timeless freedom from peril.[3] At the very least these preoccupations and this search move the focus away from the practical problem. To put the point more strongly and pejoratively: they are the elements of a quest more fit for sea squirts than people confronted by serious problems the tools for dealing with which are themselves in need of close examination.

Sea squirts are marine organisms that, in their mobile juvenile form, possess a primitive nervous system (a rudimentary brain-like ganglion). This gives them some sensitivity to light-variation, allowing them to wander the reef in search of a suitable secure location in which to make themselves at home. Once fixed on an appropriate piece of coral they absorb their brains, which are no longer needed (Llinás 1987, pp. 35f). Not that they can be blamed for this. Once securely fixed in place and taking in nutrients wafted their way on the current, they no longer need even their previous slight awareness of their environment, let alone to think about it. Once the 'brainwork' is done, the secure foundation for existence found and, mentally speaking, all is still, what is left to do with your brain except to eat it? Of course, this is hardly an adequate biological description of the relevant events in the sea squirt life-cycle, especially when expressed in exaggerated and sensationalist terms ('They eat their own brains?' 'They don't really have brains!'). But it has become a popular metaphor for bureaucratic place-seeking and keeping: most unfairly a similarity has been noted to the process of gaining academic tenure.[4]

A better analogy is to the 'quest for certainty': the preoccupation with attaining a perfect intellectual security guaranteed to be free from error, from subsequent displacement and the need for further finding. There is a similarity between the sea squirt 'goal' of a fixed security the achievement of which renders the 'intellectual' means of getting there redundant, and the goal of certainty, which suggests an end point where the possibility of error is excluded and thought's anxious striving over,

---

[3] See especially Dewey (1929, ch. 1). See Bernstein (2010) for an account of how such pragmatist concerns are also present in much of the most important philosophical work of the past century.

[4] See, for example, Rowlands (2000, p. 102) after Dennett (1991, p. 177). The neuroscientist Rodolfo Llinás refers to the mindless taking in of nutrients wafted past by the current as a 'typically bureaucratic' process (Llinás 1987, p. 34).

54   Pragmatists and sea squirts

its 'real work' completed: a point of secure mental stillness. Luckily for the subsequent evolution of nervous systems some primeval sea squirts are thought to have retained their 'brains' beyond the juvenile stage in another case of neotenic speciation. To avoid being like the sea squirts we not only have to think about our surroundings, but be very careful how we think. Unlike sea squirts we have to *continue* to think about our surroundings, and so should not think in ways that presuppose that the completion or end of thinking is itself the true goal of thought.

2.4   Constructionist nature scepticism and the quest for certainty

One way the quest for certainty can be unhelpful to environmental thought is in helping to motivate constructionist scepticism about nonhuman nature that is problematically sea squirt-like in its disregard of wider surroundings. This can happen even when epistemological and practical considerations are linked closely together. For example, some sceptical constructionism about nature is the result of considerations bequeathed by the Kant-Hegel-Marx epistemological sequence. Alarmed by Hume's cheerful critique of Reason's abilities and scope,[5] Kant sought to solve the resulting 'problem of knowledge' by means of his Copernican Revolution. Steven Vogel (2011, pp. 193ff) nicely tells familiar elements of the subsequent story as a story about alienation 'from something like nature', and, like much critical theory, his own challenging constructionist environmental philosophy is much informed by these epistemological moves. It also exemplifies their conclusion: we can only know and be on meaningful terms with what we ourselves construct – the humanized landscape. It will be instructive to consider a compressed version of his account of the sequence.

For Kant, the 'problem of knowledge' is solved by presenting the knower as actively constructing, or constituting, the known world (the empirical world) by imposing categories on sense material, rather than 'passively receiving information' as in Hume's classical empiricist model. Epistemology is advanced and knowledge secured by the radical move of bringing the empirical world within the scope of a transcendental 'act' of categorial pre-structuring that renders it no longer 'really' external.

---

[5] Hume's work has its agonized moments to be sure: 'I am confounded with all these questions, and begin to fancy myself in the most deplorable condition imaginable, inviron'd with the deepest darkness, and utterly depriv'd of the use of every member and faculty' (Hume 1969, p. 316). But these seem to be caused by his grappling with some painful Cartesian intellectual implements; the discomfort lessens when he puts some of them down.

Constructionist nature scepticism and the quest for certainty 55

Hegel then further radicalized this picture in his account of *Spirit* actively overcoming nature's otherness through a historical process culminating in its recognition of the world as itself, its own (self-) creation.

Marx comes next but, as a preliminary to that further shift, Vogel emphasizes the crucial place of the master/slave relation within Hegel's system. The slave's labour is 'structurally analogous to the active constitution of the world of knowledge by the knowing subject' (Vogel 2011, p. 193). This idea was deeply inspirational to Marx. Labouring and knowing are both active, productive processes whereby the labourer and knowing subject come to recognize themselves in a world that is no longer apparently alien, other or external, but *their* world. Work – labouring upon objects – is supposed to be a vehicle for self-realization (the actualization of self-consciousness as free personality), as the objective reality of the labourer is demonstrated to herself and others through labour-wrought changes to the world. The labourer is 'in the world' transformed by her labour into an expression of herself. Yet under slavery the labourer's product is appropriated and used by the master, and so becomes a condition of her oppression, a blockage to the very process of self-recognition it is supposed to enable. Although it should be recognizable to her as an expression of herself, it belongs instead to another and appears to her as external – as 'alien'. She is thus *estranged* from the product of her own labour, from the objective vehicle of her own self-recognition (and of her recognition by others), and so she is estranged from herself too.[6]

Vogel portrays (early) Marx's 'materialist turn' as replacing the obscurities of transcendental and absolute idealism with something much more down to earth by 'reinterpreting epistemological categories in terms of practical human activity'. 'Active concrete labourers' know the world through actually building it, rather than by 'magically constituting it'.[7] 'Alienation', by which Vogel means here 'reification' (a lack of recognition of objects as the labour products they are, such that they appear instead as 'external things' and 'alien powers') becomes an economic phenomenon. Objects created by labour function as the source of capitalist profit, and ultimately capital itself and so, rather than being labourers' means of self-expression or actualization, create conditions that stultify and impoverish them. The labourers are then 'confronted by and

---

[6] For Hegel, the recognitional conditions of self-realization involve more than the mere absence of slavery; they also require more positive institutional expression, including through the institution of private property. Issues of 'recognition' will reappear at various places in the following chapters. In Chapter 3 I consider the Hegelian picture in more detail and in Chapter 5 the place of private property in his system.

[7] That is, transcendentally, or through being vehicles of Spirit's journey to self-knowledge (Vogel 2011, pp. 193–4).

56   Pragmatists and sea squirts

yoked to a world of objects from which they are alienated'. In our terms they are estranged from the landscape.

Vogel also stresses the ways in which the economic focus of Marx's materialism brings out the social and historical character of this process (Vogel 2011, pp. 194f). Hegel's approach is historicist through and through of course, and his account of master/slave relations is an account of social relations, but the economic picture he paints remains relatively individualistic. Marx brings to front and centre the fact that all production is social production and that labourers fail to see the *social*, not just human, origin of that which confronts them as a hostile power. Economic facts, such as commodity prices, unemployment rates and so on, appear in a reified form as 'natural facts', or the product of 'natural forces', rather than as the expression of productive relations they really are. 'Alienation', in the sense of a complex of estrangements and reification, is thus a social phenomenon, and overcoming it requires recognition of the human social origin of such processes and their re-appropriation as such. Vogel (2011, p. 196) says that 'for Marx … [this] meant something like putting them under the control of a democratically organized planning process'.

Knowledge is properly secured then when 'active concrete labourers' take full social possession of that which they can know – the landscape that they and their fellows have produced. It is on this basis that Vogel argues that talk of nature as something 'beyond or before practice' that we should respect, or from which we might be estranged, is actually a further expression of our estrangement from our socially created world. Such a nature is not something we *could* know given that knowledge is achieved through social production:

The trouble … is that if knowledge is truly active then this putative substrate ['matter', or nature 'beyond or before practice'] cannot itself be *known* – which makes it quite uncertain what status the repeated claim that it exists could possibly have, or what relevance its existence might possess for a critical theory of human life given that such a life is of course a practical one. (Vogel 2011, p. 202, emphasis in original)

Now the view of thinking and knowing as active, productive and social is a central theme of the pragmatist tradition, which has generally sided with Kant and Hegel against classical empiricism on such matters as the 'spontaneity', historicity and mediated character of our cognitive life and knowledge (Bernstein 2010). This, however, does not require buying into the quest for certainty. And, at least in the case just discussed, the view that thought can only know and be on meaningful terms with what it actively constructs itself, while resonating with pragmatist ideas

Constructionist nature scepticism and the quest for certainty   57

of knowledge as social practice, was originally motivated largely by the concern to restore certainty and necessity in response to the Humean claim that we have no *rationally certain* grounds for our belief in an external world, the 'uniformity of nature' and so on.

Hume's own 'gentle scepticism' came with the advice that we should try not to worry too much about reason's inability to establish non-trivial, certain foundations for knowledge (when the anxiety wells up, do something else: have dinner with friends, play some backgammon...) (Hume 1969, p. 316). Such advice remains futile in the face of the *demand* for certainty. But the original concern to restore certainty, and so abolish the kind of anxiety produced by the absence of certainty, can paradoxically result in scepticism about nature as more than human. Given that the environmental crisis is partly constituted by the impact of human action on nonhuman species and systems, we *should* worry about *that* scepticism. There is a lesson here.

We are taking environmental philosophy to be concerned with helping us make a world for ourselves on better terms with our surroundings, including nonhuman surroundings, and so to be prepared to criticize the philosophical tradition for the condition and type of the tools it has provided for the job. Such an environmental philosophy must then be wary of transposing concepts, theories and arguments designed to secure necessities and certainties, to 'calm troubled souls', into concepts, theories and arguments for handling the ontological and normative relations of humanity and nature. They are too stiff and inflexible; they were designed for a different job: *they're the wrong tools!* As such they are likely to delineate sea squirt surroundings more than human surroundings.

It might be objected that this fails to do justice to the praxis-oriented thinking of environmental constructionism unpacked in Marxian or critical theoretical terms. After all, the goal of such thinking is a reappropriated practice and world produced by that practice and precisely not some sort of stillness or end of thought. But, left unchallenged, the epistemological moves reducing nature to the anthropogenic world in order to focus attention entirely on the project of making that as homely an expression of humanity and epistemic security as possible, *do* end thought about how the home is situated, about what is 'outside' it – how it relates to its wider environment. It is exactly as if all were still and settled as far as the outside issues are concerned. Consider that 'brainless' adult sea squirts, fixed to the coral though they are, are not therefore utterly inert; they continue to actively modify their immediate environs through living and metabolizing, but do so without even their former slight awareness of a wider world. This exemplifies the problematic 'application' to environmental questions of a given line of philosophical

58   Pragmatists and sea squirts

thought without critical regard to the implications of its colouring by the quest for certainty.

2.5   Environmental pragmatism and nonanthropocentrism

An implicit quest for certain foundations is also problematic when the environmental philosophy eschews constructionism and embraces non-anthropocentrism. To see this, consider that my association of critical environmental philosophy with pragmatism will raise eyebrows; eyebrows likely to get higher the more I emphasize critique of traditional anthropocentric assumptions. This is because the intervention of philosophical pragmatism into environmental philosophy is often associated with suspicion of, if not hostility towards, nonanthropocentric valuation of nature 'for its own sake'.

A good example of this is Ben Minteer's case for basing environmental ethics on Deweyan pragmatism. In his impressive book *Refounding Environmental Ethics: Pragmatism, Principle and Practice* (2012), Minteer plausibly presents environmental ethics, as it has developed since its origins in the 1960s and 1970s, as a primarily nonanthropocentric bastion for the defence of nonhuman nature for its own sake, independently of human interests. Despite differences (for example between a 'biocentric' focus on individual organisms and an 'ecocentric' focus on ecological systems), the field has been largely united in condemnation of a 'flawed anthropocentric ontology and ethics' – an exclusive concern with human interests and moral worth – as a major factor behind the environmental crisis (Minteer 2012, pp. 4–6). This looks like the feature of environmental philosophy that I have referred to as 'critical'. There have been dissenting voices of course; thinkers who have emphasized the resources for environmental protection available within anthropocentric traditions of thought. Minteer points to the work of John Passmore and to the development of environmental pragmatism, for example in the work of Bryan Norton and the important collection of papers edited by Andrew Light and Eric Katz (1996). Viewed in this light, pragmatist environmental philosophy itself appears as a *critical* departure; this time from a prevailing nonanthropocentric orthodoxy. Thus from Minteer's environmental pragmatist perspective, 'traditional' nonanthropocentric environmental thought suffers from some serious and interrelated defects.

One is a commitment to 'moral monism'; to finding a single normatively compelling type of environmental value, particularly a nonanthropocentric 'intrinsic value' in nonhuman organisms or systems (Minteer 2012, p. 116). Pragmatism by contrast welcomes a plurality of values as resources to help resolve problem situations. This pluralism breaks with

Environmental pragmatism and nonanthropocentrism 59

the quest for certainty as a foundationalist quest for *the* single moral end, a final truth concerning humanity's place within and obligations to nature that is fixed prior to practice and deliberation (Minteer 2012, e.g., pp. 116f). For pragmatism all claims are fallible and revisable in the face of experience, criticism and open-ended 'experimental' inquiry. Moreover, for Minteer, nonanthropocentric environmental philosophy is strangely hostile to anthropocentric values, despite the widespread appeal of such values and their efficacy for practice, including environmental practice. It is oddly insistent on the *necessity* of a reorientation of human culture around nonanthropocentric value recognition (Minteer 2012, e.g., pp. 17–19). This leaves little space for meaningful public deliberation of the merits of such claims and their relation to the actual problems and projects of concrete individuals and communities, and to the dilemmas faced by environmental managers and policy makers (Minteer 2012, pp. 19ff).[8]

Thus Minteer makes nonanthropocentric environmental philosophy seem rather sea squirt-like in orientation, with the apparent aim of fixing us once and for all securely to intrinsic value. It seems to be about establishing the one true picture of our proper place within an intrinsically valuable nature as a secure normative foundation that, once discovered, eliminates the need for further reflection and discussion beyond its mere elaboration and application. This is just the sort of thing that Dewey rejects when in *Reconstruction in Philosophy* he criticizes appeals to 'ends in themselves' as things dogmatically 'injected into the situation from without' (Minteer 2012, p. 66; cf. Dewey 2004, p. 97). These preclude the need for 'intelligent' consideration of the multiple factors and values in play in actual problem situations, where fallibilism and revisability hold sway. The assertion of foundational normative nonanthropocentrism then functions unhelpfully as a 'conversation-stopper', or as the only alternative allowed into a crude zero-sum contest with a crassly instrumental, consumerist anthropocentrism.

Minteer does accept that general claims about the noninstrumental 'considerability' of nature may contribute to the successful resolution of environmental problems. But this is only if offered alongside other considerations as revisable pointers to progress in particular problematic situations. In other words, only if their status (appraisal of their 'rightness') is offered as contextual, rather than fixed and foundational (Minteer 2012, e.g., pp. 73f). Moreover, once viewed in this light it is

---

[8] Minteer illustrates his case with quotations from such distinguished nonanthropocentric environmental philosophers as Holmes Rolston, J. Baird Callicott and Eric Katz (Minteer 2012, pp. 18f, 34ff, 84f).

60   Pragmatists and sea squirts

clear that the opposition between anthropocentric and nonanthropocentric considerations can be overdone. Viewed instrumentally, as tools for the resolution of problems, apparently nonanthropocentric considerations may be translated into an anthropocentric form that is 'weaker' and more considered than crassly economistic and consumerist forms of anthropocentric instrumentalism. Nature *is* a resource for humanity, but not just a material resource; it is a moral, spiritual and imaginative resource, a source of inspiration to be mined in order to raise the tone and efficacy of environmental problem-solving (Minteer 2012, e.g., pp. 84ff).

I return to these issues below. However, I do think that a nonanthropocentric, *noninstrumental* view of nature is a weighty and inescapable element of an adequate critical environmental philosophy. Minteer's pragmatist objections have force insofar as nonanthropocentrism presents itself in the form of an assertion of the one true moral vision that must animate all acceptable environmental attitudes. Yet a weighty (not 'weak') element of nonanthropocentrism can be contained within an environmental philosophy that eschews fixed foundational principles, ahistorical or decontextualized intrinsic value claims and does not view nature as an external authority or something to be worshipped or followed. My focus is on how 'alienation from nature' might be understood to assist in clarifying a problem situation. Again then, much obviously depends on the initial understanding of the problem situation, inchoate and revisable though this is. In terms of Dewey's account of a properly pragmatist method of inquiry, as presented and advocated by Minteer, it is a matter of the first two (or maybe two and a half) stages:

(1) the formulation of a "problematic situation", or the judgement that a particular "indeterminate" situation – that is, one characterized by a perceived instability or disturbance – requires investigation; (2) the contextual analysis and generation of various action-guiding hypotheses; (3) the reasoning through, rehearsing and testing of these hypotheses. (Minteer 2012, p. 29)[9]

If we are to go through these stages without fixed metaphysical dogmas then this applies to anthropocentric instrumental dogmas too. As Minteer says, but could emphasize more, the call to avoid mere dogmatic assertion or 'application' of given entrenched metaphysical pictures and monistic principles applies to both sides.

---

[9] The fourth stage is 'the construction of a reflective and terminating judgement resolving the problem at hand (although a decision is open to revision and replacement in the light of further inquiry)' (Minteer 2012, p. 29).

Environmental pragmatism and nonanthropocentrism   61

The nonanthropocentric focus within environmental philosophy can be read as arising from a sense that purely anthropocentric instrumental assumptions are built into much of the philosophical tradition and the surrounding culture, and that this is an important part of the problem situation – the environmental crisis. Bringing to light and criticizing these assumptions, and formulating alternative value orientations, then became very important: *someone has to do it!* It is not as if anthropocentric orientations are hard to find in wider philosophy and the intellectual culture generally. Nor is it that nonanthropocentric environmental philosophers are unconcerned with practice, although from the perspective of mainstream business as usual *outside* environmental philosophy the called-for practice might seem disconcertingly radical and 'unworldly'.[10] Yet the trace of sea squirt baggage identified by Minteer in nonanthropocentric thinking is a problem and not unconnected to a lack of worldliness.

The position here seems to me to be similar to that involved in Vogel's constructionist nature scepticism. Vogel makes a very important point: we should overcome estrangement from our anthropogenic environment so as to take control of it. This project is not helped by an environmental philosophy speaking *only* about 'nature', especially if its references to the nonhuman are unpacked in terms of intrinsic value claims fixed in advance as trumping most anthropocentric interests. Vogel's point speaks to an inescapable element of the problematic situation. But the quest for certainty in the background of Vogel's radical constructionism and its fleshing out in a praxis of knowledge and control eliminates from consideration another vital element of the crisis – our problematic relation with the nonhuman. That seems too 'radical' and 'unworldly' too.

Both anthropocentric and nonanthropocentric critique is required and both are badly served by the search for certainty and fixed foundations. Indeed, the *estrangement* between anthropocentric and nonanthropocentric seems to me to be also a deeply unfortunate part of the situation: both are needed to play their part in articulating and grappling with it. I agree with Minteer that to play their parts better both sides should adopt a more pragmatist philosophical orientation, rather than the more usual 'applied' orientation in which already fixed positions are applied to practical issues. This suggests that environmental philosophy would be better off considering itself to be pragmatist with a big 'P' (rejection of quest for certainty, fixed foundations, monism and so on)

---

[10] See, for example, Callicott's paper 'Environmental Philosophy *is* Environmental Activism: The Most Radical and Effective Kind' (Callicott 2002).

62   Pragmatists and sea squirts

rather than pragmatist with a small 'p' (simply having a concern with applying itself to practical issues).[11]

2.6   Pragmatism and constructionism

As I have mentioned however, my argument is not meant as an *exercise* in philosophical pragmatism in the sense of treating it as a given doctrine to be applied to environmental issues. Theoretical commitments peculiar to versions of pragmatism may themselves be problematic within environmental contexts and criticized as such. For example, consider the tension within environmental contexts between the pragmatist idea of theories as tools for coping with the world, and the view, also often associated with this idea, that concepts and theories are practical tools for *making* the world, more than they are for *discovering* truths about it. There is a danger, when the 'making' idea is given a strong sense, say via theories stipulating conditions of meaning, that the notion of a 'nature' that has *not* been made by humans, and with which we may have a more or less defective relationship, will appear meaningless, and so a useless tool to be discarded. Clearly the sense of us as 'world-making beings' is an important one; I am thinking of it in terms of the notion of 'landscaping'. But given that the original motivation for using such notions involves concern about humanity's relation to the nonhuman (this being at least one significant aspect of the environmental crisis), they need careful, critical handling not to eliminate the idea of 'human-independent reality' altogether and land us in sea squirt territory similar to that arrived at through the quest for certainty.

Still, it might be objected, no amount of careful handling here will be sufficient: associating my account of alienation from nature with philosophical pragmatism is misconceived because it is actually inconsistent with a genuinely pragmatist philosophical orientation. I shall discuss three objections in this area, each of which concerns my distinction between humanized landscape and nonhuman nature. They are three ways in which pragmatism might be thought to reduce nonhuman nature to landscape and so exclude the nonanthropocentric elements of my account; including the suggestion that we endorse a degree of estrangement from and alienation of nonhuman nature.

One is that as a radically constructionist philosophical doctrine, pragmatism excludes the idea of nonhuman nature as *landscape-independent* nature. Another is that their instrumental understanding of justification

---

[11] For a statement of this contrast from a 'small p' perspective, see Callicott et al. (2011). See also note 2 above.

Pragmatism and constructionism 63

commits pragmatists to an anthropocentric instrumentalism that rules out the idea of nonhuman nature in my sense of landscape independent. Third, pragmatism's humanistic orientation rules out any external non-human authority or value as a constraint on human deliberation of what is in the best human interest in any given problem situation. I shall consider these in turn, starting in the next section of this chapter.

But first it will be useful to remember that there are different versions of constructionism, and that we may distinguish more or less thorough-going forms of social constructionism about nature.[12] Let us label as 'moderate constructionism' the view that simply says conceptions and theories of anything, including nature, are formed in social contexts, and may express numerous possible interests, not all of which can be thought of as universal interests. This seems to be a truism usually worth mentioning only in some reformist or liberationist context, where one says something like 'such and such an idea, identity or practice is in the interests of *those* people over there, and against *your* interests; but it is not inevitable, or somehow built into the essential nature of things, it is a social construction'.[13] This moderate position does not entail the sweeping ontological claim that seems to animate *radical constructionism*: everything, including nature, is socially constructed. That is, there is *nothing* to nature than this or that social construction labelled 'nature'; hence there is no 'real' or 'independent' nature.[14]

Moderate constructionism as such is consistent with the landscape/nonhuman nature distinction. It allows us to interpret talk of the 'social construction of nature' as a reminder not to be naive: when the issue is 'nature' one should be aware of the landscaping that might be going on, in which nature is coopted to, interpreted in line with, this or that humanity-oriented end, cultural purpose or project. One might 'stand back' from landscaping concerns to ensure that landscape and nature are not simply being identified through one's thinking. This suggests a

---

[12] See Brian Baxter's useful discussion (Baxter 2005, ch. 2).

[13] Compare Hacking (1999, pp. 6ff).

[14] It would be a mistake to think that I am wasting time on a straw man here. I touched on some grounds for radical constructionism in the previous chapter. Vogel, exemplifies the move from moderate to radical social constructionism when he emphasizes the material sense of 'construction' suggested by 'the social construction of nature' (construction of the material landscape), and that we should always remember the contingent constructed status of our ideas of the natural, but also suggests that since we can't know a 'nature' independent of all this constructing, environmental philosophy should go 'postnatural' and drop the notion of nature altogether (in addition to the references above, see e.g., Vogel 2002, pp. 33ff). Richard Evanoff (2005) exemplifies the moderate constructionist resistance to this move when he agrees that understandings of nature are socially constructed, but argues that nevertheless these constructions are constrained by 'how things actually are'.

64   Pragmatists and sea squirts

distinction between types of intellectual landscaping; between landscaping aware of itself as landscaping, able to recognize a nature independent of landscape, and landscaping that is not self-aware in that way. This latter sees the world *only* in anthropocentric instrumentalist terms as landscaping material; only in terms of human interests and needs, or the role items in the world might play in this or that cultural project.

But now what if a radical constructionist says there is nothing to nature beyond the anthropocentric concerns of landscaping? With the distinction just made between modes of intellectual landscaping in mind, one might reply as follows.[15] Suppose that radical constructionism is true – there is nothing more to nature than this or that understanding of it. This is still not to say anything about the object of such understanding – 'nature', which, we are allowing, may be as constructed as you like. It remains open whether that object, even if constructed, is something other than landscape constructed in a specific – i.e., human-oriented instrumental – way. This line of thought expresses the plausible view that radical constructionism about nature does not strictly entail a purely anthropocentric instrumentalist view (construction) of it. For example, although one might struggle to make this position at all plausible, one might argue that (i), there is nothing to nature beyond our constructions of it and (ii), the best construction represents it as something to be worshipped *regardless* of human interests.

On the other hand, I think that purely anthropocentric instrumental landscaping is equivalent to what amounts effectively to an important kind of radical constructionism, even if the ontological claim (there is *nothing* to nature but constructions) is officially denied. An implicit or explicit assumption that the natural world is entirely 'our world' in the sense of only a resource for human use effectively reduces nature to landscaping materials. Therefore, because the idea of landscape is that of nature insofar as it is modified or interpreted for human-oriented ends, it reduces nature to landscape. Clearly, this is not equivalent to the baldly sceptical claim, 'there is no such thing as nature'. For example, the 'Cartesian' picture of objectified and instrumentalized nature does not deny nature. But such anthropocentric instrumentalism does effectively reduce the natural world to the human landscape (nature insofar as it is transformed or *interpreted* for the sake of human-oriented goals). In that respect it implies scepticism about *landscape-independent* nature. And indeed, by locking us into anthropocentric instrumentalism when it comes to justifying our beliefs and claims to each other, the pragmatist

---

[15] I am indebted to Logi Gunnarsson for suggesting this line of thought to me.

tradition can seem to enclose us within the human landscape. But I shall argue that this is not inescapable.

At this point, however, merely asserting that we don't have to confine ourselves to anthropocentric instrumentalism hardly takes us far against radical constructionism as such. For the something other than instrumental landscape is itself admitted as constructed, albeit now in a way that is 'self-aware' in being prepared to recognize more to 'nature' than our anthropocentric instrumental interpretations of it. We might still worry that this is just another human construction, and think that what is required is some way of securing the distinction between landscape and not-landscape (as a distinction between our humanized environment and independent nonhuman nature) as not just another mere construction. But this is just what radical constructionism seems to rule out: the notion of 'nature as such', as it is independently of us and our landscaping, has no application.[16] There is just the landscape (a historically developed collective cultural/material/intellectual construction); so as nature is swallowed by, identified with, the landscape, there seems no space left for the nature/landscape distinction.[17]

2.7 Rorty's neopragmatism

In considering whether pragmatism entails such radical constructionism I shall focus mainly on salient aspects of Richard Rorty's neopragmatism. My aim is not to assess the overall coherence or philosophical acceptability of Rorty's neopragmatism, or to present it as the most defensible form of pragmatism. Rather I take it to be a well-known recent version of pragmatism that seems to present the problems in a particularly strong form. His portrayal of 'independent reality' as the 'world well lost', and endorsement of Derridean talk of there being 'nothing outside the text', might well be taken as a paradigm of radical constructionist elimination of landscape-independent nature.[18] Thus it is worth seeing whether

---

[16] As Stephen McLeod has suggested to me, we can put the situation simply as follows. Given that all concepts are socially constructed, a question is: are their extensions, if they have extensions, also socially constructed? The concept money is a socially constructed concept with an extension, the concept phlogiston one without extension. Radical constructionism seems to say the extensions of all concepts (with extensions) are themselves social constructs. In the case of the concept of nonhuman (landscape-independent) nature it seems incoherent to suppose that *that* has a socially constructed extension. Thus the radical social constructionist position seems to be that that concept has no extension.

[17] Such constructionism should be distinguished from the 'end of nature' thesis, which presupposes that there at least *used to be* nonhuman nature. See Benton (2001).

[18] Holmes Rolston takes it in this kind of way (Rolston 1997, p. 39).

66   Pragmatists and sea squirts

Rorty's version of pragmatism does in fact exclude the landscape/non-human nature distinction as I understand it.

A helpful discussion of Rorty's neopragmatism should notice first that what he calls the 'world well lost' is *not* the universe of stars, planets, ecosystems and organisms (mostly) causally independent of, but causally impacting on, humanity, as investigated by science. It is the world understood as the way things *really* – as opposed to merely *apparently* – are; an Ultimate Reality posited in various ways by the philosophical tradition.[19] Rorty rejects philosophical 'realism', but without endorsing 'anti-realism' or idealism, in the sense of a denial of 'mind-independent reality', meant as a philosophical discovery finally fixing the ultimate, intrinsic nature of things as turning out to be not at all what people, especially non-philosophers, had imagined. Rather the rejection of realism is part of a case against a traditional, 'Platonist', philosophical urge to establish a special authority over other parts of culture by claiming to *fix* the limits of Knowledge, Rationality or Meaningful Discourse, and so Reality.[20] Once the goal of truth-as-correspondence-to-reality is abandoned as Rorty wishes, then philosophical claims must earn their keep through their pragmatic value, like all other claims. As with Dewey and other pragmatists the point is that the traditional philosophical search for necessary and sufficient conditions of Truth, Knowledge, Meaning, Reality no longer earns its keep (if it ever did).

So Rorty's rejection of philosophical realism (as Platonism) is not meant to entail a denial of a 'real world' pressing on us, constraining what we find useful to say. He emphatically endorses Donald Davidson's view that the relation between world and beliefs (or the vocabularies in which beliefs are expressed) is causal, not normative. Because relations like *sanctioning*, making correct/true or incorrect/false are normative, they cannot hold between world and beliefs, only between beliefs and other beliefs. If we find ourselves wanting to say more about truth, or The Truth, perhaps in order to fend off relativism then, as Rorty puts it,

Davidson's claim that a truth theory for a natural language is nothing more or less than an empirical explanation of the causal relations which hold between features of the environment and the holding true of sentences, seems to me all the guarantee we need that we are, always and everywhere, 'in touch with the world'. If we have such a guarantee, then, we have all the insurance we need against 'relativism' and 'arbitrariness'. For Davidson tells us that we can never be more arbitrary than the world lets us be. So even if there is no Way the World Is, even if there is no such thing as 'the intrinsic nature of reality', there are still

[19] Rorty (1982, pp. 14ff; 1989, p. 5; 1998, pp. 72f, 83; 1999, pp. xxvi–xxvii, 32f).
[20] See for example, Rorty (1980, pp.3, 8, ch. 8; 1982, p. 19).

Rorty's neopragmatism

causal pressures. These pressures will be described in different ways at different times and for different purposes, but they are pressures none the less. (Rorty 1999, p. 33)

All such describing goes on within historically conditioned vocabularies (hence 'everything is socially constructed'), but these may be extended, modified and brought together in novel ways, so that we 'recreate' the world and ourselves. The criterion of improvement here, *the justification*, is the pragmatic one of coping better with reality: improving human life by allowing new questions, new answers to old questions, new ways of framing things and so new possibilities of action. It would be unhelpful to try to judge success here by lapsing back into Platonism and take ourselves to be describing The Truth About What It Is (Or How) To Be Human. We just have various beliefs in this area, which we seek to justify in line with other beliefs, including beliefs about political and economic realities and consequences. So the normative kudos associated with 'truth' is to be reassigned to 'usefulness relative to the project of coping with reality and improving human life'. And Rorty associates improved human life with freedom in a pluralist liberal democracy (or 'maximal room for individual variation', which he calls 'the liberal goal' (Rorty 1999, p. 237)).

Put like this, it seems that Rorty's neopragmatism does not exclude the landscape/nonhuman nature distinction. 'Nonhuman nature' means the world insofar as it is not landscaped, *not* a finally fixed realm, ahistorically accessible by Reason through its timeless determination of Knowledge, Truth and so on: 'the world well lost'. The distinction just has to make sense (cohere with rather than contradict or exclude other beliefs to which we are committed) and be 'useful'. I return to the important issue of justificatory utility below. As for making sense, we could just refer again to matters discussed in the previous chapter, such as Lewis' account of the nonhuman as a perennial sense of nature required by our practical situation.

More than that though, consider that Rorty, like Dewey, emphasizes the affinity between his view of language (and so theory) as a set of tools for coping with and manipulating reality, rather than a device for representing reality, with a Darwinian theory of human origins and capacities. It is easier, he thinks, to understand human linguistic behaviour as continuous in this way with pre-human adaptive behaviour than in terms of the sudden emergence, with our species, of language as a device for *representing* reality (Rorty 1999, pp. 64f). Obviously, the Darwinian story requires the idea of nonhuman nature in order to fill out the ideas of evolutionary origin and of the natural environment relative to which human features and types of behaviour are adaptive (or not). This is

68   Pragmatists and sea squirts

a large part of the reality with which we are to cope. Also part of the
story about that reality must be the idea of an evolved (or evolving) set
of human capacities. These include our linguistic sophistication, which
allows culture and history and our capacity to landscape in the sense
of self-consciously transforming our environment and identifying items
within it as more or less useful in our constructing of a (better) home
for ourselves in the world. These ideas are not supposed to be The Truth
about Ultimate Reality, but particularly useful ways of talking about the
world and ourselves.[21]

2.8   Neopragmatism and radical constructionism

Consider again the distinction between moderate and radical forms of
social constructionism. The former says that all claims and theories,
including those about nature, are formed in a social context, and may
be 'interested' in various ways (so one shouldn't be naive about them,
but be prepared to criticize them). That, remember, allows for the nonhuman landscape/nonhuman nature, whereas stronger constructionism
seems to threaten it. However, *radical* constructionism, if it is taken to
have extra-linguistic ontological import – *there is nothing to X ('nature' or
whatever) but the social construction* – is not endorsed by Rorty's neopragmatism. For him, 'ontology', in the sense of the list of items we take to
constitute reality, is a function of our vocabularies. But that is not to say
there is *just* the vocabulary; i.e., reality is just language. To say that would
be to lapse into a particular form of Platonism: at last we have discovered Ultimate Reality and, you would never have guessed, it turns out to
be Language! We find ourselves with vocabularies that have ontological
commitments, but we can criticize and revise them. In this context the
pointed assertion of radical (as opposed to moderate) constructionism,
as if it were an important discovery of which we need to be frequently
reminded, now seems empty or, more precisely, unhelpful, and so unjustified. As Rorty puts it,

Of course they [human rights] are social constructions. So are atoms, and so is
everything else. For … to be a social construction is simply to be the intentional
object of a certain set of sentences – sentences used in some societies and not in
others. All that it takes to be an object is to be talked about in a reasonably coherent way, but not everybody needs to talk in all ways – nor, therefore, about all
objects. Once we give up the idea that the point of discourse is to represent reality
accurately, we will have no interest in distinguishing social constructs from other

---

[21] They are not the *only* useful ways of talking about ourselves and the world of course: there
is no commitment here to biological reductionism for example.

Neopragmatism and radical constructionism 69

things. We shall confine ourselves to debating the utility of social constructs.
(Rorty 1999, pp. 85–6, emphasis in original)

For Rorty, the social construct that is the naturalistic Darwinian view of
the world, with its ontology of organisms evolving within environments,
including humanity, the animal whose linguistic abilities are sophisti-
cated enough to allow culture and history, has great 'utility'. But that
social construct requires the idea of nonhuman nature, which is therefore
justified by the role it plays in that construct.

Now, it is important to be clear here for there is an argument that says
that given our evolutionary heritage, nonhuman nature not only must
exist, but also cannot be totally inaccessible to our sensory and cognitive capacities, or we would have been selected against.[22] This argument
might seem to beg the question against constructionism interpreted as
saying, in a spirit of unqualified relativism, that the Darwinian picture
is a *mere* social construct, *just another* social construction of 'nature': we
cannot step outside such constructions to see which best matches reality,
so we have no justification for viewing it as 'more true' than any other.
This is not how to read Rorty's neopragmatism, although he agrees we
can't step outside our vocabularies and theories to check which is best.
Referring to Darwinism as a *mere* social construct betrays a Platonist
concern with representing Reality. Evolutionary theory can be justified
(or not) as a better 'construction' than its competitors (e.g., creation-
ism) to put on the reality with which we are in causal contact; justified
in pragmatist terms. If constructionism is taken to involve the crudely
relativist claim – all constructions are *mere* constructions – Rorty's neopragmatism bolsters the Darwinian argument against it just stated. But
all interpretations of nature are interpretations. So there is nothing to
be gained by condemning one as a *mere* interpretation. We can't manage
more than interpretations; but it doesn't follow that there is nothing but
interpretation.

The issue is what interpretation to adopt, and an interpretation aware
of itself as interpretation – and able to accept the nonhuman nature/land-
scape distinction in a moderately constructionist fashion – still seems
possible. The question is whether it is useful and I contend that it is useful as a central feature of a pluralist account of alienation from nature,
the utility of which in turn lies in helping us to articulate various aspects
of the environmental crisis. For example, as we shall see in more detail
in the next chapter, talk of reification of, or within, the landscape is talk

---

[22] This, which is a traditional pragmatist line of thought, is part of Rolston's thinking too
(Rolston 1997, p. 42).

about a type of environmental problem that is part of that overall situation – the taking of landscaped items as given things rather than products of human labour and vehicles of interpersonal recognition. Such talk need not involve a distinction in the condemned Platonist sense between how things 'merely appear' (as untouched wilderness, say) as opposed to what they 'really essentially are' (a humanized home embodying human labour, say). The distinction involved can be interpreted as one that is useful to make in various environmental contexts; a distinction enabled by the landscape/nonhuman nature contrast, which is itself understood as a tool for coping with reality rather than representing it. Similarly, the suggestion to recognize nonhuman nature's difference and live with some estrangement from it does not have to be interpreted as a suggestion that we replace certain false appearances (everything is or should be used for our purposes) with a picture corresponding to the ultimate truth of our proper place in reality (not everything is or should be viewed as simply there – given as to be used for our purposes).

2.9 Neopragmatism as anthropocentric instrumentalism

But *is* the landscape/nonhuman nature distinction a helpful tool, especially with regard to the nonanthropocentric work I am attempting with it? What of the objection that I am ignoring the instrumentalism that comes with a pragmatist understanding of ideas and theories as tools? The idea of nonhuman nature that I am contrasting with landscape is not *just* the idea of a nonhuman environment with which to run, say, the naturalistic Darwinian story. It is also the idea of nature insofar as it is not viewed only in anthropocentric instrumentalist terms, as this or that kind of resource for human homemaking. As such it is supposed to allow space for some normative – nonanthropocentric, noninstrumentalist – content, such as that involved in endorsing some estrangement and alienation of nonhuman nature. Unfortunately, although the anti-Platonist, anti-representationalist aspect of neopragmatism does not exclude self-aware landscaping employing the landscape/nonhuman nature distinction in the moderately constructionist way that I wish, other aspects of Rorty's thinking threaten to make this impossible. There is a particular problem with Rorty's characterization of the pragmatist project in thoroughly anthropocentric instrumentalist terms.

As we have seen, for him, truth-as-correspondence-with-reality is to be replaced by justification-as-utility; utility specifically with regard to the human interest in coping with and manipulating reality better to improve human life. These are the terms in which the justification of any theory (or any social construct) is to be assessed. I have argued that running

Neopragmatism as anthropocentric instrumentalism

the landscape/nonhuman nature distinction does not require us to seek the truth about the intrinsic nature of ultimate reality. However, it does involve our attempting to consider nature independently of 'anthropocentric instrumentalist landscaping concerns'; i.e., as it is apart from the role it plays in serving human interests, needs and furthering human-centred projects. But if any *justified* conception of anything at all is so in virtue of its utility relative to the human interest in coping with and manipulating reality better, then it seems that an anthropocentric instrumental stance will be built into any justified conception of nature. It seems that any justified belief about reality will be of the anthropocentrically circumscribed instrumental landscape, language itself being nothing more than a handy tool for such landscaping. Whenever we try to say anything about nature as it is independently of landscape we will be led straight back into it. There seems to be no escape.

Again, I think such a picture amounts to radical constructionism. This is not because it is a form of linguistic idealism (claiming there is just the vocabulary) or involves any fixed definite ontological claim of that sweeping, Platonizing metaphysical sort. It is because ontology is said to be relative to vocabulary, and the only *justified* vocabularies concerning 'nature' are those it is in our interests to have and so may be said to construct it entirely in anthropocentric instrumentalist terms. Consequently, the only justified interpretations of nature will be in terms of the humanized landscape; something we construct physically and intellectually for our own interests. Anything extra, taking nature as other than an instrumentalized object will be unjustifiable; hence *radical* social constructionism. Thus, although the neopragmatist version of the claim that 'everything is a social construct' as such does not reduce nature to landscape, its account of justification might seem to do so. Unless, that is, it is in our interests to seek to form a view of nature as it is independently of our interests. I want to say two things about this problem before giving my main response to it in section 2.11 of this chapter.

First, especially given the context of the present environmental crisis, it can be argued that it *is* in our interests to view nature noninstrumentally. Noninstrumental reasons for respecting nature may help reinforce instrumental reasons – reasons derived from the human interest in *sustainable* landscaping, for example– and vice versa. In terms of the different senses of alienation from nature I have distinguished, the 'anthropocentric' senses (reification and pernicious forms of estrangement and alienation with respect to the landscape) are to be overcome, where this overcoming *requires* endorsing some alienation from nature in the 'nonanthropocentric' senses of estrangement from and alienation of nonhuman nature. And vice versa.

72   Pragmatists and sea squirts

It is important to consider the point that noninstrumentalism may buttress instrumentalism here also because Rorty, like Dewey and other pragmatists, might argue my thinking in this area presupposes a dualism between the instrumental and the noninstrumental, which should be ditched along with the other dualisms familiar from the Platonizing philosophical tradition (for example that between morality and prudence).[23] It is implausible, however, to suppose that at least a fairly sharp distinction between instrumental and noninstrumental (in the form of a slave/non-slave distinction, for example) *can* be ditched by pragmatists committed, like Dewey and Rorty, to liberal pluralism. That said, we needn't view the instrumental/noninstrumental distinction as an *absolute* dichotomy standing in the way of all pragmatic thought. Thus I have emphasized that the landscape/nonhuman nature distinction is a matter of degree: nonhuman nature is nature *insofar as* it is not modified or interpreted in line with human-oriented concerns. It is not the idea of pure, untouched nature or the idea of nature as absolutely useless. Again, something can be both instrumentally and noninstrumentally valuable, and there can be instrumental grounds for having a noninstrumental view of something.[24]

In the context of the environmental crisis it is reasonable to worry whether an anticipated case of anthropogenic destruction, or alteration, of a part of nonhuman nature is viewed with excessive complacency because of a not well-justified expectation that any resulting damage to human interests can be avoided or compensated for by further technological progress. A measure of noninstrumentalism here would provide at least a prima facie reason to reconsider and moderate the activity independently of any expected impact on humanity. Under the circumstances of our having an important long-term interest in sustainability, and a tendency to be complacent about our capacity to manipulate nature in a comprehensive yet sustainable way, it is not out of the question that it is in our interests to accept noninstrumental reasons (for 'nature's own

---

[23] See for example, Rorty (1999, pp. 72ff). As I mentioned above, softening the instrumentalism/noninstrumentalism and anthropocentric/nonanthropocentric contrasts is a theme of environmental pragmatist work, including that of Minteer to whom I return below.

[24] An example of the latter is John Rawls' distinction between accepting a conception of justice instrumentally as the terms of a *modus vivendi* (the parties see it is in their interests to accept it under the current, highly contingent, balance of power), and as the basis of an overlapping consensus in which the parties accept it for 'its own sake' because of the ways their various conceptions of the good life intersect on it and validate its component ideas (e.g., of freedom and equality) as politically *right* rather than simply expedient. An important *instrumental* reason for preferring an overlapping consensus is its relative stability compared to a modus vivendi. See for example Rawls (1996, Lecture IV).

Anti-essentialism, intrinsic value and giraffes

sake') to intervene less comprehensively in nature – and so to accept some estrangement from the nonhuman.

2.10 Anti-essentialism, intrinsic value and giraffes

My second response to the thought that neopragmatism is an inescapably anthropocentric instrumentalist construction tool is this: the sense in which it is in our interests to have a given conception, C, of something, X, leaves it open whether, within the terms of C, X can be viewed noninstrumentally. Here we should separate out the ideas of 'coping with', and 'manipulating' reality as they feature within Rorty's account of justification. Consider his comments on giraffes:

[The] causal independence of giraffes from humans does not mean that giraffes are what they are apart from human interests. On the contrary, we describe giraffes in the way we do, *as* giraffes, because of our needs and interests. We speak a language which includes the word 'giraffe' because it suits our purposes to do so. The same goes for words like 'organ', 'cell', 'atom', and so on – the names of the parts out of which giraffes are made, so to speak. All the descriptions we give of things are descriptions suited to our purposes. No sense can be made, we pragmatists argue, of the claim that some of these descriptions pick out 'natural kinds' – that they cut nature at the joints. The line between a giraffe and the surrounding air is clear enough if you are a human being interested in hunting for meat. If you are a language using ant or amoeba, or a space voyager observing us from far above, that line is not so clear, and it is not so clear that you would need to have a word for 'giraffe' in your language. (Rorty 1999, p. xxvi)

It is in our interests to be able to distinguish giraffes as a type of entity with relatively stable features from other elements of the environment. It helps us to cope with reality, predict what will happen next and so on; allowing us to survive and lessening our confusion and fear. Thus our giraffe conception and giraffe talk are justified – they have utility relative to the goal of our coping with the world.

Consistent with this is the possibility of refraining from a *purely* 'manipulative' perspective, caring *only* about whether giraffes are good to eat, have grazing habits that threaten our crops and so on. These features bear on our manipulating reality in the sense of engaging with, and remaking it, in accordance with our interests. In terms of the landscape/nonhuman nature distinction, the latter manipulative perspective is confined to the giraffe's role in the humanized landscape. But our giraffe talk, even if developed for our own interests in coping, rather than as a device for depicting accurately the 'intrinsic essence of giraffe-kind', also allows us to say *something* about what is typically needed for something

74   Pragmatists and sea squirts

to continue to be an example of the sort of thing we pick out as 'a giraffe'. Our giraffe talk includes a capacity to talk of interests giraffes have 'in their own right', in the sense of independent of the role they play or might play in making our lives easier or harder. This will be important when considering our estrangement from the nonhuman.

Also evident in the passage just quoted is Rorty's 'anti-essentialism', another important element of his pragmatism. Anti-essentialism here says there can be no such thing as the 'essential nature' of X, in the sense of a fixed kernel of properties all Xs have in every context, irrespective of relations to other things, i.e., describable without reference, implicit or explicit, to any non-X. Descriptions of X are always at least implicitly relational, so it is pointless to seek to distinguish intrinsic from extrinsic properties with the aim of getting at X's 'real intrinsic nature'. This is not to say it is *false*, in that anti-essentialism captures The Truth about how things really are; just that attempts to get at the 'real essence of things' are not useful, or less useful than other incompatible aims (Rorty 1989, p. 8; 1999, pp. 52ff).

It is important to notice that such anti-essentialism undermines positions in environmental philosophy and ethics focused on claims about the *intrinsic* value of nonhuman objects and organisms, where this means value possessed in virtue of their non-relational intrinsic or inherent properties.[25] But this should not be considered a disaster for nonanthropocentric environmental philosophy, even though nonanthropocentric ethics has often sought a secure foundation in intrinsic value. The relational properties that constitute nonhuman entities need not relate them to human interests only in the manner of subservient means to human interests as ends. A very convincing case has been made, by Christine Korsgaard for example, in favour of distinguishing clearly the ideas of intrinsic and noninstrumental value, and bearing in mind that the absence (or impossibility) of intrinsic value does not imply the absence (or impossibility) of *noninstrumental* value (Korsgaard 1983). This is because the idea of noninstrumental value does not require the notion of intrinsic, non-relational, properties to get off the ground. Intrinsic

---

[25] Pragmatism's inhospitality to intrinsic value was also a theme of the late-1980s exchange between Weston and Katz on pragmatism and environmental philosophy in the journal *Environmental Ethics* (see the papers by Katz and Weston reprinted with a discussion of the debate by Andrew Light in the *Environmental Pragmatism* collection edited by Light and Katz (1996)). There Katz argues that, although intrinsic value cannot function as the source of an environmental ethic, it can play a supportive role in developing a nonanthropocentric justification for environmental policies. But he worries about the subjectivism and relativism implied by pragmatism's placing of nature's value at the mercy of contingent human interests. I hope my discussion in the rest of this chapter allays the sort of worry Katz expresses.

Anti-essentialism, intrinsic value and giraffes

value (ascribed in virtue of intrinsic properties) is to be contrasted with *extrinsic* value (ascribed in virtue of extrinsic-relational-properties). The instrumental/noninstrumental distinction is a separate distinction that does different work. It concerns *how* we value X (say as a means or an end). If there is no intrinsic value, because no intrinsic properties, then all value is extrinsic. But it does not follow that all value is instrumental value.[26] If we accept that *we* have no intrinsic properties we are not thereby committed to the view that *we* have only instrumental value. Thus it remains consistent with anti-essentialism and the associated elimination of intrinsic value to, for example,

1. delineate (relationally) a class of entities – 'giraffes' – with a relatively stable set of (relational) features in common;
2. describe, and criticize (in terms of its disutility relative to the modified pragmatist understanding of justification to be discussed shortly) a tendency to refer to giraffes *purely* in terms of a relation to human interests that makes them subservient means to those interests as ends;
3. describe, and criticize this (in terms of its disutility), as part of a wider tendency to view the world only in terms of landscaping concerns, and so collapse the distinction between landscape and nonhuman nature and move from moderate towards radical constructionism.

Again, I call the tendency just mentioned *radically* constructionist because it eliminates nonhuman nature as landscape-independent (nature insofar as it is not modified *or interpreted* in terms of human-oriented ends). This idea of nonhuman nature leaves space for nonanthropocentric, noninstrumental stances such as those I associate with (endorsing some) estrangement and alienation. But the noninstrumental 'respect for nature' involved does not require positing intrinsic value. The 'rightness' of the noninstrumental stance turns on the rightness of refraining from a blanket anthropocentric instrumentalism, rather than detection of a metaphysical value present in nonhuman things in virtue of their essential nature. Nor then need it be a matter of viewing nonhuman nature is an 'end in itself', or an absolute good 'injected into the situation from without' as Minteer, following Dewey, puts it in his critique of nonanthropocentric intrinsic value. In Minteer's Deweyan terms, the noninstrumentality involved may be considered as an 'end in view': a guide to action to 'enter deliberation as a means able to structure ethical inquiry', rather than a foundational conversation-stopper (Minteer 2012, pp. 66f).

---

[26] For more on the differences between intrinsic and noninstrumental value see Korsgaard (1983) and Green (1996).

76   Pragmatists and sea squirts

2.11   Redescribing the pragmatist project

But my main response to the problem that Rorty's account of justificatory utility makes his pragmatism a purely instrumentalist construction tool is that it remains open to us to *redescribe* the pragmatist project in less anthropocentric instrumentalist terms. His rejection of essentialism makes it hard to see Rorty's own purely anthropocentric characterization of the goal of theorizing as an essential, ineliminable fellow traveller of the more definitive anti-Platonist philosophical core of his neopragmatism.[27]

Rorty himself is at pains to emphasize the gap between pragmatist philosophy and particular evaluative commitments. I mentioned above that he equates 'improved human life' (for the sake of which reality is better coped with and manipulated) with freedom in a pluralist liberal democracy. But that is a contingent commitment, for *every* vocabulary, including every political vocabulary, is historically contingent. Rorty praises Hegel for historicizing philosophy and Dewey for giving pragmatism both a definitely liberal democratic and historicist edge.[28] Still, one *could* be a neopragmatist with a different understanding of 'making human life better'. In *Philosophy and Social Hope*, Rorty goes so far as to say,

Philosophy and politics are not that tightly linked. There will always be room for a lot of philosophical disagreement between people who share the same politics, and for diametrically opposed political views among philosophers of the same school. In particular, there is no reason why a fascist could not be a pragmatist, in the sense of agreeing with pretty much everything Dewey said about the nature of truth, knowledge, rationality and morality. Nietzsche would have agreed with Dewey against Plato and Kant on all these specifically philosophical topics. Had they debated, the *only* substantial disagreement between Nietzsche and Dewey would have been about the value of egalitarian ideas, ideas of human brotherhood and sisterhood, and thus about the value of democracy. (Rorty 1999, p. 23)

Rorty is perhaps wrong here about the closeness of Nietzsche and Dewey on those 'specifically philosophical topics'. Minteer argues for a tighter relationship between Dewey's 'instrumentalist' and 'experimental' understanding of inquiry and his commitment to deliberative democracy than Rorty recognizes. Dewey's method is not confined to specifically scientific inquiry, and he holds that deliberative democracy is the best way of institutionalizing it to bring the widest range of experience and perspectives to bear upon social, political and ethical problems (Minteer

---

[27] See Malachowski (2002, pp. 2ff) for a discussion of the malleability of Rorty's position given his own rejection of essentialism.

[28] See for example, Rorty (1982, pp. 44ff; 1998, ch. 15; 1999, pp. 11f, 49).

Redescribing the pragmatist project

2012, pp. 29ff). Nietzschean contempt for democracy is thus inconsistent with the most efficacious 'intelligent inquiry' as Dewey understood it. However, for Rorty, the point of philosophy once Platonism is put aside is redescription for the sake of edification; showing interesting new possibilities for the improvement of human life. It is to help to articulate 'social hope'. So redescribing the aim of the pragmatic project itself, the utility-currency for assessing justification, must be *philosophically* allowable. The goal of improving human life encompasses the possibility of improving the understanding of what constitutes such improvement. This is a point with particular significance given our historical situation is one of environmental crisis. And, given our need to get to grips with this crisis, my suggestion is that we redescribe the goal of inquiry in line with emerging 'green', nonanthropocentric vocabularies, so that it becomes 'making human life better, where this includes a more respectful relation with the nonhuman'.

Such a redescription requires distinguishing, and detaching, the political association of social hope with liberal democracy from the encompassing anthropocentric instrumentalism. Rorty's liberalism has been fiercely criticized for complacently ignoring the urgent reality of suffering and the ways power operates in capitalist society (Geras 1995; Johnson 1998). A response to this, one offered by Rorty himself, is that extending our imaginative grasp to take in previously unnoticed – unmentioned – forms of suffering, injustice and humiliation, making them possible topics of deliberation, is crucial to the pragmatist project; and the best political/economic arrangement so far devised to facilitate this is liberal democracy with a regulated market economy (Rorty 1998, ch. 12; 1999, p. 214). Recalling the Marxian account of the multiple estrangements and reification brought by private property and labour alienation in a market economy (capitalism) we might wonder whether this response is fully adequate. But whatever one thinks of it as a response to radical critique (whether it reflects a complacency which, as Jonathan Culler put it, 'seems entirely appropriate to the Age of Reagan'[29]), it is not entailed by the anti-Platonist core of Rorty's neopragmatism. Certainly, Rorty's political thinking in *Contingency, Irony and Solidarity* and related writings, wraps up his pragmatism quite tightly with a liberal separation of public and private, and yields a particular account of that.[30] But the very separation of a public sphere of democratic deliberation from an arena of what he calls 'private irony' and 'self-creation', presupposes an egalitarian public commitment to seeking agreement and solidarity with fellow humans.

[29] Quoted by Rorty (1998, p. 212 n. 23). See also Rorty (1999, p. 4).
[30] See, for example, Rorty (1989, Pt II; 1998, pp. 307ff; 1999, pp. 170ff).

78   Pragmatists and sea squirts

This is a contingent commitment not entailed by the anti-Platonism and abandonment of truth as correspondence to reality.

In his more political writings Rorty sometimes seems to suggest that 'truth' is a matter of democratic consensus (Rorty 1989, p. 67; 1999, p. 173). However such suggestions are not meant to amount to a 'theory of truth' (see, for example, Rorty 1989, p. 84 n. 5). He is better read as claiming that citizens of a utopian liberal democracy should be happy to give the normative kudos associated with Truth as correspondence to reality over to agreements reached through domination-free democratic debate. But the prior question – why have *that* particular utopian vision – is to be answered with reference to the overall pragmatic goal, like any other belief, act or institution; although of course Rorty's contingent egalitarian (and so anti-Nietzschean) interpretation of that goal loads it in favour of democracy.[31] *Pace* Minteer then it seems that Rorty remained, as he himself thought, fairly close to Dewey on the relation between pragmatism and democracy: it is the best way we have found so far to institutionalize the open inquiry called for in seeking improvements in human life and identifying and overcoming obstacles to that ('problematical situations'). The main difference perhaps is that he emphasizes more than Dewey the contingency of the egalitarian commitment to the value of agreement and solidarity as a value commitment in addition to the valorization of democracy as an institutionalized means of problem-solving.

Putting aside the instrumental justification of democracy as institutionalized method of inquiry, my point is that the egalitarian commitment to agreement and solidarity is only contingently related to the anti-Platonism. Consequently, its redescription, whether in a more or less egalitarian direction, in the light of other beliefs and commitments, must be *philosophically* allowable; allowed that is by the anti-Platonism. Now, just as it is possible to redescribe the political terms of social hope, so it is possible to redescribe the anthropocentric instrumentalism. We can recast the goal to that of making human life better, *where this includes a more respectful relation with the nonhuman*. I take it that this would require recognition of a nonhuman world 'beyond' the landscape that is not, as it were, 'just ours' to manipulate in accordance with our interests.

---

[31] Robert Hood (1998) argues that Rorty's understanding of public democratic discourse, as distinct from assertions of private preference, is consistent with giving public weight to environmental valuation, including intrinsic valuation. He discusses this public valuation as informed by artistic representations of nature, where such representation (as when a picture represents its subject) doesn't amount to 'representing' in the condemned, Platonic, sense. Hood doesn't discuss the problem for *intrinsic* value posed by Rorty's neopragmatism.

Redescribing the pragmatist project

Presumably it would include a willingness to seek greater awareness of nonhuman interests and flourishing, and incorporate this within our deliberations. We do have serviceable vocabularies within which it is intelligible to ascribe interests to organisms other than humans and to consider their own independent flourishing requirements.[32] Perhaps this is still generally understood as a matter of accurately representing a non-human reality, but it needn't be. For example, Darwinian naturalism can be interpreted as a tool for coping with reality in a way that allows us to talk of nonhuman interests, and indeed to be suspicious of the very idea that 'having interests' was something completely new to the world when our particular species evolved. So it must be allowable to have them in mind when describing the pragmatist project.

The landscape/nonhuman nature distinction earns its keep here partly by helping to focus attention on nonhuman interests. For example, it is a way of putting the moderate constructionist warning to remember that any given theory or description is a social construct and as such may be more or less anthropocentrically 'interested' (as in descriptions of organisms as 'pests', 'weeds', 'game', etc.; I return to this in Chapter 4). More generally the distinction allows us to focus on the landscape-independence of any nonhuman form, to be able to say, for example, '*this* is not *just* the place of our ancestors, a source of raw material for our industry, a place of particular beauty' and so on.

However, our situation is such that we must also remember that we are landscaping beings out to make a better home for ourselves in the world, and should consider the *reification* of humanized things that might be going on in talk of the natural. My claim is that alienation from nature, understood pluralistically, and as something not always to be overcome entirely, earns its keep by helping to structure thought that has the redescribed goal of improving human life including a more respectful relation to the nonhuman, in the overall context of a world that is to a very significant extent, but not wholly, landscaped. In Deweyan terms it is a matter of suggesting a way to clarify a problematic environmental situation suspected to have something to do with alienation from nature where this encompasses insufficient respect for the nonhuman. As my argument in the next chapter

---

[32] It might be thought that Rorty himself uses such a vocabulary when he glosses justification and social hope in utilitarian terms. Thus he might be thought to leave the door open for something like Singer-style 'non-speciesist' utilitarianism. If so then his take on justification/social hope is not as anthropocentrically instrumentalist as I present it to be here. However, Rorty only occasionally mentions 'fellow sentients' and doesn't seem to attach much significance to them. It is important to remember that he does not accept 'utilitarianism' as a rationalistic theory of impartial moral reasoning of the sort associated with Singer's principle of equal consideration of interests. See, for example, Singer (1979, chs. 2–3); Rorty (1989, pp. 179ff; 1999, p. 81).

80 Pragmatists and sea squirts

makes clear, I am not advocating a suspension of democratic deliberation, but suggesting a way of thinking through the situation using different senses of alienation that brings out both anthropocentric and nonanthropocentric concerns and some of their relations.

2.12   Pragmatism, humanism and anthropocentrism

And yet still it might be thought that the nonanthropocentric elements of my argument remain a problem from the pragmatist point of view. The pragmatist aim to resolve problems in the way of improving human life expresses a commitment to humanism. It might be objected then that the redescription proposed above is inconsistent with humanism because any substantive nonanthropocentrism prevents the steady anthropocentric focus required of any genuine forthright humanist. This is the final objection I shall consider to the association of my account of alienation from nature with philosophical pragmatism.

One way Platonism is an obstacle to human progress, according to Rorty, is that the ambition to *conform* to external reality, by seeking to have beliefs made true by answering to it, expresses an infantile wish to be subject to an external authority. Such abasement hinders a grown-up, properly humanist focus on improving human life. Thus, even if the anti-Platonist philosophical core of Rorty's neopragmatism otherwise allows the landscape/nonhuman distinction, still it might be thought that *respecting* landscape-independent nature perpetuates an ancient urge to bow down before a nonhuman other.

This would be wrong, however, because 'respecting the nonhuman world' needn't involve abasement before it or revering it as a source of *authority* over us. We have already seen that 'respecting' giraffes, say – taking them into account in a way allowing them to exist and flourish in their own way rather than co-opting them into our plans as much as possible – need not be a matter of positing intrinsic value that we then regard as an external constraint. Nor is it necessarily to worship them, or to think of them as somehow *showing* us how to behave, or as authority figures to whom we are answerable for our linguistic and other practices.[33] Indeed, to regard giraffes, or any other features of the nonhuman world,

---

[33] Perhaps if 'answerability to the world' is purged of its association with the correspondence (or representationalist) picture, as in 'our beliefs are answerable to the world because they should get the world right, and it is the world that makes them right by making them true', it might yet be a useful phrase. One useful, instrumental, interpretation of 'answerability to the world' might be 'the world contains forces that will harm us if we are not careful'. Another, noninstrumental, interpretation would be 'we are capable of harming the world in various ways and should think about this and consider ways of reducing such harm'. Both of these interpretations seem consistent

Pragmatism, humanism and anthropocentrism

in such ways is to landscape them. Not in a grossly economistic sense of instrumentalize, of course; but to co-opt them as moral or spiritual *resources* for our homemaking projects.[34]

I am not condemning this as always 'wrong'; perhaps to some degree it is an inevitable feature of landscaping as a moral enterprise: in making our surroundings homely we take some things to symbolize virtues and vices. I am pointing out that this is not what I mean by respect for landscape-independent nonhuman nature. Along with crassly economistic forms of anthropocentric instrumentalism it is to be *contrasted* with it. This is clearer, I think, when the noninstrumental respect is couched in terms of accepting some estrangement from the nonhuman. Although presumably less destructive generally than the material transformation of things into commodities with economic use value, the degree to which something nonhuman is coopted as a resource for moral or spiritual (or aesthetic or recreational[35]) purposes is a degree to which it is 'brought within' our humanized world for our use (even if physically untouched). The degree to which we regard it as having its own way of being or flourishing that is not ours and is independent of our uses and purposes (whether economic, moral, spiritual, aesthetic or recreational) is the degree to which we remain estranged from it as landscape-independent.

It is worth emphasizing here that this goes beyond the 'weak anthropocentrism' and Deweyan 'natural piety' associated with environmental pragmatism by Bryan Norton and Ben Minteer. Norton's weak anthropocentrism turns on the idea of 'considered preferences': the value of nonhuman items is not intrinsic to them but contingent on human preferences, not all of which are crassly consumerist or crudely economistic. *Considered* preferences, rather than the 'felt' preferences of those immersed in environmentally illiterate consumer cultures, might value nonhuman nature as a source of moral, aesthetic and spiritual inspiration (Norton 1984). Minteer finds in Dewey's relatively neglected work *A Common Faith* a notion of 'natural piety' which 'far from celebrating the triumph of the human will and technoscientific mastery over nature ... advocates a normative attitude of humility towards natural conditions ... that should resonate with environmentalists of a variety of convictions including nonanthropocentrists' (Minteer 2012, p. 76). In seeking to 'redescribe' spirituality in a way that

---

with answerability *in the context of belief justification* being an entirely interpersonal, or inter-belief, intra-linguistic affair.

[34] It is a mistake to equate protection of nonhuman nature 'for its own sake' with the view that nonhuman nature itself supplies us with ethical imperatives that we can somehow read off of it. See again the discussion of 'following nature' in the previous chapter (section 1.8), and also Evanoff (2005, p. 66).

[35] Or indeed philosophical, as in my earlier coopting of sea squirts to help make a philosophical point.

82   Pragmatists and sea squirts

preserves humility with regard to wider reality while freeing it of dogmatic religiosity and metaphysical objects of worship, Dewey writes of piety that it is 'attachment to whatever in the source of man's being also serves as the natural and historic fount of the values that make that being worth having. It is a cherishing consciousness that the human spirit is derived and responsible, having its roots in nature and the past endeavour of society' (quoted by Minteer 2012, p. 80).

For Minteer this grounds a form of humanism that does not myopically or arrogantly ignore our dependence on wider nature. The naturally pious do not *worship* nature in the manner of a theistic stance towards a god who issues commands or radiates goodness from a place transcending all problem situations. Nor, for Dewey, do they worship humanity: 'A humanistic religion, if it excludes our relation to nature is pale and thin, as it is presumptuous, when it takes humanity as an object of worship' (quoted by Minteer 2012, p. 81). They have an ecological view of themselves as dependent parts of larger evolving wholes, both natural and social, that they cherish (Minteer 2012, p. 81).

So neither Norton nor Minteer want entirely to exclude nonanthropocentric perspectives from deliberation about environmental problems. Even intrinsic value claims may be useful in countering the crass consumerism and narrow economic instrumentalism of strong (as opposed to weak) anthropocentrism; as long as they are not dogmatically asserted as fixed prior to debate and immune to revision.[36] But although not 'strongly' (rather than weakly) anthropocentrically instrumentalist, their positions are still anthropocentrically instrumentalist. Deweyan natural piety towards the 'natural and historic fount of the values that make [our] being worth having' is piety aimed at the landscape: nature insofar as it has been modified by humanity and interpreted for the sake of human-oriented ends. This includes nature understood as the support of our physical being and a resource for our imagination to work on in producing moral and spiritual values. The anthropocentrism, humanism and instrumentalism here have an environmentally enlightened form that is much to be welcomed of course. In the next chapter I shall discuss some of the requirements of such an environmentally enlightened humanism as matters of overcoming reification and pernicious forms of estrangement and alienation within the landscape context.

However, it is also important that there is a tie between such human interests and respecting nonhuman nature. We don't need to think of human interest as playing a *foundational* role in the overall situation akin

---

[36] Minteer is more positive about the role of nonanthropocentric intrinsic value claims than is Norton. See Minteer (2012, pp. 59ff).

Pragmatism, humanism and anthropocentrism 83

to the role played by 'enlightened self-interest' in the less hopelessly implausible forms of egoism. Again this involves emphasizing matters of degree with phrases like 'not a mere resource' (as in: 'we have to regard nature as a resource, but not as a *mere* resource'). But the 'mere' here points to a contrast between viewing something as a resource (anthropocentric) and *not* viewing it as a resource (nonanthropocentric); rather than a contrast within an overall category – 'resource' – between (the 'strongly' anthropocentric) commodities to be consumed or exploited for economic profit versus (the 'weakly' anthropocentric) source of moral, spiritual or aesthetic uplift. To repeat: we do, of course, have to make a home in the world, in moral, spiritual and aesthetic terms, as well as in material, economic terms, but we do not have to view wider nature as a mere resource for our homemaking. Recognizing this seems to me key to genuinely welcoming nonanthropocentric contributions to deliberations about our environmental situation, even though these contributions are often couched in admittedly problematic and unnecessary terms of intrinsic value claims.

Finally, none of the above is meant to deny the notion of nature as an objective realm of regularity and law to be investigated by science is a social creation with a particular history. Interpreted in a moderately constructionist fashion, without radical qualifiers ('mere' or 'just another' social construction), such a claim is consistent with the landscape/nonhuman nature distinction presented here. For example, Neil Evernden stresses the historicity of science, tracing the main moment of construction to Renaissance Europe (Evernden 1992, ch. 3). But he also claims that we retain a sense of the presence of a nonhuman other, a sense experienced most vividly in childhood, before one's sense of things is coloured by a worldview that puts them in (an) order. He refers to this nonhuman other as 'wildness', as opposed to 'wilderness' (Evernden 1992, ch. 7; see also Evanoff 2005, p. 76). I should like to think it is nature insofar as it is not landscaped. But is this sayable in neopragmatist terms, or is it phenomenology *as Platonism*: in early childhood, before the official ontology is drummed into us, we glimpse the intrinsic nature of reality, and are awed by its otherness? Evernden's account need not be interpreted in that way. It might be justified pragmatically as a way of making vivid our acceptance of the landscape/nonhuman nature distinction, a distinction that, if the arguments of the preceding sections are sound, may in turn be justified pragmatically.[37]

---

[37] In Chapter 6 I discuss what I take to be a useful understanding of 'estrangement from the natural world' in phenomenological terms, but without relying on any suggestion

84   Pragmatists and sea squirts

Evernden also laments the way scientific understanding of nature, including ecological understandings employed on the side of preservation and sustainability, 'tames this wildness' through imposing humanly constructed categories of ordering (Evernden 1992, pp. 120ff). Indeed, it is naive to expect science to provide us with unproblematically 'disinterested', purely 'neutral' accounts of things as they are independently of how we hope, wish, fear or need them to be. Science is a human social institution and we suspect that this means it can never really attain purely disinterested neutrality. This thought might be taken to reinforce radical constructionism about nature: natural scientific theories reflect the 'interests' of natural scientists, the power relations they are caught up in, the historically contingent socio-economic matrix within which their particular institution is located, no less than any other theory or view of the world. But the question is how far to push this thought.

Like all intellectual tools perhaps scientific tools must always qualify otherness to some extent. But given its historical reality and pragmatic success, we have no choice but to treat science as the best socially created tool for understanding nonhuman nature. This is another reason for refraining from talk of *mere* social constructs. We can accept this while recognizing that any given scientific account of the world might assimilate it to landscape to some extent. The hope is that it is possible to be both pragmatic and critical by viewing these tools as the best available for getting a handle on how things are independently of how we prefer them (not) to be given our human-oriented plans, while also considering how they and their employment may be implicated in and coloured by the furtherance of those plans, by the interests of those whose interests are wrapped up in them.

This is a familiar point in relation to the privileging of the interests of some humans over those of others that might be furthered through the use of this or that intellectual model. It would be odd if no one ever mentioned the possible ideological colourings of the 'selfish gene' metaphor, for example. Similarly theories, including scientific theories, might be examined to see whether and how they shape things anthropocentrically in line with the pursuit of human interests. For example, as we saw in the previous chapter, Evernden draws upon biological science to outline our natural alien status while criticizing the Cartesian picture often associated with the 'scientific worldview'.

What is crucial is that such qualification of otherness does not necessarily amount to its elimination, or to the total reduction of nature to

---

of our *forgetting* how things were, either in early childhood or in some earlier 'primitive' state of human culture.

Pragmatism, humanism and anthropocentrism 85

landscape (to the construction of 'nature' only as something useful, available, continuous with human purposes). Scientific metaphors and depictions of natural order can be scrutinized critically with this thought in mind. To say this is simply to be a moderate constructionist; it chimes with the suggestion that the main point of constructionism talk is liberationist. Here it is nature that is to be 'liberated' from attempts, whether witting or not, to co-opt it entirely into this or that human-oriented project, and so reduce it to the human landscape. This all seems to be sayable in neopragmatic terms.

3 Landscape

3.1 Estrangement, alienation and reification within the landscape

In this chapter I consider the ways that the different senses of alienation work in the context of landscape. The idea of landscape, remember, is that of the natural world insofar as it is humanized: modified and interpreted; 'appropriated' as it were, for anthropocentric purposes. The focus of this chapter then is the anthropocentric elements of my account of alienation from nature.

For Marxists, the alienation of labour inherent to capitalism produces multiple estrangements, including that of workers from themselves, each other and from their reified environment. This is an account of occurrences within landscapes. It is a usefully stark way of emphasizing the requirement to recognize landscapes as social creations for which we need to take responsibility and that this can turn on matters of loss (alienation) of ownership. Insofar as this requirement is not met we are liable to find ourselves confronted by something 'alien', hostile to our purposes, whose contours are more like those of a prison than a genuine home, albeit a prison that is both dynamic and out of our control rather than fixed and static. Although the Marxian picture informs our understanding of alienation, estrangement and reification in the landscape, not all senses of alienation from nature are well illuminated by it. This includes senses of alienation from nature that I think should be viewed more positively, as something not to be overcome as much as possible. One such is estrangement from nonhuman nature (a topic for the next chapter). But another is a dimension of estrangement from humanized nature. Thus it is useful to consider other ways of understanding estrangement, alienation and reification and their relations in the context of landscape.

The main organizing thread of this chapter is an emphasis on landscapes as vehicles for the realization and recognition of human personhood. I give the idea of landscape this extra gloss to indicate some important senses of reification and estrangement in this context – important in that they encompass serious environmental problems. These problems include environmental (such as climate) injustice; the failure to acknowledge and take responsibility for one's involvement in landscaping; and what is sometimes called the 'crisis of place'. Alienation of ownership is part of the picture but plays a subsidiary role. Alienation in this sense is a *problem* when it involves serious estrangement.

I begin by relating the ideas of reification, estrangement and alienation to the idea of justice. Theories of justice may be interpreted as concerned with avoiding serious, unacceptable reification of and estrangement between persons (property alienation involves unacceptable estrangement when unjust). But much political philosophy understands justice in terms of principled relations between persons abstracted from the wider landscape except insofar as it is property to be owned and alienated. If reification and estrangement are to be useful notions, 'environmentally speaking', it is unsatisfactory to think of them only in terms of violated rights, entitlements and distributive principles as these are often discussed in political philosophy.

That they can have more useful environmental content I illustrate through a discussion of Axel Honneth's recent 'recognitional' account of reification (Honneth 2008). Honneth's account of what he calls 'reification of nature' is best interpreted as an account of reification of landscape in our sense; a matter of inadequate appreciation of and respect for landscapes as vehicles of recognition of persons. Drawing particularly on the work of David Schlosberg (2007), I then briefly consider some environmental problems in these terms, especially some concerns of environmental justice movements and theories of environmental justice. I argue that insofar as such theories lack a recognitional component they risk intensifying reification of landscapes. Relations of injustice, thickened by the mediating role of landscapes into relations of *environmental* injustice, also constitute an unacceptable form of estrangement between persons.

However, there may be deeply problematic estrangement constituted not so much by unjust relations between people as by the lack (or serious deterioration) of important relations between people and landscapes. Here I mean that people may fail to find themselves 'at home' in the world they are making by failing to acknowledge and especially *take responsibility for* their role in making it. This is a matter not only of reification of landscape, but of a pernicious kind of estrangement from it as reified, or indeed an impetus towards its reification. I discuss this estrangement in the context of our immensely difficult climate change situation and in the light of some themes of Hegel's philosophy, which usefully brings together ideas of being at home, recognition, responsibility and realization of personhood.

88   Landscape

In this chapter the default position with respect to the forms of reification and estrangement discussed is that they are to be avoided or overcome. Towards the end of the chapter, however, I consider a form of estrangement contrasted with the idea of making ourselves at home through the 'practice of place'. I draw upon Peter Cannavò's recent account of this practice as 'the mutual founding and preservation of place and identity' (Cannavò 2007). Presumably it is important to avoid, or overcome, 'rootless estrangement' in the sense of being at home *nowhere*, there being no place recognizable as partly constitutive of one's self or identity. But given that there is a plurality of different places and of different interpretations of places, one cannot expect to be equally at home in all of them, in all landscapes. A degree of estrangement from landscapes is required by the just recognition of human difference.

3.2   Justice and the forms of alienation

Consider that persons[1] are themselves parts of landscapes as humanized nature. Our humanized surroundings include other persons, and these important parts of one's environment are not just 'naturally given'; personhood as a status amounting to more than mere membership of a particular biological species is realized through social relations. Certain kinds of social relations thwart what is taken to be an adequate realization or development or exercise of personhood; however this is to be understood exactly. Thus Marxists point out that workers beset by the clouds of estrangement and reification generated by relations dominated by private property and labour alienation are in no position to develop in ways that clear-minded observers would describe as adequate. However, the idea that personhood is not just naturally given, but an important achievement enabled or sustained by some social relations, and blocked or undermined by others, is in one way or another more or less explicitly shared across much contemporary political philosophy.

If we take theories of justice this point seems most obvious with 'recognitional' theories, such as those of Iris Young (1990), Axel Honneth (1995) and Nancy Fraser (1997). These focus on the lack of recognition in wider social and cultural contexts, as well as formal political institutions, marked by forms of denigration, sidelining and outright exclusion of thereby oppressed individuals and communities. There are differences between these theories. For example, some (such as Fraser) understand misrecognition in terms of injuries to people's social status embedded

---

[1] Or human selves: I don't mean to invoke a specific (for example Kantian) tradition or understanding by using the term 'person' here.

Justice and the forms of alienation

in social structures and institutions. Others focus on the psychological impact of misrecognition on individuals' own sense of self-esteem (e.g., Honneth, whose recognitional account of reification I discuss in the next section). Still the importance of recognition for the development and flourishing of persons is a shared theme for these theories. This is evident, for example, in their shared emphasis on the importance of inclusive, participatory processes of decision-making. The use of the term '(mis)recognition', rather than just '(dis)respect', say, emphasizes that an important goal is the bringing in of groups or communities who had been ignored, excluded – *not recognized* as full members of the political community. As Schlosberg argues, the differences and controversies between the more 'psychological' approach represented by Honneth, and the more 'structural status injury' approach of Fraser are sometimes exaggerated (Schlosberg 2007, pp. 16ff). Exclusionary status injurious to social structures are intersubjective structures after all, and experiences of self-worthlessness occur and are reinforced or overcome in social contexts.[2]

The formulation of theories of justice as recognition was inspired partly by a perceived need to supply theoretical articulation of the concerns of actual social justice movements held to be badly served by highly abstract theories of justice focused on distribution. Distributive justice is important, of course.[3] Indeed the idea of personhood, or at least an adequate level of personhood, as something achieved or thwarted by different kinds of social relations, is also a feature of theories focused more on distributive justice. Thus for John Rawls, the 'social primary goods' to be distributed by the principles of justice as fairness are preconditions for the adequate realization of persons as free and equal citizens with self-respect and 'moral powers' sufficient to both uphold justice and frame and pursue their own conceptions of the good life (Rawls 1971). For Robert Nozick, respect for persons' definitive capacities to give shape and meaning to their own lives requires respecting their natural rights to non-interference in their voluntary arrangements and legitimate

---

[2] Things are different when we look 'beyond' the landscape. Schlosberg makes very interesting use of a non-psychological status injurious understanding of misrecognition with respect to nonhuman nature. I return to this in Chapters 4 and 6.

[3] Schlosberg also points out that the contrast between recognitional and distributive justice can be exaggerated. The wisest approach is a pluralist one that views distributive, recognitional and procedural (or participatory) elements as complementary and necessary features of justice (Schlosberg 2007, pp. 20ff). A recognitional element is necessary if not sufficient because, left to their own devices, distributive approaches tend to remain focused on abstract principles with little or no regard to actual exclusions. We shall see below that it is important not to focus on distribution without regard to recognition when considering reification and estrangement in the landscape.

90   Landscape

'holdings' (Nozick 1974). For Martha Nussbaum, principles of justice concern the rights, freedoms, opportunities and securities required to guarantee citizens' threshold levels of capabilities held to be constitutive of their flourishing with dignity (Nussbaum 2006).[4] And so on.

One way of characterizing such theories is that central to them is a contrast between persons and mere things to be used or ignored.[5] Injustice is fundamentally a matter of failing in one way or another to enact social relations held to be crucial to the sustaining of personhood at an adequate level; the level below which human beings start to be treated as non-persons, mere things to be ignored or discounted, and maybe begin to experience themselves as, if not actually become, such things.[6] To this extent theories of justice are against the *reification* of fellow humans, as if they were simply *given as things* to be used.[7] They provide accounts of the social relations – relations of justice – involved in preventing a slide towards mere thinghood, the embedding of a status of humans as mere things to be used or ignored. From this shared point of view slavery is the paradigm of an unjust social institution.

It is also meaningful to take such theories to be about avoiding a fundamentally unacceptable form of *estrangement* between persons. To treat others unjustly or be caught up in social injustice is to be involved in relationships that set oneself and others apart in ways we should not be set apart. Again, this is not confined to recognitional theories. Rawls for example wishes us to see society as a 'system of cooperation' (Rawls 1996, p. 14) the benefits and burdens of which should be distributed justly, justice being 'the first virtue of social institutions' (Rawls 1971, p. 3). This is especially so for those 'basic' institutions crucial for determining life chances and through which one ought to be able to achieve personal fulfilment in cooperation with others. Only in the just society, or in a society clearly moving in the direction of justice, can we be said

[4] The capabilities approach represented by the work of Nussbaum (and Sen) is perhaps best understood as a combination of distributive and recognitional themes. Distribution is central, but so is the impact of distribution on capability functioning and how this bears on the flourishing of those previously excluded (unrecognized), for example by the equation of personhood with strong conceptions of rational agency.

[5] Again, the terminology of person versus thing here should not be taken to suggest that all of the political philosophies involved are especially Kantian. See Nussbaum (2006, e.g., pp. 64f, 132f) for a powerful case against the equation of personhood with Kantian rational agency.

[6] That this is a shared characteristic of theories of justice has been obscured by the 'communitarianism versus individualism' debate, insofar as that suggests a clash between those who do and those who do not believe that justice is about the *social relations* proper to adequate personhood. Although of course this is not to deny the importance of debates about which political philosophies provide a sufficiently rich and plausible account of the social dimensions of their own presuppositions.

[7] I qualify the equation of reification with 'thingification' as such below.

Justice and the forms of alienation

to be genuinely 'all in it together'. The point is not that if we are in an unjust society then we are 'not really in it', but in a pre-social state of nature instead. That would have the rather too convenient implication that because we clearly are not in a state of nature we must be living in a reasonably just society. The point is that there is a serious sense in which those living in an unjust society are 'in it apart', rather than in it together; living in a state of estrangement constituted by some benefiting unjustly at the expense of others. Theories of justice are very often also theories of just ownership that define the just acquisition and exchange of private property. These issues have particular pride of place in some theories, such as Nozick's libertarianism. But they are also features of other theories of distributive justice, which are therefore also theories of proper and improper alienation of ownership. To put it very minimally, alienation is improper when it involves unjust coercion or a departure from just distribution, and it is proper when not coerced or accords with just distribution (or is a case of redistribution required by justice).

Thus despite their obvious differences in terms of requirements of adequate personhood; what is the correct account of principles, rights, entitlements, what is required to enable proper recognition and so on, and the different institutional and policy directions they suggest, such theories can be read as ways of understanding the relationship between estrangement, reification and alienation. They locate them in relation to justice. In their terms reification is always 'wrong' qua unjust and to be overcome or avoided as such. And so is the estrangement constituted by unjust relations between people or the slide towards the reification of at least some of them by depriving them of (the just) conditions required to sustain adequate personhood in contrast to thinghood. As I have said, there is an important exception to the presumption that estrangement is always to be eliminated: the just recognition of human difference imposes an important limitation on the overcoming of estrangement. I return to this towards the end of the chapter. Still, when social relations are unjust (in distributive, recognitional or whatever terms) then they constitute an unacceptable estrangement.

However, alienation is very far from being always unacceptable. It involves injustice when coerced or out of step with distributive requirements. But alienation of private property is also usually seen to be a necessary component of the just society, especially when the focus is the realization of *free* personality; and this might include the alienation of labour required by the private ownership of productive resources. For the Marxist, 'liberal' and other non-Marxist theories of justice are ideological and futile because they ignore the role of private ownership in generating multiple estrangements and thoroughgoing reification. Again,

92   Landscape

it is not my aim to adjudicate definitively here between Marxian and non-Marxian theories. It is better to see them as contributing different insights into a complex picture rather than as rivals in a zero-sum contest for total domination. If we expect the latter then it is likely that important Marxian insights will be lost, insights that remain useful outside of the Marxian picture understood as the one true picture. One is that reification and estrangement, at least, can be understood as more thoroughgoing features of intersubjective life and praxis within humanized landscapes than associating them with abstract conceptions of distributive justice might suggest. It is odd that much political philosophy abstracts away from the landscape as a material environment, except as a collection of objects to be owned, exchanged and (re)distributed. In this respect, (property) alienation is related to estrangement and reification only as those ideas apply directly to persons: as estrangement between and reification of persons. Relations between persons and the wider surroundings of the humanized landscape (or, to put it another way, relations between persons mediated by the humanized landscape) are otherwise presumably to be left to others, such as architects and social geographers.[8]

3.3   Honneth on reification

I have suggested that theories of justice may be interpreted as having a concern for reification, estrangement and alienation. Serious reification involves relations of injustice and such relations constitute unacceptable estrangement. Alienation may be unjust and, as such, involve unacceptable estrangement, depending on the terms and conditions of the alienation and how the theory views these and ownership issues in general. Putting aside (property) alienation for now though, it can be helpful to understand estrangement and reification in terms that are 'thicker' than those generally provided by theories of (at least distributive) justice. One cannot simply *equate* these notions with injustice, in the sense of violations of principles, rights and entitlements. That they encompass more than injustice so conceived is illustrated by Axel Honneth's recent account of reification (Honneth 2008). It will be helpful to devote some

---

[8] It should be acknowledged that there is some significant 'mainstream' political philosophical work about landscapes understood as more than relations between persons abstracted from their material surroundings (except insofar as these surroundings are considered as property). For example, there is important work highlighting the condition of physical public spaces unjustly inaccessible to disabled humans (e.g. Nussbaum 2006). There is also an increasing amount of work on justice in relation to climate change, some of which I consider below.

attention to this account before turning directly to more obvious environmental issues.

Honneth builds upon the classic Marxian account of reification first published by Georg Lukács in 1925 (Lukács 1971). He makes clear that reification involves more than purely cognitive intellectual errors, such as committing category mistakes, or failing to see the applicability of abstract moral principles (Honneth 2008, pp. 22ff). It cannot be escaped simply by grasping the truth of propositions or by applying abstract moral principles. Rather it is a 'distorted, atrophied form of praxis' (Honneth 2008, p. 26); an ensemble of habits, attitudes and behaviour that permeates subjectivity and the social world. For Lukács it was 'a habit of mere contemplation and observation, in which one's natural surroundings, social environment and personal characteristics come to be apprehended in a detached and emotionless manner – in short, as things' (Honneth 2008, p. 25). Honneth seems to accept this as a description of the core features of the 'distorted consciousness' in which reification consists. While noting that the notion has been mostly out of fashion since the 1920s and 1930s he points to various areas of intellectual culture he thinks involve exploration and critique of what amounts to reifying trends in contemporary life.

One area is literature, including works by Raymond Carver and Michel Houllebecq that portray 'an aesthetic aura of creeping commercialization ... [and] suggest that we view the inhabitants of our social world as interacting with themselves and others as they would with lifeless objects – without a trace of inner sentiment or any attempt at understanding the other's point of view' (Honneth 2008, p. 18). Social psychology also explores problematic reification, according to Honneth. Here, he says, investigations have noted 'an increasingly strong tendency on the part of subjects to feign certain feelings and desires for opportunistic reasons to the extent that they eventually come to experience those very same feelings and desires as genuine elements of their own personality' (Honneth 2008, p. 19). Another area is recent work in ethics and moral philosophy that is critical of 'human behaviour that ... [does not treat] other subjects in accordance with their characteristics as human beings, but instead as numb and lifeless objects – as "things" or "commodities"' (Honneth 2008, p. 19). He cites here the work of Martha Nussbaum and Elizabeth Anderson as critical of 'tendencies as disparate as the increasing demand for surrogate mothers, the commodification of romantic and familial relationships, and the boom in the sex industry' (Honneth 2008, p. 19). We might add that, once pushed to a certain point, such tendencies come within the purview of theories of justice interpreted as concerned with avoiding reification of persons

94   Landscape

as things. The fourth context in which Honneth discerns an opposition to reifying tendencies is in 'discussion concerning the results and social implications of brain research' conducted in 'strictly physiobiological' terms (Honneth 2008, p. 20).[9] These examples of contemporary intellectual life underwrite Honneth's declaration that '[l]ike a philosophically unprocessed nugget, the category of "reification" has re-emerged from the immense depths of the Weimar Republic and retaken centre stage in theoretical discourse' (Honneth 2008, p. 18). Clearly some environmental thought can be interpreted as concerned with reification too – I return to this shortly.

Part of the 'philosophical processing' Honneth provides is through his endorsement of Lukács' understanding of reification as more than a narrowly cognitive error. He also finds plausible these features of 'true', undistorted, praxis that he discerns in Lukács' text: in 'genuine' praxis subjects experience the world in a directly engaged way, as 'cooperative', and the objects within it as 'qualitatively unique' and 'particular in content' (Honneth 2008, p. 27). But he also emphasizes his departure from Lukács in several key respects. These concern unhelpful features of the classic understanding of reification that caused it to fall out of favour as a critical concept. One is Lukács' 'totalizing' Marxist explanation of reification as caused by the expansion of commodity exchange (or property alienation) into all areas of life. Engaged in commodity exchange relations (coloured, as we have noted, by the central place of labour alienation) agents are 'mutually urged' to view objects, each other and their own talents, merely as given 'things' from which they may profit (Honneth 2008, p. 22). As a general explanation of reification, that includes its manifestation as racism for example, this exaggerates the significance of commodification; and it ignores the possibility that the stance of detachment and 'strategic' action, associated with reification, is not only functional for the efficient working of developed societies, but as such may be 'legitimate' in certain areas of life (Honneth 2008, p. 28).[10]

Another problem is Lukács' identification of genuine human praxis with conditions in which objects are understood *only* as the products of subjects, or a collective subject, such that 'mind and world ultimately

---

[9] The argument Honneth refers to here 'goes that by presuming to explain human feelings and actions through the mere analysis of neuron firings in the brain, this [strictly physiobiological] approach abstracts from all our experience in the lifeworld and treats humans as senseless automatons and thus ultimately as mere things' (Honneth 2008, p. 20). He associates this argument with the philosopher Andreas Kuhlmann (Honneth 2008, p. 86 n. 11).

[10] With regard to the latter point we might say that for Honneth a certain amount of reification is 'basic' in Biro's sense, at least in large societies with highly complex divisions of labour to manage.

Honneth on reification   95

coincide with one another' (Honneth 2008, p. 27).[11] This 'idealism' is untenable for Honneth, as it is for me: it exemplifies the radical constructionist reduction of nature to humanized landscape.[12] Honneth points to the unfortunate merging in Lukács' thinking of a critique of reification with a concern to overcome the 'antinomies of bourgeois thought' taken to be irresolvable by a modern philosophy trapped in the subject/object dichotomy by its historical location in reifying capitalist culture (Honneth 2008, p. 29; Lukács 1971, pp. 110ff).[13] But Honneth also finds a more phenomenological existentially oriented depiction of engaged praxis beneath Lukács' 'official idealism'. He builds upon this by noting similarities to Heidegger's notion of 'care' and Dewey's notion of 'interaction' (Honneth 2008, pp. 29ff). For those thinkers, one of the great phenomenologists and one of the great pragmatists, humans are always already involved, prior to cognition, in practical engagements with a world of existential significance, from which the perspective of the 'neutral observer' is a distorting abstraction.

This leads Honneth to reject the view that a reifying praxis could replace *all* 'genuine' engaged praxis – a claim that sits awkwardly in Lukács' work alongside the expectation that the proletariat will be 'awakened' by their radically demeaning and reified condition into the realization that it is a set of social relations, alterable by them, and not something given that they must simply endure (Honneth 2008, pp. 31f). The possibility of such an awakening implies that 'engaged praxis' must always already exist to some extent, in however rudimentary a form, even though more or less distorted by reification. Or, rather, reification *is* the distortion of a 'primordial' engagement towards a merely observational, contemplative disengagement that views surroundings, others and self as more or less merely thing-like. The distortion must be *a matter of degree* and Honneth explains the 'habit of detachment' involved in terms of a '*forgetting*' of the primary 'empathetic recognition and engagement' with others and the world that 'precedes a neutral grasping of reality': 'Recognition comes before cognition' (Honneth 2008, p. 40). The priority here, Honneth insists, is both genetic and conceptual (Honneth 2008, pp. 41ff). Primordial *recognition* is always there but may for various possible reasons be buried and so 'forgotten' beneath a reflective layer

[11] See also Martin Jay's introduction to Honneth's text, especially Jay (2008, pp. 5–6).
[12] See, for example, Chapter 1, sections 1.9 and 1.12; Chapter 2, sections 2.4 and 2.6.
[13] We shall see in Chapter 6 that collapsing the idea of object into that of subject, by seeing the former as (simply) a construction of the latter, is not the only way to overcome a sharp separation of each that tends to represent one or both as thing-like. This will involve looking at the matter phenomenologically in a way partly informed by Honneth's account of reification.

96   Landscape

that distorts one's interpretation of others, surrounding objects and oneself into a view of them as thing-like (Honneth 2008, pp. 52ff).

3.4   Landscapes as vehicles of recognition: Honneth on reification of 'nature'

We may distinguish the following elements of this account of reification. Reification is: (i) a distortion of sensibility and praxis irreducible to
cognitive errors; (ii) this distortion is of a relation with others that one
cannot altogether leave behind; and this is (iii) 'pre-reflective' or 'primordial'; (iv) reification has a '(mis)recognitional' component that (v) relates
fundamentally to other persons; (vi) reification involves 'forgetting'. In
Chapter 6 I shall argue that, suitably modified and supplemented, the
first four of these can serve as elements in a useful conception of *estrangement* from the natural world. I discuss these elements in more detail there,
where I also discuss (vi), the 'forgetting' element. The fifth element raises
problems for Honneth's account of what he misleadingly calls 'reification
of nature'. His terminology is misleading for us because what he means
by 'reification of nature' is reification of what we are calling humanized
nature or landscape – the natural world insofar as it is modified or interpreted for the sake of human oriented ends. It will help our understanding of reification in the landscape context if we consider this now.

First we should notice a distinction between 'mere thingification' as
such and viewing something humanized as a *naturally given* thing. One
can view items as 'mere things' without failing to think of them as social
products. If someone views an artefact, a table, say, in a detached manner
as a mere thing, this does not mean she must believe falsely that it is a
naturally given thing. She might believe correctly that the table embodies
social labour and therefore is not something naturally given, while still
simply registering in a detached manner the table's existence as a mere
thing (just another commodity, say). Does this not show that Honneth's
understanding of reification must be different to the one that concerns
us, which is the taking of something humanized not just as a mere thing
but as a naturally given thing? This might be true if reification in our
sense is interpreted in narrowly cognitivist terms as a matter of false
beliefs. Thus, again, viewing social product P as a mere thing does not
entail the false belief that P is naturally given, and so a notion of reification defined in terms of the former is clearly different to one defined in
terms of the latter. As we have seen, however, Honneth emphasizes that
reification involves a distorted, atrophied praxis encompassing habitual
attitudes and behaviour rather than just narrowly cognitive errors. This
allows the familiar possibility that someone might believe truly that what

Landscapes as vehicles of recognition

is before them is a person, not a mere thing, yet fail to 'recognize' or engage adequately with her as a person. Despite truly believing she is not a mere thing, he acts and feels towards her as if she were a thing, a 'sex object', say.

Similarly, and more generally, he might believe truly that the landscape is not a naturally given thing (when asked whether his social and material surroundings are naturally given he is disposed to give the correct answer 'no', an answer he is perfectly capable of justifying), yet his praxis as an ensemble of actions, attitudes and habits expresses detachment from it, as if it *was* just a naturally given thing; as if it were something whose (re) production, maintenance and modification he is not involved in more or less cooperatively with others. His praxis shows a less than adequate recognition of the *human dimension* of his surroundings as more than a collection of things to be contemplated, endured or used as things. The condition of feeling and acting as if confronted by something with the character of a *nonhuman* alien imposition can survive the reflective refutation of it. Moreover, Honneth's understanding of reification as a distortion of engaged recognition of others seems to turn on a contrast between, on the one hand, an adequate empathetic engagement with others and the world *as having a human dimension,* and, on the other hand, 'disengaged' encounters with reified things. This contrast between *the human(ized)* and *the thing* seems to equate the reifying apprehension of X as a thing with the apprehension of X in a manner more appropriate to what is given as a thing in or by nonhuman nature: nature minus any human dimension. In which case, to reify X *is* to relate to it *as if it were a naturally given* thing.

This contrast and equation are strongly suggested by Honneth's account of the 'reification of nature', where 'nature' means, in his phrase, 'nonhuman objects'. Even if we take it that Honneth otherwise provides a fully satisfactory account of reification, one that improves on Lukács,[14] we cannot just take on board his application of it to 'nature'. He unpacks the idea of reification of nature via that of reification of human beings, where 'reification of human beings signifies that we have lost sight of or denied the fact of antecedent recognition' (Honneth 2008, p. 61).

---

[14] This cannot be decided properly on the basis of the compressed account I have provided. For critical discussion see the contributions of Butler, Guess and Lear collected in Honneth (2008), along with Honneth's replies. One difficult question for Honneth is this: why assume 'primordial' recognition is a *sympathetic* recognition? As Martin Jay puts it, Honneth's critics 'all wonder if Honneth has accounted for the less savoury aspects of precognitive interaction, those that may well frustrate any hope for beneficial mutuality' (Jay 2008, p. 10). It seems to me that this is a decisive objection to Honneth only if his account is intended as a total picture of 'social pathology', rather than a component of a wider, pluralistic picture.

98   Landscape

Crucially, the antecedent recognition that has been misplaced or denied is supposed to involve respecting the meaning given to objects by other human beings.[15] 'Reification of nature', then, consists in 'perceiving animals, plants or things in a merely objectively identifying way, without being aware that [they] possess a multiplicity of existential meanings for the people around us' (Honneth 2008, p. 63). In line with the meaning of reification as relating to treating the manifestation of human presence and activity as a merely given nonhuman thing, Honneth refers *non-reified* 'nature' back to a position *within* humanized landscapes as anthropogenic environments and fields of significance oriented *only* around the pursuit of human projects. 'Nature' then figures as a vehicle for the recognition of persons. Honneth equates 'nature' with 'nonhuman objects'. In our terms, insofar as they are invested with human-oriented existential significance 'nonhuman objects' are part of the human landscape, their natural otherness thereby qualified to some extent. It looks like any attempt to articulate concern for nature insofar as it is viewed *independently* of the human-oriented roles allotted to it within landscapes will count as a reification of nature.

Honneth's account of reification of 'nature' is then an account of reification of nature in the sense of *humanized nature or landscape*. It is nature in this sense that can serve as the vehicle for recognition of persons. Extending this to nature in the other senses (natural world and nonhuman nature) reduces them to the landscape and so counts as an exercise in anthropocentric instrumentalism. For example, compare the 'objectifying' stance that Evernden associates with the Cartesian picture of nonhuman nature as inert matter for manipulation. One might think that this involves reifying nonhuman objects, as Honneth says 'in a merely objectively identifying way', as mere things. To be sure, reduction to the status of mere thing is involved in such objectification, which is a case of anthropocentric instrumentalism: the reduction of nonhuman nature to landscaping materials. But if reification concerns non-recognition of humanization and human-oriented significance, then understanding the objectification of nonhuman nature as reification is a covert way of furthering anthropocentric instrumentalism. It presupposes that the objectification undermines, distorts or just ignores a prior humanization, or

---

[15] Honneth says he is following Adorno both in speaking of 'recognition of nonhuman objects' and in confining this to recognition of the significance such objects have for other persons (Honneth 2008, pp. 62–3). Moreover, '[b]y pursuing this line of reasoning we have the opportunity to justify this concomitant idea without having to resort to speculations about interactive dealings with nature' (Honneth 2008, p. 63). It is not obvious why he wishes to talk of 'reification *of nature*' (rather than just 'nonhuman objects') if he wants to avoid such speculations.

posing of human-oriented significance. It implies that the objectification is 'wrong' because, and only because, it negates the status of the 'nonhuman object' as vehicle of recognition of humanity, as I do in a small way when I objectify the bald eagle without regard to its status as national emblem of the United States of America.

It is necessary then to distinguish reification and objectification and disconnect more emphatically than does Honneth (who simply contrasts them directly), the perception of 'animals, plants and things in a merely objectively identifying way' from the awareness of the multiplicity of 'existential meanings' they have for people. Although reification can involve objectification (within the landscape), there can be environmentally problematic objectification that is not a matter of reification because it is objectification of what was relatively 'other', or 'outside' the landscape.[16]

3.5   Examples of landscape reification

Despite this problem, the notion of reification can be used to help articulate important problems. To be clear, it is helpful to follow Honneth and consider reification as the failure to recognize adequately the human and the humanized as the human and the humanized, where this is not just a cognitive error, such as the false belief that something humanized is naturally given; it need not even involve that false belief. It is a matter of praxis: a failure to engage adequately in the recognitional practice called for by the human and the humanized. This applies not only to persons themselves but to all elements of landscapes. Whatever else 'adequate praxis' involves in this context it at least involves respect for things as imbued with significance for others (as vehicles of recognition of others) and so more than mere things. Although success in these terms does not rule out reification, the more adequate praxis presumably also involves taking care not to believe falsely that humanized things are naturally given, and taking notice of principles of justice that might help, or indeed hinder, the maintenance of landscapes as vehicles of recognition of persons. Very importantly, it involves taking responsibility for landscapes as something the (re)production and modification of which one is always already caught up with along with others. I return to this point later in this chapter. I mentioned above Honneth's claim that reifying trends are in effect topics of exploration and critique in various domains,

---

[16] I return to nonhuman nature and the difficulties of disentangling it from the landscape at several places in the following chapters and to Honneth on 'reification of nature' in Chapter 5.

100   Landscape

including literature, sociology and social psychology and moral philosophy. We should note now some other areas of contemporary thought that concern what is in effect the reification of humanized landscapes.

One is the critique of tendencies to regard humanized nature as pure nature or wilderness, rather than the landscape of indigenous peoples. We have seen that this critique can be pushed too far – to the point of scepticism about nonhuman nature.[17] Clearly, however, the tendency being criticized should indeed be criticized. Insofar as it is not just an oversight, correctable simply by being shown evidence of human modification of the nature in question, or of its significance within a landscape, then it can involve potentially very serious reification: a more ingrained failure to take indigenous landscaping, and so indigenous peoples themselves, as worthy of recognition. It is not as if this can be safely assumed to be a feature only of a grim colonial past. For example, as Plumwood notes, postcolonial critics, such as Vandana Shiva, have pointed to the 'biopiratical' corporate practice of designating 'as "nature" seed varieties that represent the labour of hundreds of generations of indigenous farmers' (Plumwood 2006, p. 131). In Plumwood's own landscape context, '[t]he idea that the Australian continent, or even substantial parts of it, are pure nature, is insensitive to the claims of indigenous peoples and denies their record as ecological agents who have left their mark on the land' (Plumwood 2006, p. 134). And, of course, this issue has been central to the North American wilderness debate:

The movement to set aside national parks and wilderness areas followed hard on the heels of the final Indian wars, in which the prior human inhabitants of these areas were rounded up and moved onto reservations. The myth of the wilderness as 'virgin' uninhabited land had always been seen as especially cruel when seen from the perspective of the Indians who had once called that land home. Now they were forced to move elsewhere, with the result that the tourists could safely enjoy the illusion that they were seeing their nature in its pristine, original state, in the new morning of God's own creation. (Cronon 1995, p. 78)

A second area of concern is with disregarding the impact of economic activity on the landscapes of others, or only 'objectively identifying' it, as if their material environment and its condition was of no great significance to them, or indeed crucial to their basic survival needs. Examples include the siting of industrial and extractive processes and toxic dumps without regard to their disruption of landscapes and what this means to their inhabitants. This is often under the sign of 'development'. But when development is pursued in ways that reduce landscapes to economic

---

[17] See Chapter 1, section 1.10.

Examples of landscape reification   101

resources – commodified things – whose condition and sustainability is disregarded except in short-term economic terms, it fails to recognize the 'existential significance' of them for their inhabitants. This includes the disruption of ecosystems and destruction of biodiversity within landscapes through extraction of nonrenewable resources and the siting of industrial processes and their waste without adequate attention to the significance (physical and symbolic) of the biodiversity and ecosystems to those whose landscape it is. Thus, as Schlosberg says, critics of globalization like Shiva have 'argued that globalization creates "development" and "growth" by the destruction of the local environment, culture and sustainable ways of life' (Schlosberg 2007, p. 93). Another example is concern about the siting of technology and infrastructure (wind farms and railways, for example) aimed at achieving wider environmental goals without adequate regard for the impact on the local landscape.

A third area of concern for (what is in effect) reification of humanized landscape is continuous with the previous one, but focused on one's own landscape. This is concern about a tendency of people to regard their own actual humanized surroundings in a 'merely objectively identifying way' without adequately taking them on board as humanized and as vehicle of recognition of surrounding persons and themselves. One example, less trivial than it might first appear, is criticism of littering – the casual casting off of the unwanted wrappings and refuse of everyday life into shared surroundings, with a shrugging of the shoulders at any resulting deterioration of the landscape as if it was just a neutral backdrop to whatever project is the current focus of attention. Another example is criticism of the tendency to take issues regarding 'sustainability' to require only 'value-free' scientific analysis. This ignores that sustainability concerns the maintenance of things of value (not 'mere things'); items that matter within the lives of people and are likely to continue to do so for future people. The questions of 'what really matters', and in what ways, are obviously contested normative questions and not just scientific questions.[18] Even when the normativity is acknowledged it is often considered only in terms of maintaining 'natural capital'. This forces the multiplicity of significances things have into what is 'surely one of the more obviously loaded categories available to us' (Dobson 2003, p. 155).

A fourth area of concern is a specific case of the previous two: climate change. The climate change situation can be taken to involve reification

---

[18] See for example Andrew Dobson (2003, p. 147), after Brian Barry (1999, p. 101). Dobson usefully sketches the faltering turn of the millennium attempts of the UK government in various reports and guidelines concerning environmental protection and risk assessment to recognize that such issues raise questions that can be answered only by the articulation and analysis of values (Dobson 2003, pp. 146ff).

102 Landscape

of the humanized landscape in various ways, including a denial of its anthropogenic status and a shrugging disregard of the reports of the impact of climate change on human landscapes, including one's own. I return below to the issue of climate change.

3.6   Reification and environmental justice

It should be clear that the environmental issues just mentioned are not only, or even mainly, the concern of philosophers and other theorists. They are the concern of international institutions, national and local governments, non-governmental organizations, political parties, local, national and international movements and pressure groups, as well as private citizens. Such issues feed into a generalized sense of environmental crisis. My claim is that if they are held to indicate our 'alienation from nature' as a basic feature of that crisis then the alienation is best understood in terms of reification of and estrangement from our surroundings considered as humanized nature or landscape. Thus they concern the anthropocentric elements of my overall argument and account of alienation from nature.

I shall discuss estrangement shortly, but first consider again the point that when the reification is bad enough it comes within the province of justice. Calling at least some cases of reification unjust is to give them a certain weight and priority: some reification of humanized landscapes is not merely unfortunate or 'wrong' but *unjust*, and so merits urgent political action and policy formation. As I suggested earlier, the seriousness here reflects the way justice is concerned with preserving the conditions of adequate personhood and avoiding the reification of persons. To say a case of landscape reification is *unjust* then is to say that the failure to recognize the humanized as humanized, the disregard of landscape as vehicle of recognition involved, is sufficiently serious to threaten conditions of adequate personhood. In this respect, theories of climate justice and environmental justice more generally are in the same game as 'non-environmental' ('mainstream') theories of justice interpreted as at least partly concerned with avoiding the reification of persons. However, I also want to emphasize that thinking in terms of reification of landscape here – justice in the context of landscapes as vehicles of recognition of persons – underlines the importance of recognitional justice, not only distributive justice.

Of course, environmental justice movements and activists have been concerned with distributive justice; the unjust distribution of environmental burdens on poor and minority groups within affluent societies, and between more and less affluent societies. But it is not simply that

Reification and environmental justice 103

the distribution of environmental benefits and burdens fails to comply with distributive fairness. Such failure involves some benefitting from a situation in which the environmental – landscape – condition of others is either disregarded altogether or noticed in a way that is more 'merely objectively identifying' than adequately recognitional. Putting things like this brings out that environmental justice movements are concerned with recognitional justice at least as much as with distributive justice.

Reflecting on the complex scene of environmental justice movements in the US, Schlosberg notes its pluralism and pragmatic nuances in encompassing calls for justice in recognitional, participatory and capability terms as well as equity in the distribution of environmental benefits and burdens (Schlosberg 2007, ch. 3). There have been important declarations from environmental groups that make no explicit reference to equitable distribution of environmental risk.[19] Again, this is not to deny that an interest in distributive justice, as expressed in Mark Dowie's comment that '[w]hile created equal, all Americans were not, as things turned out, being poisoned equally' (cited by Schlosberg 2007, p. 55), has generally been central. However, Schlosberg emphasizes the importance of recognitional issues underlying distributive issues and how distributive inequities are bound up with recognitional injustice as a practical concern of environmental activism. For instance, he reports this 'clear example of the relationship between structural inequity and the lack of recognition' from the work of Native American activist-scholar Winona LaDuke:

EPA standards limit the level of dioxin releases from paper mills into rivers and streams. These releases are known to contaminate fish, and so the EPA based its release levels on the average consumption of such fish. Yet Native American consumption is well known to be higher than the average American, making the dioxin release a much greater health risk to Native Americans. Whether the EPA is deliberately racist is beside the point here; the fact is that there is structural discrimination in the setting of pollution limits by the EPA, based on a lack of recognition and acknowledgement of Native American practices of subsistence fishing. (Schlosberg 2007, p. 60)

In more global calls for environmental justice too, critique of the asymmetrical power relations and distributive inequities of the neoliberal 'globalization' overseen by such institutions as the World Trade Organization is often accompanied by denunciation of their lack of recognition of landscape diversity (Schlosberg 2007, p. 86). In terms of justice, the

---

[19] For example, there is no mention of it in the statement of principles arrived at by the 1991 First National People of Color Environmental Leadership Summit (Schlosberg 2007, p. 49).

104   Landscape

disregard of indigenous peoples entailed by viewing their landscapes as 'pure nature' is very obviously a recognitional and not only a distributional matter.[20] But to approach the issues under the heading of reification of humanized landscapes with a view to overcoming 'alienation from nature' *in this sense* is to emphasize recognitional matters more generally and highlight a limitation of *theories* of justice that focus only on abstract rights and distributions. These can themselves be reifying when they seek to establish principles abstracted from the nuances of different landscapes and the significances they have for the people within them. For example, in the fishing case mentioned above, it is clear that a principle of equal exposure to dioxin poisoning, based on average American fish consumption, fails to recognize the role of fish and fishing in Native American life. This is not to say that such considerations are always indefeasible, but that they should be taken into account and that justice might require compensation for their defeat.

Another example is the developing political philosophical field of climate justice. The injustice of impacts of anthropogenic climate change is frequently seen in terms of violations of basic human rights, such as those to life, health and physical security (e.g., Shue 1998, Caney 2009). As Derek Bell says, 'there is ample evidence in the latest IPCC reports to show that anthropogenic climate change is likely to kill, injure, starve and cause illness to many millions of people. In short, anthropogenic climate change will violate their human rights' (Bell 2011, p. 103). This is surely correct if human rights mean anything at all. But Bell also points out that climate justice cannot be understood adequately in terms of 'carbon egalitarianism', where this means the granting of universal equal rights to carbon emission (Bell 2008). Carbon egalitarians, such as Tom Athanasiou and Paul Baer, see it as obvious that rapid and significant restriction of global carbon emissions can be achieved *justly* only if there are equal per capita emissions rights; an equal share in the 'finite atmospheric space' in that sense (Athanasiou and Baer 2002, p. 64). Peter Singer has also defended equal emissions allowances for each person in the world; an equal 'share of the capacity of the atmospheric sink' (Singer 2004, p. 43). These suggestions apparently ignore (display no recognition of) the significances of differences in circumstances in different parts of the world. People don't live in a homogenous atmospheric sink, but in different landscapes. Carbon egalitarianism ignores such facts as that the preference to keep warm[21] has different implications for

---

[20] The exporting as an *unjust imposition* of the 'virgin wilderness' idea from First to Third World environments has been an important focus of controversy about wilderness for some time. See, for example, Guha (1989) and Cronon (1995).

[21] Or the temperature-sensitivity of the capability to be healthy, say, and of the value of 'carbon resource' allocations.

Reification, injustice and contestability 105

carbon emissions in Stockholm, as compared to Benidorm (Bell 2008, pp. 248ff).[22] Similarly, Schlosberg argues that 'the per capita approach ... does not take variation in the needs of different people living in different places into account; rather in its equal distribution of emission shares, a basic recognition of the differences of places are simply dismissed' (Schlosberg 2012, p. 448).

Notice that supplementing carbon egalitarianism with 'cap and trade' systems, whereby countries with higher emissions can buy allowances from peoples with lower emissions, does nothing to alter the problem with the initial equal allocation. Indeed the reification implied by the initial lack of recognition might even be intensified by such an economistic approach to justice; one that combines an equal allocation with the invitation to alienate it. In a critique of the universalization of economistic rational choice models of human behaviour John Dupré points out:

Only a society deeply imbued with economic thinking could suppose that a market in pollution licences was the best way to control pollution. It may, indeed, very well be the best policy for controlling pollution. But, if it is, it is surely so only because we live in a society in which a certain style of economic behaviour (maximizing profits without much concern for externalities) is considered natural and acceptable. (Dupré 2001, p. 131)

In our terms this is to say that such policies might look appropriate in a society that already significantly reifies landscapes as thing-like backgrounds to the maximization of profit. Because not everyone in every landscape relates to their landscape in this way, such policies lack a vital recognitional element.

3.7 Reification, injustice and contestability

Bringing in the idea of reification might help with the illumination and assessment of environmental injustice claims but it obviously won't end all controversy. That a case of reification is a case of injustice is contestable, like any other claim of injustice. For example, claims that the placing of wind turbines in a particular location transforms its significance for the inhabitants without any regard at all for this significance might turn out to be false. Some might even turn out to be based on a prior reification of the landscape as naturally given: the turbines 'spoil a

---

[22] As Bell points out this remains true whether carbon egalitarianism is based on welfare egalitarian (or preference utilitarian), capability justice or resource egalitarian premises. See Knight (2014) for defence of the view that departing from carbon egalitarianism does not mean that those with historically higher emissions should have lower current emission rights.

106   Landscape

pristine wilderness'. The latter kind of case also exemplifies ways of significances attributed in landscaping that can themselves be open to challenge on grounds of reification. For example, one move in the American wilderness debate is to claim that the idea of wilderness as 'Frontier', the symbolic home of the rugged individual, expresses a masculinist identity.[23] As such it might be criticized as a bulwark of a patriarchal culture that unjustly reifies gender stereotypes.[24]

Some claims that a case of reification amounts to injustice might turn on a misunderstanding of the ecological dimensions of the landscape in question. For example, Plumwood reports the argument of mountain cattlemen in Victoria against the ending of ecologically damaging grazing in the Alpine National Park, that such 'grazing represents "cultural heritage", which is just as important as "natural heritage", if not more important' (Plumwood 2006, p. 126). The National Park as 'natural *heritage*' here is the National Park as landscape. But so is the ecosystem considered as *support system* for the Alpine National Park landscape, the system allegedly damaged by the cattle grazing. The cattlemen's own cultural heritage position should not be simply ignored or dismissed. That would be an unjust failure of recognition. Still, presenting their position as one of the unjust reification of their landscape, a lack of recognition of its vital significance for them as the ongoing environmental context of their cattle-grazing economy and culture, does not make their case decisive. It invites the rejoinder that they misunderstand the significance of the ecological relations within that same landscape, which render unrestricted cattle grazing there unsustainable. Restricting the grazing to ecologically sustainable levels, or even ending it so that the Alpine National Park landscape and the *other* human significances it embodies remain sustainable would not necessarily be an unjust reification of it (or even reification at all).

Since I have admitted that bringing in the idea of reification does not resolve all such controversies it might be thought better to leave it out, and to understand cases like that of the mountain cattlemen simply as cases of clashing values instead. But this would be to ignore the bigger picture. Putting them in terms of reification locates them in the wider theoretical setting enabled by my overall argument and account of interrelated senses of alienation from nature. If one wanted an analysis and resolution of a situation like that of the mountain cattleman

---

[23] See for example Cronon (1995), who makes it clear that this is not the only idea of wilderness at play in North America. See Kirchhoff and Vicenzotti (2014) for a survey of Northern European ideas of wilderness and their intellectual antecedents.

[24] Compare the liberationist aim of moderate social constructionism (see Chapter 2, section 2.6).

Reification, injustice and contestability 107

considered in isolation, then not much, if anything, is gained by invoking the idea of reification. If one wants to think of it as located within our general environmental crisis, a predicament taken to have something to do with our alienation from nature, than I suggest it is helpful to emphasize the issue of landscape reification. It will help to connect it to other senses of alienation that capture other elements of the overall crisis situation.

In this chapter I am concerned particularly with reification and estrangement with respect to landscape. Thus I suggested earlier that theories of justice can be read as concerned with the avoiding of fundamentally important estrangement as well as reification. Unjust social relations constitute an unacceptable estrangement between persons involving (at least a slide towards) the serious reification of some of them. The same can be said for theories of environmental justice: an inadequate appreciation of the humanized as humanized, of landscape as vehicle of recognition of others, when serious enough to count as injustice constitutes an unacceptable estrangement between persons. To reify others and their landscapes, indeed to reify others *by* reifying their landscapes, is, when sufficiently serious, to participate in relations of injustice in this regard, and this is an intolerable form of estrangement. Putting things this way emphasizes certain relations – environmental relations – between people that are missed if the focus is on unjust treatment of people abstracted from their surrounding landscape. This in turn underlines again that some theories of environmental justice are less helpful than others because they abstract too much from landscapes as vehicles of recognition, for example by focusing on shares in the 'global sink' regardless of differences between different places. They stay too close to the traditional political philosophical tendency to ignore the landscape except insofar as it is a collection of things to be owned, alienated, distributed and redistributed.

From the perspective of overcoming serious (unjust) reification and estrangement within the landscape context, then, there is an important truth in the traditional Marxian objection to 'bourgeois liberal' conceptions of justice focused on rights, entitlements and freedoms of individuals abstracted from their concrete circumstances. Such theories of justice risk intensifying rather than helping to overcome reification and estrangement once the context of justice encompasses the environment as humanized landscape; our surroundings as the products of human labour. On the other hand, the recognitional aspect of reification and estrangement in the landscape context suggests that these cannot be reduced entirely to products of labour alienation. I return to this point towards the end of this chapter.

108   Landscape

3.8   Landscape as objective spirit

I have been drawing upon Honneth's recognitional understanding of reification and viewing reification of landscapes as a matter of inadequate recognition of the humanized as the humanized. And I have suggested that this can be connected to estrangement through theories of environmental justice interpreted as concerned with the condition of landscapes as vehicles of recognition of persons (not just abstract distribution). Thus so far in this chapter the emphasis has been on landscapes as vehicles of recognition. Now, the work of Hegel is an important philosophical source of the recognitional paradigm. With regard to reification of 'nature' Honneth is rather too Hegelian; this is a point to which I shall return in Chapter 5 where I discuss Hegel's account of property. But it will be useful to consider briefly how some of Hegel's themes bear on the present discussion. I shall do this shortly with reference to the climatic aspect of the environmental crisis.

Consider first that, of all the great philosophers, Hegel has perhaps done the most to emphasize our need to be 'at home' in (or reconciled to) the world. This is a very useful thing to do for we clearly are in the business of making and remaking 'our world'. That we are is a crucial frame for philosophizing about the environmental crisis. We *have* to make a home for ourselves in the natural world: we must transform our physical environment to satisfy our wants and needs; and we must interpret it, make sense of it and, in doing so, inject our surroundings with meaning and significance. The landscapes we live in – rural, urban, industrial and even 'wilderness' – mark our attempts, and those of our ancestors, to modify nature in line with human purposes. The alternative to recognizing this and taking responsibility for the results is estrangement from a reified human landscape. An important Hegelian theme is that such recognition and taking of responsibility is a condition of our full realization as free persons. For him, achieving free personhood requires being at home in a world in which we can recognize ourselves and for which we can take responsibility. Putting things this way helps illuminate some of the extraordinary difficulties raised by the climate change situation.

One of the ablest and most influential contemporary commentators on Hegel's notoriously complex and difficult system is Jürgen Habermas and my interpretation owes much to his.[25] His is a helpfully 'de-transcendentalized' and pragmatist recovery of Hegelian insights from the Absolute Idealist metaphysical trappings of Hegel's own presentation of them. I shall leave discussion of the importance of this

---

[25] Mainly Habermas (1999), but also Habermas (1988, ch. 2).

Climate change as unintended landscaping 109

recovery of Hegel from Absolute Idealism until Chapter 5. Here my point is that we can think of the idea of landscape as the human home in the world (nature modified and interpreted for human-oriented purposes) in terms of Hegel's notion of objective (or intersubjective) 'spirit'. Objective spirit encompasses and connects individual subjective minds. In its aspects of shared language and labour (understood to include technique and technology), it is both the condition of, and medium for, the historical development of consciousness. 'Consciousness' here includes practical know-how, as well as theoretical intelligence (Hegel 1977, e.g., pp. 308ff, Habermas 1999, pp. 136ff). Objective spirit then encompasses the shared, historically accumulated knowledge and traditions of practice embodied both in the discourses developed to describe reality, and in the forms of labour and tools invented to cope with reality, to modify it to suit human purposes. 'What the worker [learns] in the process of coping with reality congeals in the tools he invents for extending control over nature. The tool is what survives the vanishing moments of actual intervention and satisfaction' (Habermas 1999, p. 139).

Presumably one must say much the same for the portions of the natural world to some degree transformed into (and so to some degree brought *within*) the human home through objective spirit's encounters with it: not just the tractor, the drill, the cement mixer and power station, but the field, the city, the managed forest, the quarried mountain; and indeed the unwanted, unforeseen and unintended (by-)products of such encounters. In short, and to combine Lockean, Hegelian and Marxian metaphors, the human landscape considered as nature modified and 'mixed' with 'congealed labour', accumulated intelligence, interpretation and experience; the embodiment of humanity's historical and ongoing attempts to make itself at home in the world which, we must now acknowledge, includes the changing climate as one of its more unfortunate unintended (by-)products.

3.9 Climate change as unintended landscaping

The phenomenon of anthropogenic climate change reminds us that the 'landscaped' world we've made is more than land, buildings and scenery. It includes the atmosphere, the air we breathe, the wind and rain on our faces and the ambient temperature that now has a new kind of significance. It is not merely a given backdrop to our lives. Our landscapes are local in that their significance to us as home tends to be confined to some portion of the Earth's surface. Hence the need for environmental and climate justice to have a nuanced recognitional component. But taken together they constitute the 'human world', the global reach of objective

110   Landscape

spirit, and the warming global climate is part of that world. Hence the pressure towards conceptions of climate justice with a scope to match that global reach.

Climate change should also remind us that our world-making is a matter of transforming a natural world that exceeds our full grasp; its transformation into home can never be complete if 'home' is equated with 'fully controlled environment'. Climate change illustrates dramatically that our landscapes are partly, perhaps largely, composed of the unintended consequences and often unseen by-products of intentional action. Reflecting on the fate of the statue-builders of Easter Island, Mary Midgley has noted the tendency of people engaged in some grand project to ignore the ground on which they stand and the air they breathe (Midgley 1996a). Climate change means the grand project of industrialism can no longer be pursued, its benefits enjoyed, without regard to the air around and above ourselves and others. Raymond Williams remarks on a tendency to ignore that 'by-products' of human industry are no less its products than are its intended results (Williams 1980). Many homely landscapes contain factories, refineries, cars and motorways. They also contain slag heaps, oil spills, landfills and atmospheric greenhouse gases of sufficient concentration to cause dangerous climate change. Thus there are questions about the justice or injustice of the distribution of these environmental hazards and about their position in the landscape and how they are viewed expresses reification and estrangement.

Until recently, climate change has been easy to miss or ignore because, unlike many other (by-)products, it has been invisible. 'Climate' itself is an abstraction and, unlike its associated weather events, changes to it are detectable only through scientific analysis. Greenhouse gases themselves are invisible and disperse rapidly in the upper atmosphere. That such factors, along with the cumulative and diffuse process and effects of anthropogenic climate change, make it extremely difficult to map onto individual responsibility and generate difficult moral psychological and motivational issues, has been quite widely discussed.[26] Responsibility for the changing climate as an aspect of *humanity's world-transformative homemaking activities* seems to have been less widely discussed.

This is not to say it hasn't been touched on at all. For example, Andrew Dobson's conception of the obligations of 'ecological citizenship' in

---

[26] For example, Gardiner (2006). Some philosophers deny that individuals bear personal responsibility for climate change; because the causal complexity of the processes dissolves it and because by and large climate change and its consequences are unintended effects of harmless actions. See di Paola (2013) for a recent discussion and Kirkman (2007) for an interesting phenomenological treatment of the invisible threat of climate change as something very difficult to 'feel in one's bones'. I touch on the issue shortly.

terms of responsibility for the impact of one's 'ecological footprint' on others, including distant and future others, points in this direction (Dobson 2003). These obligations of ecological citizenship encompass those 'generated by the phenomenon of global warming' (Dobson 2003, p. 81). For Dobson, the 'space of ecological citizenship', or the community constituted by such citizenly relations, is not *given* along with the political realm of nation-states, as in liberal and republican theories of citizenship, or with abstract humanity as in cosmopolitan extensions of these theories. Ecological citizenly obligations are something whose *production* we are always already materially involved in through the production and reproduction of our everyday lives. Dobson argues that (distributive) justice is the 'first virtue of ecological citizenship': 'it is relations of systematic ecological injustice that give rise to the obligations of citizenship' (Dobson 2003, p. 132). And 'our' (i.e., affluent people's) responsibility for impacts on others generates asymmetrical, non-reciprocal obligations to them. In this respect he seems to share the egalitarian view, often associated with the ecological footprint idea, that everybody's share of 'ecological space' should be equal, at least ideally. Yet there are also strongly recognitional elements to his discussion; an emphasis on 'earthly impacts' on particular people in particular places (such as the impacts of those who are globalizing on those who are subjected to globalization), rather than on membership of an abstract world community (Dobson 2003, e.g., pp. 98f). This emphasis seems to be necessary to get the ideas of *produced* responsibility and obligation off the ground (the abstract world community and associated obligations are, he says, merely announced, not produced).

3.10   It makes a difference what we do

Now, as I have said, from the Hegelian point of view, to be at home in the world we are actually involved in producing, rather than estranged from it, we do indeed have to acknowledge and take responsibility for this concrete productive role. This requirement is deeply connected to our realization as free persons. As a way into the significance of this, consider the response to reports of climate change that goes 'it makes no difference what we do, the bad consequences of climate change will happen anyway'. This might be interpreted in a number of different ways, two of which are particularly important here. The first takes 'we' to be the citizens of a particular country (e.g., the UK) and says that because of the actions of others elsewhere (e.g., Chinese industrial development), it makes no difference if we alter our behaviour even quite drastically, so we shouldn't impose pointless costs on ourselves now. Whatever we do

112   Landscape

to limit our emissions, the relatively vast scale of theirs means the consequences of climate change will be nearly as bad anyway.

I will come to the second interpretation shortly,[27] but notice that this one suggests a picture of us as what Bernard Williams (1973) called utilitarian 'agents of the satisfaction system'. It makes us look like agents of the satisfaction system in the rather awkward position of noticing that, because of the pursuit of certain projects, a very bad thing is happening; yet our own contribution to which is sufficiently small, compared to that of others, that any benefit of our reducing or ending it is outweighed by that of continuing as we are with our own current projects. The bad outcome will be pretty much just as bad as a result of others' activities whether or not we restrain our own similar projects. Therefore we should not restrain them, especially since doing so will produce significant immediate dissatisfaction in our own part of the world.

Interestingly, although in this case it seems that the 'agent of satisfaction' mentality counsels us to maintain our current commitments, despite their contributing to a great harm, it has been taken, by Bernard Williams and others, to be generally at odds with the ongoing commitment to projects required for personal integrity. Utility can demand that we disown our projects, even those to which we are deeply committed and that are most constitutive of one's own sense of self. Given the impartial goal of maximizing overall utility, the agent's own projects are only 'one set of satisfactions among those which he may be able to assist from where he happens to be' for, as an agent of the satisfaction system, he is but 'a channel between the input of everyone's projects, including his own, and optimific decisions' (Williams 1973, p. 115). Williams objects that this ignores 'the extent to which his acts and decisions have to be seen to flow from the commitments he most closely identifies himself with in order to avoid serious self-alienation and loss of integrity' (Williams 1973, pp. 115ff). However, in the case of anthropogenic climate change, viewed from the perspective of satisfaction agents who assume others will continue their carbon-heavy projects, it seems this status as channels between the inputs of everyone's projects and 'optimific decisions' absolves us with respect to our own similar projects. The scale of the consequences to the climate of others' projects means it makes no difference what *we* do.

---

[27] Another interpretation of the response is that it is denying anthropogenic climate change altogether: either the world is not warming up or it is but the cause is nonhuman (solar radiation, say) and so it will continue with or without our help. I note this interpretation simply to put it aside; let us give the strong scientific consensus its due and take anthropogenic climate change to be a reality.

My aim here is not to endorse or discuss Williams' objection to utilitarianism (or, say, the relation between utilitarianism and cost-benefit analyses generally). It is to bring out that even if we don't have to abandon our own projects for reasons of climate change, *on this way of thinking* (that of agents of the satisfaction system) we are to put aside our own responsibility for our contributions to climate change. 'It makes no difference what we do', on this interpretation, apparently ignores the notion of responsibility. If we assume that it *really makes no difference* whether or not we contribute to the production of harm because the harm is going to be produced anyway by others, then it seems to follow that it makes no difference whether or not we bear any responsibility for its production. There is no significant difference between a world in which a very bad thing happens and I or we bear no responsibility for it, and a world in which the same thing happens but I or we do bear some responsibility for it. This in turn presupposes that responsibility either doesn't or shouldn't play any *necessary* role in our thinking about the knowing production of harms. To think like this is to be in danger of disowning (I am tempted to say *alienating*) responsibility for the less than perfect world we are in the process of helping to make, and this is highly problematic (partly for reasons that do end up connecting with the issue of integrity).

Responsibility does matter – no doubt for many reasons. Here we are interested in this Hegelian reason: if we don't see ourselves as responsible for the alterations we make to the world around us, if we don't, as it were, *recognize ourselves* in the world we are in fact making, this will tend to undermine the possibility of our full realization as free persons. To be fully self-consciously real as a person, one needs to be recognized as a person, by others and oneself. To be more than a merely subjective daydream, free individual personality must be identifiable objectively, expressed in public form so as to be recognizable to oneself and others. This is a matter of participating in and upholding the practices and institutions of objective spirit, which is also a matter of participation in physical landscaping. To be recognized as a person one must *do something to or with something*. Making alterations to the things around us reveals our distinct free personalities to ourselves as well as to others as objectively real (*I/we* did *this* to or with *that*).

These are the guiding thoughts of Hegel's justification of private property as a central institution of objective spirit (Hegel 1991, pp. 75ff). I touched on them in Chapter 2 when discussing Vogel's argument for replacing talk of 'alienation from nature' with talk of 'alienation from something like nature' (the humanized landscape). The fully realized free labourer is at home in the world recognized as the product of her labour, an expression of herself. I noted there that for Hegel more is required

114   Landscape

for this than the mere absence of slavery; objective spirit must incorporate positive institutions able to foster the recognition of free personality. Central to this picture is the ownership and alienation of things within a system of private property rights. We shall see in Chapter 5 that the Hegelian argument connecting ownership with personal realization can be pushed too far; i.e., to the point where nature figures *only* as something to be owned for the sake of the human interest in realizing free personality.[28] Still, the relationship between recognition, responsibility and ownership is an important consideration, and apparently threatened by the second interpretation of 'it makes no difference what we do' response to climate change.

People need to be at home in the world as objective spirit –the landscape – otherwise they are estranged from it and unfree. Being at home in humanized nature requires them to 'see themselves in it' as something they endorse and whose construction and maintenance they are actively involved in and so partly responsible for. It is a vehicle of recognition not only of others but of oneself. To the extent that it is taken to be something 'happening anyway', then one is estranged from the landscape in a way that interrupts free personhood. Given that only free persons with commitments can have personal integrity, it follows that this is also a threat to personal integrity. Integrity preserved by not allowing climate change to undermine continuity of commitment to ongoing carbon-heavy projects (on the grounds that 'it makes no difference...') is also threatened by losing sight of the conditions of realizing free personhood in the first place.

3.11   Responsibility and reconciliation

But we can hardly leave things like that. It is at least unhelpfully incomplete or one-sided, if not excessively harsh and moralistic, to emphasize threats to such big things as personhood and responsibility without also acknowledging another relevant interpretation of 'it makes no difference what we do...'.

On this second interpretation 'it makes no difference what we do...' expresses confused powerlessness in the face of demands generated by the world's problems, which now must include climate change; demands apparently requiring us to make dramatic changes to our lifestyles, personal projects and so on, for the sake of something for which, as

---

[28] This raises the same issue of anthropocentric instrumentalism as Honneth's account of 'reification of nature'. In Chapter 2, section 2.4 I discussed Vogel's argument as exemplifying the problematic quest for certainty. The problem is intensified and a radically constructionist instrumentalism even more firmly fixed in place when that quest is conjoined with an ethico-normative focus only on interpersonal recognition.

Responsibility and reconciliation

individuals, we bear very small responsibility. Here (as indeed on the previous interpretation) the thought is perhaps an individual one: 'it makes no difference what *I* do' (any 'we' is a collection of individuals all saying this). This sense of confused powerlessness in the face of problems one is aware of having a hand in but that are also too overwhelming in size and complexity to grip clearly, and indeed map personal responsibility onto, is surely a form of estrangement from the humanized environment that can motivate a tendency towards reification. It just seems *much easier* to treat this dimension of humanized nature as a given backdrop to personal and professional life, rather than a set of relations and processes one is actively involved in reproducing.

We might usefully think here in terms of Thomas Nagel's account of the tensions between personal/impersonal standpoints (Nagel 1991). For Nagel what we need are political institutions that effectively integrate the personal and impersonal (collective or objective) aspects of responsibility through the articulation and implementation of norms and effective policies (Nagel 1991, ch. 2). Without such *political* institutions and measures, as individuals we are left exposed to demands generated by a radically imperfect world; demands too weighty to internalize while retaining acceptable continuity of commitment to personal projects. Not addressing such demands, or ignoring them by focusing on the thought that one is not personally responsible for all of the world's problems, including climate change, seems only reasonable. Perhaps it is not mere selfishness or abdication of responsibility but an understandable, even forgivable, self-defence mechanism to be expected under conditions of serious political failure. What is needed is a politics able to address such demands in a satisfactory way collectively (in Nagel's terms helping to 'shape the self' so that the personal may harmonize with the impersonal), making it possible for us to face our responsibilities together and recognize ourselves in the world we're making.[29] Otherwise that taking of responsibility, even supposing a convincing way to individuate it, can appear more like a route to personal suicide than one to a more adequate personal realization. Put another way, we need political institutions, processes and policies to help dissolve the clash between different requirements of integrity: some continuity of commitment to personal projects and commitment to satisfying impersonal demands and accepting responsibility for participation in world-making. The need to reconcile abstract morality (*moralität*) and subjective motivation is also a theme of Hegel's

---

[29] See the illuminating exchange between Marion Hourdequin (2011) and Baylor Johnson (2011) on the relationship between individual and collective responsibilities in the context of climate change.

116   Landscape

Philosophy of Right. The ethical (*sittlichkeit*) dimension of objective spirit embodied in norms and institutions is supposed to do just that. I return to this in Chapter 5.

However the reconciliation between what Nagel calls the personal and impersonal standpoints is unpacked, whether in the liberal terms Nagel himself suggests or those of a more radical form of participatory democracy, for example, *some* conception of justice must be operating. If the earlier discussion was along the right lines then the relations involved must be just, or on the road to justice, or they will reproduce serious forms of pernicious estrangement and reification. Moreover, the justice involved must include environmental justice. Justice marks our 'all being in it together', where 'it' is the humanized landscape, not 'society' abstracted from the rest of the landscape. We can put an (if not *the*) aim of the environmentally just society, and of ecological citizenship in Dobson's sense, as that of avoiding or overcoming a situation of estrangement between people reified as more or less merely thing-like, and so of avoiding a situation of estrangement from landscapes that have been reified out of their role as vehicles of recognition. Given this aim it is easy to see why there is such emphasis in environmental politics on participatory processes and grassroots involvement.

3.12   Estrangement and the practice of place

So far in this chapter the discussion has conformed to the assumption that estrangement is to be overcome. Although in the next chapter I reject this assumption more emphatically with regard to nonhuman nature, it is important to notice that the aim of overcoming estrangement from the landscape needs to be qualified too. In general, such estrangement involves a lack of justice, homeliness and identification with regard to what in our surroundings is the expression of humanity. I have emphasized the importance of being at home in the sense of recognizing oneself in the world one is involved in making, and of estrangement as the absence of this. But not all estrangement as lack of homely identification with humanized surroundings involves that lack of recognition. Nor does such estrangement need to involve reification as the general failure to recognize adequately the humanized as humanized. One might be only too aware that one's surroundings embody human labour, not at all inclined to misrecognition of those whose landscape it is, and still fail to identify with them and find oneself at home within them; indeed one might have good reason not to be at home there.

Before returning to this important point it will be useful to consider the idea of estrangement from the landscape in terms of what some call

Estrangement and the practice of place

the 'practice of place'. For example, in his book, *The Working Landscape*, Peter Cannavò explains that 'place' is a *practice* for 'the creation and identification of something as a defined place is inevitably a process of social construction' (Cannavò 2007, p. 21).[30] The practice of place is inescapable because we need a 'home' – some degree of meaningful familiarity and coherence in our environment – rather than rootlessness and estrangement. This is what we have been calling 'landscaping' and the talk of 'home' here is clearly influenced by the ultimately Hegelian emphasis on the importance to us of making ourselves at home in the world. Thus, as Cannavò puts it, all places are *founded*, as opposed to simply *found*. To view places as given things we simply find around us is to reify them, of course. The founding of place occurs through (re) description, (re)interpretation and, usually, transformation. Again, we do this to be 'at home'. Indeed our identities are partly defined in relation to our surroundings interpreted as elements of place: the 'boundaries between place and person are not absolute'; there is 'mutual founding of place and identity' (Cannavò 2007, p. 33). There must then be mutual preservation of place and identity. Founding must be balanced with such preservationist activities as 'physical care and maintenance, ranging from wilderness management ... to housekeeping'. Otherwise places become too unstable to be vehicles of meaning, identity and physical security, rather than 'stress, disorientation and existential homelessness' (Cannavò 2007, p. 41); that is to say estrangement as a lack of homely identification with place.

Although in tension founding and preservation are equally integral to place and, Cannavò emphasizes, they ought to complement rather than confront one another in an either/or opposition: 'Founding must not destroy the meaningful world we have created or cut off connections to nature and history ... Preservation must not freeze our environment in time, turning it into an unusable, untouchable museum piece' (Cannavò 2007, p. 47). Both founding and preservation are mostly collective endeavours that should be pursued democratically rather than through authoritarian imposition (Cannavò 2007, e.g., pp. 202ff). Cannavò clearly has more sympathy with preservation. Particularly in the form

---

[30] At least as much as that of 'landscape', the notion of 'place' has been widely discussed in a variety of disciplines, including geography, anthropology, phenomenology and political theory, as well as environmental philosophy. Meaningful engagement with this range of literature is beyond the scope of this book and I won't attempt it here. Cannavò's work is particularly useful because of its interdisciplinary synthesis. He draws upon insights from a range of thinkers including political theorists Iris Marion Young and Hannah Arendt, philosopher Edward Casey, humanist geographer Yi-Fu Tuan and Marxist geographer David Harvey. For another useful interdisciplinary synthesis see, for example, Norton and Hannon (1998).

118   Landscape

of commodification of place founding has had the upper hand in recent decades. Still, 'preservationists must recognize ... others may disagree on what to preserve or ... be more interested in founding activities' (Cannavò 2007, p. 41). His main point is that founding and preservation have not been in 'complementary tension' within recent land-use politics, but too often pursued by opposing political actors in crude zero-sum contests, with insufficient regard for the plurality of interpretations of place(s) and of interests in founding and preservation.

Cannavò develops this point through a detailed study of three controversial land-use cases in the US: the Pacific North-Western 'timber wars', the redevelopment of Ground Zero and the phenomenon of 'sprawl'. The 'timber wars' encompasses a spectrum of positions. The Forest Service and the timber industry, pushing utter transformation of forests and timber communities to maximize short-term yield, are at the radical founding end. Intransigent preservationism, concerned to minimize human impact on ancient forests without regard for local livelihoods or wider economic considerations, is at the opposite extreme (Cannavò 2007, ch. 2). Constructive possibilities such as those favoured by timber workers who combine attachment to their profession with regard for the ancient forest, are drowned by a rancorous, polarized 'debate' between these extremes (symbolized by Mark Rey's infamous 'stark choice between people and owls' (Cannavò 2007, p. 92)). The post-9/11 redevelopment of Ground Zero has also been characterized by a tendency to zero-sum opposition between founding (for the sake of short-term financial and political gain) and preservation (especially the 9/11 families' wish to freeze that place as a permanent memorial to the casualties and heroes of that awful day); with both sides paying insufficient regard to the multiplicity of founding and preservation interests at stake (Cannavò 2007, ch. 4).

Cannavò's other case study concerns 'sprawl' – the low-density, automobile-dependent, highly privatized, centreless development with separated residential, commercial and industrial land use, which is rapidly consuming open farmland, forests and wilderness while draining vitality from urban areas (Cannavò 2007, ch. 3). Sprawl expresses a narrow short-term founding imperative without regard to preservation. Thus it involves such 'fundamentally dysfunctional' processes as 'cycles of abandonment' within interchangeable, homogenized and commodified (reified) places that are increasingly like abstract – existentially meaningless – space rather than meaningful *places* within which one can be at home (Cannavò 2007, pp. 105ff). Resolute preservationism is an understandable reaction to this, notes Cannavò, but it tends to be too intransigently reactive, ad hoc and piecemeal. 'New Urbanist' alternatives, on

Basic estrangement from the landscape

the other hand, seek to *force* mixed-use places into existence and *fix* them there through 'rigid planning and architectural design', and so represent an 'unpalatable combination of extreme founding and extreme preservation' (Cannavò 2007, p. 122).

For Cannavò these cases exemplify a generalized 'crisis of place' with four historical moments (Cannavò 2007, ch. 5): top-down governmental attempts to plan and control landscapes, assisted by philosophical and scientific reconceptualizations of place as abstract space; the increasing power of international capital to commodify places; the 'postmodern turn' to electronic global flows of economic and political power; and an environmental movement overemphasizing preservation as a response to these radical founding tendencies. At the latter extreme are bioregionalists and others whose undemocratic radical preservationism is often unhelpfully focused on preservation of wilderness, as if environmental problems in other places may be discounted.

3.13   Basic estrangement from the landscape

It is tempting to introduce the idea of labour alienation at this point and argue that it is the intensifying exploitation of labour and general commodification involved in the increasing power of international capital (the second of Cannavò's historical moments) that is fundamental to explaining estranging 'crises of place'. Indeed it might be thought that the Marxian view of the relationship between alienation of labour, estrangement and reification in general is the best way to understand all cases of reification and estrangement within the landscape. This would include those considered above in terms of environmental and climate justice, Hegelian recognition and responsibility and now in terms of problematic practices of place. To rephrase a point made earlier: the vast majority subjected to the labour alienation imposed by capital are hardly in a position to take responsibility for the world they are making, engage in environmentally just relations, participate in adequate practices of place or the like. They are inevitably mired in estrangement and reification from and of themselves, each other and wider landscapes. This claim seems particularly telling with respect to some issues, such as sprawl and globalization. For example, even without the Marxian emphasis, effectively forced or otherwise unjust alienation of ownership, even outright theft (as in cases of 'biopiracy'), must be important parts of the picture of globalization as something involving unjust landscape reification and estrangement. Yet Honneth is surely right when he argues that the Marxian account does not capture all cases and aspects of reification of persons. It also seems that giving unjust alienation of labour pride of

120   Landscape

place obscures the recognitional issues associated above with reification and estrangement in the landscape.

This brings us to the point that an aim to overcome estrangement from the humanized world needs to be qualified. Landscaping as practice of place is not pursued as a project of *homogenous* abstract humanity as such but – as Cannavò, for example, emphasizes – in different concrete ways in different locations. That the *homogenizing* pressure of international capital manifested in sprawl is a problem presupposes that something important is lost in the loss of difference between different places. That we can register this loss and see the homogenizing pressure of international capital as a threat to homely identification with place presupposes that we recognize different identities and places. Now, seeing the situation only in Marxian terms makes estrangement a consequence of the alienation of labour required by capitalism and, as such, something always to be overcome. Seeing estrangement as something always to be overcome is problematic because recognition of human difference entails some respect for the difference of different places, of the different human identities wrapped up in them, and so entails that one (or 'we') should not expect to be equally at home in all of them. This is not *only* a matter of noticing that although one (or some collective 'we') has an impact on another place, one is not the home*maker there* and does not hold rights of ownership, and so shouldn't steal things or otherwise unjustly accomplish their alienation. It means that one should not expect 'there' to be altogether shaped by the same purposes and significances as one's own home place. Where estrangement from the human world consists in not being fully at home in it, then acknowledgement of human difference as manifested in different homemaking projects requires accepting some estrangement from those 'other' places. This applies even in the same location as one's own place when the location encompasses cultural heterogeneity as tends to be the case especially in modern urban areas.[31]

This then is an environmental context in which overcoming estrangement is to be limited. The thought that humanity should overcome estrangement from its own humanized world might make sense as an abstract ideal, especially when overcoming estrangement is understood in terms of recognizing ourselves in and taking responsibility for our contributions to making that world.[32] Even so, it does not equate to each concrete human being or group finding themselves equally at home in every humanized place. In this respect some estrangement from

[31] See Iris Marion Young (1990, ch. 8).

[32] It makes most sense perhaps to view the complete elimination of estrangement in interpersonal relations as an ideal when the relations are considered entirely in abstraction from the rest of the landscape.

Basic estrangement from the landscape 121

humanized landscapes is 'basic' in the sense of necessary to the recognition of human difference. Here I am adapting Biro's claim that some 'alienation from nature' is basic in the sense of required by civilization, to say that some estrangement from landscape is necessary for civilization, assuming that just recognition of human difference is necessary for civilization.[33] Consider these remarks of William Cronon:

> We need to embrace the full continuum of a natural landscape that is also cultural, in which the city, the suburb, the pastoral, and the wild each has its proper place, which we permit ourselves to celebrate without needlessly denigrating the others. We need to honor the Other within and the Other next door as much as we do the exotic Other that lives far away-a lesson that applies as much to people as it does to (other) natural things. In particular, we need to discover a common middle ground in which all these things, from the city to the wilderness, can somehow be encompassed in the word 'home'. Home, after all, is the place where we finally make our living. It is the place for which we take responsibility, the place we try to sustain so we can pass on what is best in it (and in ourselves) to our children. (Cronon 1995, p. 88)

As I hope will become clear over the following chapters, if it is not clear already, I am very sympathetic to these ideas. But I am arguing that they are not well-served by reaching for an all-encompassing idea of 'home'. Putting aside the otherness of nonhuman nature until the next chapter, 'honouring the *other*', whether next-door or far away, requires accepting their difference. This requires living with some estrangement from them and their place as different; which means in turn that one cannot be fully at home with them and theirs. It might also be that one ought not to be at home in the places of others, not out of respect for difference, but because the places symbolize or express a dubious identity, or are organized in accordance with unacceptable projects. Perhaps one ought to be estranged from the wilderness qua site of macho individualistic Frontier Spirit, for example; and surely one ought to be estranged from surroundings configured as a death camp to enable genocide. But these cases involve estrangement as something to be overcome: the dubious identities are to be challenged; the unacceptable projects prevented. Estrangement required by the just recognition of difference is to be endorsed as something to live with.

This is also to reinforce the requirement, discussed above, that theories of environmental and climate justice have a nuanced, recognitional component. A homogenous global sink, for example, is an abstract space, not a meaningful place in which concrete human beings can be at home;

---

[33] See Chapter 1, section 1.6.

122   Landscape

even if they are taken to have individual, common or collective property rights in it. Even if it is deemed necessary to posit it as a 'shared resource', access to which is to be distributed justly, the justice of the distribution cannot be assessed without attention to impacts on different homely places, including those that are exotically other.

The consideration of human difference applies also to the requirement for reconciliation of 'personal' and 'impersonal' standpoints noted above in connection to climate change. Just as some estrangement is necessary to the recognition of human difference in the landscaping practice of place context, so each individual or group cannot find themselves expressed fully in political processes and institutions appropriate to the accommodation of human difference. Given that they have different commitments, they cannot reasonably expect to identify the totality of their commitments with such processes and institutions if these are to justly accommodate human difference. This rules out strongly holist or expressivist conceptions of the proper relation between individual and state, such as that of Hegel.[34] Because the reconciliation of personal and impersonal has to leave room for this basic estrangement, its accomplishment, should that occur, cannot be taken as fixed and final.[35]

It might be thought that the way forward here would be tightly communitarian and homogenous, perhaps bioregional, political structures. But these would need to be very small to track human difference and this simply pushes the question back to the framework of relations between the political communities; a familiar problem for anarchism and other radically 'decentralist' political thought. Cannavò's democratic solution to crises of place involves what he calls 'working landscapes' with open-ended constructive interplay between founding and preservation; the proper mix being decided democratically through deliberative procedures involving diverse voices and yielding revisable decisions. Although he rejects bioregionalism's radical preservationism as anti-democratic, Cannavò suggests that the best level for this is the region: areas on the scale of metropolitan areas and watersheds. Enduring democratic

---

[34] Hegel (1991). See Larmore (1987, ch.5); Patten (1999, p. 2).

[35] In an earlier book I emphasized the way Rawlsian political liberalism, as a 'free-standing' political conception that is not the expression of a particular comprehensive doctrine of the good, is intended to accommodate human difference in the guise of the fact of reasonable pluralism. In this picture citizens do not fully identify with the political as the expression of their total commitments, and the degree of necessary 'distance' from the political this involves is, I argued, a foothold for the development of 'respect for non-human nature's otherness as a political virtue'. See Hailwood (2004, ch. 4). But maybe the Rawlsian or any very determinedly liberal framework is, as Habermas puts it, too 'monological': too much the final verdict of an individual philosopher and in that respect too fixed and final.

Basic estrangement from the landscape 123

regional structures on this scale, rather than ad hoc shifting coalitions and local jurisdictions, are required for coherent landscape planning (Cannavò 2007, e.g., pp. 230ff).

Cannavò critically discusses a range of ways of organizing such regional politics and the policies they might pursue, and in fact have been pursued in the US, although in fragmentary ways including by collaborative conservation and environmental justice groups (Cannavò 2007, e.g., pp. 259ff). The defects of such movements can be ameliorated and their working landscape tendencies enhanced and coordinated through formal regional democratic structures, he hopes. It is not my intention to discuss political structures and policies here. Cannavò offers us one picture of a balanced, pragmatic eschewal of absolutes, zero-sum oppositions and authoritarian fixedness within environmental political practice; a way of finessing the needs to overcome estrangement from the humanized landscape, as expressed in terms of crises of place, without envisaging the total overcoming of estrangement within the landscape that would be equivalent to the elimination of human difference. This is not to say that Cannavò's account is wholly unproblematic and I shall discuss one problem with it at the beginning of the next chapter.

4 Nonhuman nature: estrangement

4.1 Introduction

In this chapter I turn to the nonanthropocentric elements of my overall argument about alienation from nature. The discussion of the previous chapter mostly bracketed relations to nonhuman nature. Not everything exists only as 'landscaped', however; as the embodiment of human labour and purposes or as vehicle for the recognition of persons, or in virtue of playing some other human-oriented role. It doesn't follow, however, that insofar as things are considered as more than (or not at all) landscaped then they must be taken to be '*mere* things'. That would suggest that 'mere-thinghood' was the given 'natural' status of nonhuman entities and processes; a default status problematic only in the context of humanity, its reification and estrangement from landscape. This brings us to the idea of estrangement from nonhuman nature.

The humanized and nonhumanized are intertwined and continuous in many ways within overall nature of course. However, the natural world, *insofar as it is a nonhuman as opposed to landscaped world*, precisely is not a reflection of human purposes or set up to satisfy our interests or to provide us with a given natural slot to fill. Hence our *estrangement* from it and situation as 'natural aliens' in Evernden's sense. Given that to be 'at home' in our surroundings involves having arranged them in accordance with our interests and to reflect our values and purposes, then to the extent that they are 'wild' – embody nonhuman processes or a more than human agency[1] – we cannot be fully at home in our surroundings. The important point here is that, whereas within the limits of human difference it seems right to say we should be at home within our surroundings insofar as they are humanized (and criticize such estranging and reifying obstacles to that as sprawl and environmental injustice), it is not right

---

[1] Remember that 'wildness' in this sense should not be confused with 'wilderness' even understood as specific regions in which wildness is more evident than in more thoroughly humanized places. Wildness is not confined to wilderness. See for example Hettinger and Throop (1999).

Introduction   125

to say our overcoming of estrangement from the nonhuman should be limited only by recognition of *human* difference. We should be prepared to view *estrangement from* the nonhuman as at least a qualified good. We should also be prepared to countenance some *alienation of* nonhuman nature in the sense of abandoning the assumption that nonhuman nature should enter into considerations of property only as something to be owned for the sake of human interests. These claims, which entail one another, are the topics of this chapter and the next. It is largely through them that I try to bring out the nonanthropocentric content of my overall argument. I discuss property and alienation in the next chapter having first discussed estrangement from nonhuman nature in this one.

Estrangement from, and alienation of, nonhuman nature concern our relation to nonhuman nature, of course, and to focus on them as modes of relating to be endorsed, rather than avoided or overcome entirely, requires that we try to view them in a nonanthropocentric light. It requires that we emphasize them in a way amenable to what we might call 'respect for nonhuman nature'. The theories and concepts we use to understand our environmental situation partly in terms of such estrangement and alienation viewed positively must then give weight to, or at least leave space for, such respect. This can be lacking in theories that focus on our landscaped surroundings, even when they offer promising ways of understanding such notions as estrangement and reification within that environmental context. For example, I doubt that it is merely idiosyncratic of me to prefer more emphasis on respect for nonhuman nature in both the founding and preservation elements of Cannavò's account of the practice of place.

It will be remembered from the previous chapter that Cannavò emphasizes the 'encumbrances' of place, the mutual embeddedness of place and personality, and that he doesn't want the mutual embeddedness of place and personality to be static and reactionary (to permanently privilege preservation over founding). This mutual embeddedness suggests that we can think of types of personality accompanying types of place, but if we do that then presumably we don't want collections of egoists recognizing nothing outside themselves other than resources for their own perfection, freedom and homemaking. Nor do we want places that embody such egoism. Presumably we want *reasonable* democratic types respectful of plurality and difference or otherness. At least this seems clear enough when our attention is confined to political relationships between persons: such reasonableness is presupposed by a commitment to democratic pluralism.

Our attention is not so confined, however, and given that we have no fixed a priori commitment to anthropocentric instrumentalism it seems

126 Nonhuman nature: estrangement

arbitrary to stop there and eschew an analogous reasonableness when it comes to the relationship between landscaped places and wider non-human nature. Absent a prior commitment to anthropocentric instrumentalism then we should expect places to be 'reasonable' places in the sense of *not* equating wider nature with themselves or resources for themselves, but rather recognizing and respecting nature's otherness. And we might ask for this reasonableness to be nurtured along with democracy, even though what it requires of particular places should be resolved democratically in the light of the other values and interests at play. Cannavò is prepared to grant nonhuman nature's independence and value, while rightly rejecting any, for example bioregionalist, 'finding' of moral and political imperatives inherent within it. As we have seen, he wisely wants to avoid pitting respect for nature 'for its own sake' against viewing it as a resource as an either/or zero-sum contest: we must do both. But the moment of respect for the nonhuman could be more emphatic and weighty in his picture of the 'working landscape'. That it isn't very emphatic and weighty is perhaps simply because Cannavò's primary focus is precisely the landscape and not the relationship between that and wider nonhuman nature. But that relationship is part of our overall environmental situation. How then should we understand estrangement from nonhuman nature and its connection to such notions as respect for nonhuman nature?

4.2 Estrangement and anti-domination

Notice that the distinction between nonhuman nature and landscape as humanized environment generates a sense in which we must be estranged from nature by definition. As long as there is something *nonhuman*, then trivially it remains nonhuman and, apparently equally trivially, so does our estrangement, our 'separation' or 'distance' from it as the 'different', the not-human. This also seems to drain alienation in this sense of normative significance and so rob it of its status as a critical concept with which to evaluate situations and practices. For *all* human situations and practices by definition involve alienation in this sense of estrangement from the nonhuman. Thus Steven Vogel refers to what he calls 'tragic' conceptions of humanity's 'alienation from nature' that lament our being in such a condition while making it conceptually impossible to escape (Vogel 2011). This apparent triviality and undermining of critical efficacy in relation to nonhuman nature, together with the difficulty of making sense of the idea of our being alienated from nature in the overall sense (of which we are inescapably a part), leads him to argue that

Estrangement and anti-domination 127

we should confine the idea of alienation from nature to alienation from 'something like nature' – the humanized landscape.[2]

Now my suggestion is that we remove the air of triviality here by emphasizing matters of degree, and by reversing the expected direction of the critical bite, so to speak. This gives us the idea of estrangement from nonhuman nature as a qualified good. What is not at all trivial is that we can always try further to 'overcome' such estrangement in the sense of eliminating more of nature as *nonhuman*. The more the natural world is humanized, so as to have less of the nonhuman about it, the less estrangement from nonhuman nature there is. Presumably something like this has in effect been the 'domination of nature' agenda considered as the determined pursuit of anthropocentric instrumentalism: we should view the nonhuman world only instrumentally, tame it to eliminate its unruly otherness and so reduce nature to the humanized landscape as much as possible. A purely anthropocentric radical constructionism about 'nature' would view this project as always already complete, so that a properly 'post-natural' environmental philosophy and politics should be about conditions within the humanized environment (as Vogel says, 'something like nature') and not about the relation between that and the nonhuman elements of a 'wider environment' called 'nature'. If instead we assume there are nonhuman items and processes from which we are estranged – wildness encountered even in the heart of the city – then we can make sense of this estrangement as a qualified good: living with it, rather than always seeking to overcome it, is equivalent to rejecting domination.[3] This can only ever be a matter of degree, however, given that *some* interpretation and transformation of the world for the sake of specifically human needs and interests is 'basic' in Bìro's sense. So it seems appropriate to call it a *qualified* good. Thus one might claim for example that nonhuman nature (whether large-scale – ecosystems, species – or local particular wildness encountered on the street) should not be eliminated for the sake of *trivial* human interests. This seems to me to be an important sense in which 'alienation from nature' can be good: good in the guise of the *estrangement from the nonhuman* maintained by resisting the wholesale unqualified assimilation of the natural world to the humanized landscape.

Consider again the environmental occurrence that was the arrival of a large splat of bird droppings on my window while Liverpool was the European Capital of Culture. The culprit-bird – a gull – and its

---

[2] See the Introduction, section 0.3 and Chapter 1, section 1.2. I return to his argument with regard to overall nature in Chapter 6.
[3] Or equivalent to rejecting what Mick Smith calls 'ecological sovereignty' (Smith 2011).

128 Nonhuman nature: estrangement

product were at least relatively wild. Certainly such wildness can be irritating: I had to decide whether to go to the trouble of cleaning the outside of a second-storey window, difficult to do from the inside, or to put up with an excremental view until the regular window cleaner was due (or until another significantly non-anthropogenic process – the rain – did the job first). I might interpret the gull as a marvellously complex evolved nonhuman organism, the occasional intrusion of whose waste products is a small price to pay for its presence, or as a nasty little flying excrement-generator. Either way, although perfectly familiar and obviously affected by human activity, it is relatively *other*. One may speak of being *estranged* from the bird and its produce: they intrude and confront me as an alien presence that, although not all that powerful, frustrate my purposes by obscuring the spectacle of human genius outside my window. I might seek to overcome this *entirely* by both cleaning the window and advocating the extermination of the gull and its kind. Or I could just live with much of that estrangement, live my life around it rather than seek to overcome it; except of course insofar as it is important and convenient to just clean the window. Or I might seek to overcome the estrangement to a greater extent, short of eliminating the gulls: perhaps we would not mind so much having our view obscured by better coloured bird-droppings, for example. In which case maybe we could intervene more in the relevant circuits of relative wildness: contrive to get the local birds to eat special food that colours their droppings. The estrangement would then be overcome somewhat as some human genius is mingled with the splat on my window.

There could be reasons for and against a variety of possible courses of action here. If we reduce the options to three – wiping out the gulls altogether, causing their droppings to be more pleasing to look at or simply putting up with them – and take living with some estrangement from the nonhuman to be the only consideration, the third option would prevail. Presumably the usual position is to put up with them until there are reasons (e.g., aesthetic considerations or issues of hygiene) to do something about them. However, one point I am making here is that even looking out of the window to recognize and appreciate what is highly humanized can require looking around, or past, what is much less humanized, even in highly humanized urban environments. Another is that the estrangement from nonhuman nature involved in such situations should not be on a list of impediments to be eliminated without qualification or question.

These points both rely upon and help constitute, a *dynamic* picture that acknowledges the transformative power of human activity and

Estrangement and anti-domination 129

does not equate nonhuman nature with untouched nature; and consequently does not equate respect for the nonhuman (or preparedness to live with some estrangement from it) with a completely 'hands off' stance towards pure wilderness. This cannot be emphasized enough. For example, Ben Minteer worries that a nonanthropocentric position concerned to preserve pristine nonhuman intrinsic values cannot deal with our actual 'post-stationary' situation. The increasing stress on ecosystems and threat of extinctions caused by anthropogenic climate change, for instance, might well require such measures as 'managed relocation' of especially vulnerable species, subject to an assessment of their impact on their new environment (Minteer 2012, pp. 162ff). Given they are not motivated by purely anthropocentric concerns, such measures are not at all ruled out by the nonanthropocentric elements of my overall argument, which do not rely on 'intrinsic value' any more than pristine nature or wilderness.[4]

For example, say it turns out that anthropogenic factors (climate change, disruption of the relevant food chain, presence of easy pickings from human food waste) cause very large numbers (a 'plague') of gulls to inhabit Merseyside, where their guano and importunate scavenging is found intolerable. The human inhabitants of this place are now simply *too* estranged from their newly gull-dominated surroundings. The option to relocate as many as possible to some other, less humanized coastal environment (assuming a suitable one can be found) 'for their own sake' might then function as an alternative to the purely anthropocentric measure of exterminating an unwanted pest without regard to the interests or flourishing-requirements of this species of nonhuman organism, or to its larger nonhuman ecological relations. That the presence and behaviour of the gulls has a large anthropogenic component does not mean they are no longer relatively wild and other. Nor is it necessary to refer to anything in this scenario as 'untouched nature', including the alternative coastal environment, even though that is less humanized than Merseyside. It might not be possible to relocate the gulls of course; and it might be impossible to find a suitable alternative environment that would not be too damaged by their introduction – damaged to a degree unjustifiable in the nonanthropocentric terms motivating the relocation exercise. The question then becomes how much estrangement is liveable with in this context: what should be done to the Merseyside gulls in situ; how many of them should be culled?

---

[4] See Chapter 2, sections 2.5 and 2.10.

130   Nonhuman nature: estrangement

4.3   Anti-domination and the Frankfurt School

I am suggesting then that one way of thinking of 'respect for nonhuman nature' is in terms of resisting domination and that resisting domination can be thought of in terms of living with, rather than seeking always to overcome, some estrangement from nonhuman nature. I don't mean that respect for nonhuman nature and a positive view of estrangement from it can be connected only by the idea of resistance to domination. There are various ways to understand such respect that might help to unpack the idea of maintaining a degree of estrangement from nonhuman nature and lend it critical content, although, as we shall see, they need careful handling to be helpful in these terms. However, 'resistance to domination' is associated particularly with the critical theory tradition, especially the early Frankfurt School, which, while taking much of its inspiration and general historical materialist orientation from Marx, to some extent saw him as caught up in the domination of nature agenda. It will help to clarify my own argument further if first we look briefly at some difficulties arising from this tradition's approach to the issue of the domination of nature, and then at the matter in more orthodox Marxian terms before turning to more recent environmental philosophy.

Whether traditional Marxism, or Marx himself, is *inextricably* caught up in the domination of nature agenda is a matter of dispute. As Ted Benton says, 'Marxism has been berated for its "productivism"; its reliance on scientific and technical advances (the famous "development of the forces of production") to deliver a future paradise of material abundance; and for its commitment to the modernist project of the "mastery of nature"' (Benton 1996, p. 243).[5] The early Frankfurt School theorists are generally regarded as stern critics of traditional Marxism in these terms. Thus, in an influential work of green political theory, Robyn Eckersley (herself an 'ecocentric' critic of Marx and his followers) reports that the Frankfurt School criticized Marxism for viewing

nature as little more than raw material for exploitation, thereby foreshadowing aspects of the more recent ecocentric critique of Marxism. Horkheimer and Adorno argued that this stemmed from the uncritical way in which Marxism had inherited and perpetuated the paradoxes of the Enlightenment tradition – their central target. In this respect, Marxism was regarded as no different from liberal capitalism. (Eckersley 1992, p. 101)

---

[5] See the papers in Benton (1996) and Benton's introductory sections for discussion of the extent and depth of Marx's commitment to dominating nature, and the prospects for 'greening Marxism'. I will discuss shortly an interesting suggestion of Benton's in this regard.

For those thinkers the central 'paradox of the Enlightenment tradition' is that the domination of 'outer nature' through a purely instrumental rationality focused on its manipulation is accompanied inescapably by a distorting domination of 'inner nature' that undermines the subjective conditions of freedom (Eckersley 1992, p. 102). Eckersley proceeds to condemn the Frankfurt School for failing to live up to its critical potential with regard to the environmental crisis. For example, the early theorists, such as Adorno and Horkheimer, were deeply pessimistic of any 'reconciliation' between humanity and nature, although they did insist on the importance of maintaining the idea of it as a 'somewhat vague utopian dream' as an alternative to mere 'passive surrender to the status quo' (Eckersley 1992, pp. 102–3).[6]

4.4 Nature, alienation and non-identity

Some more recent scholarship has sought to recover the 'critical ecological' dimensions of the work of the early Frankfurt School thinkers and has also painted a more nuanced picture of their view of Marx's position with regards to nature.[7] But this scholarship is also characterized by differences of interpretation.

For example, Vogel takes Adorno to exemplify the 'tragic conception of alienation' from nature, which, as we have seen, views it as a condition both regrettable yet impossible for us to overcome; impossible because nature is defined in terms of nonhuman otherness. For Adorno, on Vogel's interpretation, 'nature' stands for the remainder 'left over' by the failure of concepts to fully capture their objects and of actions to fully realize their intended goals: the recalcitrance of nonhuman reality with respect to human thought and action.[8] 'Identity thinking' is Adorno's term for an assumption he believes central to the dominating stance of instrumental reason that concepts can and do 'go into their objects without remainder' and actions unambiguously and unqualifiedly achieve their ends. Resistance to this then has to take the form of 'non-identity thinking', a 'negative dialectics' in which reason is deployed not instrumentally, but critically so as to expose the irreducible remainder of nature's otherness. Vogel emphasizes that for Adorno this cannot amount to the

---

[6] The *later* Frankfurt School, represented by the views of Habermas, is committed to retaining instrumental rationality as *the* mode of reason appropriate to our engagement with nonhuman nature (the sphere of labour, science and technology), while non-instrumental 'communicative' rationality pushes it out of the intersubjective, human social sphere thus liberating *only that sphere* from domination (Eckersley 1992, pp. 106ff). See also the discussion of Honneth on 'reification of nature' in the previous chapter.

[7] See, for example, Biro (2005; 2011), Cook (2011).

[8] Vogel (1996, 2011).

132 Nonhuman nature: estrangement

formulation of precise concepts and a systematic theory without itself lapsing back into identity thinking. And again Vogel argues that understanding alienation from nature in terms of non-identity, or the ultimate ungraspability of nature's otherness, makes it ineliminable ('tragic') and robs the notion of alienation of its critical purchase. Better then to return to (early) Marx's conception of alienation as focused on what can be grasped, at least in principle: the human landscape produced by human labour.[9]

Vogel's interpretation of Adorno is questionable on a number of grounds. He suggests that Adorno regrets something called 'alienation from nature' where 'nature' is 'non-identical remainder' and the regrettable alienation consists in being confronted by its unknowability or ungraspability. A more plausible interpretation perhaps is that Adorno regrets the domination of nature brought by instrumental reason's attempt to override non-identity, to reduce everything to the graspable. Regrettable alienation in this picture would then be more a matter of the failure to 'respect' non-identity than the 'fact' of non-identity itself and, as such, something we might overcome to some extent through negative dialectics. Thus D. Bruce Martin draws upon Adorno to criticize the strong forms of identification with nature, through 'enlarging the self', proposed by deep ecologists such as Arne Naess as a way of overcoming alienation from nature: for Adorno '[t]he danger consists in projecting characteristics of the self onto the other, subjecting the other to the needs of the self as yet another extension of the domination of nature' (Martin 2011, p. 123).[10] Such a critique of strongly holist ecocentric thinking builds on the theme of non-identity as something to be 'respected' rather than overcome. It chimes with similar criticisms of deep ecology made by environmental philosophers such as Peter Reed and Val Plumwood, some of whose views on the matter I consider below.

Moreover, Vogel agrees with Biro's reconstruction of the early Frankfurt School's conception of alienation from nature as consisting in our (to some basic extent unavoidable) self-conscious transformation of nature (Vogel 2011, pp. 190, 192). Vogel is right to say this conception

---

[9] In terms of twentieth-century critical theory then, Vogel favours Lukács' account of reification as the more satisfactory theory within which to understand 'nature'. This is also a theme of Vogel's (1996) book *Against Nature*: we should stop worrying about nature as an unknowable other and concentrate on what we can know through our participation in its literal construction (i.e., the landscape) and focus resistance to domination in terms of overcoming the reification of landscape into a 'second nature', rather than alienation from *nature*.

[10] See also Deborah Cook's detailed exploration of the differences and affinities between Adorno and deep ecology (Cook 2011, pp. 122ff).

Nature, alienation and non-identity

of alienation from nature is problematic.[11] But to ascribe it to Adorno seems inconsistent with interpreting him as making non-identity itself a matter of inescapable and regrettable alienation. It suggests instead that Adorno understands alienation from nature in terms of domination – remorseless transformation powered by instrumentalism and identity thinking – rather than non-identity and ungraspable otherness. And given the interdependence between domination of 'outer' and 'inner' nature in the Frankfurt School view, it seems that Vogel's interpretation of Adorno as equating 'nature' with non-identity is also questionable. This is especially so with regard to *nonhuman* nature. Thus Deborah Cook and Alison Stone argue that for Adorno non-identity encompasses humanity and human culture (what we are calling the landscape) as well as (nonhuman) 'natural' things (Cook 2011, p. 43; Stone 2006, p. 242). The recalcitrant otherness of non-identity is not then a matter only of nonhuman otherness. If so, and we still want to say that nature is non-identity, then the nature in question is more like the natural world in our sense, which encompasses both the human and nonhuman.[12] And if, with Vogel, we interpret Adorno to mean we are alienated from the non-identical qua non-identical, then we are taking Adorno to claim that we are necessarily alienated from the natural world. But then this seems to make Adorno a target also of Vogel's other argument, the argument focused on the idea of alienation from the natural world: non-identity is a feature of our 'natural' condition in that it does not put us 'outside' the natural world. So, again, why call it 'alienation from nature'?

Now, pointing to such interpretative difficulties does not in itself undermine Vogel's overall claim, which is that whatever the proper interpretation of Adorno turns out to be, the conceptual problems involved in running alienation from nature (whether nonhuman or natural world) as a critical concept make it advisable to think instead in terms of alienation from 'something like nature', the humanized landscape. My way through these issues is to keep the distinctions between landscape, nonhuman nature and the natural world in mind and take it that the sense of 'alienation from nature' presently at stake is estrangement from nonhuman nature. Nonhuman nature, remember, is nature insofar as it is not transformed and assimilated to, and interpreted in terms of, human-oriented interests and purposes. In this sense it is 'other' and we are estranged from it by definition. But this is far from trivial because it means that

---

[11] See the Introduction, section 0.3.

[12] Presumably this could not be an identity claim: two things, non-identity and the natural world, are themselves really identical. Rather 'natural world' would be functioning (perhaps implausibly) as a label for the non-identical remainder left over when concepts fail to capture their objects, regardless of whether they are designated human or nonhuman.

134 Nonhuman nature: estrangement

self-conscious transformation of surroundings, rather than constituting 'alienation from nature' as in Bíro's reconstruction of the Frankfurt School view, is a way of *overcoming* estrangement from *nonhuman* nature by the progressive elimination of nonhuman nature through its progressive transformation into humanized landscape. This is a matter of degree and can't be completed; there will always be a 'remainder' and so, although I shall qualify this shortly, there is some affinity here with the Adornian line on non-identity, at least where non-identity is confined to nonhuman nature as in Vogel's (questionable) interpretation of Adorno.

There is rather more affinity perhaps with the critique of domination understood as unrestricted transformation and instrumentalization of nature: the *identification* of the natural world with the human landscape and accompanying elimination of the idea of nonhuman nature as more than landscaping resources. Again, I am thinking of such domination as a matter of overcoming estrangement from the nonhuman. In saying that this can only be a matter of degree I am agreeing with Vogel at least to the extent of saying that alienation (in this sense of estrangement) from nonhuman nature is to some degree ineliminable. But I am also claiming that it is unhelpful to call it 'tragic' and wrong to say that it must lack critical bite. The bite is kept by associating respect for nonhuman nature and critique of its domination with resisting the aim of always seeking to overcome estrangement from nonhuman nature.

Vogel is also right to worry about very strong notions of the otherness of nonhuman nature, which treat it as *absolutely* other, a kind of *unknowable*, effectively noumenal, remainder. One problem with this is that, as he points out, it is at odds with the assumption of continuity within the natural world. I return to this below where I consider a similar point made by Plumwood. But it is not a problem for our distinction, within the natural world, between humanized landscape and nonhuman nature, which is meant to be a pragmatic matter of degree.[13] It is not meant to be an 'ontological distinction', if that means a dichotomy between absolutely distinct substances.[14]

The idea of nature as unknowable other is also problematic insofar as it is associated with the philosophical quest for certainty I criticized in Chapter 2 for its sea squirt tendencies.[15] A problem then with trying to understand estrangement from nonhuman nature in terms of the critical theory of the early Frankfurt School and their more respectful

---

[13] See Chapter 1, section 1.13 and Chapter 2, section 2.1.

[14] This seems to be what Vogel has in mind when he complains of thinkers who begin 'by assuming an essentially ontological distinction between humans and nature and then [call] that distinction "alienation"' (Vogel 2011, p. 192).

[15] See Chapter 2, sections 2.2–2.4.

Nature, alienation and non-identity

interpreters and critics is that this locates it in a debate already coloured by epistemological considerations headed unhelpfully in the sea squirt direction. The extent of this colouring is also open to interpretation of course. For example, Cook emphasizes the role in his case against identity thinking played by what Adorno calls the 'fallacy of constitutive subjectivity': 'the illusory view (which takes many forms) that mind, or spirit, constitutes nature' (Cook 2011, p. 9). Adorno is against idealism then, and so against attempts to complete the quest for certainty by reducing the real to the mental so that it can be grasped securely and finally. In fact Adorno's rejection of identity thinking seems to be a rejection of all forms of the quest for certainty considered as a *completable* quest for an absolutely secure *grasp* of things. In this respect he appears to be a profoundly anti-sea squirt thinker.

On the other hand, insofar as the non-identical is contrasted emphatically with things 'grasped' *in the form of known*, then a covert sea squirt ideal is discernible in the background. We can see that this is unhelpful when we think of the 'non-identity' of humanized landscape and non-human nature. If we say that a fox is 'more than' the set of interpretations and roles foisted onto it through our landscaping – 'pest', 'wily quarry' and so on – then we are saying there is more to the fox than the place it has in relation to our human-oriented purposes. Our awareness of this 'more than', or 'remainder' left over by our landscaping of the fox, marks our estrangement from it in the sense I am interested in here, and which I am suggesting we should not seek to overcome entirely. And clearly, as I have said, there is an affinity here with Adornian non-identity with regard to the nonhuman. But the extent to which the fox is more than its place in the landscape (its role *for* us) need not be the extent to which it is *unknowable*; a meaningless, inexplicable occurrence of shape and colours, say. When asked in virtue of what is the fox more than its landscaped role, we can say things like this: well, we know that the fox is a type of mammal, a member of a species with its own mode of flourishing and its own natural history that, although to a significant degree intertwined with and affected by human history, is not reducible to it. We can admit that this knowledge is partial, provisional and revisable and we can consider the extent to which in its partiality it is coloured by landscaping interests (in pest control or the availability of satisfying 'country sports', for example).[16]

The point here is that such provisionality and revisability is much weaker than non-identity as unknowability. The latter calls for a far

---

[16] Compare 'moderate constructionism' (Chapter 2, section 2.6).

136 Nonhuman nature: estrangement

more emphatic perpetual repetition of the 'more than' refrain; one that seems to betray an unhelpful sea squirt tendency. Having said that the fox is more than a wily chicken-killer and set out something of its own way of living and flourishing and ecological needs, it can be unhelpful to be told it is 'more than that'. We might agree that it is more than that, but still wish to dwell on our provisional knowledge and employ it to help unpack our sense of estrangement from non-human nature. So at this point we might wish to resist the impulse to emphasize the 'more than' of non-identity. This is especially so if we suspect the reason the impulse is so insistent is not the wish to resist the dominating reduction of the nonhuman to the human landscape, but a drive to complete a quest for thorough, unassailable knowledge of each particular thing in its total particularity. We might suspect that the completion of this quest, which is blocked by identity thinking's attempt to grasp things by placing them under general concepts, is the only condition under which the repeated emphatic 'more than' refrain will be allowed to pause and relax its hold on our attention. Insofar as Adorno's negative dialectic is like this then it has an unhelpful sea squirt tendency.

4.5   Labour, estrangement and domination

In bringing together resistance to domination, living with estrangement from nature and respect for nature we are not then simply taking on board the early Frankfurt School view of things. Although there are obvious resonances in terms of resistance to domination and instrumentalization, and some affinity with Adorno on non-identity, for example, there are features from which we must distance ourselves: hints of a sea squirt tendency and, most obviously, an understanding of alienation from nature as something to be overcome as much as possible. What of more classical Marxism? Is it committed irredeemably to the domination of nature? None of my discussion so far rules out the possibility that the idea of *accepting* a degree of estrangement from the nonhuman might be informed helpfully by traditional Marxian materialism. One initially promising route in this regard is suggested by Ted Benton's discussion of the importance of an 'eco-regulatory', as opposed to purely transformative, conception of labour (Benton 1992).

Benton argues that Marx's own vulnerability to the charge of anthropocentric 'productivism', of seeking the complete subservience of nature to the forces of production, is due largely to his focus on a purely transformative conception of human labour. This gives the labour process a particular 'intentional structure':

Labour, estrangement and domination 137

one in which labour uses some instrument to bring about a change in raw material. This raw material, having undergone the transformation, now meets some human purpose: it has a 'use value'. The point or purpose of the labour process is to transform raw materials into use values. (Benton 1992, p. 59)

But there are other forms of labour that aim to produce use value without conforming to the 'raw material -> transformation -> product' model (Benton 1992, p. 60).[17]

One such is 'eco-regulatory' labour,[18] which is labour 'primarily devoted to optimizing and maintaining the *conditions* under which some organic transformations take place', as in various agricultural and horticultural practices. Here human labour doesn't itself transform a seed into a plant, say, but optimizes the conditions for that to occur by itself, by tilling, irrigating and so on. 'Contrast this with the carpenter who works with tools to change the form of a piece of wood' (Benton 1992, p. 60). On the one hand, these conditions and associated causal mechanisms, such as the topographical and climatic requirements and biological features of certain crops, are not themselves transformed into commodities or products with use value. On the other hand nor are they utterly non-manipulable 'untouched nature'. Benton points to the '*relative* non-manipulability of certain contextual conditions and causal mechanisms' involved in, say, agriculture. 'For any given socio-technological organization of the labour process, some things can be altered but others just have to be taken as "given" and adapted to as well as possible' (Benton 1992, p. 61). We cannot coherently envisage this general fact as something that might be transcended by further 'socio-technological developments'. The idea of human mastery over all nonhuman processes is 'the purest idealism', Benton says, and to seek to realize it is 'to court ecological catastrophe' (Benton 1992, p. 63).

He discusses the situation of English Lake District hill farmers in the early 1990s in these terms. They responded to low market sheep prices by increasing their flock sizes, which, given topographical constraints, increased grazing density and so degraded pastures and progressively reduced the quality of grazing for future stock. Thus they were trapped in a downward economic spiral. Benton's eco-regulatory analysis

shows how, for this *particular* sociotechnical organization of sheep farming, the forms of economic calculation imposed on farmers qua petty-commodity producers in a capitalist economy contradict the forms of calculation imposed by the

---

[17] Benton's claim isn't that Marx did not know this, but that he did not appreciate its significance for an understanding of the conditions of human labour.

[18] Another is domestic labour, he says (Benton 1992, p. 59).

138 Nonhuman nature: estrangement

requirement to sustain sheep farming as an 'eco-regulatory' labour-process. The biological nature of the breeds of sheep capable of thriving under prevailing ecological conditions, the size of the available land, the quality of the grazing and so on, are ecological constraints which combine together with and overdetermine socioeconomic and cultural ones to constrain the range of options open to hill farmers. They are among the conditions which are, for the current sociotechnical organization of the labour process, not available for manipulation. They are constraints which have to be *adapted* to as far as is possible. (Benton 1992, p. 62, emphases in original)

New breeds of sheep and forms of fertilizer and so on may be developed to enhance the grazing potential of the hills of course. But any new hill-farming labour process will still face further ecological as well as socio-economic constraints, even if profitable: 'fertilizer run off may pollute water supplies, the greater density of grazing may encourage spread of sheep parasites and diseases, or induce unforeseen social behaviour in the sheep. Unpredictable or harsh weather conditions will still be encountered, weathering will still generate tasks of farm maintenance, and so on' (Benton 1992, p. 62).

The point is generalizable. Imagine that we could genetically engineer gulls to excrete in ways less intrusive than the one I complained of earlier. They would still likely find other ways of being annoyingly intrusive. Thus Benton uses the example of genetic engineering to illustrate his argument that 'no matter how "deep" we go into the structure of the materials and beings with which we work, it remains the case that transformation both *presupposes* constancy of structure and causal powers at a *deeper* structural level, and are *limited* by the nature of that deeper level structure' (Benton 1992, p. 66, emphasis in original). When units of DNA (molecular genes) from one genome are recombined with those from another it is to produce a specific phenotypical result otherwise absent from the now 'engineered' species. This presupposes some awareness of what phenotypes result from what DNA combinations. GM technology thus presupposes the *non-engineered* propensities of molecular genes themselves, which cannot be combined in any old way to produce a viable version of whatever type of organism we prefer (Benton 1992, pp. 66f; see also O'Neill 2012).

We might say then that any given historically specific organization of the labour process leaves an ecological 'remainder' that, although not unknowable, escapes its grasp and mastery and has to be adapted to. To fail to acknowledge this is to indulge in the incoherent 'promethean' dream of total human mastery over everything, and acknowledging it requires supplementing the transformative conception of labour with eco-regulatory considerations. In terms of estrangement, we have seen

Labour, estrangement and domination

that the forms of estrangement considered by traditional Marxism are those produced by the alienation of labour. As such they are to be overcome along with the abolition of private property and so of the alienation of labour required by that form of ownership. However, the eco-regulatory conception of the labour process brings with it a form of estrangement – estrangement from nonhuman nature – that cannot be overcome, at least in the guise of an always present limit to the material transformation of nonhuman entities and processes in accordance with human-oriented interests and purposes. Therefore once the transformative conception is supplemented by eco-regulatory considerations Marxism can accept at least the inevitability of a degree of estrangement in this sense.

But this isn't quite the sense of estrangement we are after. The *normative* stance I am associating with the idea of accepting some estrangement from nonhuman nature – that of respecting nature, for example by resisting its domination – is not *given* with an eco-regulatory understanding of labour. Benton shows that this understanding makes total mastery of our surroundings a conceptual impossibility: eco-regulatory labour by definition occurs against a background of conditions that cannot be transformed and have to be adapted to. But this remains consistent with anthropocentric instrumentalism as an *agenda* of domination. Any given ecological constraints revealed by a particular stage of productive technology might still be viewed as an obstacle to be overcome, a condition to be transformed *at some point*, after further 'research and development', even though it is accepted that such overcoming and transformation will always be against the background of further constraints and conditions that cannot (yet) be overcome and transformed. Accepting the impossibility of total mastery is consistent with always wanting as much mastery as possible and a perpetual effort to extend the range of the mastered. Because it remains consistent with a blanket anthropocentric instrumental agenda, the eco-regulatory conception is consistent with remaining entirely within an instrumental landscaping perspective that interprets its surroundings only in terms of potential resources and obstacles.

For example, consider the suggestion that we now live in a new geological era: the Anthropocene.[19] Even if we accept this label we can hardly take it to mean that we have 'ended nature' in the sense of replacing all previously nonhuman processes with human labour processes and products. Rather the label marks the massive scale of anthropogenic impacts upon the Earth. But it remains an open question whether we take it as a cause for concern at the domination it represents and against which we may assert the virtue of living with some estrangement from nonhuman

---

[19] See the Introduction, section 0.2.

140   Nonhuman nature: estrangement

nature as a counter-value. We might take it instead as a welcome sign that human control is proceeding apace and the prospect is opening of ever more profound and comprehensive control, for example through bio- and geo-engineering technologies. The eco-regulatory conception of labour is consistent with the latter, which remains the stance often associated with traditional Marxism. Benton's emphasis of the ineliminable structure of eco-regulatory labour is a necessary corrective to change the agenda from one of unqualified mastery of nature, to our '[c]apacity to bring technology itself, the mediation between human social relations and natural mechanisms under communal control...the distinctive hoped for ecological virtue of socialism' (Benton 1992, p. 67).[20] But this is not sufficient.

However, Benton speculates that more 'romantic' and 'ecocentric' attitudes to nature[21] can be made consistent with the historical materialist notion of the human 'species being' by thinking of them as general human needs alongside those for creative, non-estranged labour (Benton 1992, pp. 67ff). He notes that this is in keeping with some of Marx's writings on humanity's relations to wider nature, not all of which express an unrestricted promethean fantasy. For example, at times in the *1844 Manuscripts* Marx envisages the development of wider aesthetic and 'spiritual' aspects of human/nature relations and an almost Romantic resolution of the 'conflict' between humanity and nature.[22] If something like this is right then the Marxist tradition does appear to be consistent with my claim that we should seek to overcome pernicious estrangement from the humanized landscape *without* seeking to overcome estrangement from the nonhuman as much as possible. The space for estrangement from nonhuman nature as a normative stance of respect and resistance to domination is provided by a conception of labour modified by eco-regulatory considerations; and the normative basis supplied by 'respect for nature' as a component of the human species being.

And, of course, considering things in Marxian terms reminds us not to neglect interconnections between forms of alienation, reification and

---

[20] Here Benton echoes the critical theorist Walter Benjamin, who writes at the end of *One Way Street*: 'The mastery of nature, so the imperialists teach, is the purpose of all technology. But who would trust a cane wielder who proclaimed the mastery of children by adults to be the purpose of education? Is not education above all the indispensable ordering of the *relationship* between generations and therefore mastery, if we are to use this term, of that relationship, and not of children? And likewise technology is not the mastery of nature but of the *relation* between nature and man' (quoted by Gunster 2011, pp. 223–4).

[21] These are his terms: he seems to mean attitudes that involve a denial of anthropocentric instrumentalism. But by 'nature' he seems to mean the natural world. I return to this point shortly.

[22] See Marx (2007, e.g., pp. 102, 105), Benton (1992, p. 68).

Labour, estrangement and domination

estrangement. This places estrangement from the human species being (in the guise of negation or denial of its respect for nature component) among the cluster of estrangements associated with private property and alienation of labour, which all need to be overcome if the domination of nature is to be halted. It closely connects considerations of estrangement from nonhuman nature with other considerations of alienation made familiar by traditional Marxism. It suggests that we might understand 'living with some estrangement from nonhuman nature' as a part of what is required to overcome estrangement from the human species being.

That said, there are at least two related reasons for not resting content with the (modified) Marxian position here with respect to estrangement from the nonhuman. First, even if modified to incorporate an eco-regulatory understanding of labour and a species being need for 'eco-centrism', the resulting commitment to respect for nonhuman nature and resisting its domination is not very emphatic. As with Cannavò's idea of the working landscape, the main focus is on the landscape. Notwithstanding the prospects for some significant 'greening' of Marxism and for interpreting Marx himself as a less than wholehearted anthropocentric instrumentalist, it is at least clear that respect for nonhuman nature is very much an afterthought and not a priority for traditional Marxism. Second and related, as with the Frankfurt School, the thrust of Marxist thinking on estrangement is that it is to be overcome. It is no accident that Benton refers to those aspects of Marx's thinking that seem 'friendlier' to nature as 'almost romantic' and about reconciliation and 'ending the conflict between man and nature'. Meeting the need for ecocentric respect for nature – overcoming estrangement from our species being in *that* way – is associated here with estrangement from nature as something to be overcome: *overcoming* estrangement from species being and from nature are two sides of the same coin. It is best then to interpret 'nature' here as meaning the natural world, encompassing humanity and nonhuman nature, rather than specifically nonhuman nature. Estrangement from the latter should not be overcome entirely: I am arguing that living with some of *that* estrangement is equivalent to resisting the domination of nonhuman nature.

As part of my overall argument I shall claim in Chapters 6 and 7 that overcoming estrangement from the natural world *requires* accepting some estrangement from the nonhuman. Although, as we have seen, it is to put the point too strongly to say that Marxism rules this out as a possibility, its concentration on overcoming estrangement primarily within the landscape and then when 'greened' from the natural world, makes it hard to focus on estrangement from nonhuman nature as something to be lived with. It will be helpful then to look outside the Marxian tradition

142   Nonhuman nature: estrangement

at positions that are more emphatic about 'respect for *nonhuman* nature'. We can do this while accepting that a concern to live with estrangement from nonhuman nature should not neglect reification, alienation and estrangement within the humanized landscape: we need to keep the various senses of 'alienation from nature' in mind. For example, preparedness to live with some estrangement from nonhuman nature should not exclude concern to overcome pernicious estrangement from other persons and the reification of unjust global social and economic relations as simply given things to be endured.

4.6   Estrangement, anti-domination and recognition

I have already suggested that, at least on the face of it, a number of environmental philosophies seem available to unpack further the normativity of the idea of estrangement from nonhuman nature. Some point to 'naturalness', or the 'autonomy of nature' – the origin and capacity for continued existence and direction of growth and development that nonhuman natural items and processes have independently of humanity – as itself grounding intrinsic value.[23] This seems to provide a normative basis for accepting estrangement from nonhuman nature, including when couched as a form of resistance to domination: we should stop dominating nonhuman nature and viewing it only instrumentally because it has intrinsic value 'in its own right' and intrinsic value is to be respected wherever found. We have seen, however, that the notion of *intrinsic* value is problematic. There is the worry about it functioning as a pragmatically unhelpful conversation-stopper or sea squirt goal.[24] Moreover, in the present context nonhuman nature is being 'valued' in virtue of a relation to us (non-humanity), rather than in virtue of intrinsic properties.[25] To fit our purposes, this approach needs at least to reconsider the idea of intrinsic value and focus instead on non-instrumental value.

A different approach is involved in David Schlosberg's suggestion to extend recognitional justice to nature. Under the headings of reification and estrangement in the landscape I discussed in the previous chapter some of the ways Schlosberg uses recognitional theories to inform his pluralistic approach to environmental justice. But now I have in mind particularly his modification of Nancy Fraser's status injury model of the kind of misrecognition that can stand in the way of human justice, into

---

[23] See for example, Elliot (1992), Goodin (1992), Lee (1994) and the papers in Heyd (2005) for a good sample of this position.
[24] See Chapter 2, section 2.5.
[25] This is a problem even if one does not want to go as far as to reject the notion of intrinsic value altogether. Compare Chapter 2, section 2.10.

Estrangement, anti-domination and recognition 143

a recognitional component of his pluralistic account of *ecological* justice: justice to the nonhuman (Schlosberg 2007, pp. 139ff).

Fraser's approach prioritizes status injurious misrecognition as *domination* rather than the psychological consequences of a *felt* lack of recognition. This makes it potentially applicable beyond humanity without inviting charges of excessive anthropomorphism: we might think of what it is to do nonhuman nature an *injustice* in terms of the injurious status ascribed to it through our institutions, norms and practices (Schlosberg 2007, pp. 140f). Thus we might routinely fail to recognize nonhuman entities and processes adequately, where this needn't be understood in terms of hurting their feelings or undermining the sense they have of their own worthiness to exist and develop in their own way. We can run the idea without being committed either to the Cartesian assumption that only humans have subjectivity, or the opposite assumption that *everything* has subjectivity; or to restricting its scope to those nonhuman entities and processes we feel sure do have subjectivity. It is a matter of our 'dominating' them by not considering them at all except insofar as they are useful, or present an awkward obstacle to our landscaping projects.

Such misrecognition might be implicit in thought and action and only occasionally stated explicitly. Like reification, we can think of it as a matter of praxis, of routine practices and habitual attitudes towards nonhuman entities and processes that either ignore them altogether or reduce them to *mere* things to be landscaped. Thus Schlosberg applies Fraser's three types of status injury to nonhuman nature: 'a general practice of cultural domination'; 'a pattern of non-recognition equivalent to rendering invisible'; and 'disrespect or routine disparagement in stereotypic public and cultural representation'. In the following quotation the terms 'nature' and 'natural world' seem to refer to nonhuman nature:

In the causes of, and discussions surrounding, global climate change ... we see all sorts of status-injurious misrecognition – the domination of nature by extractive industries, the invisibility of nature in political planning ... and the disparaging of the natural world in discussions of the mitigation of impacts on human communities at the expense of nature. (Schlosberg 2007, p. 140)

Tackling 'ecological injustice' in this sense clearly involves resisting the project of being fully at home in the world through overcoming all estrangement from the nonhuman. It fits well with the basic move of accepting estrangement from nonhuman nature as a critical normative stance respectful of the nonhuman and opposed to domination: we should not *identify* landscape and nonhuman nature, or reduce the latter

144 Nonhuman nature: estrangement

to the former. We should *recognize* that there is more to the nonhuman than its (potential) place in the human landscape. The world is 'more than human', and we should be prepared to live with this without disparaging the nonhuman or ignoring it except to contemplate its transformation into humanized landscape.

4.7 Extensionism, continuity and difference

While environmentalists have identified many sources of ... destructive alienation from nature-from philosophical systems like Cartesian dualism to the capitalist labor process-some form of alienation, in the sense of a recognition of varying patterns of difference/distance among the self, other humans, and more-than-human-others is an important aspect of the very possibility of ethics. (Smith 2011, p. 230 n. 15)

Notice that employing recognitional justice in this way is a form of 'extensionism'; a matter of taking a moral/political notion, in this case a notion of (in)justice, formulated for inter-human (intra-landscape) relations and extending it to nonhuman nature. We need to be careful about this. Remember we are not doing 'applied ethics' in the sense of applying what is taken to be a given already formulated and settled position to 'environmental problems'.[26] That extensionism can trap us into a focus on sameness and continuity (or what we take to be sameness and continuity) between humanity and the rest of nature, rather than difference or otherness, illustrates how the 'applied' method can be problematic in the present context.[27] It can do this in a way that threatens to transform the issue from that of (accepting) estrangement from nonhuman nature to that of (overcoming) estrangement from the natural world, and in a way that helps us with neither of these issues. Thus we may distinguish two ways in which recognition can be extended to nature.

One concerns the recognition of *similarities* between human and nonhuman and emphasizes *continuity* between them as parts of the same overall natural world. Often this is a matter of taking some feature held to ground moral considerability in the human case (for example, integrity, sentience, flourishing capabilities or sheer life) and pointing to aspects of nonhuman nature, or nonhuman beings, with the same, very similar

---

[26] See Chapter 1, section 1.4.

[27] Smith makes a similar point when he argues that an 'ecological difference-based ethic ... potentially offers a radical alternative to all attempts to enclose the nonhuman in an economy of the Same' (Smith 2011, p. 44). The quotation at the start of this section is of a footnote to a discussion in which he criticizes 'biocentric' approaches that further the anthropological machine by exemplifying the continuity form of extensionism I am about to touch upon (Smith 2011, p. 44).

Extensionism, continuity and difference 145

or strongly analogous features. Given the similarity or continuity of features between the human and nonhuman it then becomes perniciously anthropocentric, a matter of mere arbitrary or 'speciesist' prejudice, to withhold recognition of the nonhuman version of such features and the moral considerability associated with them in the human case. The impetus here is towards 'expanding the moral community' to include beings that have been arbitrarily or unjustly excluded from it. This emphasizes that 'we are all in it together' and should engage in those relations, of justice for example, held to be appropriate to the declared community, and eschew forms of praxis that involve viewing and treating the nonhuman members as mere things to be moulded in accordance with our plans. Putting aside the landscape context,[28] in terms of estrangement from nature such approaches focused on continuity, similarity, and so inclusivity, speak most clearly of *overcoming* estrangement from the *natural world*.

A contrasting way of understanding recognition of nature, one that speaks more to the idea of *accepting* a degree of estrangement from *nonhuman* nature, concerns the recognition of difference more than continuity. Here the focus is on recognition of the otherness of nonhuman entities and processes, the fact that they don't embody or confirm specifically *human* purposes, interests and ideals (their landscape independence), as the feature to be respected. I take Schlosberg's extension of the status injury model of recognitional injustice to be an example of this approach.[29] The normative emphasis here is on *not* viewing nonhuman beings and processes as defective simply insofar as they don't seem all that similar and continuous with ourselves and our plans, or lack in any developed form the features we take to underwrite our own moral considerability. This makes explicit the potential for further domination involved in the continuity-based approach to extending recognition to nature. Unless qualified by the difference-based approach, an approach

---

[28] The discussion of justice and estrangement in the previous chapter confined them to the landscape. There an important point was that, within the limits marked by just recognition of human difference, injustice as the failing to live up to the implications of our 'all being in it together' marks a form of estrangement to be overcome.

[29] Schlosberg's pluralistic approach to ecological justice also encompasses more continuity-based kinds of extensionism. For example, he endorses Tim Hayward's (1998) integrity ethic, interpreting the integrity of nonhuman beings and systems as something to be recognized (Schlosberg 2007, pp. 137–8). And he further extends Martha Nussbaum's (2006) extension of capability justice to animals to encompass the capability functioning of ecosystems (Schlosberg 2007, pp. 147ff). I touch briefly on Nussbaum's problematic extensionism shortly. Because he tempers them with the far more difference-based extension of recognition involved in the status injury approach, Schlosberg's appeals to continuity recognition don't generate the problem I associate with unqualified versions of them.

146   Nonhuman nature: estrangement

focused on continuity risks buying into the assumption that nonhuman beings and processes are *for us* to organize and perfect in accordance with (our idea of) their own good conceived by analogy with, or as an extension of, our own good. This would be a further landscaping project, albeit one that is intended benevolently and that needs to be neither crudely anthropocentric nor crudely instrumentalist. But when unqualified it does count as a form of anthropocentric instrumentalism in the sense of reducing things to their place in the humanized landscape.

Like the distinction between humanized landscape and nonhuman nature itself, the contrast between continuity and different versions of extending recognition to nature is a matter of degree and not a strict dichotomy. Both involve the extension of normative ideas beyond humanity after all. There is, however, a real contrast. Extending the status injury understanding of recognitional justice is particularly appropriate as a way of unpacking the normativity of accepting some estrangement from nonhuman nature, precisely because it involves a strong emphasis on accepting difference or otherness; on the injustice of discounting, denigrating or seeking the transformation or improvement of others because they are 'not like us'.[30] This form of extensionism remains 'anthropocentric', of course, in that the idea of nonhuman nature and its difference is defined relative to us. In and of itself this doesn't show it to be perniciously 'centric'[31] though. To claim that it does would be like claiming

[30] Again we should think in terms of matters of degree. We can identify a spectrum of views, as I do very roughly and crudely here. First, consider Mill's (uncharacteristic) depiction of nonhuman nature as 'replete' with all sorts of unpleasantness and injustice (Mill 1904, e.g., p. 16; see Chapter 1, section 1.8), a view seemingly endorsed recently by Nussbaum (2006, pp. 367ff). A milder, although still discernible, blanket denigration of most of nonhuman nature is implicit within views like that of Tom Regan (1983), who extends rights to those organisms who, *like us*, are 'subjects of a life' with beliefs, desires and a conception of the future. Paul Taylor's (1986) biocentric egalitarian 'respect for nature position' is more promising. The egalitarian component involves both an emphasis on continuity (humanity is no less subject to laws of genetics, natural selection and adaptation than any other organism) and a denial of humanity's special status, whether grounded in Greek humanism, Judaeo-Christian Great Chain of Being or Cartesian dualism. The biocentric component asserts that each organism has inherent worth qua 'teleological centre of life'. Taylor's 'respect for nature' involves recognizing this continuity and worth; but one of the principles it generates is a duty not to interfere with nonhuman (wild) life. Putting aside the problematic 'inherent worth' (intrinsic value), the resulting picture is a nuanced one in which elements of continuity sit with and inform significant recognition of difference (expressed in a duty of non-interference). But the main focus is on 'respect for nature' on the basis of its continuity with us, and entities and process that *fall outside the circle of life* have only instrumental value. In this chapter I am concerned with respect for *nonhuman* nature whether living or not. See also Smith (2011, p. 44).
[31] See Chapter 1, section 1.4. See Plumwood (2002, pp. 97ff) for a critique of 'centrism': views that place humanity (or the male, or the powerful, the colonizer) at the centre with others defined in terms of their distance from that centre, which thus defines the yardstick for measuring their worth. This is a problem with the more continuity

Extensionism, continuity and difference

that a rejection of egocentrism in one's dealing with others necessarily remains egocentric because it is a stance defined in relation to oneself: necessarily it is still 'all about me' at the centre of a web of relations. Of course it is, but only in the sense that the issue is all about the terms in which one understands and acts out one's relations with others.

Something like the status injury understanding of recognition, considered as part of the normative content of *living with some estrangement from nonhuman nature*, is required to temper moral extensionist drivers of the project of overcoming estrangement from the natural world. Otherwise that project is in danger of becoming another landscaping project and transforming itself into a concern with overcoming estrangement from the humanized landscape. Consider again the question of how to interpret the news that some scientists claim we are now in the Anthropocene: is it a welcome confirmation that human mastery is proceeding apace and promises to become ever more comprehensive; or is it a worrying reminder of the power of the domination agenda that calls for renewed resistance, for example by asserting the need to live with some estrangement from nonhuman nature? We noted earlier that the eco-regulatory conception of labour does not in itself decide this question. But nor does extensionism as such settle the issue. It depends how much focus on continuity, as opposed to substantive commitment to respecting difference and tolerating human/nonhuman discontinuity, there is in a given version of extensionism.

Imagine that eco-regulatory labour is performed not for the sake of securing narrowly instrumental use values, but for the sake of delivering justice to nonhuman animals in the form recommended by Martha Nussbaum (2006, ch. 6). One of Nussbaum's most striking claims is that the extension of her capability theory of justice requires the 'gradual supplanting of the natural by the just' (Nussbaum 2006, p. 400). Left to their own, nonhuman devices, wild animals often behave in ways that are inconsistent with each receiving their just entitlements in capability terms. Predatory behaviour, for instance, obviously deprives prey animals of the threshold levels of such capabilities as life and bodily integrity required for them flourish in accordance with their kinds. Equally obvious is that, unless handled very carefully and with adequate knowledge and technique, intervening in wild predatory relations is likely to undermine the flourishing of both predators and prey (through overpopulation, for example). Nevertheless the clear message of Nussbaum's extension is that we have duties to be on the lookout for opportunities to

---

based and landscaping forms of extensionism. I discuss the affinity between her views on these matters and the position I am advocating shortly.

148   Nonhuman nature: estrangement

intervene and 'police nature' in the name of justice as far as we can. The project to supplant nature by the just has to be gradual because it is constrained by ecological and biological conditions that current technology cannot overcome but must operate within.

From this standpoint, the Anthropocene announcement is presumably welcome because, although the huge anthropogenic impacts it signals have not occurred for the sake of justice, they suggest the potential for more and more comprehensive interventions for its sake: we are profoundly affecting wild animals and we should make sure that we do so justly.[32] Thus we might contemplate a range of radical measures (short of the delusion of total control of everything), including ecosystem management, bio-engineering, laboratory-grown meat for predators, birth control for prey species and so on, to make the lives of previously (at least relatively) wild animals more continuous with those of citizens of well-ordered liberal democratic societies. This imposition of continuity is extensionism as landscaping.[33]

4.8   Too much continuity: deep ecology

I want to emphasize again that in suggesting we reverse the direction of critical bite associated with estrangement in the context of nonhuman nature, I am not claiming that overcoming 'estrangement from nature' in non-domineering ways is impossible or that talk of it is always misplaced or meaningless. I am suggesting that, where *nonhuman* nature, as opposed to the overall natural world, is concerned, it is more helpful to think of ideas of respect and resistance to domination in terms of living with, rather than overcoming, estrangement. This is not to deny that there are places – perhaps especially those designated as 'wilderness' where nonhuman wildness is most evident and welcome rather than prevented,

---

[32] Nussbaum appears to be committed to something like the end of nature thesis: there is no pure untouched (nonhuman) nature on earth and the issue then is how to temper the touch with justice (Nussbaum 2006, e.g., pp. 368–9).

[33] It is no caricature (see, for example, Wissenburg 2011), although we should note hesitations in her position; for example she does attach weight to 'the sovereignty of species' and expresses repugnance at the idea of 'benign despotism' over the nonhuman (Nussbaum 2006, p. 373). She is far less enthusiastic about 'policing nature' than is Tyler Cowen, for example, who argues on broadly utilitarian grounds that predators have had things their own way for long enough (Cowen 2003). Yet her call for the gradual supplanting of the natural by the just is a call for such police action (Hailwood 2012). Although he endorses Nussbaum's extension of capability justice, Schlosberg criticizes her 'sanitized' view of nonhuman flourishing. He argues that this can be remedied by a further extension of the approach to encompass the capability functioning of ecosystems themselves, which casts predation in a different light (Schlosberg 2007, pp. 150ff). This further extension raises problems of its own: see, for example, Cripps (2010).

Too much continuity: deep ecology 149

begrudged or ignored – where some might see their attachment to place as constituted partly through respect for the nonhuman, for nonhuman agency and productive contribution to place making.

For example, Val Plumwood's (e.g., 2002, pp. 186ff) eco-feminist ethic of care involves 'identifying' with nonhuman coinhabitants of place, and this might be described as a matter of overcoming estrangement from them. I don't want to *condemn* such a description (much less the practice so described), but I do suggest that things are clearer when 'overcoming estrangement from nonhuman nature' denotes a relatively thorough humanization of surroundings to make them reflect specifically human-oriented purposes and values. The estrangement is overcome as the nonhumanity is overcome, as it were. It is particularly important not to confuse overcoming estrangement from nature in this sense with overcoming estrangement from nature in the different sense of the overall natural world, or to consider one without regard to the other. It will be helpful to consider some of the issues here in the light of Plumwood's own very useful critical discussion of the contrasting positions of Peter Reed and deep ecologist Arne Naess. With regards to the latter, Plumwood says that

Deep ecology, and especially the work of Arne Naess, has helped shift the discussion away from conventional extensionist ethics towards activist-inspired issues of how we can account for and develop our capacity for solidarity or 'standing with' earth others, and also towards the broader and more philosophically productive ethico-ontological issues concerning the analysis of human identity, alienation and difference from nature that underlie many ethical stances. (Plumwood 2002, p. 196)

But she also argues that Naess' account of solidarity seriously overemphasizes human/nonhuman continuity by positing a supposed identity of human and nonhuman interests. This account centres on the ideas of the self as the 'totality of our identifications' and of 'enlarging' this self to encompass nonhuman interests. The self (or what thereby becomes the Self) is enlarged by 'identification', a process 'through which the supposed interests of another being are spontaneously reacted to as our own interests' (Naess 1990, p. 187). It is not that continuity is pursued here to the point of total unity, the fusion of human and nonhuman 'selves';[34]

---

[34] Some strands of deep ecology seem to have gone down the road of a strong metaphysical holism that views distinctions as 'ultimately' illusory: to perceive boundaries between things at all is to fall short of deep ecological consciousness. Some of Naess' own early statements suggest this picture (see, for example, Naess (1973, p. 95)). Plumwood rightly rejects such strongly holistic metaphysical understandings of 'identification' with nonhuman nature, as suggesting the assimilation of nonhuman others to the self (Plumwood, e.g., 1993, pp. 176ff).

150   Nonhuman nature: estrangement

but it is pursued to the point of identity of human and nonhuman interests. 'Selves may not be fused, but interests are, and the other is included ethically to the extent that a kind of equivalence to self is established through identification' (Plumwood 2002, p. 199). This is too much continuity; too much overcoming of estrangement.

As Plumwood argues, we need to distinguish between 'identifying in solidarity' with someone or something in the sense of being prepared to act in support of their interests, from 'identifying' in the much stronger sense of acquiring identical interests (Plumwood 2002, pp. 199f). When we identify in solidarity with wombats (Plumwood's example), say, and seek to 'remove them from "vermin" status ... we do not thereby acquire identical specific interests, in grass eating, for example' (Plumwood 2002, p. 200). In terms of our earlier example of recognizing the fox as 'more than' its landscape role, as a matter of living with estrangement, one cannot think of this as acquiring interests identical to the fox. This is not just a matter of physical or biological impossibility given current technology, which we might dream of developing to the point of *making* human and fox interests coincide; identifying with the fox as it is independently of human landscaping purposes (i.e., as a being with interests of its own) is logically incompatible with acquiring identical interests.[35] Solidarity and identification here must be with the other in their difference. This means there is an important sense in which we cannot be *completely* at home with the nonhuman other, even if we take such identification in solidarity to partly constitute the self and its relation to its therefore not fully humanized surroundings.

The kind of identifying Plumwood has in mind then emphasizes care for others 'in their otherness'. This retaining of otherness seems to me a retaining of estrangement analogous to that involved when, as in the previous chapter, we bracket the nonhuman and consider the estrangement/ being at home contrast in the context of encountering human difference and human places that aren't one's own. Caring for the other does not entail, and should not be thought to require, assimilating them, or enlarging oneself to encompass their interests to make them and their home as smoothly continuous as possible with us and ours. On the contrary, caring for them in their difference requires preserving a degree of estrangement. Similarly, I want to say that even in locations where nonhuman processes and entities are accommodated and cared for 'partners' in place-making, there is an element of estrangement from (not being fully

---

[35] Moreover, given that nonhumans themselves have conflicting interests (as predators and prey for example), encompassing *all* nonhuman interests is a logical impossibility however large the Self (Hailwood 2004).

Too much discontinuity: 'Man Apart'

at home with) them and their *different* interests and active tendencies of growth and development. Otherwise there is a risk of either equating the *domestication* of nonhuman nature with 'caring' for it, or of reading human values into nonhuman nature. There is surely a danger that in seeking the (impossible) acquisition of interests identical to those of the nonhuman other the enlarged Self picture will motivate the (only too possible) reading of our interests onto them: *of course* foxes relish being hunted by hounds.[36]

4.9   Too much discontinuity: 'Man Apart'

In rejecting Naess' imposition of excessive continuity through strong identification, Plumwood draws partly on the 'Man Apart' position articulated by Peter Reed partly in response to the deep ecology of Naess and others (Reed 1989). According to Reed 'it is our very *separateness* from the Earth, the gulf between the human and the natural, that makes us want to do right by the world' (Reed 1989, p. 56). Thus Reed very strongly emphasizes the nonhumanity of nonhuman nature. He refers especially to the work of theologian Martin Buber as 'a call back to a common-sense idea that there *is* something that is not just part of us, a solid something we can kick in refutation of Berkeley's *esse es percipi*. It is a reminder of the power and being that exists independently of the human mind'. This seems helpful. And it is, up to a point, given that we want to reject radical constructionism and to emphasize the 'more than human' aspects of the world and the delusional quality of the promethean dream of total mastery.

Unfortunately Reed unpacks his 'Man Apart' position in ways that involve *too much* separation between humanity and (the rest of) nature. He draws on Buber's views to present our relation to nonhuman nature as an 'I–Thou' relationship in which nature as Thou is '*wholly* other', an awesome and 'total stranger' who is 'radically apart' from us (Reed 1989, p. 54). Plumwood states Reed's position fairly when she says 'in the right spirit, we can meet this other, but only as "two ships that pass in the night", since the "I" and the "Thou" do not depend on each other' (Plumwood 2002, p. 198). One does not need to adopt a very

---

[36] Again, as Martin, drawing upon Adorno, puts it, '[t]he danger consists in projecting characteristics of the self onto the other, subjecting the other to the needs of the self as yet another extension of the domination of nature' (Martin 2011, p. 123). But one need not take oneself to be engaged in negative dialectics to worry that the enlarged Self might turn out to be an enlarged human ego: some significant emphasis on the independence and difference of nonhuman entities, systems and processes is required to preserve a sense of *their* 'value' as opposed to ours. See, for example, Plumwood (1995, pp. 158ff).

152 Nonhuman nature: estrangement

strong form of continuity, such as that of Naess, to reject the dualism this involves. Reed's position does more than respect nonhuman nature's difference, it embeds a radical separation. All we have in common with the nonhuman is a 'mere' physical nature or a nature that is, as Plumwood says

both 'mere' (in the human case) and the object of what amounts almost to worship (in the case of the other). We are left wondering why the supposed radical difference of the other should be a basis for awe and wonder in the one case and something like disdain or indifference in the other. (Plumwood 2002, p. 198)

His indifference to human–nature continuity also leads Reed to focus on wilderness as the site of truly awe-inspiring nature as Thou, and unable to acknowledge adequately the crucial matter of degree in the human landscape-nonhuman nature contrast. As Plumwood points out, it is 'hard to see how this kind of orientation to "the Wholly Other" can provide a basis for the consideration of nature in the large number of situations where it is less impressive and more vulnerable – precisely the kind of context, one would have thought, where activists especially need a respect ethic' (Plumwood 2002, p. 199). I have suggested that Schlosberg's extension of status injury-based recognitional justice is an appropriate basis for such an ethic in the context of living with estrangement from nonhuman nature. But equating any such ethic in turn with awe in the face of pure wilderness is bound to leave it drowned out by talk of the End of Nature and beginning of the Anthropocene.[37] More than this, as Plumwood (2002, p. 199) also notes, Reed's austere view of the awesome majesty of nature as Wholly Other also led him to the unhelpfully misanthropic thought that nature might be better off in our total absence. This curious reversal of the status injury view of ecological justice, to the point of radical misrecognition of humanity, seems the result of pushing estrangement from nonhuman nature to the point of abasement before the all-powerful Total Stranger: there is a real question whether mere humans could ever be worthy participants in an I–Thou relationship with it.

4.10 Continuity and difference both in play

Plumwood sums up her view of the opposed positions of Naess and Reed like this:

Neither Reed nor Naess distinguishes sufficiently between difference and normative hyper-separation, an emphatic form of differentiation associated especially

---

[37] It also raises the problem of reifying indigenous labour and its products of course.

with the view of the other as inferior. The outcome is that Reed treats difference, on his account the basis of the other's value and of their ethical recognition, as implying the denial of continuity and the maintenance of the existential gulf, while Naess treats removing the existential gulf as meaning the expulsion of difference and the basing of value on forms of identity or equivalence to self. (Plumwood 2002, p. 201)

She is correct to underline the vital importance of keeping hold of both continuity and difference with regard to the rest of nature and to portray Naess as exemplifying a stress on continuity to the detriment of difference and Reed as exemplifying the opposite stress on difference to the detriment of continuity. I am thinking of the stress on continuity in terms of overcoming estrangement from the overall natural world *within* which we are inescapably located and I take it that we should seek to overcome estrangement in this sense. This is a matter for Chapter 6.

But I am also thinking of the stress on difference in terms of another worthy pursuit: retaining some estrangement from nonhuman nature. Without this, which has been the focus of my discussion in this chapter, the project of overcoming estrangement from the natural world is distorted by strong versions of continuity and extensionism into another landscaping project. This is so even if the reduction of nature to humanized landscape involved is a more 'benign' form of domination than that of more obviously reductive and economistic forms of instrumental anthropocentrism. For example, Nussbaum's extension of capability justice to animals is far more impressive when divested of the proposal to make all of nature just and limited to our intra-landscape relations with animals already relatively highly humanized (domesticated, selectively bred, tamed, controlled and confined). On the other hand, as Reed's Man Apart position suggests, too much positive stress on estrangement from nonhuman nature as other risks undermining our appreciation of continuity. It thereby risks embedding estrangement *from the natural world*. This is another reason to view living with estrangement from nonhuman nature as a *qualified* good.

So I am suggesting that it is useful to approach the tricky issues of sameness and difference in our dealings with (the rest of) nature, the need to keep both in play without confusing one with the other, reducing one to the other or losing touch with either, through ideas of estrangement from nonhuman nature and the natural world; in terms of 'alienation from nature' in these senses. My overall argument is that this allows us to put these issues in terms of connections that are of significance to a 'joined up' environmental ethics and politics. For example, overcoming estrangement from the natural world entails living with (a degree of) estrangement from nonhuman nature, and these

154   Nonhuman nature: estrangement

forms of living with and overcoming estrangement require overcoming pernicious forms of estrangement, reification and alienation within the landscape context. I return to these matters in the final two chapters. In the next chapter I consider the idea of *alienation of* nonhuman nature, which is itself entailed by that of living with estrangement from nonhuman nature.

5   Nonhuman nature: alienation

5.1   From estrangement to alienation

This chapter concerns alienation in the sense of loss or renunciation of ownership. It continues with nonhuman nature as the environmental context and with the nonanthropocentric elements of my overall argument captured through viewing this type of alienation in a positive light. *Alienation of* nonhuman nature is to be encouraged in that we should renounce an anthropocentrically oriented presumed ownership over it; let go an assumption that the nonhuman is *ours* in a possessive sense, to be owned only for the sake of our interests. We should 'alienate' nonhuman nature by rejecting the assumption that the nonhuman should enter considerations of ownership and property rights *only* as something to be owned for the sake of individual or collective human interests. Such alienation is entailed by living with estrangement from nonhuman nature. If the latter is viewed positively as an anti-domination commitment, involving recognition of the landscape-independence of the nonhuman with something of the normative force of, say, ecological justice, then so must a 'letting go' of purely anthropocentric understandings of ownership over the world for the sake only of human interests. Indeed, we could think of this alienation as a particular exercise of living with estrangement. But given the great importance of ownership in mediating relations between persons and their surroundings, humanized and nonhuman, it is worth distinguishing property alienation from estrangement and considering it separately.

To reject the assumption that the world is ours to be owned for our interests is to give up the anthropocentric instrumentalism at the heart of traditional thinking about property. Traditional political philosophy, whether the tradition is Lockean or Hegelian for example, has just such an anthropocentric instrumental conception of ownership. Ownership, perhaps the key concept through which the human/nonhuman relation is mediated in political contexts, has been filled out with accounts of nonhuman 'things' penetrated by, 'mixed with', human labour and thereby

155

156   Nonhuman nature: alienation

'improved' – imbued with human spirit and use value – and so brought within the humanized landscape. Such an understanding of ownership has been the unqualifiedly anthropocentric agenda-setting moment of much of the instrumentalization and domination of nature in political thinking. At that moment there is no *recognition* of the nonhuman as anything more than, say, a vehicle for *interpersonal* recognition and realization of personality. In this context the idea of nature not used is the idea of nature *unemployed*, 'wasted', awaiting completion through subservience to humanity.

I am not suggesting the notion of property should be dropped. That hardly seems possible or desirable. Nor am I denying that property can play an important role in the securing of environmental goals. For example, Elizabeth Brubaker has provided evidence and arguments in favour of strong property rights as a better device than government regulation and intervention for avoiding pollution and other forms of environmental degradation (Brubaker 1995). There is of course a traditional argument that says holders of property, whether common or private, and especially landowners, generally have the strongest motivations to care about the condition of their holdings and are able to assert rights that are often upheld by courts; for example in the form of claims against trespass and nuisance under English Common Law (Brubaker 1995, pp. 29ff). Brubaker calls her book *Property Rights in the Defence of Nature*, although in our terms the cases she cites concern landscaping issues: the preservation and sustainability of various kinds of environmental resources, aesthetic or economic, and the preservation of the places of traditional, indigenous cultures. Give them strong rights of ownership, whether common or individual, and then they will be able to defend their holdings against at least many kinds of environmental ills.

It is not impossible that this is also an effective way of preventing the wholesale physical transformation of nonhuman nature into humanized landscape: those concerned to preserve their holdings in a relatively wild condition might be able to assert their rights to do so. This, however, does not make the idea of alienating nonhuman nature as I understand it redundant. If the argument is that strong property rights is an effective tool for resisting the domination of nature (retaining some estrangement from the nonhuman) then alienation of nonhuman nature, in the sense I mean, is *entailed* by the same thought that motivates the argument as a justification of strong property rights; thought being that we should resist the domination of nature and live with some estrangement. Alienation of nonhuman nature, as I am understanding it, is not a matter of rejecting property, or of suspicion of property as such. It is a matter of rejecting the assumption that only human interests, or intra-landscaping

From estrangement to alienation

considerations, should enter into justifications of ownership and property rights, whether these are strong or otherwise. It is a point mainly about political philosophy and the background assumption it has generally made concerning the nonhuman with regard to issues of ownership, the importance and role of property in our political life; and what form it should take – private, common or collective.

As with living with estrangement, negating this assumption must be a matter of degree, a qualified good; to some degree taking ownership for the sake of human interests is obviously 'basic' or inescapable. If we think of the practice of place, for example, this seems inconceivable without some such taking ownership, whether private, common or collective. Alienation as a positive movement here is a matter of rejecting the assumption that the nonhuman is *merely* something to be owned for the sake of human interests, a matter of a *qualified* release of the grip of anthropocentric possession. Running the idea of alienation in this way requires distinguishing the notion of relinquishment or renunciation of ownership from that of transfer of ownership. The latter concerns the interpersonal exchanging, buying, selling, gifting, swapping and taking of property. The rightness or wrongness of such occurrences is very often thought a matter of justice, itself understood in terms of crucial human interests; for example our interest in achieving adequate personhood as discussed in Chapter 3. A case of property alienation might or might not bring the interpersonal estrangement marked by relations of injustice.

For the Marxist, the alienation of labour (the wage/labour relation) necessitated by private ownership of productive resources brings a series of pernicious estrangements that are unjust, if anything is unjust. However, the renunciation of ownership involved in the alienation of the nonhuman as I am understanding it is not a matter of transferring that ownership. Although it might be helpful sometimes to talk of 'giving nature back to itself', this cannot be a matter of selling or giving nonhuman nature ownership rights over itself. Moreover, because it concerns what has not been produced by human action, alienation of nonhuman nature is better thought of on the model of recognizing what is already 'external', rather than on the model of the externalization (*entäusserung*) of human will or labour. But clearly alienation of nonhuman nature, in this sense of a relinquishment of presumed blanket anthropocentrically oriented ownership over it, is necessary to any attempt to resist the unqualified overcoming of estrangement from it. And vice versa: there is mutual entailment between alienation of and estrangement from nonhuman nature considered as qualified goods and ways of countering domination.[1]

---

[1] Equally clearly there is mutual entailment between alienation of the nonhuman and natural worlds. The natural world encompasses both nonhuman world and humanized

158   Nonhuman nature: alienation

On the one hand we need to take 'ownership' of the landscaped world we are making, in the sense of recognizing we are making it and taking responsibility for how it is turning out. In Chapter 3 I discussed this in terms of avoiding reification and pernicious estrangement, including unjust forms of property alienation in the landscape context. On the other hand, to live with estrangement from the nonhuman (avoid domination) we need to take ownership in that sense without also seeing the nonhuman merely as 'something to be owned' as property by humans for the sake of human interests. But, as I have said, traditional approaches to property precisely do tend to present nonhuman nature as *just* something to be owned for the sake of human interests. In this way they take a certain, anthropocentrically coloured, idea of ownership too far. Some taking ownership is necessary, but at the same time some *alienation* of nature is also required if we are to avoid domination or anthropocentric instrumentalism.

I will be discussing this issue mainly in relation to Hegel's account of private property. We saw in Chapter 3 that Hegel usefully emphasizes the human requirement to 'be at home in the world'. It will be useful also to dwell on Hegel in this chapter because he also emphasizes the importance of property to our being at home in the world as concrete individuals with objective freedom. But even without a specifically Hegelian focus, it is clear that property is fundamental to the process of homemaking. This is not only because property systems profoundly affect the shape of landscapes as economic endeavours, as well as the just or unjust distribution of human life chances. Again, the notion of ownership itself encompasses a fundamental relation, mediating the human/ nonhuman as much as the interpersonal, through which we construct our surroundings, at least through political thought and action. Because of this, philosophical accounts of property, which factors they see as relevant and important, and the way they treat them, are telling indicators of the status given to nonhuman nature. At least in its treatment of ownership political philosophy *is* environmental philosophy, whether it realizes this or not and however abstractly it presents itself. When armed

---

environment. To reject the assumption that the nonhuman is significant only as ownership material for human interests is to reject it with respect to the natural world too: insofar as recognition of nonhuman nature as more than a means to human ends enters into considerations of ownership, then so must such recognition of the natural world, simply in virtue of the nonhuman being part of the natural world. However, whereas living with estrangement entails alienation with respect to nonhuman nature, the situation is different for the relationship between estrangement and alienation in the context of the natural world, where that mutual entailment does not hold. I return to the idea of estrangement from the natural world in the next chapter and to the connections between different senses of alienation from nature in the final chapter.

Ownership and reification 159

with a purely anthropocentric treatment of ownership, political philosophy pushes aside and obscures the possibility of *political* consideration of nature as more than landscape or potential landscape.

5.2 Ownership and reification

Matters of ownership very often lurk close at hand, even when not the main focus of attention. For example, consider again Honneth's recognitional account of 'reification of nature' that, remember, for him consists in 'perceiving animals, plants or things in a merely objectively identifying way, without being aware that [they] possess a multiplicity of existential meanings for the people around us'. 'Nature' here figures as a vehicle for the recognition of persons; and thinking of nature only in this way appears to reduce it to humanized landscape, to nature insofar as it is modified and/or interpreted for the sake of human-oriented interests. In Chapter 3 I argued that this is unacceptable to us because any attempted recognition of nature as it is *independent* of human-oriented roles allotted to it (independent of its 'existential meaning' for other humans) risks being condemned as reification.

But it might be argued that this magnifies the risk too quickly. Say some do invest nonhuman items with a specific form of existential significance; i.e., as 'other', with a reality independent of human-oriented purposes and interests, which should be respected as such. Say then that, in the terms of the previous chapter, they hold a form of difference-based approach to recognitional justice with regard to nonhuman nature, or at least hold an ethic of this kind, and so they are prepared to endorse some estrangement from the nonhuman. If so then Honneth's account seems to imply that to view nonhuman items as simply resources for landscaping, as mere things lit up with significance only once allocated to a human-oriented purpose, is to fail to recognize adequately those persons holding the difference-based view. Thus it might be argued that Honneth's account of reification of nature need not require a total anthropocentric instrumental reduction of nature to humanized landscape; in fact it cannot require it when there are people around who hold anything like the difference view.

Unfortunately this seems an insufficiently robust barrier to such a reduction. The barrier consists in recognition of persons, and through that the existential meanings things have for them, plus the possibility that some such meanings encompass welcoming estrangement from the nonhuman because some of the persons recognized hold a different view. The interpersonal recognition is a given constant; the difference in view and the estrangement are highly contingent optional extras. What then

160 Nonhuman nature: alienation

if people in fact view their surroundings *only* as a collection of human landscaping resources of one kind or another; that is what their 'natural' environment means to them? How can we escape the thought that in failing to respect *that* meaning our recognition of *them* is defective? With the political dimensions of the issue in mind we might ask how we are to respond in general to *conflicting* meanings bestowed on surroundings. Whose should we recognize; what is the 'official' meaning?

These questions raise matters of ownership; they lead us to the idea of property and so to the topic of this chapter: the tendency for political thought to remain trapped within the humanized world by an anthropocentric instrumental understanding of ownership. If that understanding is taken for granted in the background, to be filled in by Honneth's account of reification, for example, then ownership will be understood *only* in relation to interpersonal recognition and the avoidance of reification as the absence of that recognition. Whose meanings I should respect for a given object or portion of nature will be decided by *whose* object or portion it is within a property system set up for the sake of enabling interpersonal recognition. Given such a system, it is up to them, the owners, how to interpret it, and in respecting that (and their interpretation) I am recognizing them. You reify me and *my* rabbit, me and *my* car, us and *our* (commonly owned) National Park, when you view these things as *mere* things rather than *my* cuddly companion, *my* vehicle of personal freedom, *our* site of beauty and tranquillity. It is still possible to claim that you reify me and my plot of relative wildness when you eye it as a mere thing to be exploited, rather than my site of respect for the nonhuman. But such a claim is likely to be muted, inarticulate or odd-seeming against the background of anthropocentric instrumentalism driving the idea of ownership itself. Honneth's account of reification owes much to Hegel in its focus on recognition. More than that, Honneth's account of reification of nature, once viewed in the light of the ownership issues it raises, risks being trapped in the same anthropocentric instrumentalist agenda set by Hegel's considerations of abstract right. I discuss these considerations below, where it will be useful to delve a little into Hegel's metaphysical system to illustrate that, in the absence of the sort of ultimate grounding provided by that system, there is no a priori reason to embed anthropocentric instrumentalism in our thinking about ownership.

5.3 Concept of property

Before that it will be useful to consider briefly the concepts of property and private property in general and as landscaping devices. Following Jeremy Waldron I shall take the central idea of property to be that of

Concept of property 161

rules determining interpersonal relations with regard to access and control over things (Waldron 1988, ch. 2). Generally, the 'things' in question are at least relatively scarce goods and resources. The concept of *private* property as a particular way of organizing property systems, distinct from collective and common property, is the idea of things correlated with named individuals in relation to a social rule upholding as final their decision as to how the things should be used (Waldron 1988, pp. 38f). The idea of collective property, by contrast, is that of a system of allocation based on a 'social rule that the use of material resources in particular cases is to be determined with reference to the collective interests of society as a whole' (Waldron 1988, p. 40). I say a little more towards the end of this chapter about how my argument relates to collective ownership.[2]

To be the 'owner' of something in a system of *private* ownership is to be in a privileged position *in relation to others* with respect to the things one owns. Particular bundles of rights, liberties, powers and duties associated with ownership in particular systems of private property (defining just what is entailed in owning a car, say, in a particular society: the training, maintenance and insurance requirements, restrictions on who might drive it and where and how fast it may be driven and so on), are particular *conceptions* of the abstract concept of private property (Waldron 1988, pp. 52–3). Such bundles are 'held together' by the concept of private property, which is the underlying idea capturing the basic commonsensical sense of private ownership (notwithstanding the legal complexities of car ownership, *this* car is *mine, I own it*).[3] We live our lives, pursue our personal projects, within a framework of rules constituted in large part by these bundles that define who gets to do what with what.

Notice that although things are owned and we often refer to our property as 'our things' (my property as 'my things'), what constitutes something as property is itself a relation – a relation established and upheld by persons between persons – not a thing. To view property itself as a given thing, rather than a rule-governed interpersonal relation, is to reify a product of human agency. The thing owned as property may or may not

---

[2] For Waldron, common property differs from collective ownership in that it does not give special status to either collective or private interests. Common ownership consists in rules of access to and control over resources 'organised on the basis of them being in principle available to each person alike'. He points to parks and 'national reserves' as examples of this form of ownership (Waldron 1988, pp. 41f).

[3] Waldron reports that because they are concerned mainly with issues arising within particular systems (conceptions) of private property, lawyers and legal theorists sometimes deny there is such a concept over and above the bundles. But, as Waldron points out (1988, pp. 52f), the concepts of property and private property *as such* are analytically required if one wants to consider the justifiability of specifically private property. They are also very helpful if one wants to bring out the purely anthropocentric instrumental role played by the standard accounts of property within political philosophy.

162   Nonhuman nature: alienation

be (more or less) a product of human labour; the relation constituting it as *owned* most definitely is a product of human effort and activity. Now, let us take it that the property relation is not being reified – it is viewed as what it is, a human construction. In Chapter 3 we saw that reification – the viewing of humanity and human labour products as merely given things – may be distinguished from objectification, understood as the instrumentalization of items as mere inert material for manipulation. Reduction to '*mere* thinghood' is involved in both; indeed we might consider reification to be a particular case of objectification. But not all objectification involves reification. The absence of reification does not preclude objectification in the guise of a reduction of things to mere things to be owned for human interests. One might objectify tables and yet be fully aware that they are products of human labour. I argued at the start of the previous chapter that although not everything embodies human labour it doesn't follow that whatever is nonhuman and relatively landscape-independent should therefore be considered a *mere* thing, as if that was its 'natural' status, a status problematic only in the context of reified humanity and landscape. That follows only if the dominating stance of anthropocentric instrumentalism is itself given.

5.4   Shaping the bundles

Notice also that the general constraints on harmful behaviour, including harmful uses of owned items, which determine the private ownership bundles and so define the specific shapes of property relations and allowable movements of owned things, are themselves external to the concepts of property and private property. Otherwise, as Waldron points out, these concepts would cover most of what people do; the content of morality would be more or less given with the concepts of property and private property (Waldron 1988, pp. 32f). Rather property rules are themselves located *within* such wider constraints so as to determine which generally allowed or encouraged acts may be performed with what and by whom. So, for example, the moral prohibition of stabbing people is not part of the concepts of property or private property themselves, which concern access to things like knives within the context of such constraints. Such constraints include those over what is allowable in terms of interpersonal alienation of property and they shape ownership bundles accordingly. The mere fact that certain things are mine does not give me carte blanche to sell them or give them away to anyone in whatever manner and circumstances I please. If they are dangerous weapons, for example, then their rightful transfer might be limited by certain licensing requirements. Considerations of justice constrain property alienation too, at

Shaping the bundles 163

least in ideal theory. For example, transfers might be required for the sake of redistribution or compensation in accordance with a principle of distributive justice. These general considerations are external to bare concepts of property themselves.

As Waldron notes, this externality means that it would be incorrect to build the distinction between person and 'thing to be owned' into the concept of property, such that our view that persons cannot be property becomes trivially true in virtue of the definition of property. Persons and their labour are in fact material resources and it is a mistake to rule out slavery a priori simply with reference to the concept of property. That human beings should not be viewed *only* as a material resource is a normative commitment external to the concept of property (Waldron 1988, p. 33 n. 15). Similarly, although nonhuman things and processes are material resources, within some limit we do not have to view them as *only* material resources, view them only through landscaping eyes as *mere* things to be owned for our own interests. The claim that we should not view them only in that way is central to the idea of accepting some estrangement from nonhuman nature. This claim also should not be rendered true or false by definition, with reference only to bare concepts of property. But it is in danger of being ruled out of court, precipitately and without appeal, by assumptions surrounding such concepts in our thinking about ownership.

Particularly crucial are the types of considerations allowed in to determine the move from the bare idea of property (systematic rules concerning allocation of goods) to derive the more specific ideas of private, common or collective property. Also crucial, given that we have derived private property, are the considerations allowed in to determine the more concrete conceptions – bundles of rights, entitlements, duties and so on – defining ownership of X in a particular society. The considerations used to derive private property will set the agenda for determining the bundles. When purely anthropocentric instrumental considerations are used in the derivation then it will tend to be the case that only such considerations will inform the nature of the bundles, which will then reflect the same anthropocentric inwardness shaped only by landscaping concerns. Although this might happen occasionally, it will tend to seem out of place to, for example, place restrictions on the use of privately owned things for the sake of ameliorating the impact of climate change on ecosystems and nonhuman species independently of impacts on human interests.

This is not to deny, of course, that ownership bundles should be and sometimes are shaped by such environmental *landscaping* concerns as climate justice and other forms of environmental justice. In a liberal society the considerations used to determine private property and the shape of

164 Nonhuman nature: alienation

specific ownership bundles will be centred on individual freedom. Other things being equal, and within the constraints of justice, the ideal shapes are those that maximize individuals' negative freedom to use their property in pursuit of private goals without interference. Even so, as we have seen, precisely because of the wider constraints of morality and justice it is obviously not the case that once ownership of X is allocated the owner can do whatever he happens to feel like doing with X. Even in Nozick's libertarian utopia, where the idea of negative liberty shapes virtually the entire political landscape, what one may do with one's legitimate 'holdings' is limited by rights preserving others' negative liberty and holdings: 'my property rights in my knife allow me to leave it where I will, but not in your chest' (Nozick 1974, p. 171). Radical, including Marxian, critique notwithstanding, private property is consistent in principle with overcoming reification and pernicious estrangement and unjust alienation within the landscape.[4]

Things are different, however, when we remember that the natural world encompasses more than the humanized landscape and consider the anthropocentric inwardness brought to the situation via the tradition on ownership. This does seem to be an important obstacle to recognitional *ecological* justice and other ways of unpacking the idea of accepting some estrangement from nonhuman nature. For example, compared in relation to property, there is an important difference between the normative status of slavery and that of a dominating anthropocentric instrumentalist stance regarding nonhuman nature. The general, widely accepted, considerations against slavery, although external to the bare concepts of property and private property, are broadly continuous with *standard justifications* of private property. The very same normative considerations involved in justifying private property tend also to rule out systems of private property incorporating slavery. In the case of the nonhuman, the situation is reversed: justifications of private property tend to reduce nonhuman things to the status of mere resources, *just* 'things' to be owned. It is the negation of this tendency, which is a dominating tendency towards the complete *overcoming* of estrangement from nonhuman nature that I am referring to as alienation of nonhuman nature.[5]

Consider the issue of rights to 'ecosystem services' as 'non-excludable' benefits. The benefits of some crucial services, such as the climate regulation by CO_2 uptake and water evaporation provided by vegetation, are

---

[4] The realization of this principle does assume many things of course, including progress towards the personal/impersonal reconciliation noted in the discussion of climate justice in Chapter 3.

[5] As will be made clearer below this is not to be restricted to considerations of specifically private property.

enjoyed well beyond their immediate sources. They are non-excludable in that the owners of the land from which they proceed cannot prevent others from benefiting from them. Do benefit recipients owe something to landowners for these services? Do landowners have a duty not to do anything to end or seriously degrade them? If they do end or degrade them, do they owe the former recipients compensation? These questions concern the appropriate shape of property bundles regarding ownership of important 'natural resources'. Answers to them can be found, or at least debated, within the terms of standard property derivations and accounts of the relation between property, freedom and justice.[6] In addition to any other considerations appealed to in deriving private property, how such notions as freedom and justice are understood, and the weight given them, will colour the ownership bundles designed to handle the issue of non-excludable ecosystem services. If, within the terms of the derivation of private property, nonhuman nature has the status *only* of provider of services to free human beings then this will colour decisions regarding the relevant ownership bundles such that it will be prima facie problematic to place limits on the use of things for reasons independent of such human interests (e.g., in continued receipt of important eco-services).

Such a purely anthropocentric approach to ownership makes it a powerful instrumental landscaping tool then. Not *all*-powerful: it is still possible to shape ownership bundles partly for the protection of relative wildness, to allow it to run its course in designated ways and areas. But still very powerful; sufficiently so to warrant a critique, in line with anti-domination recognitional justice, for example: it is a status injury to the nonhuman to reduce it to provider of services to humanity and embed this in norms governing property. Resisting this through *alienation* of the nonhuman in the sense I mean involves, for example, taking account of the nonhuman recipients of ecosystems themselves when shaping ownership bundles bearing on those services. A set of purely anthropocentrically derived rules requiring those who degrade or end services to compensate previous human beneficiaries won't necessarily compensate the previous nonhuman beneficiaries.

5.5   Property derivations as landscaping devices

It is hardly surprising that justifications of private property have been couched in purely anthropocentric terms, given the importance of the

---

[6] See for example, Marc Davidson's recent analysis of these matters in libertarian terms (Davidson 2014).

166   Nonhuman nature: alienation

issues they encompass, considered as aspects of the enterprise of making ourselves at home in the world. They locate crucial seams in the human landscape, as it were, considered as the expression and vehicle of this enterprise.

Thus we might take aspects of the moral and material process of establishing ourselves as free individuals to be captured by the Lockean tradition on property. For Locke not only must we labour to secure our subsistence and 'enjoyments', we have a duty to do so because we were made by God to 'last in accordance with His pleasure and not our own'.[7] We secure our subsistence and fuller enjoyments through labour. In labouring we transform, improve, nature through a process in which (an aspect of) humanity and parts of nonhuman nature become intertwined as people 'mix' their labour with those parts of nature, paradigmatically land. Individuals who mix their labour with parts that are not yet privately owned acquire exclusive property rights over them, given the satisfaction of certain provisos. One of these is the 'enough and as good' proviso: the acquisition of private property must leave enough and as good portions of nature for others as appropriate. Another is the 'no-wastage' proviso: the nature appropriated should be used productively. Important here is Locke's claim that God gave the world to the 'industrious and the rational'. Rightful private ownership is underwritten not only by the mixing of labour with nature; it is a matter also of desert. The productive – industrious and rational – improvement of nature for human purposes demonstrates that the owner deserves rights over it. The notion of desert plays a role in a number of derivations of private property. In the Lockean picture, for private property to get off the ground as a rightful institution there has to be occurrences of useful labour-mixing with what was previously held in common rather than already privately owned. Homemaking in this way then is fundamental to the enactment of individual liberty, understood as the natural right to live, and do with one's private *possessions* as one sees fit, so long as it is productive and consistent with respecting the same rights of others.

I have already noted (in Chapter 1) that the Lockean account of ownership provides a strong motivation to see the landscapes of indigenous peoples and those produced by 'lower class' labour as 'wasted' or unproductive; indeed to reify it as *terra nullius*: virgin wilderness, awaiting rightful 'enclosure' or colonization through mixture with the labour of the industrious and rational. Notice, however, that despite the references to 'nature' and the 'natural' and the tendency towards reification of the already humanized

---

[7] Locke's arguments are in chapters 2, and especially 5, of his *Second Treatise of Government* (Locke 1960).

Property derivations as landscaping devices 167

as nonhuman, there is an important sense in which the Lockean story all happens within the human landscape. It is a story in which all of nature is already landscaped, in the sense of viewed only through the landscaping lens; in terms only of serving human interests. God made humanity to last in accordance with His pleasure, and God made the Earth and, so far as original interpersonal ownership relations are concerned, He *gave* it to humanity in common, not to Adam and his heirs and successors. He gave it to humanity to secure our subsistence and enjoyments. The whole world is *ours*, the issue being under what conditions parts of it should be allocated to individuals as private property. Ultimately, of course, we are God's property (made to last according to *His* pleasure) and so therefore is the rest of nature, we being its intermediary owners or lease-holders for our own good; and, as with ourselves, we are to look after it, and develop it industrially and rationally. There is nothing outside this world so understood except the *supernatural* – only such entities as souls and God Himself. In our terms there is nothing known as landscape-independent.[8]

Now Locke thought it important to justify private property against the background of a given 'original' common ownership. We might say that for him this is the context in which we achieve adequate personhood. We achieve it through individual liberty, itself analysed largely in terms of 'natural' private property rights. But however feeble we consider the Lockean story as a justification for actual private property rights (isn't most productive human labour a collective endeavour, for example?), and for shaping private ownership bundles so as to maximize individual negative liberty, it is speaking to crucial landscaping imperatives. It is not surprising that such imperatives crop up in a variety of classic derivations of private property rights.[9] Presumably most agree that securing such

---

[8] We cannot necessarily say the same thing about the theistic stewardship tradition in environmental philosophy, which can be read as modifying the position. Yes, we are to look after the world for the sake of human interests, having being commanded to secure our interests and those of our descendants; but we are also commanded to look after it because it is *God's* creation. It is possible to interpret this story as preserving at least an element of nonhuman landscape-independence within the natural world, which God is commanding us not to dominate: he is commanding us to alienate it in the sense I mean here and live with some estrangement from it in the sense discussed in the previous chapter.

[9] See Carter (1989) for a useful discussion of some main philosophical derivations of private property, distinguished and attached to their respective advocates; including Locke, Hume, Kant, Hegel, Bentham and Mill. For example, for Hume, our general selfishness and limited capacity for generosity and the fact that we are faced with a moderate scarcity of desired and necessary external goods, mean that we need the institution of private property (the 'artificial' virtue of justice) to ensure a level of stability of enjoyment of such goods similar to that of bodily and mental pleasures. When with Bentham landscaping is considered as an explicitly utilitarian moral enterprise, human happiness requires subsistence, security and abundance, as well as equality. Subsistence and security, in

168   Nonhuman nature: alienation

human goods as subsistence, a measure of enjoyments and individual negative liberty and the wherewithal to reward the deserving, is a reason why we both must and ought to transform our surroundings into something of a home for humanity. Again, given their importance, it is unsurprising that the theories involved with them focus on them to the exclusion of anything else and thereby embed anthropocentric instrumentalism. Although we are considering alienation of nature as a way of resisting this as a *complete* reduction of nature to landscape we should remember that some system of ownership, whether private, common or collective, is required to achieve them to some basic degree.

Presumably, however, we can at least suspect when things are going beyond the basic. Suppose we are tempted by the Lockean derivation of private property. We should not confine our attention to the initial acquisition of property rights over land. Suppose, for example, we have the GM technology to modify a gull genotype to make phenotypes that produce more aesthetically pleasing droppings. Despite the benefits of this mentioned in previous chapters, it is unlikely to happen in the present state of technology because the process is expensive and the benefits non-excludable. But suppose we are inclined to press on anyway to see where this line of research and development leads. Given the Lockean framework, this seems to presuppose our coming to own the gull genome, as if the deep genetic structure of this organism had been a commonly owned item in a state of nature, awaiting mixture with the labour of the industrial and rational to vastly increase its use value. But even if we think it reasonable for such genotypes to be privately owned on this basis, we might also think it reasonable that the relevant ownership bundles be shaped partly by recognition that we are dealing with a nonhuman organism with its own way of flourishing and slotting into wider ecosystems. The latter consideration is defeasible by serious human landscaping interests, but perhaps not by a preference for differently coloured droppings.

Another area of overlap between different derivations of private property is freedom in the sense of individual autonomy: actively willing or endorsing the principles, rules and duties one lives by, rather than being simply subjected to them. Thus the Kantian tradition on property speaks in a particularly profound way to the morally necessary business of making a home fit for autonomous beings. Here the main idea is that what we

particular, require private property rights in order to motivate labour; human happiness therefore requires private property. And of course there is the claim that both subsistence and the greatest total sum of enjoyment are best served by the most efficient allocation of resources and goods in accordance with the demand for them; which in turn requires a 'free market' of privately owned goods.

Hegel, objective spirit and property 169

might refer to as 'doing something to a thing' (appropriating and labouring on, or at least using, something) is necessary to our autonomy. For Kant, autonomy requires that at least some 'external' things be subject to the individual will; to enable a system of designating such 'objects of the will' as mine as opposed to yours is also required. The views of Hegel fall within this tradition.

5.6 Hegel, objective spirit and property

In Chapter 3 I discussed the need to recognize and take responsibility for the world we are making – humanized landscape(s) – as our creation. I suggested there that we might think of humanized landscape in terms of Hegel's notion of 'objective spirit', because this notion is particularly helpful in bringing together the themes of recognition, homeliness, responsibility and the realization of free personality. In his work *Elements of the Philosophy of Right* Hegel presents ownership as central to objective spirit (Hegel 1991). As I said above, it will be useful to dwell on Hegel's account because it brings out the central landscaping role of property. Looking briefly at Hegel's grounding of anthropocentric instrumentalism in his larger Absolute Idealism will also help to show that in the absence of such a metaphysical system there is no a priori reason to embed anthropocentric instrumentalism within our thinking on property.

In constituting shared traditions of practice and enabling the transmission of norms, objective (intersubjective) spirit encompasses the 'ethical life' of society, and serves as the medium of reconciliation between subjectivity, autonomy and the abstract requirements of moral duty. Hegel agrees with Kant that individual autonomy, involving the agent 'standing back' from his 'determinations' (including desires and perceptions of self-interest) to reflect critically on them, to be able to endorse them or not, is essential to true freedom (Hegel 1991).[10] But a purely 'subjective' freedom, *unqualifiedly* abstracting away from all given determinations, necessarily has little content in itself, and so an account of freedom that stays at the level of abstract autonomy risks vacuity. To be fully actualized (and so, in Hegel's language, 'concrete' or 'absolute'), freedom has to be grounded in shared, historically conditioned life. It must be exercised through participation in communities whose practices and institutions encourage and preserve both subjective and objective freedom. To

---

[10] Here I am indebted to Alan Patten's clear and elegant 'civic humanist' reading of Hegel's complex views on freedom (Patten 1999), as well as to Habermas' discussion (Habermas 1999).

170   Nonhuman nature: alienation

have objective freedom is to have *rational* determinations, those the fully rational person would have. And Hegel's view is that objective freedom in this sense is achieved through willing participation in communities and institutions that serve to protect and promote subjective freedom (critical reflection about and endorsement or rejection of determinations) (Hegel 1991, pp. 189ff; Patten 1999, ch. 2). He takes the modern institutions of family, civil society and state, including private property, to be rational expressions of objective spirit in this sense.

Moreover, simply posited in the abstract, individual autonomy and the universal categorical morality Kant derived from it, generate excessive motivational and cognitive demands on individuals.[11] Positing formal, purely impersonal, abstract duties that are supposed to bind the wills of all rational agents in all circumstances, as Kant had it, underestimates the significance of the pre-existing motives, needs and commitments with which agents find themselves already encumbered; their already existing entanglements with communities and institutions. It underestimates also the massive complexity and unpredictability of moral action and of the situations to which competing abstract duties might apply. The major social institutions constituting the ethical life of objective spirit, 'an actually existing form of reason which reaches beyond the limited horizons of subjective spirit', as Habermas puts it (1999, pp. 150f), are thus required to relieve what otherwise would be the impossible motivational and cognitive demands made on individual moral agents by formal morality in the Kantian style. To participate willingly in such institutions, private property included, is to accept the concrete duties they specify and the coordination of these duties with one another and with the various other projects one might pursue. But, again, a justificatory condition of this is that objective spirit is indeed rational, that it does indeed foster and preserve both subjective and objective freedom for all, so that its component institutions and practices can be perceived by their individual participants to be justified (Habermas 1999, p. 150).

For Hegel, the importance of private property within this picture lies in its necessary role in the actualization of free personality (Hegel 1991, pp. 75ff). For him, as we have seen, this requires one to be recognized, by others and oneself. This in turn requires one to do something to or with something. It requires that one has *one's own thing* to do something to or with. This is not just a matter of securing subsistence and enjoyments; of needing to use things for physical survival, or requiring resources to pursue desired projects. To be a concrete reality free individual personality

---

[11] Hegel (1991): Hegel's criticisms of Kantian moral philosophy run through the sections in Pt. II and pp. 189ff.

Abstract right and anthropocentric instrumentalism 171

must be identifiable objectively, not merely subjectively. It must be underwritten intersubjectively, or registered, as it were, at the level of objective spirit. Owning things allows this. By acquiring and using things recognized to be mine, I myself am recognized and *what* I own, what I do with it, and how I do it, discloses my free personality as an objective reality: *I/he* am/is the owner of *that* and did *this* with it. As Dudley Knowles puts it, 'private property becomes a necessary element of freedom as it permits such appraisals of the self as are required for self-determination. As we acquire, use and alienate property, we work on the self in a manner that demonstrates our freedom to ourselves and others' (Knowles 2002, p. 117). Private property allows the required disclosure of free personality through its recognized embodiment in particular objects correlated to named individuals. Thus when one sells the old banger, one first had to drive and acquire something that, with a little accessorizing, a new paint job, bigger wheels and a louder exhaust, will serve to establish as an unchallengeable concrete reality (rather than subjective dream or abstract possibility) one's being *this* free-wheeling speed merchant. Or not. Different people will need to do different things with other things.

What Waldron calls 'conceptions' of private property, which specify bundles of particular rights, entitlements and so on, add concrete complexity to this picture. They define the possible – recognizable – shape of genuine objective freedom in given circumstances. Assuming the rationality of objective spirit then, forms of alienation and use of owned things that are contrary to the requirements of the ethical life informing the bundles express irrationality and unfreedom, however autonomous they seem merely subjectively. For example, my life on the road, pursued without regard to insurance requirements and speed limits, establishes me as subject to irrational subjective impulses, rather than an objectively free person.

5.7   Abstract right and anthropocentric instrumentalism

Again, property is a relational idea: rightful property implies correlative duties of others to respect that ownership and thereby uphold an objective space of interpersonal recognition. This defines a tripartite relation locating the relative positions of owners and non-owners with respect to the owned thing. Alan Carter, who also emphasizes this relational aspect of property, quotes approvingly the legal theorist Morris Cohen:

[T]he essence of private property is always the right to exclude others ... whatever technical definition we may prefer, we must recognize that a property right is a relation, not between an owner and a thing, but between the owner and other

172   Nonhuman nature: alienation

individuals in reference to things. A right is always against one or more individuals. (Cohen 1978, cited by Carter 1989, p. 130)

This is not quite correct, however. Given the anthropocentric instrumentalism at the heart of traditional thinking about property, it is appropriate to say that it is also a right *against what is owned*. An initial focus on the owner – items owned – non-owner relation, viewed *only* in the light of anthropocentric concerns leaves the nonhuman items involved with the status *only* of 'things to be owned' for the sake of human interests. From this perspective there is *nothing* to them beyond that role. So, for example, within Hegel's account the property relation transforms items into things for enabling the recognition of free personality; there is nothing else to the items involved. Thus for Hegel in private property derivation mode, since we have a duty to realize ourselves as individual persons, we have a duty to transform the world around us (those parts available through the property system), to make ourselves at home, as persons, by moulding it in accordance with our will. This duty is limited only by considerations of human interests; otherwise nature is a moral void to be penetrated as much as possible to allow humanity maximal objective self-recognition. Hegel gives his main account of this in the section on 'abstract right' at the start of his *Philosophy of Right*. At the level of abstract right, self-consciousness is so concerned to actualize itself in the highest sense as free personality that everything else is material to that end.

Interestingly, Hegel's own philosophy of nature seems to disappear at this moment too. If we consider Hegel's wider preoccupation with the yearning to be at home in the world, clearly this is not just a matter of modifying surroundings to make them more comfortable, pleasing and efficient satisfiers of physical needs. But nor is the yearning always to be thought of in terms of our need for human interpersonal recognition through the ethical life of objective spirit. The *philosophical* achievement of a fully satisfactory homeliness is through intelligibility: attaining a form of thought (Hegel's philosophy) that allows us to see the world – the apparently external, nonhuman natural world as well as the obviously human social and artefactual world – as rational through and through. In her book *Petrified Intelligence*, Alison Stone shows how Hegel's philosophy of nature posits 'intrinsic value' to natural forms in a way that looks as if it might ground a nonanthropocentric environmental philosophy, but is then trumped by considerations of abstract right when he turns to explaining private property (Stone 2005, ch. 6). This suggests an interesting tension between different senses of making ourselves at home in the world: between the concrete actualization of

Abstract right and anthropocentric instrumentalism 173

free personhood on the one hand, and forming a conception of wider nature adequate to our pre-theoretical sense of its own value on the other hand.

Within Hegel's metaphysics of nature all natural forms have a rational element, recognition of which brings a homely satisfaction (Stone 2005). The natural world is intelligible to reason because it expresses a developing rationality.[12] And, because Hegel employs a Kantian theory of value, which says that whatever is rational, or acts for the sake of reason, is 'intrinsically good', this view of the world is satisfying not only qua intelligible, but because in its intelligible rationality it answers to our pre-theoretical sense of nature's own value. Hegel treats this answering as a criterion of adequacy for a metaphysic of nature; grounds for preferring it to the disenchanting, value neutral metaphysic he believes is presupposed by empirical science (Stone 2005, pp. 135f, 166f). We might have expected this satisfying view of the natural world as a surrounding field of value to inform an account of the more straightforwardly practical aspects of making a home in the world: to be truly satisfying homemaking activity, *our* transformation of our wider, more than human surroundings should be performed with its given value at least partly in mind. Our landscaping should not then be without limits other than those provided by human interests, but constrained or qualified by the value posited in nature as it is independently of human interests and transformations effected for the sake of human interests. One might have expected this to inform the content of the ethical life, the norms and institutions of objective spirit. But it is effectively denied, or rendered invisible, in the account of property as abstract right, the central context for understanding our making a satisfying home in the world as free persons.[13]

It is this exhaustive preoccupation with realizing free personality and the role of ownership within this that constitutes the foundational moment for Hegel's political philosophy. It sets in thoroughly anthropocentric instrumental terms the agenda for his account of the more concrete manifestations of Right at the levels of ethics and the social institutions required to cultivate human motivations and shape action in accordance

---

[12] Stone presents the 'forms' involved in Hegel's metaphysical theory of nature as very general stages of development (sheer materiality, bodies, physical qualities and life) that emerge as a matter of rational necessity out of the contradictions of previous stages; a process that mirrors that involved in Hegel's dialectical account of the development of consciousness (Stone 2005, ch. 2).

[13] Even if it wasn't trumped by abstract right, the thoroughly rationalist terms in which nature is evaluated here (natural forms are intrinsically valuable qua rational) make it a problematic form of extensionism; the nonhuman is valued for its closeness, qua rational, to the human. See the discussion of extensionism in the previous chapter.

174   Nonhuman nature: alienation

with duty (Stone 2005, pp. 154ff). So, in Hegelian terms, the crucial agenda-setting moment of abstract right is when, for the sake of a political philosophy able to resist unqualified domination of nature, some recognition of nonhuman reality as more than mere material for the realization of free personality should be attempted. In our terms, it should be an attempt to endorse some *estrangement from* nonhuman nature and therefore some *alienation of* it in the sense of letting go of an unqualifiedly anthropocentric instrumental understanding of ownership over it.

5.8   The absolute sea squirt

What stops *us* from endorsing such alienation? Is it that we hold assumptions something like those Hegel seeks to reconstruct systematically through his philosophy? Within Hegel's philosophical system, it is his Absolute Idealism, his concern for the realization or completion of '*absolute* spirit' that stands in the way of a robust recognition of nonhuman nature. Hegel posits absolute spirit partly to provide an overarching justification of modern objective spirit. Rather than being left in the position of justifying itself to itself intersubjectively, objective spirit is given a crucial role to play in the largest, most fundamental process of unfolding reality. This role provides it with a special foundation and legitimacy. As Habermas puts it, rather than leaving objective spirit to its own (self-) legitimating devices,

[b]y the end of the *Phenomenology of Spirit* … Hegel was presupposing a subject as the basis of the history of consciousness. This subject is thought of as the One and All, the totality which "can have nothing outside itself" … absolute spirit must internalise the shaping processes which were anonymously guided up to that point, as the history of its own emergence, restoring the primacy of subjectivity. It can no longer tolerate the "other of itself" as the constraining opposition of a resistant reality, or as an alter ego with rights *external to* itself. It can accept such an other only *within itself* downgraded to the status of raw material for the purposes its own development. (Habermas 1999, pp. 148f, emphasis in original)[14]

Notice that maximal elimination of estrangement, maximal realization of a subjectivity free from external constraint and maximal

[14] Cf. Hegel (1977, Pt. VIII). Stone challenges the popular interpretation of Hegel's absolute as itself a cosmic *subject*. She points out that Hegel defines absolute idealism in his *Encyclopaedia Logic* as 'the view that things "have the ground of their being not in themselves but in the universal divine idea". Here the "idea" is understood as a comprehensive ontological structure that is not merely "subjective"' (Stone 2005, p. 22). Moreover, 'Hegel does not equate the omnipresent "idea" with mind: rather the idea develops *into* mind' (Stone 2005, p. 32, emphasis in original). But whether absolute spirit is interpreted as a mega-subject or as a comprehensive ontological structure completed by our recognition of our place within it does not affect the force of Habermas' point, nor mine.

The absolute sea squirt   175

knowledge (which is ultimately self-knowledge) all come together in the self-recognition of the 'One and All that can have nothing outside of itself'.[15] Modern objective spirit is *absolutely* justified through the role it plays as the final stage in the realization of this, the Absolute: it enables the self-recognition of the 'One and All that can have nothing outside itself' by enabling self-consciously free human personality capable of understanding Absolute Idealism. And central to modern objective spirit as a political phenomenon is the notion of property understood in purely anthropocentric instrumental terms. Habermas' concern is with the threatened repression of the intersubjectivity otherwise characterizing Hegel's objective spirit: its being locked into a position of subservience to absolute spirit. This must be a concern for us too.[16] But our main concern here is with the repression of the external other, that is, nonhuman nature. The concept of property functions as the *politically* central case of this overall tendency of Hegel's Absolute Idealism. The objective spirit of political community cannot sanction any estrangement from or alienation of wider nonhuman reality while, subject to the requirements of absolute spirit, it is unable to tolerate that reality as a constraint on the project of personal self-realization. Habermas points out that Hegel would not be satisfied with a post-metaphysical (indeed, pragmatist) reading of spirit that does away with the overarching absolute mega-subject, thereby leaving objective spirit to an *always ongoing* project of justifying itself to itself intersubjectively (Habermas 1999, pp. 149f). Leaving modern objective spirit without an *absolute* justification would not answer to Hegel's ambition to secure a final unification in which spirit is *fully* at home in the world in the least estranged way possible, in which nothing in the world is outside or beyond itself.

[15] In his *Philosophy of Nature* Hegel says that 'Nature is mind estranged from itself' (quoted by Stone 2005, p. 57).

[16] As noted above and in Chapter 3, section 3.11, Hegel offers a way of understanding the reconciliation of personal and impersonal concerns. However, his treatment of 'ethical life' notoriously presents it as a very 'thick' set of shared values and traditions; as Patten suggests, too thick for liberals sensitive to what Rawls calls the 'fact of pluralism' (Patten 1999, p. 2) or for others concerned with human plurality and difference. It seems much too thickly *communitarian*. Now Rawls does provide an explicitly Hegelian account of one role of political philosophy being to *reconcile* citizens with their political society (Rawls 2001, pp. 3f) and he presents his project of 'political' liberalism as one of articulating and entrenching an 'overlapping consensus' on basic, 'thin' political ideas, in the context of modern pluralism, where such ideas are held to be *already implicit* within the political institutions of democratic societies (for example, Rawls 1985, p. 288). But it is hard to see any such project surviving the further Absolute-delivered intensification of the already thickly communitarian picture of ethical life suggested by Hegel's account of objective spirit. This is hard to reconcile with the need to recognize human difference we noted in the context of estrangement in the landscape, let alone nonhuman otherness.

176   Nonhuman nature: alienation

This final unification might seem to offer a way of overcoming the tension noted above between a 're-enchanted' nature, valuable in its own right qua rational, and the picture of it as a mere ownership resource for the actualization of free personality. The valued rationality inherent to intelligible natural forms is recognized as an element within the very same absolute spirit that is developing towards completion through the actualization of free human personality enabled by modern objective spirit. This is necessarily the case given that absolute spirit is all-encompassing. But although the recognition involved is of Spirit (or consciousness) and Nature as ultimately One, it is most definitely Spirit that is to do the recognizing, and do it through the vehicle of self-conscious free personality. And the 'natural' *political* fuel for this is things conceived solely as subject to the possessive will of free personality, the 'highest' element of absolute spirit. It seems that the nonhuman processes of the natural world are to be assimilated entirely to our own big home for persons, an ideal home designed to allow maximal self-realization.

Thus we can see again that this is a sea squirt project.[17] The picture is one of the absolute completion of what intellectual progress has been about all along: attaining a vision of the self as all-encompassing. No further fundamentally important intellectual work, or significant historical change, is required. All is quiet on the outside, with which there is no possibility of contact. Given the epistemologically privileged status of this final self-knowledge, there never really was any such possibility of contact, because no outside ever really existed. William James famously likened the 'through and through' universe of Hegel's absolute idealism to a 'large seaside boarding house with no private bedroom in which I might take refuge from the society of the place' (James 1912, p. 277). The place is a fully humanized place, of course, and there is no escape because there is no outside to escape to. Given the aim of realizing such a fully humanized home, an environmental problem like climate change must appear as an inconvenient glitch in the absolute project; a troublesome delay while the central heating thermostat and other environmental controls are set to optimum comfort levels. Talk of the Anthropocene and the 'end of nature' must be very welcome in this context: once the controls are set to the optimum then there will be no further serious environmental problems or obstacles to negotiate and spirit may finally rest and eat its brain.

I take it that we cannot believe in absolute spirit, and do not want to saddle ourselves with such a gigantic burden of metaphysical idealism. But in the absence of some such large metaphysical picture establishing

---

[17] See Chapter 2, sections 2.3–4.

Unflattering disclosures 177

the whole of reality as ultimately us or ours, there seems no reason a priori why we *must* talk about the world, including when we are justifying property, *only* in terms of its relations to human interests. As far as Hegelian *absolute* spirit is concerned, it seems best to assume that it always already has eaten its own brain, that the idea of it does no useful work and should be dropped. This leaves us with objective spirit with the absolute lopped off, and allows us to think of objective spirit as the historically unfolding landscape, with the fuzzy, matter of degree distinction between landscape and nonhuman nature unthreatened by the absolute's positing of itself as everything. The resulting situation is, as Habermas says, an open-ended one of objective spirit justifying itself to itself intersubjectively. Unlike Habermas, however,[18] we are emphasizing the importance to any such justification of getting to grips with the unfolding environmental crisis and considering how to understand ideas of alienation from nature in these pragmatic terms. I have argued that this understanding should involve endorsement of some estrangement from nonhuman nature as a way of resisting its domination and total assimilation, and therefore also some alienation of nonhuman nature in the sense I have explained.

5.9   Unflattering disclosures

In discussing Hegelian objective spirit as landscape I have followed Habermas in emphasizing that it encompasses the 'material infrastructure of society',[19] which includes nature *insofar as* it has been transformed and assimilated to that infrastructure. This might be taken to suggest a Left Hegelian move from private to collective forms of property. However, I am not arguing that in ownership terms human landscapes really ought to be collective property systems. Hegel's views on property hardly seem to justify a purely private system of ownership; however, my intention here is not to reject private property but to consider the status of nature within Hegel's derivation of private property that, I think, is questionable in a way that is illustrative of traditional thought on property, yet not to be answered by simply changing the terms from private to collective or common ownership. In and of itself this change won't affect the alienation of nature in the sense I mean. I return to this issue shortly.

We have seen that, for Hegel, our surroundings *as possessed* disclose our reality as free persons. If we also recall from the previous chapters

---

[18] Recall Eckersley's critique of Habermas' perpetuation of the domination agenda mentioned in Chapter 4, note 6.

[19] Habermas (1999, p. 138); see again Chapter 3, section 3.8.

178 Nonhuman nature: alienation

the idea of a mutual embedding of place and personality then we might say that human landscapes, as results of ongoing human practices of place, disclose the historical personalities, or multiple personalities, of societies as property systems. We may then distinguish between: (1) the idea of landscaped places as disclosing personality; (2) the idea that there is nothing more to nature than it being a means to disclosing (and so realizing) personality; and (3) the matter of what kind of personality is disclosed. With regards to the latter we might make a further distinction between (a) an egoistic, self-regarding personality-type that either ignores what is outside itself altogether, or views it with contempt and/or considers it *only* as a resource; or (b) a type more open to recognition of difference as something to be respected and tolerated. On its own (1) does not entail (2), but it *seems to* do so from the perspective of (3a). It is (3a) that is taken for granted and embedded by much traditional thinking on property, which then blocks thinking in the direction of (3b). I am thinking of the removal of this blockage as *alienation of* nonhuman nature.

No doubt human landscapes involve combinations of, and changing balances between, different forms of ownership. But most, if not all, of the Earth is owned in some way, and if the environmental crisis discloses something about current and historical human personality, it is not very flattering. If we consider climate change, for example, we haven't been able to see ourselves in this and therefore our impact via this mechanism on others, human and nonhuman, without scientific analysis. We can *see* factories, cars, airplanes and so on, and we can *see* flooded islands and polar bears struggling to locate dwindling Arctic ice, but not the anthropogenic climate link. Nevertheless the scientific analysis is available: *we* are doing *that* to *them*. In the case of climate change (and perhaps other features of the crisis too) the novelty of the problem is itself a problem. We have been used to thinking of the weather as something 'nature does to us'; we have to live despite the storms, heat, cold, floods and droughts. Our home in the world is a *shelter from* the elements. We are less used to thinking of the weather as something we do to ourselves and others via anthropogenic climate change; or of our home as a profound *disruption of* the elements impacting the rest of terrestrial nature, from which others might be in need of shelter.

5.10   Is collective ownership necessary?

For a Marxist, the preceding arguments probably seem to take place within an ideological perspective already coloured by the reification and

Is collective ownership necessary? 179

estrangement generated by alienation of labour. And this might prompt the Marxist to object to them in the following way:

The bundles of rights, duties, liberties and powers that define who gets to do what with what merely trace the particular reified contours of the prison of estrangement and exploitation imposed under specific historical conditions by private property. Although one might draw an abstract analytical distinction between the concept of property and the content of wider morality, this is a trivial, merely formal distinction. In concrete reality, a bourgeois morality – based on a reified and estranged vision of 'human nature' – will be given within the historical fact of private property. If that historical fact renders trivial such distinctions as those between the concepts of property, private property and general morality involved in the discussion above, it renders equally trivial the issue of what considerations relating to nonhuman nature are allowed to interpose between them. The formal declaration that no human being should be viewed as a mere resource may or may not be distinguished from the abstract concept of private property, but the alienation of labour implied by private property means that most humans will be in the actual position of 'wage slaves' whose productive activities and abilities are thoroughly commodified. What chance then for anything more than a merely formal declaration that *nonhuman* nature should be 'alienated' in the sense I mean?

I mentioned earlier that the anthropocentric instrumentalist focus of philosophical accounts of property is unsurprising given the way they speak to important issues, and so locate crucial seams in landscapes as human homemaking projects. Yes, it might be said, but humanized landscapes whose 'crucial seams' include private property relations reified into natural facts, partly through the assumptions reconstructed in philosophical derivations of private property, are necessarily unfit as proper homes in the world for humanity. The Lockean labour mixing story, for example, presupposes the idea of 'natural' self-ownership: to be in the position of potentially acquiring ownership over previously unowned things by mixing one's labour with them, one must own one's own labour in the first place. The idea of ownership of oneself and one's labour is both established as a 'truth' for ideological purposes and negated as a concrete reality by the private property relation, which imposes the alienation of labour as a *requirement* of existence. If labour *must* be a commodity to be alienated, it must first be owned as a commodity, but one that *must* be alienated. So anything like the Hegelian 'realization of free personality' is prevented by the very institution of private property said to be necessary for it, and the resulting objective spirit perverted into a degraded Lockean form predicated on 'natural' and yet inevitably

180   Nonhuman nature: alienation

alienated self-ownership. This is an objective spirit underpinned by alienation and shot through with reification and estrangement. Ownership must then be collectivized if anything like genuinely free personality is to be realized. It must then be collectivized for us to be free to endorse some estrangement from and alienation of nonhuman nature: control over the mediation of the human/nonhuman relation has to be collective control.

There are two main kinds of objection to my argument here. One is that to talk in the abstract way that I have been talking about estrangement from and alienation of nonhuman nature is to indulge in ahistorical chatter that is either trivial or ideological or both. Second, such talk ignores the fact that private ownership, at least of important productive resources, has to be abolished and ownership collectivized if there is to be real resistance to the domination of nature; whether or not one wants to describe such resistance in terms of estrangement from and alienation of nonhuman nature. I discussed the objection that I am indulging in ahistorical abstractions in Chapter 1.[20] I will finish this chapter with some discussion of the second objection. This will allow me to further illustrate the alienation of nature argument by showing how it applies to the Marxian tradition too.

Even if collective ownership is held to be necessary to resist the domination of nature, it is obviously not sufficient. The alienation argument of this chapter can be refocused easily to apply to collectivized ownership viewed as necessary for human liberation – including the realization of free personality, this time in the materialist guise of the human species being. This line of thought also tends to be confined within anthropocentric instrumentalist parameters. It is just that the free development of each as bound up with the free development of all is now the crucial seam to be brought forth and reinforced by collective ownership of the landscape as a productive enterprise. The abstractness of the idea of property as such arises from the generality of the thought that under circumstances of relative scarcity of goods – i.e., in all known and foreseeable human societies – there will be rules concerning access to them. The rules might embody private, common or collective ownership, or some combination of these, and they will vary accordingly. If the claim is that collective ownership is superior to private ownership, then it is reasonable to ask what sanctions the move from the idea of property as such to the view that it should be collective, not private, property. In other words, it is reasonable to ask for a derivation of collective property that explains why it is necessary. One might then consider whether what is provided is a purely anthropocentric instrumentalist derivation.

---

[20] See Chapter 1, sections 1.7–8.

Is collective ownership necessary? 181

The considerations provided by the Marxian critique of private property and in favour of collective property precisely do seem to involve the assumption that 'natural objects' should enter the picture only as things to be owned for the sake of human interests. As for Hegel, they are vehicles of realization of free human personality; it is just that this requires ending the alienation of labour and the associated estrangements and reification in order for the human species being to be liberated. This requires the abolition of private ownership: the very need to reconcile subjective and objective spirit presupposes an estrangement between those perspectives that may be overcome only by eliminating labour alienation. But the reconciliation involved is unpacked in anthropocentric terms.

Thus I mentioned earlier Waldron's definition of collective property as a system in which allocation is 'determined by a social rule that the use of material resources in particular cases is to be determined with reference to the collective interests of society as a whole'. Waldron points out that this definition leaves open both what counts as the collective interest and, given some conception of this, what should be the procedure for applying that conception of collective interest in particular cases (Waldron 1988, p. 40). I am taking it that the conception of collective interest operating here is the need to avoid or overcome estrangement and reification within the landscape so that the human species being – the human capacity for creative cooperative labour – may be liberated and the free development of each becomes the condition of the free development of all. This sanctions the move from the idea of property to the idea of collective property[21] and presumably also determines the proper procedure for applying it as a thoroughly democratic, rather than, say, an authoritarian centralized system of planning.

As with 'liberal individualist' private property, it is not that such a picture *necessarily* precludes (this time collective) ownership bundles accommodating 'environmental imperatives' regarding nonhuman nature. But if the background story about the nature and point of such ownership is an entirely anthropocentric one, with the nonhuman featuring only as instrumentalized resources, then it will tend to seem out of place to restrict the use of collectively owned resources for the sake of ameliorating impacts on nonhuman species, ecosystems and interests. Whatever may be the relation between the abstract idea of property as such and the ethical case against slavery, the Marxian considerations offered in favour of collective ownership are derived from those condemning the *human*

---

[21] This probably puts the point in terms too idealist for the Marxian, who will prefer to say that the actual move required is a historical material move from private to collective ownership, not from the idea of property to the idea of collective property.

182   Nonhuman nature: alienation

wage slavery wrapped up with the alienation and commodification of labour. In conditions of private property, the acquisition, use and alienation of property does not allow workers to 'work on themselves' in ways that 'demonstrate their freedom to themselves and others', rather the necessary alienation involved demonstrates their lack of freedom as they are *worked on* and the world they produce and reproduce confronts them in the appearance of an alien being. The Marxian perspective of course emphasizes the homemaking, world-transformative character of ownership but, as we have seen, often – although not always – in an anthropocentric and promethean tone.

My point is not that the Marxian perspective is entirely false and private property always justified, but again that the status of nonhuman nature in theories of property such as that of Hegel is not to be changed *simply* by changing the terms from private to collective ownership. Not every case of alienation and estrangement that interests us can be reduced to the Marxian private ownership-labour alienation-estrangement nexus. For example, we are interested in estrangement from nonhuman nature as a qualified good. Under conditions of collective ownership *understood in purely anthropocentric instrumentalist terms,* such estrangement requires alienation of nonhuman nature in the sense of rejecting that background understanding, no less than it does when that understanding is in the background of private ownership. This is not necessarily impossible for the Marxist. It depends on whether something like Benton's proposal to draw out the nonanthropocentric elements he sees in the idea of the human species being (the operative conception of collective interests) can be made to work.[22] We touched upon this in the previous chapter where we also noted that any such respect for the nonhuman is very much an afterthought in the Marxian system.[23] But nor is the situation necessarily altered by distancing oneself from the Marxian tradition by seeing as totalizing or reductive its explanation of social estrangement and reification in terms of the alienation of labour. This is illustrated by Honneth's recognitional account of 'reification of nature' that, unless conjoined with what I am calling alienation of nonhuman nature, risks remaining within the anthropocentric instrumentalist terms set by Hegel's treatment of abstract right.

Finally, I have not yet addressed this question directly: granted that collective ownership is not sufficient to change the background status of

---

[22] See Chapter 4, section 4.5. It also depends on the Marxian conception not going too far down the radical constructionist sea squirt road we saw in Chapter 2, section 2.4.

[23] We also saw that moving from a purely transformative to an ecoregulatory conception of labour is not necessarily to move away from an agenda of domination. See Chapter 4, section 4.5.

Is collective ownership necessary? 183

nonhuman nature in considerations of ownership, is it necessary? I have occasionally hinted that derivations of private property intended to justify it as uniquely and universally right are unsatisfactory. For example, much of our landscaped surroundings have been produced by cooperative and social, rather than individual, labour. And the ownership of vast resources by multinationals in a 'neoliberal' global capitalist system is a huge problem, whether we are thinking of respect for human or nonhuman difference. This strongly suggests a need for more collective, democratic control over productive resources than there is at present. Yet a pragmatist approach concerned to capture plurality, nuance and difference, and suspicious of fixed, final answers cannot be comfortable with the assertion of collective ownership as a universal principle. A presumption of total victory for either side – individual (private) or collective ownership – seems out of place and unhelpful. Given human difference, it seems better to expect difference in this matter of ownership type; a mixture of ownership types depending on local situations and already existing understandings.

Notice also that the abolition of private property to eliminate pernicious estrangement and reification and so liberate the human species being does not necessitate a purely *collective* system of ownership. There could also be some common ownership mixed in with the collective. This is perhaps especially so if considerations of nonhuman interests are allowed in to influence conceptions of ownership. It might be easier for them to get a foothold given that neither individual nor collective human interests are privileged in situations of common ownership as defined by Waldron.[24] Waldron refers to parks and 'national reserves' as examples of common ownership; many might (in fact do) say '*nature* reserves', 'wilderness reserves' or 'wildness reserves' instead. But there could be more such areas where ownership is constrained for the sake of allowing nonhuman organisms and processes to flourish and develop in their own ways. Obviously, this idea needs to be considered alongside those of unjust reification and dispossession (of indigenous peoples' landscapes, for example). I am not advocating more troublesome applications of the notion of wilderness, but an adjustment of ownership bundles determining the use of land and other owned items in human landscapes *generally*, so that the areas they occupy may serve to some extent as nonhuman as well as human reserves.

I have been trying to bring out in this and the previous chapters the importance of *endorsing* some estrangement from and alienation of nonhuman nature, given a concern to resist the domination of nature and

---

[24] See note 2 above.

184   Nonhuman nature: alienation

'respect nature' as key normative positions in play with regard to the environmental crisis. In my view, this provides some utility to talk of 'alienation from nature'. The 'universal' significance of estrangement and alienation in these senses is due to the global scope of the crisis and the fact that, the Anthropocene and the alleged 'end of nature' notwithstanding, there is no place in which nonhuman nature has been eliminated entirely. Moreover these ideas of estrangement and alienation themselves express directly a concern for difference, nuance and matters of degree. They do this particularly with respect to avoiding the intended or inadvertent elimination of nonhuman nature's difference by reducing it in thought or deed to humanized landscape as much as possible. I am taking it that this is an ever-present concern.

6 Estrangement from the natural world

6.1 Introduction

In the Introduction I mentioned that 'alienation from nature' often seems to refer to a mistaken view of humanity as not really part of a wider natural world; as if we were not one type of natural being among others similarly embedded within and utterly dependent upon a complexity of processes that gave rise to them, sustains them and which they in turn affect more or less profoundly. Perhaps many, if not most, people would answer 'yes' to the bald question: 'is humanity part of and utterly dependent upon a wider natural world?' Yet it might be that they participate in ways of life that seem to presuppose that the correct answer is really 'no'. In terms of our distinctions between types of alienation from nature, this raises the matter of our 'estrangement from the natural world'.

Remember that central to my overall argument is that distinguishing different senses of alienation from nature, and observing relations between them, allows us to capture different (anthropocentric and non-anthropocentric) environmental concerns and note some important relations between *them*. The previous two chapters sought to capture critical nonanthropocentric anti-domination or respect for nature perspectives by focusing on the discontinuity of landscape and nonhuman nature and viewing estrangement and alienation in a positive light. The notion of *estrangement from the natural world* resonates with critical environmental perspectives in a different way. Here the main idea is that the environmental crisis involves our being somehow 'cut off from nature' in a way closely associated with domineering, hubristic attitudes that prevent adequate awareness of both the harm we do to the natural world and our utter dependence upon it. Thus we should do what we can to overcome *this* estrangement. But the terms in which I suggest we understand this underline the importance of bearing in mind the other senses of alienation from nature and the relations between them. The latter issue is a matter mainly for the next chapter.

185

186   Estrangement from the natural world

Here the focus is on the continuity brought by the fact that both land-scape and nonhuman nature are *within* the natural world. Capturing and helping articulate nonanthropocentric concerns is still an issue, but this time in a context of continuity. 'Anthropocentric matters', in the sense of matters pertaining to our landscaped surroundings, must also be issues here, because of this continuity. Because landscapes are within the natural world, the idea of what it is to be estranged from the nat-ural world must be applicable to the landscape as well as to nonhuman nature. However, I shall concentrate mainly on the estrangement as it applies to the more than human dimensions of the natural world, as it captures nonanthropocentric respect for the nonhuman. I do this to avoid the danger of reducing nature to landscape through an account of this estrangement.

As with the other senses of alienation from nature discussed in this book, my aim in this chapter is to consider the idea of estrangement from the natural world as a potentially useful tool for getting to grips with our problematic environmental situation. One issue to be faced then is this conceptual problem raised in the Introduction: estrangement from the natural world seems impossible if, by definition, we always remain part of nature in that sense, whatever we do. It is not as if we could ever *leave* the natural world or become really separate from it. Even if we are excep-tional, a one-off among natural species in virtue of our 'instinct-denying' historical and technological ways of carrying on, it is still the case that we and these ways of carrying on remain *within* the natural world. This suggests that the idea of estrangement from the natural world might be empty and so not a helpful notion.[1]

My main claim in this chapter is that we can see how our relation to overall nature might involve estrangement by interpreting the situation in terms of Merleau-Ponty's phenomenological ontology of 'flesh'. If we understand the natural world as the 'fleshy' 'perceptual world', then our estrangement from it might be a matter of *inadequate participation* within this world, without this involving our actual or ontological separation from it. Understanding the estrangement like this allows us to connect it closely with environmental worries about anthropocentric instrumental-ism and attitudes of mastery and disregard of our inescapable immersion within wider nature. This is important if a satisfactory account of the estrangement is one that helps to articulate such critical worries. Indeed,

---

[1] As we have seen (Introduction, sections 0.3–4), this conceptual problem is part of Steven Vogel's case for focusing concern about 'alienation from nature' on our relations to and within the humanized landscape. Another part of his case is that our alienation (or, in our terms, estrangement) from *nonhuman* nature is trivially true by definition. I dealt with the latter in Chapter 4, section 4.2.

Misperception 187

given this condition, we need to be able to understand the central normative issue of what counts as '*adequate*' participation in nature as flesh in terms that are continuous with that critique. I think the flesh account is useful because it enables this: it suggests a picture of participation such that the criteria of adequate participation can be shaped by the critical environmental perspective. The point is not that the flesh account in and of itself *entails* the environmental critique. Rather it is a philosophical tool that can help clarify it as a critique of our estrangement from a wider world within which we are inescapably located. We shall also see that understanding things like this connects them closely with the ideas of *accepting* some estrangement from and alienation of the nonhuman.

On the other hand, even if this idea of estrangement from the natural world is a useful way of broaching environmental worries, it is important also to consider any project of *overcoming it* in relation to other environmental goals; especially those involving the overcoming of pernicious reification, estrangement and alienation in the landscape context. Again, I consider in the next chapter how these goals relate to that of overcoming estrangement from the natural world. Before that I shall build up the idea of estrangement as 'inadequate participation in the flesh'. This will involve some further discussion of Honneth's account of reification as a distortion of primordial recognition. Suitably modified, some elements of his account helpfully point to aspects of the idea of estrangement I have in mind, one that assists in the articulation of environmental critique. Others don't and have to be excluded altogether. I discuss these modifications and exclusions and relate them to salient aspects of Merleau-Ponty's accounts of 'perception' and 'flesh'. This will take some time and philosophical effort but will result in an account of estrangement from the natural world as a condition collecting together several features of the problematic environmental situation.

6.2 Misperception

Firstly, recall how the idea of estrangement cashes out in relation to nonhuman nature. Estrangement from the nonhuman consists in (being confronted by) the landscape-independence, or otherness or difference, of nonhuman nature. Here the discontinuity, distance or apartness of the estrangement denotes our 'separation' from nature in that *nonhuman* entities and processes do not embody human will and are not set up to serve human interests. In this respect nonhuman entities and process are 'other'. To some degree overcoming this estrangement through landscaping, in terms of both physical transformations and anthropocentric instrumental interpretations of nature, is 'basic' in the sense of being

188 Estrangement from the natural world

necessary for human life and civilization. But this precisely *is* a matter of degree and, again, my suggestion is that we need to live with some of this estrangement rather than seek to reduce nature to landscape entirely in either physical or anthropocentric instrumentalist interpretive terms. It is better then to think in terms of refraining from 'surplus' *overcoming* of estrangement from nonhuman nature.

Thus the drive to overcome all estrangement from nonhuman nature and view it simply as 'ours' to transform and interpret for our own interests (the 'domination agenda') is part of the environmental problem situation. If we think of the problem situation in terms of failure of perception, then this part of it involves failing to perceive nonhuman nature as other, or ignoring its otherness and seeing it only in landscaping terms. However, estrangement with respect to nonhuman nature does not *itself* consist in a failure of perception; it is the *problem* (or this part of the overall problem situation) that consists in either ignoring the estrangement involved in landscape-independence or perceiving it only as something to be overcome as much as possible. There is no recognition of nonhuman difference of the kind that can supply a normative underwriting to living with it, or 'letting it be'.

In the case of estrangement from the natural world I think it is helpful to say that the apartness or distance *is itself* a matter of misperception of our situation; a lack of appreciation of our immersion within and dependence upon a wider more than human world. This move allows us to evade the conceptual problem raised by our inescapable location within the natural world. But, as with the other kinds of estrangement discussed in this book, estrangement from the natural world should not be understood in *purely* cognitive terms. It should not be considered only in terms of lack of knowledge, or holding false beliefs and principles. It is also a matter of praxis, sensibility and habitual practice. Thus we may distinguish two kinds of misperception: one consisting in cognitive, epistemic errors, the other involving matters of praxis and phenomenological issues. I shall spend more time on the latter in this chapter because it requires more clarification.

This is not to say that the cognitive, epistemic dimension is unimportant and unnecessary.[2] Rather it is *insufficient* for a satisfactory account of estrangement from the natural world. Take the conceptual problem raised by our always remaining within wider nature whatever we do. It might be asked why, if this is supposed to be a difficulty in the way of understanding how we could ever be estranged from the natural world,

---

[2] I make more of this 'cognitive estrangement' in the next chapter.

Misperception 189

we can't get around this simply by defining the estrangement in terms of ignorance of the ecological relations that come with our inescapable location in wider nature? If the 'error' involved is simply a cognitive error (ignorance or denial of our ecological impacts and dependencies, say, or failure to give them sufficient weight in decision-making) then this is obviously consistent with our always remaining within overall nature. It is also easy to see why we should avoid it: our future prosperity, if not survival, depends upon it. Remaining in a state of avoidable ignorance is generally bad policy and particularly foolish in the specific case of ecological facts.

Putting things like this does chime with the picture of alienation from nature mentioned at the start of this chapter (a mistaken view of humanity as not really part of and utterly dependent upon a wider natural world). But it is insufficient if a satisfactory account of the estrangement is one that captures and helps to articulate a critical perspective on the environmental problem situation. Even if it is partly a matter of ignorance or neglect of ecological facts, this may not capture everything helpfully encompassed by the idea of estrangement from the natural world. It is not just obvious that even highly eco-literate people with detailed knowledge of ecological relations and dependencies cannot be estranged in a problematic way from wider nature simply in virtue of having that knowledge and a willingness to act on it. For example, it would be unsatisfactory to limit the picture to human desires for survival and prosperity, ecological knowledge and instrumental rationality, so as to make the estrangement a matter of deficiencies in the latter two. That reduces nature to landscape. It suggests a view of knowledge as power, and a wish to overcome all estrangement, *including from the nonhuman*, by reordering ecological relations to maximize human security and prosperity. Left like this it expresses, or is at least consistent with, attitudes of domination and hubris that are themselves to be associated closely with the idea of estrangement from the natural world (given that the latter is to help articulate a critical perspective on the environmental crisis).

This in turn suggests that the relevant 'interrelations', in terms of which we are to understand (mis)perception of our embeddedness within that wider world, are *not only* causal relations, such as those determined by ecological science. It suggests that they also involve something else, something to do with lived meaning; something we enact or fail adequately to enact, even though we do not thereby remove ourselves from them any more than we can remove ourselves from causal ecological relations simply by ignoring them. The question is how to fill this in.

6.3 Honneth again

To begin to see how it might be filled in, consider again the main features of Honneth's account of reification discussed in Chapter 3. For Honneth (2008, p. 26), reification is a 'distorted, atrophied form of praxis', and so more than a narrowly cognitive error correctable simply by grasping the truth of propositions or the applicability of abstract moral principles (Honneth 2008, pp. 22ff). He accepts Lukács' account of it as 'a habit of mere contemplation and observation, in which one's natural surroundings, social environment and personal characteristics come to be apprehended in a detached and emotionless manner – in short, as things' (Honneth 2008, p. 25). By contrast in 'genuine' praxis subjects experience the world *directly* in an *engaged* way, as 'cooperative' (Honneth 2008, p. 27). Indeed, Honneth notes similarities here to Heidegger's notion of 'care' and Dewey's notion of 'interaction' (Honneth 2008, pp. 29ff). From these phenomenological and pragmatist perspectives, humans are always already involved in practical engagements with a world of existential significance. Thus there is no suggestion that reification could *wholly replace* genuine praxis (Honneth 2008, pp. 31–2): 'engaged praxis' must *always already exist*, in however rudimentary a form, reification being the twisting of this 'primordial' engagement in the direction of a merely observational, contemplative disengagement that views things as mere things. Honneth explains this 'habit of detachment' in terms of a 'forgetting' of the primary 'empathetic recognition and engagement' with others and the world that 'precedes a neutral grasping of reality'. Recognition is both conceptually and genetically prior to cognition (Honneth 2008, pp. 40ff) and yet may be 'forgotten' beneath a reflective layer that distorts one's perception of others, surrounding objects and oneself into a perception of mere things (Honneth 2008, pp. 52ff).

In Chapter 3 I distinguished various elements of this understanding of reification: (1) a distortion of sensibility and praxis irreducible to cognitive errors; (2) the praxis of which reification is a distortion involves an always already existing relation with others; (3) this always existing relation is a 'primordial' relation; (4) it has a 'recognitional' component; (5) the recognition involved in 'genuine' praxis is fundamentally of other persons; (6) reification involves a 'forgetting' of this always already existing recognition. I argue that, suitably modified and supplemented, the first four are also elements of a satisfactory conception of estrangement from the natural world. The modifications and supplements I have in mind are mainly with reference to Merleau-Ponty's notion of 'flesh', discussed below, but notice that the first two elements speak to matters already touched upon above: a satisfactory conception of estrangement

Forgetting 191

from the natural world can neither reduce it to narrowly cognitive errors nor have it involve an actual departure from nature; we are always already involved in the natural world.

The fifth element (the recognitional component of 'undistorted' praxis is fundamentally recognition of other persons) has to go, however. It is excluded by the stipulation that a satisfactory conception is one that helps capture and articulate nonanthropocentric environmental concerns. As we have seen in Chapters 3 and 5, Honneth unpacks what he calls 'reification of nature' via reification of persons, such that 'nature' figures, in Hegelian fashion, as a vehicle for the recognition of persons. I am taking it that, to capture critical environmental concerns in a satisfactory way, any recognitional element involved in (overcoming) estrangement from the natural world cannot be focused only on recognition of persons, with the nonhuman dimensions of nature entering the picture only as a means of achieving that. Otherwise the account of estrangement would be just another way of reducing nature to landscape, however helpful it is for understanding estrangement and reification within the landscape context.

6.4   Forgetting

I return soon to the issues of primordiality and recognition. Consider first the matter of 'forgetting', the sixth element of Honneth's account just distinguished. Should we think of estrangement from the natural world as a case of *forgetting* something? I think not. Although a discussion of this will help to bring out something that is of central importance, it is misleading to say that the estrangement necessarily involves forgetting something. For Honneth, the 'forgetting' of the primary recognition of other persons at least partly expresses the genetic priority of recognition over reification: one is more focused on empathetic recognition as a child prior to later developments that bring the risk of reification. I think it is neither desirable nor necessary to claim that anything like this must be part of our picture of what it is to be estranged from the natural world. To see this we should distinguish some senses of 'forgetting', each of which might have been thought essential to our picture.

First, in one sense, forgetting involves an inability to answer questions that one could answer before; a loss of propositional knowledge, or knowledge *that* ('remind me: what is the capital of Bulgaria?'). Estrangement from the natural world might involve this. Perhaps having been told the ecological facts about humanity's dependence upon and interconnectedness with wider nature, one keeps forgetting them, including in the relevant decision-making contexts. Perhaps having read studies of

192   Estrangement from the natural world

the ecological consequences of a policy aimed at maximizing economic growth one reads a memo warning of Big Businesses' reaction to changing the policy and forgets all about the ecological studies. But making this the central definitive feature of the estrangement pushes us in the direction of a narrowly cognitivist account in which overcoming it consists in learning and remembering ecological facts. We saw above that this is consistent with a thoroughgoing anthropocentric instrumentalism and so does not establish the close association with critical environmentalism we are seeking.

In another sense, forgetting involves a loss of the knowledge *how* involved in a practice at which one was previously adept. This is the sense of forgetting involved in the alleged impossibility of forgetting how to ride a bicycle. And this might seem helpful given that we are seeking to understand estrangement in praxis-oriented, rather than narrowly cognitivist, terms. Thus it might be thought that a pertinent example here is a lost ability to live a previous way of life that was in some way 'closer to nature'; our estrangement is a matter of our culture having forgotten how to do this: 'alas, we have forgotten the ways of our ancestors; if only we could remember how to be like them, *at one with nature*'. But we need to remember here the pluralism involved in the overall argument of this book. To be helpful to us the idea of 'closeness to nature' has to be distinguished carefully from that of a unity with nature that obliterates the otherness of its nonhuman dimensions. If overcoming estrangement from the natural world is to be a matter of 'getting closer to nature' then the idea of 'closeness' involved must be consistent not only with our always remaining within the natural world (however lacking in 'closeness' we are), it must be consistent also with recognition of nonhuman difference. That is, it must be consistent with accepting some estrangement from nonhuman nature. The conception of estrangement from the natural world I am proposing in this chapter allows us to see a sense of getting closer to nature through the overcoming of estrangement from it as something that entails recognition of the nonhuman (and estrangement from nature in *that* sense). Or so I will argue.

However, the present issue is the helpfulness or otherwise of making forgotten know-how an essential element of our conception of estrangement from the natural world. Clearly there is a temptation to interpret talk of (overcoming) estrangement from the natural world in terms of retrieving an imagined previous unity with nature, from which we have fallen in that we have forgotten how to live it. For example, recall the strands of 'anarcho-primitivist' thought that call for a recovery of the mode of human existence 'within nature' that prevailed before the invention of agriculture; a way of life held to be superior to subsequent human

Forgetting 193

cultures in most ways and not only in terms of 'harmony with nature' (e.g., Zerzan 1994).[3] But I am taking it that the need to avoid saddling our account of estrangement with mythologizing and excessively romanticized pictures of prehistoric human existence is an important reason to be careful about the idea of 'forgetting' here, and to distance our account from the idea of *forgotten* know-how.[4]

Consider also a further sense of forgetting as consisting this time in inadequate attention to, or participation in, a still current relation or practice. We do speak of 'forgetting' in this sense, for example when we say things like 'don't forget you are in a relationship' to someone we think is inadequately 'involved' in the relationship in question. Clearly this need not be a matter of lost propositional knowledge, such as no longer knowing the answers to such questions as: 'are you married; what is the name of your spouse?' But nor need it be a matter of *lost* know-how in the area; it might be that the person has *never* been 'good at relationships'. Rather the point seems to be inattention, the focus of energy being elsewhere as when someone is distracted by career, or some other obsession.[5] Calling this 'forgetting' emphasizes the possibility of remembering as a drawing of attention back to what one is already engaged in. And, again, this might seem helpful in the context of estrangement from an overall nature with which we are always already involved. But calling it *forgetting* also suggests a loss or deterioration of something one 'had' before in superior form; a more adequate attention to or participation in the relation in question. And, also again, I don't think the idea of such loss or deterioration of some previous superior relationship should be considered *essential* to the notion of estrangement from the natural world.

---

[3] See again Introduction, section 0.2.

[4] Much primitivist thought can be read as a radicalization of ideas associated with NDD and the biophilia and savannah hypotheses, combined with Jared Diamond's famous claim that the agricultural revolution was 'the worst mistake in the history of the human race' (Diamond 1987). Not only would returning to an anarcho-primitivist Pleistocene way of life vastly reduce our impact on nature, it would be highly beneficial to the genuine flourishing of animals like us: 'we must return to being animal, to glorying in our sweat, hormones, tears and blood ... [and] struggle against the modern compulsion to become dull, passionless androids' (Dave Foreman, quoted by Cronon 1995, p. 83). Although he also emphasizes and praises its capacity to enrich our political imagination, especially with regard to subverting the assumption of total human sovereignty over nature, Mick Smith is surely right to argue that taken at all literally such primitivism merely and naively appropriates and reverses traditional myths of humanity leaving a 'state of nature' in order to realize its potential for civilized culture and assume its (or the relevant subset of humanity's) rightful place as sovereign master of nature (Smith 2011, pp. 70ff).

[5] Gilbert Ryle (1971, p. 388) mentions a sense of forgetting as a 'ceasing to notice things' in his discussion of the impossibility of 'forgetting the difference between right and wrong'. He mentions this in a way that suggests a contrast with both 'non-retention of information' and 'loss of skill', but he doesn't develop the point.

194 Estrangement from the natural world

It seems to me that the important point to take is *inadequate participation* within an (always) already existing relation. This speaks to two requirements of a satisfactory conception of estrangement here: that it should have a praxis orientation and should capture the impossibility of escaping the natural world however estranged we are. We must always participate in nature in this sense and the possibility of estrangement marks the issue of the adequacy of our participation. Know-how – being able to do something well (or badly) – remains important, and I shall return to this and discuss what counts as (in)adequate participation below. But here the point is that maybe one has *never* participated adequately. Overcoming the estrangement, getting 'closer to nature', in the sense of 'becoming a better participant' within it, would then be more like learning than recovering or remembering. Although the negligent husband was never a good husband, our telling him not to forget he is married suggests we assume that at some point he *used to be* more focused on at least trying to be a good husband. Similarly our telling each other not to forget we are always already involved in nature, with the thought in mind that the quality of our involvement could be better, suggests we assume that we used to at least try to achieve a better involvement. But there seems no good reason to assume this, at least as a general fact about humanity. A better analogy for coming to grips with the idea of estrangement from the natural world, one without any necessary reference to forgetting and remembering anything, would be coming to recognize that a certain older person had been one's cousin all along and then living this particular familial relation more or less well.[6]

6.5 Primordiality and phenomenology

I am suggesting then that the estrangement consists in inadequate participation in an ongoing relation. I am suggesting also that we adapt the third element of Honneth's account of reification distinguished above and understand the relation involved as a 'primordial' relation. So I think we should understand the natural world in terms of this primordial relation and estrangement in terms of inadequate participation within it. But what does 'primordial' mean? Before considering how to understand the idea of (in)adequate participation, I need to clarify the notion of primordiality involved here. This requires a foray into phenomenology, which will take us in the direction of Merleau-Ponty's account of the primordial perceptual world as 'the flesh'.

---

[6] I am grateful to Steven Vogel for suggesting this analogy to me.

Primordiality and phenomenology 195

For Honneth, reification is a distortion of primordial recognitional praxis. In his account of reification 'primordiality' seems to denote the genetic and conceptual priority of recognitional praxis. The latter is not only always there even when 'distorted' by reification; it is there *before* any reification: an occurrence of reification involves recognitional praxis lying forgotten beneath a reifying reflective layer that both presupposes and buries it. Adequate recognitional praxis then comes to involve remembering and restoring what was always already there though buried and forgotten. But I have just argued that forgetting is not an essential feature of estrangement from the natural world. The notion of primordiality involved in our understanding of the natural world should not then denote something temporally prior that has been forgotten and calls for retrieval and remembering. Nor, however, need it involve conceptual priority in the sense of being logically presupposed without logically presupposing anything itself. The kind of priority involved is that of 'things themselves' that constitute the world experienced prior to abstraction, where 'prior' need denote only what is left once an attempt is made to put aside the determinations of abstract thought and theorizing. The resulting 'world of things themselves', or the attempt to bring it to the centre of philosophical attention, is the starting point for the phenomenological tradition inaugurated by Edmund Husserl.

Now it might be thought that such matters are too rarefied and 'philosophical' to be of interest or use to people with practical environmental concerns on their mind. This would be a mistake. In their introduction to the collection *Eco-Phenomenology: Back to the Earth Itself*, Charles Brown and Ted Toadvine (2003) provide a useful discussion of the affinity between environmental concerns and ideas central to the phenomenological tradition. It will be instructive here to quote from this discussion:

One point of agreement among phenomenologists is their criticism and rejection of the tendency of scientific naturalism to forget its own roots in experience. The consequence of this forgetting is that our experienced reality is supplanted by an abstract model of reality-a model that, for all of its usefulness, cannot claim epistemological or metaphysical priority over the world as experienced. The return to 'things themselves' and the critique of scientific naturalism both point to much contemporary environmental thought. (Brown and Toadvine 2003, p. xi)

Once again, we need to distance ourselves from such talk of 'forgetting'. This general characterization of phenomenology as a rejection of the tendency of abstract thought (such as natural science) to *forget its roots in experience* should also remind us that Honneth's view of reification as distortion of primordial recognitional praxis is inspired in part by Heidegger's notion of 'care'. However, Brown and Toadvine also bring

196   Estrangement from the natural world

out that phenomenology speaks to features of critical environmental philosophy:[7] 'For environmental philosophers, phenomenology suggests alternatives to many of the ingrained tendencies that limit our inherited perspectives: our myopic obsession with objectivity, our anthropocentric conceptions of value, and other legacies of Cartesian dualism' (Brown and Toadvine 2003, p. xii). This becomes especially clear once phenomenology takes the environmental crisis seriously and so becomes '*eco*-phenomenology':

> With other radical ecology movements, eco-phenomenology shares the conviction that our cultural detachment from our natural roots rests on the very structure of our current modes of thought, that we are weighted down by the ballast of tradition, by the assumptions and commitments carried forward from Platonism, Christianity, capitalism, Cartesian dualism and the like. Part of the solution to our current situation must lie in tracking down these philosophical land mines, scattered through the landscape of our cultural history, in order to defuse them. (Brown and Toadvine 2003, p. xix)

Indeed, they also go on to say:

> The rediscovery of a natural world that is inherently and primordially meaningful and worthy of respect might help us to overcome our cultural *estrangement* from the world around us. This new vision of nature might also allow us ... [to circumvent] intractable puzzles concerning intrinsic value and anthropocentrism. For far too long, humanity has envisioned itself as an *alien* presence in nature ... Having constituted ourselves in opposition to nature, we adopt values and purposes that threaten the earth itself. Only a reconceptualization of our place and role in nature can work against this tragic *disconnection* ... To begin this task by *reconnecting* us with our most basic and primordial experiences of the natural world—such is the power and promise of eco-phenomenology. (Brown and Toadvine 2003, p. xx, emphases added)

Unfortunately they don't say very precisely what the estrangement consists in beyond the reference to a 'tragic disconnection' from 'our most basic and primordial experiences of the natural world' as the world around us. I think that we can understand it through an idea of natural world as 'experienced reality', constituted by 'things themselves', with the estrangement consisting in inadequate participation in this world. We shall see that an excessive focus on abstract and virtual 'worlds' is part of the picture of estrangement understood in these terms. However, let me say yet again that the estrangement is not essentially a matter of *forgetting* experienced reality, as if 'we' (or our ancestors) used to live out an adequate (non-estranged) form of participation that we now need to remember.

---

[7] See Chapter 1, section 1.5.

Primordiality and phenomenology

Nor should 'experienced reality' be thought of as the 'root' of abstract models of reality, if by root is meant a foundation that has epistemological or metaphysical priority over abstract (for example, scientific) models in virtue of its self-supporting certainty. Neither the experienced world nor abstract models have that kind of foundational priority, because nothing has that kind of foundational priority. The kind of priority involved here is rather methodological: a matter of what is being focused on, and so not bracketed and, for the sake of such focusing, other things *are* being bracketed. The pragmatic rationale for the bracketing is to use it to help to clarify a praxis-oriented, perceptual sense of estrangement from nature. Thus the aim here is to bring out aspects of estrangement from nature that are irreducible to purely cognitive errors because they involve more 'lived', praxis-oriented matters. This does not require a *rejection* of 'scientific naturalism', to which we might look to provide much of the content of the cognitive picture of our overall ecological situation, or even of the possibility that theoretical reflection might show that the phenomenological world presupposes something else (including something posited by natural science). It is a matter of putting scientific naturalism and other theoretical constructs (including those of 'commonsense') aside, or bracketing them, in favour of describing the more immediate world of practical significance with which we are always already engaged.

Important also is that this is not a matter of simply reaching for a certain given philosophical approach (here phenomenology) and 'applying' it to solve a problem (the 'environmental crisis' or estrangement from nature as a feature of that crisis). Our interpretation of the philosophical approach is coloured by our sense of the problem as much as the other way around. For example, we are not taking it that there *might* be an environmental crisis and thinking of doing some 'phenomenological description' to check whether there is and, if so, discover the solution. We wish to clarify an already present sense of an environmental crisis or serious environmental problem situation involving human domination and somehow connected with estrangement from the natural world.

This requires us to be cautious and selective in our choice of phenomenological approach. Partly this caution just follows from our pragmatism. Thus we cannot understand primordiality here in terms of a secure foundation for everything else; a foundation of certainty from which we have become adrift and to which we should return and cling in the manner of sea squirts. And partly the caution is imposed by our critical environmental philosophical take on the problem situation.[8] For example, it is generally supposed that the phenomenological 'world' of experienced things

---

[8] See Chapter 1, section 1.5.

198   Estrangement from the natural world

themselves should not be identified with *anything* prior to investigation of immediate, concrete experience, and this seems risky given that we want to understand the natural world from which we might be estranged as encompassing both humanized landscape and nonhuman nature. It looks as if the phenomenologically disclosed world will be centred on oneself (or, intersubjectively, ourselves), precisely because it is the world with which one is *always already engaged*. As with Honneth's account of 'reification of nature', the focus seems *bound to* remain on human-oriented concerns within the humanized landscape. Perhaps this is true of much of the phenomenological tradition,[9] but some recent eco-phenomenology, inspired particularly by Merleau-Ponty, refers to a reality both human and decidedly 'more-than-human'.[10] His phenomenological ontology of the 'flesh of the world' in *The Visible and the Invisible* (Merleau-Ponty 1968) has seemed particularly suggestive in this regard. This difficult, unfinished and posthumously published work continues and develops Merleau-Ponty's earlier preoccupation with 'perception' or the 'perceptual world' (e.g., Merleau-Ponty 2002). I turn now to Merleau-Ponty's work as this speaks directly to our concerns.

6.6   Merleau-Ponty and primordiality

We can distinguish two senses of 'primordiality' in Merleau-Ponty's account of perception. First, primordial perception is non-inferential: the world of primordial perception is not inferred from something else ('sense data', say). Nor is it the world as 'worked over' by reflecting on what can be inferred from it: it is the thing itself, not what can be inferred from the thing itself.[11] For example, insofar as our view of the world as 'God's world' is the result of an inference from certain features of the world (as apparently designed, say) then the 'world' so viewed is not that of primordial perception.

Second, primordial perception is non-conceptual in the sense of not being constituted by conceptual thought (e.g., Merleau-Ponty 1968, pp. 35ff). Obviously, talk and description of it is conceptually mediated, a matter of groping for the concepts and metaphors to do it justice, or that seem most helpful given some issue regarding it. In

---

[9] See, for example, Mick Smith's critical discussion of the anthropocentrism of Levinas' account of 'the face' (Smith 2011, pp. 46ff) and John Llewellyn's (2003) discussion of the anthropocentrism of Husserl and (early) Heidegger.

[10] This phrase is used often by David Abram (1996), perhaps the most popular eco-phenomenologist drawing on Merleau-Ponty; but see also, for example, Brook (2005), James (2007), Toadvine (2009) and the papers in Cataldi and Hamrick (2007).

[11] Merleau-Ponty (e.g., 2002, p. xiv; 1968, pp. 28, 50).

Merleau-Ponty and primordiality

this connection Merleau-Ponty emphasizes the importance of what he calls 'hyper-reflection', as reflection mindful of its own situatedness (Merleau-Ponty 1968, p. 38). Reflection is mediated by its historical, cultural and linguistic 'location' (Merleau-Ponty 2002, p. 71). Indeed, 'primordial contact' with the perceptual world is not a matter of 'immediacy' in the sense of an unmediated 'absolute proximity' to things that would be equivalent to fully fusing or coinciding with them (Merleau-Ponty 1968, pp. 122ff). I shall return to this below.

I shall return also to Merleau-Ponty's view that reflection should be mindful not only of its historical and linguistic location but mindful as well of how it is situated relative to the 'perceptual faith' that is the experience of 'inherence' in a world 'that is *more than* the correlative of my own vision, such that it imposes my vision on me as a continuation of its own sovereign existence' (Merleau-Ponty 1968, p. 131, emphasis added). Always already renewed within primordial perception, this 'faith' is badly served by the deployment of philosophical tools designed to reconstruct it as certain knowledge, as a shield against radical scepticism. Philosophy that is 'critical' in the Kantian sense, for example, shares the sceptic's dissatisfaction with the non-demonstrable status of our inherence within the world, and so attempts to 'undo our natural bond with the world in order to remake it' by portraying the constituting of intentional objects by a transcendental subject (Merleau-Ponty 1968, p. 32). So Merleau-Ponty rejects the picture of the world as product of the synthesizing subject, and Husserl's phenomenological method insofar as that reduces the world to objects correlated to subjects within intentional consciousness (e.g., Merleau-Ponty 2002, pp. xii–xvi). Such a constructed world is not the primordial perceptual world. It is the latter world, especially as glossed in terms of the notion of 'flesh' that I want to equate with the natural world. This equation is an act of reflection, a conceptual move, of course, rather than something given in primordial experience, but it is a move with the aim of clarifying a useful sense of alienation from nature, rather than that of transforming the perceptual world into a secure, certain foundational home.

Merleau-Ponty's notion of flesh will point us in the direction of the idea of estrangement as inadequate participation. Before proceeding to consider that notion we should consider some more features of his better-known account of perception and the perceptual world in his book *Phenomenology of Perception*. We should do this not only to be better placed to understand the flesh, but because some of these features seem to confirm the suspicion that phenomenological approaches require careful handling if they are to be more than anthropocentric construction tools.

200   Estrangement from the natural world

6.7   The perceptual world

The perceptual world, the world as revealed to primordial perception, is a holistic world of elements internally related to one another and to ourselves. Merleau-Ponty rejects the empiricist account of perception as built up out of atomic sensations such that perception of things involves the combination of distinct qualities 'observed' to accompany each other. According to that account, my perception of my carpet is a matter of my awareness of various distinct qualities – a shape, a light green colour and, if I touch it, a fairly smooth texture – that happen to appear together. The shape, colour and texture are only contingently and externally related to each other and to me. My perception is explained in terms of a causal process resulting in the sensory qualities appearing as sensations in my experience when I am suitably located relative to the carpet under normal light conditions, and so on.

Contrary to this, for Merleau-Ponty, primordial perception is always of things against a background, as part of a field of things within which they are internally and not merely externally (e.g., causally) related to each other and to oneself. This goes for the particular qualities of things too. My initial perception of the carpet is not of various qualities (an oblong shape, shade of green, smooth texture) that then happen to combine into a familiar collection. They modify each other and appear in the ways they do in virtue of being qualities of this carpet.[12] Moreover, my perception of my carpet is of it against a background and as part of a wider meaningful field: it is on top of, and partially covers, another darker green carpet that in turn covers the whole floor of the room. It is really more of a rug then and is itself partially covered by a small, low brown table and an armchair. The perceived shape and colour of the smaller carpet or rug present themselves in the ways they do in virtue of relations to the other items in the room (it is smaller, underneath, on top of; its green is lighter than that of the larger carpet and in contrast to the brown of the table and so on). Its place in relation to my projects is also part of my perception, and not something entirely additional to, or 'after the fact' of, my primordial awareness. The light green rug shows up in the way that it does in virtue of its place in a field of practical relational meaning: the contrast between the lighter smoother rug and the darker, more wiry carpet pleases me; the rug covers a worn patch on the carpet and was a gift, and so on. Primordial perception is not a passive taking in of information or reception of stimuli, but of involvement with things that

---

[12] Merleau-Ponty's example is of a woolly red carpet, the specific redness of which would not be what it is without the specific woolliness and vice versa (Merleau-Ponty 2002, p. 5).

The perceptual world 201

appear in the ways they do in light of their role in our practical affairs. My primordial perception of my rug is not of something I simply contemplate, or whose presence I *first* register and whose significance I *then* come to a view about. I perceive it straightaway as something I am doing things with and that does things for me.

This then is an account of perception that emphasizes it as a matter of praxis, of *lived* practical engagement within the primordial world. Merleau-Ponty refers to the traditional alternative to empiricism as 'intellectualism' (Merleau-Ponty 2002, e.g., pp. 30ff). This also emphasizes the active nature of perception but assigns it to intellectual acts of judgement that impose unity on otherwise distinct sensations. Although this emphasis on perception as active marks an improvement on empiricism, intellectualism remains committed to the empiricist idea of atomic sensations as the building blocks of perception. For Merleau-Ponty, primordial perception is not of atomic sensations, and the unity of perceived things and the primordial world is not imposed by judgement. Again, the primordial world is not constituted by thought. Perception does not always involve judgement and for Merleau-Ponty, as far as our primordial experience is concerned, judgement is secondary. In this respect, again, primordial perception is not primarily a cognitive affair.

Moreover, in being internally related to our practical engagement with(in) it, the primordial world is the world as revealed to *embodied* perception. Merleau-Ponty's phenomenology is distinctive in this emphasis on embodied perception. The perceptual world is an embodied world, and his later notion of flesh is in a way the further radicalization of the sense of our embodiment, at least in inspiring a focus on our presence within a wider more than human world of embodiment. I return to this shortly. But even without that further step, primordial perception cannot take the form of an external surveillance from a perspective cut off from the world in the manner of a disembodied mind. In that respect what is *my world* cannot be foreign to me (cf. James 2007, p. 505). We might say here also that things in the primordial world cannot be the 'mere things' encountered in what Honneth calls reified praxis. These latter and the praxis in which they show up must be something of a departure from the perceptual world, as the significance-rich context of an always already ongoing primordial life as one of *engagement*. The stance of observational 'detachment' that Honneth associates with reification seems *disembodied* in the sense of inhabiting a perspective distanced from that of primordial embodied perception. The reifying stance appears as if stuck in a position brought about by a reversal of the bracketing process required to focus on primordial perception. But once the reflective stance and its deliverances are bracketed then one is not simply 'in' the perceptual world,

202   Estrangement from the natural world

alongside a collection of objects primarily there to be surveyed; one *has* a perceptual world always already related to the body as a sphere of practical engagements.

6.8   Embodied coping

Clearly then the notion of body here is not that of body as scientific object. The primordial world is centred on the 'lived body', and one does not posit the existence of one's *lived* body in an act of reflective thought (for example, as the mechanism that turns causal input from the external world into sensations). In this sense one's lived body is pre-theoretically given and given as always already entangled with the perceptual world. Primordial perception is inescapably lived bodily perception. It should be clear also that this is not a matter of metaphysical materialism (as in 'I am a material body rather than an immaterial mind'). That metaphysical commitment (or any metaphysical commitment) is no more given in primordial experience than is the scientific model of the body. Like the latter, a metaphysical materialist understanding might be more or less useful given particular purposes but both are products of theoretical reflection rather than features of lived primordial perception. If the lived body is not the body as scientific or metaphysical object, what is it? In *Phenomenology of Perception* Merleau-Ponty characterizes it as that through which 'I am at grips with the world' (Merleau-Ponty 2002, p. 353). David Cerbone usefully summarizes Merleau-Ponty's claim like this:

According to Merleau-Ponty, the world is manifest in experience in accordance with our bodily structure and skills: things are manifest as near or far, here or there, in reach or out of reach, above or below, available or unavailable, usable or unusable, inviting or repulsive, and so on in relation to our ways of inhabiting the world, and such inhabitation is always bodily in nature. Things are not encountered primarily in terms of a detached gaze, as if our main relation to the world were one of staring; on the contrary, things are manifest, arrayed before and around us, in relation to our bodily abilities, our many ways of getting a *grip* on the things we encounter. I use the word 'grip' here both literally and figuratively, as when I grip the coffee cup, hammer, steering wheel, etc., in my hands (literal) and when I 'get a grip' on things and situations, putting things in order, getting things under control, and optimizing my perceptual access (figurative). The latter, more figurative, kind of grip involves myriad bodily skills. (Cerbone 2008, pp. 128–9, emphasis in original)

If one wants to speak of knowledge in this context then it is more a matter of 'I can' than 'I think' (Merleau-Ponty 2002, e.g., pp. 177, 366): one can get around in the world – one *copes*.[13] One does this, not by staring

---

[13] See Taylor (2004) for illuminating discussion of this point.

Embodied coping 203

at it from a detached point of view; one gets to grips with it. As Cerbone puts it, 'to perceive, to be embodied, to be "at grips with the world", are not three separate or separable notions for Merleau-Ponty, but are three overlapping, interconnected, internally related aspects of our existence' (Cerbone 2008, p. 129).

The lived perceptual world of embodied coping is the inescapable 'background' to the more 'conceptually minded' orientation of reflective knowledge. Again, however, it is not an indubitable epistemic foundation from which to deduce other things as certain. As Richard Dreyfus has emphasized, the relationship or movement between the primordial perceptual world of embodied coping and conceptually mindful reflection is meant to be a 'horizontal' one, not a 'vertical ascent from epistemic ground-floor to upper-storey' (Dreyfus 2007, pp. 376–7). Nor is it that primordial coping and conceptual mindedness are utterly divorced from one another, or that in thinking of one as inescapable the other becomes a dispensable optional extra. To avoid foundational metaphors and think instead in terms of horizontal, 'same level' rather than vertical or hierarchical relations, we should avoid fixing the status of either as inescapably in the background in a way that implies the other is inescapably in the foreground. We might think of this as a matter of where along the horizontal line between the two we place the bracket that puts one side in the foreground and the other in the background. Is it right up against the reflective side leaving the focus on the primordial, or at the other end to bracket the primordial, leaving the field to reflection? Presumably it depends on what we are up to. The point is that there is no need to think that either side should or could have total priority over the other or permanent background or foreground status. Nor indeed is it necessary to think that either side could ever be *entirely* bracketed or left behind, even temporarily, thereby leaving the field entirely to the other.[14]

We should expect the pragmatist requirement to be comfortable with matters of degree to apply here too: reflection never completely leaves behind the lived body and primordial perception is never completely removed from reflection (clearly not when it is reflection guiding the bracketing to bring the primordial into foreground focus). So if we agree that absorbed embodied coping is an 'inescapable background' to our

---

[14] As Merleau-Ponty says, where phenomenological 'reduction' refers to the bracketing of common sense explanations of things and scientific and philosophical theories about them in order to focus on the primordial world, the first thing one discovers is the impossibility of a complete reduction (Merleau-Ponty 2002, p. xv). In Eric Matthews' words, phenomenological methodology cannot 'fully recreate' the perspective 'of a child who has learnt nothing, can take nothing for granted, and so confronts the world directly and naively in wonder' (Matthews 2002, p. 34).

204 Estrangement from the natural world

reflective life, in that we always already have a primordial perceptual world, this does not commit us to denying that reflection is an inescapable background to our absorbed coping, in that we are always ready to be conceptually minded about what it is we are coping with and how we are coping with it. Again, we are not taking primordiality to be a matter of priority, whether temporal or conceptual.

6.9 Perceptual world as landscape

But there is a problem for us here. I mentioned earlier the worry that a phenomenological approach will turn out to be an anthropocentric instrumental construction tool, precisely because it concerns the world with which we are always already engaged. The primordial world of Merleau-Ponty's *Phenomenology of Perception* is centred on our lived bodies. The world that we have a grip on through primordial perception is the world *we have a grip on*. It is 'our world': the realm of the 'I can' in the sense of a world we know how to use; a holistic world centred on ourselves and our practical concerns. This suggests an anthropocentric reduction of the natural world to humanized landscape. The suspicion seems further confirmed when we consider that another important feature of primordial perception for Merleau-Ponty is its character of 'generality' or 'anonymity', such that it can often seem better to say 'one perceives', rather than 'I perceive':

> I cannot say that I see the blue of the sky in the sense in which I say I understand a book or have decided to devote my life to mathematics ... Every time I experience a sensation, I feel that it concerns not my own being, the one for which I am responsible and for which I make decisions, but another self, which has already sided with the world, which is already open to certain of its aspects and synchronised with them. (Merleau-Ponty 2002, pp. 215–16)

References to 'another self' (as opposed to the one for which I am personally responsible) might suggest an intersubjective self, and phrases like 'one sees' and 'one can' might suggest a world correlated to 'our' vision and practical engagements, such that the perceptual world remains fundamentally *ours* as an anthropocentrically oriented humanized world of things for us.[15]

---

[15] Another problem here is that Merleau-Ponty's account of 'anonymous' embodied perception smuggles in and universalizes hetero-normative and racially specific assumptions regarding embodied experience (see for example, Young (1989) and Fanon (2008)). I shall not discuss this issue here other than to say that the conception of estrangement I am developing through an appropriation of Merleau-Ponty's ideas has a recognitional component that avoids this problem, and is part of an overall account of alienation that

Perceptual world as landscape 205

That said, there is *some* place for nonhuman otherness within this account of primordial perception. For example, we can be aware of something's being open to an uncompletable perceptual exploration that is a matter of its 'brute presence' irreducible to how it does or could appear to us.[16] As Simon James puts it, this 'ungraspable depth' of things 'for its part intimates, as a horizon, the presence of a single wider world' (James 2007, p. 507). Indeed, Merleau-Ponty refers to this wider world as the 'nature [that] constitutes a nonhuman presence in the background of our daily lives' (Merleau-Ponty 2002, p. 382). This includes the nonhuman aspect of otherwise highly humanized things around us as well as the nonhuman world (James 2007, pp. 507f). Insofar as it encompasses the more than human dimension of things it *must* be in the background of daily lives, lived within a world centred on the practical significance things *are designed* to have. The element of nonhuman otherness of the objects around us in daily life discloses itself only to a 'metaphysical and disinterested attention', Merleau-Ponty says in *Phenomenology of Perception*, and is particularly difficult to perceive within mass-produced objects.[17] The 'nonhuman element' of such things around us thus seems evident only if we bracket our absorption in the (landscaping) projects they are designed to enable. But the 'metaphysical and disinterested' attitude this requires seems somewhat distanced from the primordial world of embodied coping. On the other hand, this account does allow us to claim that the 'nonhuman element' is perceptible more readily in the case of nonhuman, non-artefactual objects, whose otherness has not been qualified by transformative action and instrumental interpretation. Items not fashioned by humans to serve some human interest unsurprisingly tend to show up in primordial perception as having a reality less wrapped up with anthropocentric utility. Thus James claims that such 'independent' reality can be perceived primordially, rather than indirectly inferred, and may come 'in all manner of ways – in the strange gaze of a wild animal, perhaps, or in the stark indifference of the desert, or in the "mysterious presence of surrounding things" that so captivated Wordsworth' (James 2007, p. 511).

So the account of primordial perception in *Phenomenology of Perception* does not impose a blanket anthropocentrism that blots out nonhuman otherness altogether. But it does have a general anthropocentric thrust that is problematic for our account of estrangement from the natural world, where the natural world is to be the primordial perceptual world and yet encompass both humanized landscape and the nonhuman.

---

further reinforces the importance of recognizing difference. See for example Chapter 3, section 3.16.

[16] Merleau-Ponty (2002, pp. 370ff); see also James (2007, pp. 506ff).

[17] Merleau-Ponty (2002, p. 376); James (2007, pp. 508f).

Perception of the nonhuman turns out to be either 'disinterested' in the case of the remaining nonhuman element within landscaped things, and so rather removed from the primordial – or a matter of encountering relatively non-landscaped or wild – things. But the latter kind of primordial experience seems to fall under the heading of estrangement from nonhuman nature, which we don't want to overcome entirely. Being struck by the otherness of things lying markedly outside the holistic network of things centred on our interests (hence their 'strangeness', 'mysteriousness' and 'stark indifference') is not a type of *misperception* or *inadequate* participation in the primordial perceptual world.

In terms of alienation from nature then, the *Phenomenology of Perception* account seems useful primarily as another possible way of filling out estrangement from the landscape, as a lack of grip on one's surroundings, a lack of meaningful place to inhabit and get around in as a living body subject; or as something akin to a breakdown in the practice of place or to reification in Honneth's sense. Such estrangement might be overcome in the same way or breath as the latter, by achieving a more lively engaged praxis with respect to the people and landscaped things around us; a *delight* in their presence, nature and employment as entangled with one's life projects and pleasures and those of other persons (rather than the mere registering of their presence and utility). In addition to this, but very much secondary to it, the account provides some possible phenomenological gloss to estrangement from nonhuman nature as primordial encounter with relatively landscape-independent things.

6.10   The flesh

But what of estrangement from a natural world understood to encompass both landscape and nonhuman nature? It is difficult to see how to unpack this in terms of the picture provided in *Phenomenology of Perception*. This is where the flesh comes in. As I have mentioned, the notion of flesh is difficult to interpret, not least because Merleau-Ponty's main presentation of it is in the unfinished and posthumously published *The Visible and The Invisible*. It is not my intention here to attempt a full analysis of the notion or enter into the scholarly debate about its correct interpretation and place in the development of Merleau-Ponty's thought or of phenomenology more generally. I am approaching it with the aim of clarifying 'estrangement from the natural world' as a tool for critical environmental philosophy. In doing this I shall follow the thrust of recent *eco*-phenomenological interpretations of Merleau-Ponty's later thought.[18]

---

[18] See note 10 above.

The flesh

The move in Merleau-Ponty's work to the notion of flesh has been interpreted as one to a less anthropocentric position that portrays a more intimate relation between perceiver and perceived, a more radical transcendence of the subject/object dichotomy, and to a more definitely non-anthropocentric atmosphere of anonymity.[19] Lived embodiment remains central to this account of perception, which is said to involve what Kenneth Liberman (2007) calls 'reciprocal intercorporeality',[20] a 'brute contact' that is a primordial bodily contact. The flesh as '[p]rimordial nature is non-constructed, non-instituted ... [it] is what has a sense without this sense being posited by thought',[21] and this primordial nature 'in every respect baffles reflection'. It is an 'ever present phantom' resisting capture by rationalist categories and constructions (or definable in relation to the limitation of their reach as in the Kantian noumenal). But it is not imperceptible to the body (Liberman 2007, p. 44). This 'baffling of reflection' and 'resistance to capture by rationalist categories and constructions' hardly helps in the articulation of clear philosophical statements, of course. It is as if the bracket is pressed up as far as it will go against reflection in a determined attempt to leave the field as open as possible to the primordial.

The 'flesh' is difficult to interpret then, but it at least refers to the 'intertwining' of perceiver and perceived within primordial perception. As such it is neither subject nor object, nor substance, nor 'weird life-force posited as running through all things', and certainly not simply the stuff 'lying between the bone and skin'.[22] We saw above that for the earlier Merleau-Ponty, the holism of the primordial perceptual world was a matter of the internal relations holding between perceived objects and centred on the perceiving embodied subject. Within this picture subjects and objects are in an internal (hyphenated subject-object) relation, rather than a *slashed* fully dichotomized (subject/object) relation. Isis

---

[19] Although such writers, for example, Brook (2005), James (2007), Liberman (2007) and Toadvine (2009), also stress that the seeds of the later position were established in *Phenomenology of Perception*. See also Merleau-Ponty (1968, p. 142).

[20] In Lefort's translation of *The Visible* the term is 'intercorporeity'.

[21] Liberman is quoting here from Merleau-Ponty's *In Praise of Philosophy and Other Essays* (Liberman 2007, p. 40).

[22] See Brook (2005, pp. 356f). Merleau-Ponty suggests we think of flesh as an 'element' of the 'earth' (like air, fire, water) rather than a substance (like matter or 'mental stuff') (Merleau-Ponty 1968, p. 139). 'Earth' is the 'ground of being'; that which makes the subject-object possible, but which is not itself either subject or object (Brook 2005). Although frequently referred to by eco-phenomenological commentators, I mention the notions of element and earth here just to set them aside: I am not going to explore them here or compare Merleau-Ponty's use of these terms to that of other phenomenologists, such as Heidegger and Arendt. They seem too much like an attempt to fix in place a secure foundational ontology.

208   Estrangement from the natural world

Brook explains that, whereas for the earlier Merleau-Ponty the hyphenated subject-object was conjoined as the holding and the held (or, as it
was put earlier, the gripping and the gripped) within experience, in the
later position they are conjoined in a more intimate way as 'necessarily
intertwined' (Brook 2005, pp. 356f).[23]

The flesh then involves a closer 'kinship' between perceiver and perceived now related as an intertwining within primordial perception. It
is this that is particularly significant for us. The central feature of perception as fleshy intertwining is denoted by terms like 'reversibility' and
'reciprocity', and explored by Merleau-Ponty through a discussion of
certain emblematic experiences. One is that of touching one hand with
the other hand: I feel my right hand touching my left hand, my left hand
being touched (Merleau-Ponty 1968, pp. 9, 133f). But then my right
hand feels touched by my left hand, which is touching my right hand, and
so on. Perception of one hand being touched flips to that of the touching
hand itself being touched. There is an oscillation of touched and touching, a reversibility within the tangible. This reversibility expresses what
may be called the 'kinship of touchability': what may touch must also be
touchable, where this is something experienced in primordial perception
without being postulated or inferred (James 2007, p. 512). In touching
I perceive myself and the touched as touchable and touching. Touching
and touched are intertwined and the flesh *is* that intertwining or 'coiling over' (Merleau-Ponty 1968, p. 146) of aspects of perception usually
assigned separately to perceiving subject and perceived object.

On this view, reciprocity is a general feature of perception and not confined to the specific sense modality of touch: all primordial perception is
the self-reflexive coiling over of the flesh. In seeing and so being visible the
body participates in a wider visibility, the lived body being a 'fold' in the
flesh through which the perceptual world reveals itself (Merleau-Ponty
1968, pp. 146, 152). There seems to be a kind of agency involved in this
reciprocal fleshy intertwining of perception that is more than just my (or
our) own. Hence Merleau-Ponty's comment that the world 'imposes its
vision upon me as a continuation of its own sovereign existence'.

6.11   Estrangement from the flesh

The brief and compressed description of Merleau-Ponty's notion of flesh
I am providing here is deliberately tailored to the task at hand. Rather

---

[23] In the working notes accompanying the posthumous *Visible*, Merleau-Ponty (1968,
p. 200) states that his position in *Phenomenology* remained problematic because it still
implied a distinction between 'consciousness' and object as its point of departure for the
exploration of primordial perception.

Estrangement from the flesh

than dwell further on the notion independently, I want now to press on with that task and consider how we might understand the idea of estrangement from the natural world in its terms. What happens if we take 'overall nature' to be the flesh? What is estrangement from the flesh?

As perceiving beings we must be always already in the flesh, where this is a matter of participation in a relation, and not simply a matter of taking in information. The flesh is the primordial intertwining of perceiver and perceived, a relation involving kinship and reciprocity. My claim is that we can think of the estrangement as a less than fully adequate participation in this inescapable relation. But what is (in)adequate participation; what is the criterion of adequacy here? I pointed out earlier that this also must be tailored to the task at hand: the normative content expressed in the criterion of (in)adequate participation must also be coloured by the environmental critique, so as to link the critique with the conception of estrangement. This allows us to see the condemned domineering instrumentalization of nature as *a matter of estrangement from the natural world*.

We should note firstly that the flesh account suggests a view of perceptual adequacy in terms of retaining an awareness of our inherence within a wider more than human primordial world. This is not without environmental significance. Thus, although it is not reducible to them, we can refer here to cognitive – including philosophical – errors as part of the picture of estrangement. For example, we might point to a weakening of 'perceptual faith' through a determined attempt to transform it into sceptic-proof certainty, and a resulting tendency to idealism and ultimately to the view that we can be on meaningful terms only with what we ourselves 'construct'.[24] Relatedly, we might point to a reflective focus on situatedness only in historical and linguistic terms, which then ignores or dismisses our primordial situatedness in a wider world.

But the flesh account also lets us talk of more emphatically praxis-oriented matters that bring together the environmental critique and the question of the (in)adequacy of our participation within the natural world. Thus we might think of 'adequate participation' as a praxis of relative openness to the kinship and reciprocity of the more than human flesh. And so it is a praxis relatively free from (or, to borrow from Honneth, 'undistorted' by) a breakdown in this kinship and reciprocity. This means that the adequate participation is a praxis relatively free of obsession with virtual realities and abstract models of reality, of self-regarding egoism and instrumentalism, and of misrecognition of the more than human dimensions of the world. These then are the interrelated features of *inadequate* participation. In the rest of this chapter I shall

---

[24] Compare the discussion of constructionism in Chapters 1 and 2.

210   Estrangement from the natural world

give more content to the idea of estrangement from the natural world by discussing these interrelated features of inadequate participation in the more than human flesh.

To avoid some possible misunderstandings here let me emphasize again that in and of itself the flesh account doesn't entail anything about *valuing* openness to reciprocity or generate any normative commitment at all in a straightforward way (Toadvine 2009, pp. 133f). It is just meant to be an account of how it is with primordial perception. It says that such perception always involves the kinship and reciprocity of the intertwining flesh. This is helpful because we are committed to the idea of our always remaining within the natural world (here understood as the primordial flesh). As perceiving beings we are always involved in reciprocal fleshy relations. Moreover, the normative aspects of this discussion in this chapter intended to unpack the estrangement as *inadequate* participation are consistent with the flesh story; stronger than that, I would say that they resonate with it, at least as it is interpreted by *eco*-phenomenological commentators. For example, if in primordial perception we are, as Isis Brook puts it, engaged in 'an embrace of the earth'; 'where this is not just as an optional extra—a lifestyle choice—but just how it is' (Brook 2005, p. 361), then this invites us to consider the *quality* of the 'embrace', insofar as it is up to us, and to understand (overcoming) the estrangement in these terms: for example in the terms of the breakdown of kinship and reciprocity, seduction by the abstract, excessive self-regarding agency and misrecognition of the nonhuman, which I am about to discuss.

Still these normative features are not *entailed* by the flesh story as such; they are imported with the critical environmental concern: we are in an environmental crisis that is something to do with human domination of and alienation from nature. The flesh story is being used to help articulate and clarify that *given* concern as a story about estrangement from the natural world.

6.12   Breakdown in kinship and reciprocity

Primordial perception is said to be 'reciprocal' because the 'reversibility' involved reveals an agency more than our own. Not all of the activity – the work involved – appears to be done by oneself. In the context of primordial perception, the *activity* of touch appears, as James puts it, part of 'a single moment of "Tangibility"' from which oneself *as touching agent* and thing touched are abstractions (James 2007, p. 513). Thus we can say that *adequate* perception as participation 'in the flesh' involves openness to this agency that is more than our own. We might speak of a preparedness to be acted upon as much

Breakdown in kinship and reciprocity 211

as to act, such that we can be disengaged from the world in tending not to allow such reciprocity. What the openness reveals is an active body-in-environment know-how that, because of the primordial context, is again more of an 'I can' than an 'I think'. And, because the primordial context is 'fleshy', the activity involved is not confined to the isolated 'I'. According to Liberman, for example,

the body's knowing occurs in the form of the 'I can'; however, the *agency here ... equally belongs to the earth*. The landscape tells me where my legs can carry me, what is too far or too high. A breeze or lack of breeze collects me ... The earth's body engages my body, and my space is moulded, which is to say the truth of my world is presented to me. (Liberman 2007, p. 41, emphasis added)[25]

Clearly, the point cannot be that the 'agency that is more than our own' is *rational* agency, as if the fleshy reciprocity of primordial perception was somehow a matter of a contract between such agents, the terms of which we might honour less than strictly. Rather, for example, having designated ourselves as the only source of agency in town – a rational agency to be exercised against a backdrop held to be inert except for merely mechanical causality – we might find ourselves attending to everything else *only* as a collection of objects to be 'surveyed' and dominated: mere things entirely and properly subservient to our purposes.[26]

It is useful here to consider again Evernden's account of our status as 'natural aliens'.[27] We have seen that he explains our natural alien status partly in terms of evolutionary biology: as members of a neotenic species we do not mature into a form fitted to any specific ecological niche. This doesn't place us 'outside nature', but as ecologically 'placeless' we do have to think up and act out our own place in the world. I have mentioned also that Evernden is influenced by Merleau-Ponty (and Heidegger): the environmental crisis consists in a 'Cartesian' view of nonhuman nature

---

[25] Liberman is not using 'landscape' in our particular sense here. Also it is not clear whether by 'earth' he means the 'ground of being' of which the flesh is an 'element', or the natural world in our sense. For the purposes of this account of estrangement from the natural world I am equating the natural world with the primordial more than human fleshy world, rather than with some further thing ('earth') that is taken to be its ground. See note 22.

[26] For discussion of the 'backgrounding' of nonhuman agency see, for example, Evernden (1993) and Jane Bennett's (2010) employment of Latour's category of 'actant' (of which rational agency is a subset) as part of her theory of 'vital materiality', which is intended to recognize the 'active participation in events of nonhuman bodies and forces'. Plumwood discusses the traditional understanding of agency as a 'stuck elevator concept': the traditional strong association of agency with rational self-consciousness serves to background the active contribution of nonhuman entities and processes in the production of our surroundings (Plumwood 2006, pp. 116, 124). See Chapter 1, section 1.13.

[27] See Chapter 1, section 1.6.

212 Estrangement from the natural world

as a collection of inert manipulable objects and a tendency to take this picture 'inauthentically' as the unquestionable truth.

Evernden also discusses how our tool-making propensities and consequent exoticism are of a piece with our natural alien status.

A person with a tool is capable of a kind of behaviour which was formerly difficult or impossible ... The consequences of technology are subtle but extensive, and one such consequence is that humans cannot evolve *with* an ecosystem anywhere. With every technological change we instantly mutate into a new – and for the ecosystem, an exotic – kind of creature. (Evernden 1993, p. 109, emphasis in original)

This suggests that some technology and associated attitudes might express and reinforce a condition of alienation from nature. For example, Evernden cites some of Susan Sontag's remarks on photography: 'through photographs the world becomes a series of unrelated, freestanding particles'; 'the camera makes reality atomic, manageable and opaque'; 'the habit of photographic seeing – of looking at reality as an array of potential photographs –*creates estrangement from, rather than union with, nature*' (Sontag quoted by Evernden 1993, p. 87, emphasis added). He considers these remarks in relation to 'objectification' – the stripping of 'subject-ness, of any vestige of kinship' – involved in the stare of a predator at its prey. This is a very temporary stance for nonhuman (social) predators (Evernden 1993, pp. 90ff). We however have been remarkably successful in 'prolonging our existence in a state of objectivity' (Evernden 1993, p. 94), a state in which we regard objects 'neutrally', as 'things' from which we are 'totally apart', and towards which we have no obligation (Evernden 1993, p. 88). Thus photographic technology might be said to reinforce a certain observational-distanced stance towards nature that sees it as separate.[28] And given that we, along with our thought and whatever technological control and distancing apparatus it furnishes us with, remain entirely within nature, such tendencies can seem to involve a kind of mistake, or rather a cluster of mutually reinforcing 'errors', perhaps revolving around a core of Cartesian assumptions, that deserves the label 'alienation from nature'.

Evernden does not really analyse the ideas of 'alienation' and 'alienation from nature', however, beyond the evolutionary neoteny account that presumably makes our natural alien status permanent whether or not we come to live out that status better. I have argued that, in some of its senses, alienation from nature is something we should live with rather than seek to overcome entirely. But here I am locating it, as estrangement

---

[28] Evernden does allow that not every exercise of photographic art might be objectifying in this way.

Seduction by the abstract 213

from the natural world *as flesh*, in terms of features more 'primordial' than those determined by evolutionary biology. This provides a sense of alienation from nature as something we might and ought to overcome, at least to some extent. As primordial reciprocity, the flesh is inescapable, but living out the Cartesian dream as 'masters of objects', however technologically enabled, appears as an *inadequate* participation in primordial reciprocity that is not inevitable. A natural alien in Evernden's sense does not have to accept estrangement from the natural world in our present sense.

Again, this is not simply a matter of narrowly cognitive errors, such as believing too many Cartesian propositions, but of habitual attitudes and praxis. The central feature of estrangement from nature as flesh as inadequate participation is lack of openness to a wider reciprocity. This is exemplified in the overwriting of primordial perceptual kinship by the much more circumscribed kinship holding between fellow rational agents whose agency is exercised *upon* (mere) things. If this is right then presumably we *can* think of it as further exemplified and intensified by the habitual praxis associated with highly technological landscapes excessively focused on abstract realms, such as those discussed by David Abram.

6.13   Seduction by the abstract

Abram mentions various abstract 'bodiless worlds' vying for our attention, with those enabled by the digital revolution only the latest on a list that includes the realms of 'pure mathematical truths' and Platonic forms, various kinds of religious afterlife, the 'supersmall' and 'ultravast' worlds of quantum and cosmological physics and the microbiological realm of genetics. He argues that such cognitively and technologically accessible realms have been given primacy over (as more real, important, or simply more interesting than) the primordial world in which we are 'bodily immersed' (Abram 2007, pp. 152ff).[29] Of course, such focus away from the world of primordial embodiment does not actually remove us from it (Abram 2007, p. 162). It is clear also that seduction by the

---

[29] Although Abram doesn't use the terminology of alienation or estrangement, in his well-known book *The Spell of the Sensuous* (1996) he discusses at length various aspects and sources of our 'distance' from the more-than-human primordial fleshy perceptual world. One interesting theme of the book is the development of written languages from pictographic and ideographic representations through the Semitic aleph-beth, to the Greek alphabet as one of the 'progressive abstraction of linguistic meaning' to the point where '[h]uman utterances are now elicited, directly, by human made signs; *the larger, more-than-human life-world is no longer a part of the semiotic, no longer a necessary part of the system*' (Abram 1996, p. 101, emphasis in original). See Abram (1996, chs. 3–5).

214   Estrangement from the natural world

abstract should not be equated with a '*deadened*' lack of engagement with anything: people can be passionately attached to their virtual and other abstract pursuits. Thus powerful forces distract us from the primordial fleshy world:

> We turn back to our computer screen, or toward the next page of our latest book on how to survive in the digital economy ... we dial our colleagues on the cell phone to ask if they can join us at next week's conference on the most recent gene-splicing techniques; or perhaps we plunge our attention back into our meditations on the transcendental unity hidden behind the experienced world. It never occurs to us that the most profound unity may reside in the very depths of the experienced world itself, in the unfolding web of interdependent relations that ceaselessly draws the apparently disparate presences of the sensuous cosmos, ourselves included, into subtle communion with one another. (Abram 2007, pp. 162–3)

Insofar as such attachments take attention away from our fleshy embodied existence, as if to replace it, they risk something of ethical importance. At least this is so given that ethical action has a primordial location within the flesh, with moral rules and principles being more or less useful abstractions from the concrete primordial presence of particular others – of 'creative agencies' other than one's own – some, but not all, of which are fellow humans (Abram 2007, pp. 166ff). Flight from this context into the company only of the abstract and virtual appears then as a flight from the primordial context of ethics as 'immediately felt and compelling' (Abram 2007, p. 168). Here the account of estrangement under development joins with the idea of inadequate primordial recognition of persons central to Honneth's account of reification. But it also goes beyond it by including the more-than-human. Indeed, it is a way of bringing that concern with reification as misrecognition together with the concern to avoid overcoming estrangement from the nonhuman. I return to recognitional matters below.

Thus adequate participation in the flesh is not just a question of, say, agreeing with Hegel that abstract morality requires concrete ethical specification through the institutions of objective spirit. Nor is it simply a matter of a Marxian overcoming of the opposition between valorized intellectual labour and degraded manual labour. Those critical perspectives are focused on concrete freedom, interpersonal recognition and the realization of the exclusively *human* species being. More to the point is Dewey's pragmatist critique of the separation of abstract intellectualism from practical activity motivated by the quest for certainty, a quest for a perfect intellectual security unhelpfully divorced from practical problems. As I argued in Chapter 2, there is no need to confine 'practical

Seduction by the abstract

problems' to those visible from a purely anthropocentric instrumentalist perspective. Here the problem is environmental and the critical perspective focused on domination as connected to estrangement from the natural world. If the estrangement is understood as inadequate participation, a praxis not open to the kinship and reciprocity of the fleshy more than human world, then seduction by the abstract, in the sense of a tendency to inhabit 'disembodied realms' treated as superior to that world, is part of this problem, an aspect of this estrangement.

It is tempting to refer here to 'eco-psychological' problems such as Nature Deficit Disorder (NDD). In the Introduction I mentioned that a range of human problems, including depression and diabetes, has been blamed on NDD: a lack of interaction with nature. And at first glance it does seem to chime with the idea of estrangement as the inadequate participation in a wider world of primordial embodiment threatened by too much time online or passively consuming daytime television. But we need to be careful here for a number of reasons. First, we cannot simply identify inadequate participation in the flesh with NDD because the 'nature' of which there is said to be a deficit is at least relatively *non-human* nature, in the guise of woodland, parks and gardens, for example. But we are taking nature as flesh to be the overall natural world encompassing the humanized world (including the great indoors) as well as the nonhuman.

Second, insofar as the focus of overcoming NDD is on encountering nonhuman nature as a component of human well-being, or as a 'cure' for ailments caused by 'modern life', it cannot be identified without qualification with overcoming estrangement from nature as flesh. For example, Abram also refers to children placed for long periods in front of TV and computer screens, which, for him, distracts from the 'early, felt layer of solidarity with other bodies and with the bodily Earth that provides both the seeds and the soil necessary for any more mature sense of ethics' (Abram 2007, p. 169). This again is the point about seduction by the abstract threatening something of ethical significance. But notice that it is a different story to the NDD story, as a story focused unqualifiedly on *human* well-being. Abram holds up excessive immersion in a digital world as an obstacle to the development of an ethical sensibility appropriate to what we are calling adequate participation in the *more than human* flesh, rather than one focused on maximizing human well-being. Certainly we are thinking of a more adequate participation as one open to reciprocity and so prepared to accommodate, rather than completely dominate, its surroundings, including nonhuman surroundings. For example, consider gardening, or landscaping more generally, as a practice that seeks to 'work with' the tendencies of growth and activity of the nonhuman

216   Estrangement from the natural world

organisms and materials involved, as opposed to a practice that seeks to impose a pre-ordained order.[30] Perhaps this more adequate praxis has a payoff in human well-being understood in terms of the healthy functioning of the human body as biomedical object. There might also be an important payoff in terms of developing virtues required for more sustainable and environmentally just landscaping.[31] But seeking interaction with the nonhuman *only* as the means to these anthropocentric payoffs suggests an instrumental landscaping perspective at odds with adequate participation, especially given that our criterion of adequacy is coloured by the environmental critique.

6.14   Excessively self- (or human-) regarding agency

Consider also that, as we saw in the Introduction, the idea of NDD is associated with the biophilia hypothesis. It is only a lack of contact with particular aspects of the nonhuman that is a problem for human well-being: those consistent with human flourishing and that our evolutionary heritage has predisposed us to prefer (as in the savannah hypothesis, for example). This puts those we are not so 'programmed' to like at risk of the kind of misrecognition I shall discuss shortly. In and of itself, emphasizing biophilia and a lack of exposure to specially favoured nonhuman entities and features raises the question of why not give similar weight to *biophobia* – a predisposition to fear and dislike of various nonhuman entities and features in virtue of our evolutionary heritage – and 'humanize' them: remove them or modify them accordingly. Speaking on behalf of arachnophobes generally, the fantasy of removing spiders from the world and replacing them with less monstrous GMOs and nanobots designed to replicate their ecological functions has a certain appeal. But the attraction is of a purely anthropocentric instrumental kind at odds with overcoming estrangement from the natural world as inadequate participation.

Thus such adequate participation is not the same as an instrumental grasp on surroundings sufficient to achieve one's anthropocentric purposes. That is the notion of adequacy suggested more by Merleau-Ponty's earlier account of primordial perception in *Phenomenology of Perception*. One's purposes might be self-regarding and require reordering the world in accordance with them, as when I remove spiders from my living room to make it easier for me to relax. No doubt there are worse

---

[30] See, for example, Goodin (1992, pp. 50f).

[31] See, for example, di Paola's (2013) discussion of gardening as a way of addressing the moral psychological obstacles to effective coordinated environmental stewardship.

Excessively self- (or human-) regarding agency 217

forms of egoism. But when I suggest that the *in*adequate participation involves 'excessively self-regarding agency' I don't mean just *personal* egoism in the sense of individuals focused only on controlling their surroundings and manipulating others in pursuit of personal projects. There may also be a more general 'species egoism' focused only on more general human-oriented projects. For example, the redesigning and arranging of surroundings to help combat NDD and maximize forms of exposure to 'green space' held to be beneficial to well-being might be a good idea, but it is an anthropocentric instrumental, landscaping matter.[32] To take another example, when we accept principles of justice to regulate our pursuit of projects where they impact those of others, this is usually presented as the securing of shared but specifically human interests. The just securing of human interests is a weighty matter of course, one discussed in Chapter 3 in terms of overcoming reification and pernicious forms of estrangement and alienation within humanized landscapes. But adequate participation in the *more than human* flesh presumably must involve the surrender of purely *human*-regarding agency focused on manipulating the world for its own *collective* ends, as well as purely self-regarding agency as something in the way of a wider reciprocity.

Consider these remarks of Merleau-Ponty on reciprocal visibility in the flesh:

I feel myself looked at by the things, my activity is equally passivity ... not to see in the outside, as others see it, the contours of a body one inhabits, but especially to be seen by the outside, to exist within it, to emigrate into it, to be seduced, captivated, alienated by the phantom, so that the seer and the visible reciprocate one another and we no longer know which sees and which is seen. It is this Visibility, this generality of the Sensible in itself, this anonymity innate to Myself that we have previously called flesh. (Merleau-Ponty 1968, p. 139)

Such talk of being 'seen by the outside', 'seduced, captured, alienated by the phantom' and so on will strike some as unappealing and unhelpfully obscure. Indeed, it is difficult to interpret very precisely. Liberman interprets it as a call for '[u]s to "emigrate" out of our narrow conjuring acts and, even at the risk of feeling "alienated" engage in reciprocal relations, so that we can come to collect the "anonymity" that is our heritage' (Liberman 2007, p. 45). 'Alienation' here seems to mean estrangement from a world 'conjured' to serve our interests and egotistical concerns, the world as ordered by us for us. This seems to capture a movement *from* a humanized world centred on ourselves and our own concerns *into*

---

[32] Not necessarily instrumental in the narrow economistic or consumerist sense, of course. See Chapter 2, section 2.12.

218 Estrangement from the natural world

a world precisely not set up by, and for the sake of, only our own agency; a world in which, although 'looked at', one is (or we are) no longer the distinct, central be-all-and-end-all, but a relatively anonymous presence within the primordial more-than-human flesh. As suggested above, the movement seems to be to a less anthropocentric sense of anonymity. We shall see in the next chapter that this movement raises problems when understood as an unqualified attempt to overcome estrangement as inadequate participation in the flesh. But it seems more than resistance to a complete seduction by the abstract; it is also surrender of a purely self or human-regarding agency that would stand in the way of a wider kinship and reciprocity.

We can put this in terms of theoretical errors by considering moral and political principles and the theoretical apparatuses behind them as more or less useful abstractions. Again, within the terms of this discussion, a way of being less useful is to lock in place an anthropocentric instrumentalism centred on the absolute sovereignty of rational agency. For example, we might side with Martha Nussbaum's rejection of the disembodied rational agency conception of 'dignity' in favour of the embodied 'animal sort of dignity' to understand what it is to do justice to nonhuman animals as well as to a range of previously excluded humans (Nussbaum 2006, e.g., pp. 133ff). But here also the exclusion is a matter of habitual thoughts, feeling and practice, not just the holding of false theories.

6.15 Misrecognition of the nonhuman

Thus we might adapt another feature of Honneth's account of reification (the fourth element of his account distinguished above) and speak of failure of recognition as an aspect of estrangement from the natural world. We are taking the natural world to be the primordial more than human fleshy perceptual world characterized by primordial kinship and reciprocity between perceived and perceiver. Against this background, a perspective on the natural world that either ignores or denigrates its more than human character, or notices it only as something manipulable for human-oriented ends, appears a perniciously anthropocentric form of participation in that world that suggests a form of injustice. In this respect it seems an *inadequate* form of participation within the natural world; one calling for the extension of recognition-discourse to nonhuman nature.

In the discussion of estrangement from nonhuman nature in Chapter 4, we saw that David Schlosberg advocates this extension as a requirement of ecological justice. It will be remembered that he draws

Misrecognition of the nonhuman 219

upon Nancy Fraser's status injury approach to misrecognition, the focus of which is on damage to the status, rather than damage to the subjectivity, of the misrecognized (Schlosberg 2007, pp. 139ff). The focus is on the sub-optimal praxis of those failing to do the recognizing, rather than psychological damage done to those not recognized.[33] Remember also that Schlosberg applies Fraser's three types of status injury to nonhuman nature: 'a general practice of cultural domination'; 'a pattern of non-recognition equivalent to rendering invisible'; 'disrespect or routine disparagement in stereotypic public and cultural representation'. Status injurious practices of these kinds may be built into our lives in various ways. Our lives would then be less than fully adequate ways of participating in the more than human world of fleshy reciprocity. We would be 'distanced' from the natural world understood in those primordial terms. For example, consider again Schlosberg's comment that,

In the causes of, and discussions surrounding, global climate change ... we see all sorts of status-injurious misrecognition – the domination of nature by extractive industries, the invisibility of nature in political planning ... and the disparaging of the natural world in discussions of the mitigation of impacts on human communities at the expense of nature. (Schlosberg 2007, p. 140)

These misrecognitions are perhaps to be expected within a culture of estrangement from a fleshy nature that includes more than the human, given that, as Abram says, this is the world we have most 'thoroughly forsaken', and 'conventionally ... construed as the most derivative and drab dimension of all – the only realm consistently vilified by our traditions' (Abram 2007, p. 166). I should perhaps rather say that such

---

[33] See Chapter 4, section 4.6; also Chapter 3, section 3.2. We need not claim that *no* nonhuman beings have subjectivity sufficient for the notion of *felt* damage to dignity, integrity, self-respect or self-realization brought by their misrecognition to have some grip. But it is wise to avoid the charge of anthropomorphism invited by references to the psychological plight of misrecognized nonhuman things *as such* (Schlosberg 2007, p. 139). By following Schlosberg in this respect we are, to that extent, distancing ourselves from Abram's animistic 'sensuous world' interpretation of the flesh as sentient through and through (Abram 1996). Abram derives from his reading of Merleau-Ponty an animist view of the whole sensuous world as a conscious presence. Various scholars have pointed out that this ignores the status of 'remarkable variant' Merleau-Ponty gives to what he calls the 'sentient sensible'. See Merleau-Ponty (1968, pp. 136–7) and, for example, Clarke (2002), Brook (2005) and Evans (2008). Everything's being sentient to some extent does not entail that everything has subjectivity of the sort that can *feel* status injurious misrecognition, of course, but the potential slide to that position is best avoided, if possible. Similarly, we are accepting that fleshy perception involves an agency that is more than our own but without thinking that this must always be a conscious purposive agency, that being the only alternative to the mechanical causal impacts of otherwise inert mere things on one another. See note 26 above.

220 Estrangement from the natural world

misrecognitions partly *constitute* a culture as a culture of estrangement from the natural world.

Drawing upon Schlosberg's extension of recognitional justice in this way indicates an important relationship between estrangement from the natural world and estrangement from nonhuman nature, my discussion of which in Chapter 4 also drew upon extending recognitional justice to the nonhuman. In the latter case, the extension of recognitional justice was a matter of *living with* some estrangement as a way of resisting the domineering reduction of nature to humanized landscape and landscaping materials. In the present case, extending recognition is wrapped up with *overcoming* estrangement from the natural world. Misrecognition of nonhuman nature is a mark of inadequate participation. One might also say that because other people and their landscapes are part of the natural world, misrecognition of them is also a mark of inadequate participation in fleshy primordial nature, a mark of estrangement from the natural world. That would be right except that with estrangement from the natural world the emphasis is on estrangement from a *wider* world that incorporates us but, crucially, goes beyond us to incorporate the more nonhuman too. This is why I said earlier that the account of estrangement here encompasses but goes beyond Honneth's account of reification. The just recognition of *nonhuman* difference is a relatively neglected topic of recognitional justice.

Misrecognition of the nonhuman is a feature of *overcoming* (or seeking to overcome) estrangement when the estrangement is from specifically nonhuman nature. That is a kind of overcoming of estrangement to be resisted. Misrecognition of nonhuman nature is a feature of *being* estranged when the estrangement is from the natural world. The overcoming of this kind of estrangement is to be encouraged. Thus we can understand that part of what it is to be estranged from the natural world is to seek to overcome, or otherwise negate, all estrangement from the nonhuman by assimilating everything to the human landscape. By the same token, living with some estrangement from the nonhuman is part of what it is to overcome (or avoid) estrangement from a natural world that both encompasses and goes beyond us. Such relations between different senses of 'alienation from nature' go to the overall argument of this book and I say more about them in the next chapter.

6.16   Difference and continuity again

They also raise again the issue of difference and continuity discussed in Chapter 4 in the context of different kinds of extensionism.[34] Some ways

---

[34] See Chapter 4, sections 4.7–10.

Difference and continuity again 221

of 'extending the moral community' out into the nonhuman are problematic (for example, some strands of deep ecology and Nussbaum's aim to 'supplant the natural with the just'). Where the emphasis is on (estrangement from) the nonhuman then difference predominates, although not to the point of an absolute dichotomy or hyper-separation. Continuity is prominent when the emphasis is on (estrangement from) the natural world. But I am understanding the continuity here in terms of our being part of the more than human primordial fleshy world. The 'kinship' and 'reciprocity' here is of the flesh and do not involve a problematic extension in the form of 'applying' human-oriented ideas in order to *impose* continuity or posit a supposed identity of human and nonhuman interests. The continuity is lived through adequate participation rather than an imposition or application that would be features of inadequate participation.[35] So status injurious misrecognition of nonhuman nature can be associated with both estrangement from the natural world (to be overcome) and the overcoming of estrangement from nonhuman nature (to be resisted). Adequate participation in the flesh requires refraining from imposing continuity even though being in the flesh 'alongside' the nonhuman, as it were, is to be in a primordial relation of kinship and reciprocity with it.

My claim then is that estrangement from the natural world can be understood as a way of expressing critical environmental concerns by viewing nature in that sense as the more than human fleshy world, where the flesh is a primordial relation that we can participate in more or less adequately. The idea of our estrangement here marks the possibility of less than fully adequate participation on our part. This has various interrelated aspects including: a relative lack of openness to the kinship and reciprocity involved (by inhabiting a perspective that is more like the surveyor of objects); a tendency to obsessive focus on abstract 'bodiless' realms; an excessive focus on self or human-regarding agency and on the humanized and potentially humanized world as an expression of this agency; a tendency to 'misrecognition' of the nonhuman. The absence of these would then signal a more adequate participation within nature as flesh.

Notice that the absence of these features of estrangement would not involve 'total unity' with (or within) nature or the rejection of civilization and reflective thought as such. Adequate participation in the flesh open to its kinship and reciprocity does not require total immersion within

---

[35] The same could perhaps be said about imposing continuity in an attempt to eliminate all estrangement from human landscapes out of contempt for, or disregard of, human difference. See Chapter 3, section 3.13.

222   Estrangement from the natural world

the primordial or a complete and permanent horizontal movement from conceptual mindedness to 'absorbed perceptual oneness'. In fact it cannot require any such thing; to suppose Merleau-Ponty's own understanding of flesh points to a *realizable* total unity between, or identity of, perceiver and perceived is to ignore key features of that understanding. We have already noted that for him primordial perception is not a matter of the absolute coincidence of perceiver and perceived. Despite the intimate kinship of subject-object within the Tangible, the Visible and so on, the 'coiling over' of fleshy perception always involves a division ('dehiscence') into the 'flesh of the world' (sensible object) and 'flesh of the body' (*sentient* sensible) (Merleau-Ponty 1968, p. 154). Reversibility as completed in unity can never be more than imminent. Even the touching hands can never *quite* touch themselves touching, as the perception oscillates between one hand touching the other and being touched by it (Merleau-Ponty 1968, p. 147).[36] We have also seen that the flesh might be supposed to involving a primordial recognition of *others* central to engaged ethical praxis. The fleshy perceptual world precisely is differentiated (Brook 2005, p. 361). From this point of view, 'oneness' with the world as an adequate participation within it can never be more than a matter of sharing the flesh with others, and 'overcoming estrangement' in these terms cannot require a *thoughtless* immersion, but that thought, praxis and their cultural and technological accompaniments should help maintain a more, rather than less, adequate engagement.

[36] See also, for example, Evans (2008, pp. 188f), Toadvine (2009, pp. 110ff).

7 Entailments and entanglements

7.1 Introduction

In this chapter I bring things together by discussing some of the relations between the senses of alienation from nature I have distinguished and between some of the environmental issues encompassed by them. The previous four chapters have been mostly about how the different senses capture anthropocentric and nonanthropocentric concerns in the different environmental contexts of landscape, nonhuman nature and the natural world. Occasionally I have pointed to relations between the different senses; for example, estrangement from nonhuman nature entails alienation of nonhuman nature[1] and estrangement from the natural world entails accepting some estrangement from nonhuman nature.[2] But such relations have not been the main focus. They are in this chapter where I want to show how they support the main claim of this book: despite the problems it raises talk of alienation from nature can be justified, useful and important. It can help us to think through our environmental situation when understood in a nuanced, pluralistic way involving different *interrelated* senses of alienation from nature, some of which are to be viewed positively, as something to be accepted or even encouraged, rather than avoided or overcome.

7.2 Starting in the armchair

Whichever sense of alienation from nature is taken as a starting point the others appear more or less quickly as part of the overall scene. As a way into the relational issues here, consider the idea of participatory estrangement from the natural world discussed in the previous chapter. Overcoming this entails overcoming pernicious estrangement, alienation and reification in the landscape.[3] This is unsurprising because the

---

[1] Chapter 5, section 5.1.   [2] Chapter 6, section 6.14.
[3] See Chapter 6, sections 6.3 and 6.13–14.

223

224   Entailments and entanglements

natural world encompasses landscape and that the notion of participatory estrangement takes Honneth's recognitional account of reification as a main point of departure. The connection is more vivid and concrete, however, when we consider the overcoming of such estrangement from the natural world as a single-minded unqualified personal project. That sense of estrangement draws on Merleau-Ponty's account of perception 'in the flesh', with the estrangement consisting in relative lack of openness to the primordial reciprocity involved (and such related issues as seduction by the abstract). But our environmental situation has more sides than those emphasized in that particular story. We have seen that overcoming estrangement from nature as flesh does not require a thoughtless immersion within nature. However, *taken as an unqualified personal imperative* it does apparently require that one escape the distractions, including political distractions, of highly humanized landscapes and go where they are less imposing. It seems to require that we go off to wherever seems most like the wilderness. This is very problematic. Consider the following, admittedly self-indulgent example:

Pausing while writing this to allow my attention to be absorbed into present bodily experience I am 'collected' by the mutual pressing and yielding of my body with the armchair in which I sit, and by the quiet 'writing music' emerging from the hi-fi and mingling with a swishing sound (of the washing machine a couple of rooms away) to fill the room with a sort of soft stillness. I could easily allow this fleshy envelope to lull me into dozing off. I should probably change the CD. But also present is anticipation: once it reaches the spin part of the wash-cycle the washing machine will *yell* at me through the intervening walls to do something about the faulty bearings in its guts. If we are in the flesh then this must all be in the flesh. As embodiments of human agency and intentions, however, these items – my washing machine, armchair and hi-fi – are also reminders of one's own (or humanity's) power and quest for comfort and convenience. As such they appear as vehicles of control whose tendency is to pull one back from the acquiescence or openness to reciprocity involved in a more adequate kind of participation in the flesh.

True, my armchair has been known to comfort me, my washing machine to yell at me; there is bodily engagement. But it is not all that reciprocal. Rather it tends to centre on those of my concerns and interests wrapped up with the items in question; their status as 'equipment'; my reasons for having them around in the first place: considerations always in the wings of my dealings with them, even when not the subject of conscious reflection. My armchair *had better* be comfortable (without being *too* comfortable), or I'll get rid of it. My washing machine is recalcitrant: it won't wash my clothes speedily and efficiently without making

Starting in the armchair

a big fuss. Well I'll have to have it *seen to*, or replaced, then. It might well yell at me to fix it, but my perception of its yell is hardly a matter of my openness to a presence independent of my narrowly instrumental plans for it and conception of its whole reason for being there. The yelled demand *to be fixed* is intelligible as such only against that background. What is revealed then when these things 'look at me' might not be my primordial anonymity in the flesh so much as my own plans for the world around me, as confirmed and enabled or, annoyingly, interrupted and thwarted. I seem very much to be in the position of coping more or less well in the more anthropocentric instrumental terms of Merleau-Ponty's earlier *Phenomenology of Perception*.

Insofar as this is so such appliances are presumably distractions from or obstacles to the reversibility required for what we have been thinking of as adequate participation in the primordial fleshy more than human world. This is compounded when my experience of them is coloured by an awareness of the political or power relations they embody.[4] My awareness of the armchair and washing machine as *mine* already brings the political relation of ownership to bear. And this relation is implied by the reasons for their presence that designate their role in my life and that are always at the edge of even my most primordial perception as this involves them. But so may be wider political questions. For example, as 'parcels of congealed labour', the things around me potentially raise questions of alienation, domination and exploitation within the humanized environment. They raise questions about *my* place in a structure of domination and exploitation, and so within a context of reification and multiple estrangements (from self, others, our surroundings as the product of human labour and so on) associated with alienation of labour in the Marxian sense.

Perhaps it is worse than I thought then: instead of emerging from my agency, the considerations waiting in the wings of my bodily engagements might express more the agency of other persons. Moderating whatever self-regarding agency I have in the presence of the artefacts around me might be more a matter of my subservience to the agency of other humans than of achieving any 'anonymity in the flesh', or participation in any genuine reciprocity. The thought occurs that the plans for the world reflected back by the items surrounding me are not really *my* plans at all, or not plans that are in my best interests: my 'coping' in or with this environment consists in simply acting out the 'appropriate'

---

[4] I am not referring here to ecological relations involved in the sustainability and impact of the systems of extraction, construction, distribution and energy generation required to produce, run and maintain these things, although these are important issues too, of course.

226 Entailments and entanglements

habitual behaviours the artefacts are designed to enable with 'convenience'. Once I begin to put aside the self-regarding, instrumental aspect of my engagement with the appliances of daily life, then they begin to confront me as 'alien beings' in the sense of raising the question of what on earth they are doing there. Once I consider my relation to them as a part of a wider political landscape they can seem even more like alien beings: instruments of control over me rather than enablers of my free personality.[5]

7.3   Ending in the wilderness

So I cannot take myself naively as someone coping reasonably well in humanized surroundings that embody justice and include possessions straightforwardly enabling my recognition and realization as a free person; that everything else is fine and I just need to overcome some estrangement through a more adequate participation in the primordial flesh. Attempting the latter in this environment raises doubts straightaway about that description of my situation. If I am to focus *only* on overcoming participatory estrangement from the natural world then I need an environmental context different to my present one; even though my present environment is within the natural world. The required openness to primordial kinship and reciprocity will be achieved best in places uncluttered by things that embody our quest for comfort and control and raise the uncomfortable political questions mentioned above. If my overriding goal is to achieve the most adequate participation I can in the natural world as flesh, then clearly I had better pack as few things as possible and go somewhere less humanized. That is, I should go somewhere where perceptual reciprocity is with the definitely 'more than human', with the most adequate participation involved in the reversibility afforded by the *hardly any human*, as in whatever relative wilderness I can reach.

This seems to be why there is a tendency to privilege 'wilderness experience' as 'truly revealing' and to valorize indigenous peoples as 'closer to the Earth', in this strand of eco-phenomenological literature. Liberman, for example, draws upon Merleau-Ponty's appropriation of Bergson's term 'plunging' to characterize those seeking the 'wilderness experience' as *plunging* into the world, rather than 'surveying' it as a prelude to domination (Liberman 2007, pp. 42f; see Merleau-Ponty 1968, pp. 38f). Plunging seems to be a praxis of openness to primordial kinship and reciprocity *par excellence*; one markedly free from seduction by the abstract,

---

[5] Compare the Hegelian understanding of ownership (see especially Chapter 5, section 5.6).

Ending in the wilderness

self-regarding agency and misrecognition of the nonhuman. Seekers of wilderness experience plunge in, Liberman says, to 'feel penetrated' by something 'more primordial than culture and ego', to learn from the 'resistance it offers' and the 'relinquishment of agency' it requires, 'what is the meaning of our world' (Liberman 2007, p. 42). He also argues that truly 'revealing' perception requires an 'engagement with the earth [that] exceeds the idea of "conserving nature" or the English notion of nature reserves that also underlies the American conservation movement, for in those affairs the agency remains exclusively human, and so there is no revealing' (Liberman 2007, pp. 42f).[6]

If overcoming estrangement from the natural world as flesh is my over-riding aim then I should go to the lightly humanized 'wilderness'. But then any resulting overcoming of estrangement appears as a paradox-ically *self-absorbed* isolated minority achievement; a prize to be secured by *evading* problematic forms of alienation within the humanized world, including those encompassing matters of environmental justice.[7] Clearly, overcoming estrangement from the natural world as a shared, *environmentally significant* achievement requires progress in overcoming other forms of alienation preventing a more adequate participation in the more highly humanized parts of nature as flesh. Thus, even if one does approach our environmental situation *initially* with the idea of estrangement from the natural world, this quickly brings our other ideas of alienation from nature onto the scene.

Pointing to this issue with (overcoming) participatory estrangement from the natural world does not amount to taking back that understanding of alienation from nature, of course. It can be seen as a further exercise in what Merleau-Ponty calls 'hyper-reflection', this time concerning the interplay between different sides of our situatedness: our inherence within both historical humanized nature and a wider overall nature. Neither of these calls for a permanent foundational priority over the other. Given that the idea of participatory estrangement from the natural world as flesh makes sense as a way of bringing out features of the environmental crisis, then any overcoming of pernicious forms of alienation, estrangement and reification within the humanized world shouldn't be

---

[6] Quoting these claims rather bluntly like this might suggest that Liberman sees what he calls the 'remaining untamed forests and deserts' in the US as *pure* untouched wilderness and so is guilty of reifying the products of indigenous human labour. However, the rest of his article suggests that he means (in our terms) *relative* wilderness and is aware of the philosophical and political dangers of reification.

[7] Compare Cronon's critique of the wilderness idea as 'offering the illusion that one can escape the cares and troubles' of historical landscapes and a way to 'give ourselves permission to evade responsibility for the lives we actually lead' (Cronon 1995, pp. 79f).

228 Entailments and entanglements

understood or pursued in ways that lose sight of our primordial situatedness within that wider nature.

One way to put the main point here is that to focus only on one kind of alienation from nature is to risk exchanging one lack of appreciation of situatedness for another. This applies to each of our ideas of alienation from nature. Each of them focuses on an aspect of our environmental situation consideration of which should be in play without excluding the others, at least permanently. Each does some work. For example, the idea of (overcoming) participatory estrangement from nature might seem redundant for a critical environmental philosophy given that an anti-domination perspective is expressible in terms of (endorsement of) estrangement from and alienation of nonhuman nature. But this is not the case. The overall picture would be seriously incomplete, and to that extent unhelpful, if it focused only on the otherness of the nonhuman in relation to the human and humanized, and did not capture the continuity between ourselves and the rest of nature, our inescapable entanglement with the nonhuman *within* a wider world of which we are a part. It is the aspect of our situation that consists in continuity with and within a wider more than human world that the account of estrangement from the natural world is supposed to help with.

Before considering further relations between them, it will help to remind ourselves briefly of some more of the work the different ideas of alienation from nature are supposed to do, and some of their associated environmental problems.

7.4   Ideas and issues in play

Take first the context of humanized landscape. To be concerned about reification is to be concerned about the misrecognition of human products as given things, rather than meaningful and revisable results of human labour, creativity, ingenuity or stupidity. Associated environmental problems include failure to take responsibility for human modification of surroundings (landscaping), with anthropogenic climate change a particularly pressing case of this; failure to recognize indigenous landscapes as landscapes (rather than 'pure wilderness'); and lack of consideration of relations between humans and humans and nature because the broad contours of these relations are held to be fixed by 'nature'.

Estrangement in this context encompasses matters of 'homeliness' and 'place', the environmental dimensions of the realization of free personality, the reflection of human-oriented values, interests and purposes within humanized surroundings such that we can (fail to) 'recognize ourselves' in them. We can interpret justice as at least partly about enabling

Ideas and issues in play

free personality. Landscape estrangement therefore also encompasses matters of justice; pernicious estrangement is associated with injustice, although the just recognition of human difference involves an element of acceptable, or even required, estrangement (from others and their homes). The environmental problems approachable in these ways include the phenomenon of sprawl as a degraded type of place; landscapes too unsustainable to be stable vehicles of identity; the unjust distribution of environmental goods and bads, including climate injustice; and recognitional injustice in the sense of failure to acknowledge human difference including as this is manifest in landscaping. A lack of democratic control over important landscape features can also be considered under the heading of pernicious estrangement from the landscape. Problematic alienation in the landscape context concerns unjust and coerced transfers of property and, as such, can underwrite reification and estrangement, as in the Marxian account of the relations between these. The environmental problems involved here include forms of environmental injustice concerning ownership, for example biopiracy and dispossession of land.

Because we have rejected radical constructionism about nature and the 'end of nature' thesis,[8] the idea of *reification* is absent from our picture of contexts emphasizing the presence of the nonhuman. With regard to nonhuman nature, the idea of estrangement focuses attention on issues connected with the matter of degree, although indispensable, distinction between humanized landscapes and the nonhuman at the heart of our environmental situation. These include the intellectual and physical dimensions of the distinction, the recognition of the 'otherness' of nonhuman nature, and the apparent triviality of the idea of estrangement in this context. The environmental problems highlighted through the idea of estrangement from nonhuman nature include a blanket anthropocentric instrumentalism with regard to nonhuman nature (the 'domination agenda'), ecologically unjust impacts on nonhuman nature (including anthropogenic species extinction and excessive habitat destruction), and the Anthropocene discourse insofar as that expresses a deluded and despotic assumption of total human mastery over nonhuman nature.

The idea of *alienation* from, or rather *of*, nonhuman nature concerns the assumptions functioning specifically within understandings of property and the derivation and justification property rights. It is focused on the issue of purely anthropocentric instrumentalist assumptions in this area; the way the notion of ownership itself can function as an intellectual device for reducing nature to landscape by representing the nonhuman only as something to be owned for the sake of human interests.

[8] See especially Chapters 1 and 2.

230 Entailments and entanglements

This idea of alienation addresses the same environmental problems as those addressed through estrangement from nonhuman nature, but with a special focus on them as wrapped up with a (perhaps often hidden) assumption that nature has been given to us to take possession of for our own purposes.

As we have seen, estrangement from the natural world focuses attention on our continuity with the rest of nature, in contrast to the difference of the nonhuman. One issue here is the meaning of estrangement given that this environmental context is inescapable and precisely one of our being always already continuous, entangled even, with wider nature. I have suggested thinking of it in terms of misperception of our place within wider nature, and in the previous chapter I distinguished a cognitive sense in terms of ignorance or discounting of ecological facts and relationships and an eco-phenomenological sense of it in terms of 'inadequate participation'.

The environmental problems associated with the idea of estrangement from overall nature understood in these ways then must include ignorance of ecological facts and of the relations that we are a part of whether we realize it or not (or whether we choose to ignore them or not). When the participatory sense of the idea is emphasized, as it must be if the account is to capture critical environmental concerns, then it joins forces with idea of estrangement from nonhuman nature to address issues of domination and ecological injustice (especially recognitional injustice). I have not dwelt on the idea of *alienation* from (or *of*) the natural world: it contributes to this joint effort by serving as an emphatic corollary to alienation of nonhuman nature. If it is an issue whether we should view nonhuman nature as 'ours', something to be owned by humanity for the sake only of human interests, then whether we should view the entire natural world as ours in that way must also be an issue.

It is also important to be clear that for these ideas of 'alienation from nature' to address environmental issues in the way that I have suggested they must have particular normative orientations. That is, the alienation, estrangement and reification must be considered as something 'bad' and so to be combated and overcome, or as something 'good' and so to be encouraged, or at least lived with. The normative orientations I have suggested are as follows:

Reification of or within landscape is bad and to be overcome.[9]
Estrangement within the landscape is bad and to be overcome, except

---

[9] Again, given that nonhuman nature and the natural world refer to genuine realities, reification in the sense of viewing humanity and human products as naturally given things is not applicable to them. Reification in the sense of 'objectification', or the instrumentalization of 'mere things', is dealt with under the headings of alienation and estrangement.

Connections, tight and loose

in relation to human difference. With regard to nonhuman nature it is a qualified good, to be lived with to some extent, rather than overcome. Estrangement from the natural world is bad and to be overcome. *Alienation* within landscapes is bad when unjust, for example when coerced or exploitative. In relation to nonhuman nature and the natural world it is a qualified good to be encouraged.

7.5 Connections, tight and loose

Presenting ideas in a compressed form like this can help to summarize a complex picture. But it can also mislead by making the ideas seem absurdly static and abstract when they are meant to be about environmental contexts and normative stances that are dynamic, concrete and interrelated.

That we should expect them to be interconnected is suggested by the relationship between alienation, estrangement and reification made familiar by the Marxian tradition, which is a very useful tradition if for no other reason than that. If there is such a thing as a purely unqualified 'capitalist' perspective then presumably by definition it would recognize nonhuman nature only as raw material for profitable transformation. We have seen that the Marxian tradition is not entirely free from anthropocentric instrumental tendencies either. Perhaps, as Benton wishes, it can be made consistent with 'ecocentrism' and focused more unambiguously on collective control and transformation of the terms of our interaction with nonhuman nature, as opposed to the mastery and transformation of nonhuman nature itself. However, for the Marxian, estrangements are generally products of pernicious (unjust, coercive and exploitative) labour alienation. It is not obvious whether this needs to be the case for all forms of estrangement, or only those that are to be overcome along with such alienation of labour. If the latter then a Marxian analysis appears to be consistent in principle with my claim that overcoming estrangement from the natural world requires overcoming pernicious estrangement from the humanized world, *without* overcoming all estrangement from the nonhuman; if the former then my position is inconsistent with the Marxian analysis.

Either way, whereas the Marxian tradition gives a more or less permanent pride of place to labour alienation, none of these ideas of alienation *from nature* has an a priori foundational status in our overall picture. Which is taken to be central depends on what are taken to be the specific problems in specific situations, and whatever idea is taken as the starting point others are waiting to appear as needing to be dealt with (although not necessarily as designating conditions to be overcome). If

232   Entailments and entanglements

the environmental crisis, as the total overall problem situation, involves our alienation from nature in any of the senses set out here, it involves all of them. The interconnections between them also represent a pragmatic dissolution of anthropocentric versus nonanthropocentric and instrumental versus non-instrumental oppositions; not as important distinctions and differences of emphasis, but as strict dichotomies.

Some of the relations involved are relatively tight and immediate matters of logical entailment. For example, positive acceptance of some estrangement from nonhuman nature entails some alienation of nonhuman nature, which in turn entails some alienation of the natural world. And these entail some overcoming of participatory estrangement from the natural world (even if we *try* to retain a purely cognitive view of the latter – I return to this point below). If we consider environmental problems associated with these ideas of alienation from nature then, for example, protection of wild species, habitats and ecosystems for the sake of resisting domination or as a matter of ecological justice (under the heading of living with some estrangement from nonhuman nature) *entails* relinquishing a presumed blanket anthropocentric instrumental understanding of ownership of the nonhuman (and so also of the natural world) in the background of property systems. That is, it requires some alienation of nonhuman nature and of the natural world.[10] These matters also raise immediately the question of the adequacy of our participation in the wider more than human world (and so the issue of overcoming our estrangement from the natural world). And vice versa: overcoming participatory estrangement from the natural world, seeking ecological justice and opposing domination *for this reason*, also *entails* alienation of the natural world and nonhuman nature, and endorsing some estrangement from the nonhuman. That is, it requires a preparedness to live with some nonhuman otherness or difference.

Other connections seem a little looser, more contingent and less immediate. But it is still important to notice that they are part of our situation. For example, I argued above that progress in overcoming participatory estrangement from the natural world requires progress in overcoming pernicious estrangement, reification and alienation with respect to the landscape. I pointed out above that this is an unsurprising logical entailment, given that the idea of the natural world encompasses that of landscape and that the idea of estrangement is informed by Honneth's recognitional account of reification. But there is also the connection brought by our actual situation: a project focused only on overcoming

[10] Remember that the point here is not give up ownership altogether, but to give up purely anthropocentric instrumental ways of understanding and justifying property.

Landscape and natural world 233

participatory estrangement is limited to the 'wilderness experience' of those able to get there. Adequate participation involves openness to primordial kinship and reciprocity, and this is undermined by reification and (unjust) estrangement and alienation within highly humanized landscapes. This suggests that actual large-scale sustainable improvements in such (nonanthropocentric) matters as ecological justice, as a form of overcoming estrangement from the wider more than human world, requires significant progress in such (anthropocentric) matters as securing environmental justice within and between landscapes and achieving a better practice of place.

Can we say 'and vice versa' here? Does achieving environmental justice in a sustainable humanized world that functions well as a vehicle of free human personality and responsible will *require* progress in overcoming estrangement from the natural world and therefore that we also welcome estrangement specifically from the nonhuman? This would be a particularly interesting connection to establish. Does progress on the anthropocentric front *require* progress on the nonanthropocentric front? It seems not to entail it logically in the abstract: the *idea* of a humanized world in that happy state seems logically consistent with that of the domination of nature agenda understood as the aim to overcome estrangement from the nonhuman as much as possible (to make our surroundings as humanized as possible), and so hostile to the notion of a more adequate participation in the more than human world. Hostile, that is, to the thought of overcoming estrangement from the natural world in those terms. So it seems that the anthropocentric project of improving human life by overcoming undesirable estrangement, reification and alienation within the landscape does not itself logically entail the normative orientations I have attached to the other ideas of alienation from nature.

7.6   Landscape and natural world: estrangements and entanglements

It would be wrong, however, to conclude that improving the humanized world in such terms bears no important relation to those other ideas. Take estrangement from the landscape and from the natural world. Here are two arguments for thinking that satisfactory progress regarding the former requires progress in overcoming the latter:

I have already touched on *argument one*:[11] landscapes exist within a wider natural world. To be free of pernicious estrangements landscapes need to be homely embodiments of human will that ground stable

---

[11] Chapter 1, section 1.3.

234 Entailments and entanglements

identity and responsibility. Without appreciation of the wider more than human ecological realities it is only by happy accident that landscapes are sustainable and free from the radical loss of homeliness and control following ecological catastrophe. Therefore, homely landscapes require an appreciation of wider more than human ecological realities.

Argument two: encompassing such problems as degraded practice of place, environmental injustice and lack of homeliness, the idea of pernicious landscape estrangement to some extent comes together with that of participatory estrangement from the natural world in the idea of inadequate participation in primordial nature as flesh. Features of the latter – seduction by the abstract, excessively self-regarding agency and misrecognition – undermine primordial kinship and reciprocity with what surrounds us whether this is human, humanized or nonhuman nature. Overcoming them with respect to the humanized context requires getting rid of them in the nonhuman context; these being the two environmental contexts that jointly constitute the natural world. This is because, as the first argument emphasizes, the human and nonhuman are continuous, or indeed intertwined, within the natural world. They are not utterly divorced dimensions of being. Thus it is most implausible to suppose that a tendency to exhibit features of inadequate participation with regard to the nonhuman dimensions of the natural world can be simply switched off when it comes to the human dimensions.

Notice that the first argument turns on a cognitivist understanding of estrangement from the natural world as consisting in ignorance and/or the irrational discounting of ecological realities. On its own it reduces nature to landscape by regarding the nonhuman only as a support mechanism for sustainable human landscaping. Again, in this respect it is insufficient for the more radical sense of our environmental situation as an environmental crisis. This is where the second argument above comes in. On the face of it, however, the second argument comes in as available only to those already interpreting the situation as a crisis involving human domination of nature and so on. If we don't interpret the situation like that then conceding that overcoming landscape estrangement requires overcoming cognitive estrangement from the natural world seems not to commit us logically to overcoming it in anything like the more radical participatory sense. But we can perhaps establish a stronger connection between these kinds of estrangement with reference to the following two further considerations:

The first is not very decisive, but still worth mentioning. Talk of '*alienation from nature*', or, in this context, '*estrangement from the natural world*', lends itself to radical interpretation by suggesting that something is seriously and thoroughly amiss with our relations to nature or the natural world. This is so even if those talking are not normally associated with

Landscape and natural world   235

radical critique of contemporary society and attitudes. Otherwise why not refer just to common or garden ignorance and irrationality and leave it at that, rather than gloss the situation as one of 'alienation from nature'? The response to this might be to simply shrug and agree that the alienation gloss is pointless and may as well be dropped.

The second point is more substantive and builds on a point central to both of the arguments above: we and our landscapes are part of the natural world. The distinction between landscape and nonhuman nature, which I have emphasized many times is a matter of degree, is a distinction between parts of the overall natural world. We can talk in the abstract of overcoming (pernicious) estrangement from the landscape and cognitive estrangement from the natural world, without these entailing a commitment to overcoming participatory estrangement from the natural world. However, our actual concrete environmental problem situation is one in which the human and nonhuman parts of overall (terrestrial) nature are closely entwined. Partly this is precisely because of considerations motivating talk of the Anthropocene and 'end of nature' claims: the enormous scale of human presence and 'interventions'. But it is also because of 'interventions' in the other direction, as in the example of the gull and its mess on my window discussed in earlier chapters. Given our concrete situation involves such human/ nonhuman entanglement, then taking the lack of logical entailment between the ideas of estrangement considered in the abstract to be the end of the matter, or as grounds for discounting the issue of participatory estrangement, looks itself to be an instance of regrettable seduction by the abstract.

Now, argument two above said it is implausible to suppose that features of inadequate participation exhibited towards the nonhuman dimensions of overall nature can be switched off in the context of the human dimensions. This gives a reason for those concerned to overcome landscape estrangement (insofar as that also involves inadequate participation) to be concerned also to overcome participatory estrangement from the more than human natural world. The point I am making now is subtly different and intended to refute the reply that someone disinclined to care about participatory estrangement from the natural world is not *logically* committed to doing so in virtue of wishing to overcome pernicious estrangement from the landscape. The point is that this reply presupposes we can isolate the humanized sufficiently from the nonhuman so that the praxis of overcoming landscape estrangement[12] can be achieved without also

---

[12] Including as this involves adequate participation: openness to reciprocity, avoidance of purely self-regarding agency and so on. Recall again that the idea of participatory estrangement encompasses much of what Honneth refers to as reification.

236   Entailments and entanglements

achieving it with regard to the nonhuman. This is a merely abstract possibility; isolating and emphasizing it to give it a central role in the overall picture of our situation suggests a preoccupation with fixed and secure dichotomies – in this case between humanized landscape and nonhuman nature. If we drop that preoccupation and consider the actual situation, which is more fluid and indeterminate, the suggestion that we cannot disentangle things so as to make much progress on the landscape front without also making progress in overcoming participatory estrangement from the *more than human* natural world looks very plausible.

Notice also that because the latter entails living with some estrangement from the nonhuman then the point just made suggests that overcoming landscape estrangement in our actual situation requires endorsing some estrangement from nonhuman nature too. In the following sections I reinforce and illustrate this point that the entanglements of our actual situation mean that progress on the anthropocentric front (overcoming pernicious landscape estrangement and cognitive estrangement from nature) entails progress on the nonanthropocentric front (overcoming participatory estrangement from more than human nature and endorsing some estrangement from the nonhuman). These two fronts are not well understood as isolated opponents in a zero-sum contest.

7.7   On what nature 'does for us'

Argument one in the preceding section said that we should avoid or overcome cognitive estrangement from the natural world: a concern with pernicious landscape estrangement requires an appreciation of wider ecological dependencies. A recent popular book by Tony Juniper (2013) illustrates how, even if it is thought of initially only in those cognitivist terms, starting off with a concern for overcoming estrangement from the natural world brings the other ideas of alienation from nature onto the scene, including the more radical participatory sense of estrangement. Juniper's book is called *What Has Nature Ever Done For Us? How Money Really Does Grow On Trees*. As the title suggests, he seeks to show the massive contribution to human well-being, especially economic well-being, of the multiplicity of 'services' provided by nonhuman nature. It is an attempt to bring ecological dependencies into mainstream thinking, including mainstream economic and political thinking and policy-making. Even the most hard-headed economists and 'realist' politicians must sit up and take notice of the vast scale of nature's economic contribution; surely this is not something of interest only to 'environmentalists' or 'conservationists'.

On what nature 'does for us' 237

Juniper's discussion underlines both the complexity of our interrelated ecological dependencies and that when we think of relations between ideas of alienation from nature, we cannot cut through the complexity of interrelated normative considerations they speak to either by a domineering reduction of nature to landscape, or indeed by asserting an imperative to overcome alienation from nature in some single sense. However, in our terms, the main explicit thrust of Juniper's discussion is the need to overcome cognitive estrangement from the natural world in the sense of ignorance or discounting of the many ways humanity is dependent on nonhuman nature. Nonhuman service activities are so ubiquitous and vital to the human economic enterprise that their economic value has been estimated as equivalent to that of nearly double the total global (human) GDP (Juniper 2013, p. 274).

One has to be very careful here, of course. Putting aside the propriety of such claims in purely economic terms,[13] there are the dangers of reification and instrumental reductionism to be avoided. I am taking the costings seriously only as way of emphasizing the intertwining dependence of ourselves and our projects upon the nonhuman. But *reducing* the nonhuman items to their costed services first reduces them to landscape and, second, reifies them, both in the sense of allowing their economic significance to override what Honneth calls their 'existential significance', and in the sense of ignoring the human labour input into the 'service provision'. 'Natural service provision' occurs only when human effort and technology is such as to employ it. Viewing the nonhuman items involved *only* in terms their service function is a strong, crassly economistic form of anthropocentric instrumentalism. I hope that my discussion shows that one can avoid these dangers while using talk of natural service provision to emphasize the scale and complexity of our dependence upon nature.

There is some explicit questioning of current political and economic power structures in Juniper's book. For example, he mounts a version of the familiar argument that a combination of economic and political short-termism is a major factor behind the frequent discounting of the value of natural services and failure to conserve and replenish 'natural capital' (Juniper 2013, ch. 11). An interesting example here is the case of the rapid decline of Indian vultures since the 1990s: by 2007 the population of long-billed vultures had dropped some 97 per cent and that of the oriental white-backed vulture 99.9 per cent (Juniper 2013, pp. 1–2, 132ff). This is believed to have been caused by the use in livestock of the anti-inflammatory drug diclofenac. Diclofenac has highly beneficial

---

[13] Juniper bases the claim about total global GDP on the work of Costanza et al. (1997).

238   Entailments and entanglements

effects on cattle and water-buffalo (and humans), but the traces of it left
in livestock carcasses are highly toxic to the vultures that consume them.
Juniper reports that before their decline the 40 million-strong vulture
population consumed about 12 million tonnes of flesh per annum, and
the dramatic reduction in this carrion-disposal service has had various
expensive consequences for human health and the wider Indian economy. For example, for the very poor the remains of dead cattle are an
important economic resource: they are skinned for their hides and the
vultures then efficiently dispose of the flesh and pick clean the bones
then sold to the fertiliser industry.[14] The absence of vultures curtails this
economic activity and large putrefying livestock carcasses are a health
hazard that must be disposed of as quickly as possible; with the costs of
doing so borne by local communities.

Substantial numbers of large putrefying, fly-blown carcasses littering
the countryside in the hot sun are indeed a drawback from the point of
view of maintaining a homely landscape. An obviously serious hazard to
human health they are a breeding ground for anthrax and other harmful bacteria. A reduced vulture population also leaves room for larger
populations of other scavenger species that are less efficient at reducing
carcasses to clean (and so more valuable) bones and that are themselves
a hazard to human health. For example, the feral dog population has
increased dramatically in India during the decades of vulture decline,
and this has produced an increased incidence of dog bites and fatal rabies
infection.[15] Juniper reports that, according to the RSPB charity, although
vet-formula diclofenic has been banned in India, companies producing
the drug for human use still make it in 'vet-sized bottles': use of the drug
is down but still at a level preventing a recovery of the vulture population
(Juniper 2013, p. 136). Reflecting on such cases, Juniper says:

Given what we now know about the value of nature and natural systems in dealing with waste, helping to manage disease and control pests, we need to ask why
we find it so difficult to protect assets that are so evidently valuable ... In the case
of India's vultures it is poor people who have suffered the biggest direct impacts,
while the main beneficiaries of business-as-usual are those who make and sell

---

[14] As Juniper says, 'not nice work, but for very poor people at least a source of income'
(Juniper 2013, p. 133).

[15] Juniper quotes a study by Markandya et al. (2008) that estimates the number of additional rabies deaths between 1992 and 2006 in India caused by this route at between
47,395 and 48,886, and the total economic cost of the vulture loss during the period
at about $34 billion. Such figures are contesable but, as Juniper says, even if the actual
economic cost is an order of magnitude lower banning the use of dicoflenic in cattle and
restoring the vulture population would still be economically rational: the benefit would
greatly outweigh that gained for cattle farming by continued use of the drug (Juniper
2013, pp. 134f).

On what nature 'does for us'   239

diclofenic. Meanwhile, the action to support vulture populations has come mainly from a British charity, the RSPB, which is spending about £400,000 per year to start a captive breeding programme. Novartis, the company that originally developed and managed diclofenac, has expressed no interest in supporting such work. (Juniper 2013, p. 151)

Juniper's pointed reference to Novartis' lack of interest in reintroducing the vultures and mention of the unequal distribution of benefits and burdens between the rich and powerful and poor and powerless indicates a familiar scenario. Clearly, in our terms, environmental injustice – *that* form of pernicious estrangement in the landscape context – can be a self-reinforcing obstacle to economic rationality and sustainable landscaping. Environmental injustice can lie at the heart of a set of mutually supporting estrangements from the landscape, which is not then a homely satisfier of human needs.

Still, Juniper's focus is mainly on economic rationality and its relation to sustainable and environmentally just landscaping given the 'full economic costs' of our ecological dependencies. From the critical point of view, this illustrates the problem of thinking of alienation from nature only in terms of cognitive estrangement: it reduces nature to landscape, with the nonhuman viewed only as a bundle of resources and service providers to be called upon to benefit human interests. Juniper gathers together various examples of these resources and services and estimates of their monetary value so as to emphasize in a dramatic and accessible way the scale of our dependence upon them. *That's* how embedded we are in the more than human natural world: to the tune of many trillions of dollars' worth of nonhuman service provision. Thus Juniper's book can be read as making an economic case for our *taking this into account* (rather than discounting it) and for thereby adopting a more ecologically informed, and in that respect more rational, form of anthropocentric instrumentalism.

On the other hand, his case also illustrates that such an ecologically informed and rational anthropocentric instrumentalism is not equivalent to an *unqualified* domination of nature programme. For example, it must at least involve an eco-regulatory, rather than purely transformative, conception of human labour.[16] This is because of the scale of the economic case for 'setting aside', protecting or conserving a significant amount of only lightly managed nonhuman wildness (even within otherwise highly humanized landscapes) to 'allow' it to provide services more efficiently. Examples of this in Juniper's discussion include the Indian

---

[16] See Chapter 4, section 4.5.

240   Entailments and entanglements

vultures mentioned above (the cost of protection of which is far less than that of alternative methods of carrion disposal, or of not disposing of the carrion); protecting cloud forests, the Columbian paramo and other high-altitude ecosystems that regulate the supply of fresh water to many densely populated regions (Juniper 2013, pp. 154ff); and protection or provision of habitats for nonhuman plant (crop) pollinators[17] and pest controllers.[18]

This is not only a matter of refraining from such absurd and disastrous programmes as Mao's full scale 'war on pests' that sought to eliminate various species, including sparrows, and generally 'demonized nature as man's adversary, a force to be resisted, subjugated and finally overcome' (Juniper 2013, pp. 148f).[19] It is a matter of positively acknowledging the value to us of such nonhuman service provision as pest control and so the economic case conserving it by, for example, restricting the use of pesticides for short-term benefits and providing habitat corridors through otherwise intensively farmed landscapes. Thus refraining from physically transformative landscaping for short-term gain is often the rational route to long-term sustainable profitability.

7.8   Estrangement and impatience

Even so, this apparently remains a purely anthropocentric instrumental line of thought. Although it favours eco-regulatory over purely transformative human labour, it is still about instrumental landscaping within the current limits of technology; limits we might resent and that we might hope to push back as far and quickly as possible. Notice though that it does require we accept *some* estrangement from nonhuman nature in virtue of our accepting some nonhuman service-provision, given that the provision hasn't been designed and set up to serve our interests. And this is a significant point to take on board: our *actual* situation means that rational landscaping involves accepting *some* estrangement from nonhuman nature, rather than rushing in to make our surroundings as fully humanized, controlled and artefactual as possible as quickly as

---

[17] Juniper (2013, ch. 4). At the beginning of that chapter Juniper writes in bold: '$1 trillion – annual sales dependent on animal pollination. $190 billion – annual services provided to farming by animal pollinators. Two thirds – major crop plants that rely on animal pollination' (Juniper 2013, p. 105).

[18] Juniper (2013, ch. 5). At the beginning of this chapter it says: '$34 billion – costs associated with the loss of vultures in India. $310– annual value per hectare of pest control by birds in a coffee plantation. $1,500 – annual value per hectare of pest control by birds in a timber producing forest' (Juniper 2013, p. 131).

[19] This was bound to backfire, of course, and to result in terrible famine as locusts and other pests were no longer preyed upon by the sparrows.

Estrangement and impatience 241

possible. Still, without some more positive endorsement of it as involving recognition of nonhuman nature independently of its role as service provider, such estrangement looks entirely conditional on nonhuman nature continuing to play that role efficiently within an overall framework of human-oriented management and regulation.

Does this force upon us an anthropocentric instrumental reduction of nature to human landscape? I think not. Our situation is complex, with a plurality of dimensions. The dimensions described by those like Juniper who emphasize the many things that 'nature does for us' cannot be appreciated adequately without some overcoming of participatory, not just cognitive, estrangement from the natural world (and so without a more positive acceptance of estrangement from nonhuman nature). For example, although the 'letting be' of relatively wild nonhuman nature for the sake of efficient service supply suggests an instrumentality at odds with the most adequate participation imaginable, it does also suggest an attitude more akin to openness to reciprocity than to an unqualifiedly domineering 'techno-capitalist' approach indifferent to both environmental and ecological injustice. Indifferent, for example, both to the position of those suffering the consequences of the decline in the Indian vulture population and to the status of the vultures themselves as 'more than' carrion-removal operatives.[20] A praxis of openness to nonhuman nature's 'contribution' and recognition of it as more than organisms to be enslaved and inert matter to be made useful through transformation would be masked by the fixed assumption of a countervailing domineering attitude. For example, a reaction to the Anthropocene idea that welcomes it as a sign that human control of nature is intensifying, and that nature is bending more and more to the human will, looks a less useful attitude than one that worries it underlines the dangerous damage being done to nonhuman systems. Less useful, that is, *including* from a perspective that emphasizes how much we rely on services supplied by relatively unmodified nonhuman nature.

Thus we might understand estrangement from the natural world as often wrapped up with impatience with the estrangement involved in being confronted by the otherness of nonhuman nature; of what has not been fully humanized and controlled, as an obstacle to satisfaction or to feeling fully at home. Will someone please do something about those gulls whose annoying activities I have mentioned? If only the Earth's climatic system had an easily operated thermostat, like my home central heating! If estrangement from the natural world is to be overcome then so must

---

[20] Compare the discussion (in Chapter 4, sections 4.4 and 4.8) of foxes as 'more than' their landscaped roles.

242   Entailments and entanglements

such impatience. And if the drive to be fully at home through unqualified humanization and control of the world (elimination of nonhuman otherness) itself expresses estrangement from the natural world, then overcoming estrangement from the natural world cannot be equated with being fully at home in it. Overcoming estrangement from the natural world and overcoming (all) estrangement from the nonhuman mutually exclude one another.

This is the case when estrangement from the natural world is given the more radical normative gloss of inadequate participation. But the point I wish to emphasize here is that it looks very plausible also when understood initially in the cognitive sense of failing to appreciate the importance of allowing relatively wild nonhuman nature to persist and continue to function to a significant extent in its own way. That also requires overcoming impatience with the estrangement involved in being confronted by what hasn't been fully humanized as an obstacle, whether to short-term profit or to being at home in a more expansive sense. Thus, given the extent and complexity of our actual dependence on nonhuman services, overcoming estrangement from the natural world *even in the cognitive sense* and overcoming all estrangement from the nonhuman mutually exclude one another. The need for the cognitive approach to moderate impatience at the presence of nonhuman difference also requires it to move at least some way towards embracing something like the adequate participation understanding. Starting from the cognitive understanding of what it is to overcome estrangement from the natural world does threaten to impose an anthropocentric instrumentalist reduction of nature to landscape. But this reduction is interrupted by an appreciation of the actual form and extent of our dependence upon nonhuman nature, the ways our lives and economies are intertwined with what is still relatively nonhuman nature. This appreciation requires consideration of the distinction between basic and surplus overcoming of estrangement from nonhuman nature.[21] It also requires that attitudes of hostility, contempt and impatience towards (surplus estrangement from) nonhuman nature be reined in as counterproductive. This also accords with our redescribed pragmatist goal of as that of 'improving human life, including a more respectful relation with the nonhuman'.[22]

Consider again the Indian vulture case in the following terms: (1) overcoming cognitive estrangement in this case is a matter of understanding the vulture's ecological role as consumer of carrion. This is necessary to (2) economically rational landscaping in that environment, and to (3) the

---

[21] See Chapter 4, section 4.2.   [22] See Chapter 2, section 2.11.

Nature deficit

environmentally just treatment of those whose way of life, livelihood or lives are threatened by a rapid decline in vulture numbers. I am arguing that overcoming participatory estrangement within the natural world and living with estrangement from the nonhuman is also necessary to (2) and (3). In this case the 'overcoming' and 'living with' involve (4) an attitude of 'respect' towards the vultures, recognition of their own way of being and a willingness to coexist with it, rather than ignore it, denigrate it, view it as dispensable or as an obstacle to be overcome. (4) is not in conflict with (2) and (3); its presence is *required* as an element within the situation in which (2) and (3) are achieved to any satisfactory extent.

This does not mean that (4) has the status of a mere means to (2) and (3). Compare a situation in which dependence upon slave labour is woven into one's whole way of life and economy. Understanding the extent and nature of one's dependency upon slave labour is better than not understanding it or ignoring it. Otherwise one might end up with a dangerously false sense of security and power. It would be particularly irrational if, in the impatient pursuit of short-term goals, one ignored or dismissed the slaves' own needs, including their needs to do some things themselves in their own ways and for some time off. One would receive sub-optimal service; probably even catastrophic disruptions and failures of service. To help avoid these unsatisfactory outcomes, it might be better not to consider and act towards the service providers simply as mere slaves – *mere living tools* – in the first place, but beings accorded some degree of recognition 'in their own right'. Once in place this status precludes a view of it as one accorded *only* as a means to sustainable service provision.

7.9   Nature deficit

The point that (overcoming) cognitive estrangement from the natural world, in the sense of failing to appreciate ecological dependencies, quickly brings in the other ideas of alienation from nature is further reinforced by another of Juniper's examples of nonhuman service provision: the payoff in human well-being and health-related economic savings to be had from the presence of relatively nonhuman nature. This brings us back to the issue of Nature Deficit Disorder.[23]

Juniper cites a range of studies that indicate how 'being exposed to nature' (meaning *nonhuman* nature) enhances human well-being (Juniper 2013, pp. 247ff). It reduces anger, anxiety, stress and the many chronic diseases associated with stress, such as cardiovascular disease,

---

[23] See the Introduction and Chapter 6, sections 6.12–13.

244   Entailments and entanglements

depression and diabetes. There are then huge benefits in terms of health and reduced treatment costs and illness-related costs to industry to be reaped by planning development with plentiful access to 'green space', or significant presence of nonhuman nature, in mind.[24] To ignore this is to ignore a dependency on wider more than human nature and so is a case of cognitive estrangement from the natural world.

When discussing the human need for exposure to nonhuman nature Juniper refers to such facts as that approximately 99.9 per cent of human history has occurred within non-urban environments and some 95 per cent of it has involved a hunter-gather mode of living '*in* nature' (Juniper 2013, p. 254, his emphasis). 'In nature', that is, in the sense of modes of life within lightly humanized landscapes that required people to be 'competent naturalists'; knowledgeable of the workings of nonhuman nature and thoroughly and continuously aware of their dependency upon it (Juniper 2013, p. 255). Subsequent agricultural ways of life also turned on such knowledge and awareness, he says. Day-to-day proximity to (very significantly) nonhuman nature, involving detailed knowledge and awareness of it, has thus been the context for human health and well-being for some 99.9 per cent of history. At least it was the context for such health and well-being as there was through all that time: Juniper emphasizes that he is not romanticizing the past or ignoring the improvements in the health and security of many gained through the development of agriculture and especially through the massive acceleration in urbanization over the past two centuries (Juniper 2013, pp. 256f). The point is that this has been at the cost of problems associated with environments where the nonhuman is often far less present and where the focus of life is 'distanced' from – not frequently informed by appreciation of connections within and dependencies upon – the nonhuman dimensions of the wider natural world. And a large part of the most cost-effective solutions to NDD-related problems is through a 'reconnection with nature':

Such modern health challenges are not easy to address with technology alone ... And the more research that is conducted the more clearly it seems that nature could be a large part of the solution. Yet at no point in our history have so many humans spent so little time in physical contact with animals, plants and the processes that govern the natural world. (Juniper 2013, p. 257)[25]

---

[24] Chapter 10 of Juniper's book is called 'Natural Health Service', and on its first page he says: '£105 Billion – Annual Costs Caused by Mental Illness in England. £630 Million – Annual Cost of Maintaining 27,000 Parks and Green Spaces in the UK' (Juniper 2013, p. 245).

[25] Of course, we must be no less 'in physical contact with the processes that govern the natural world' in our sense of 'natural world' than we have ever been or could be. We are less in contact with those processes insofar as they govern the nonhuman dimensions

Nature deficit

Again, if this is true then to appreciate our reliance on exposure to (some) nonhuman nature is to appreciate a dependency on the wider more than human world. Thus it is part of what it is to overcome cognitive estrangement from the natural world. The question is whether arranging things so as to ensure exposure to nonhuman nature sufficient to avoid NDD can be seen also as a matter of overcoming estrangement from the natural world in the participatory sense. If so, then this illustrates how a concern for overcoming the cognitive estrangement brings in a concern for overcoming the participatory estrangement.

In the previous chapter I distinguished NDD from participatory estrangement for a number of reasons. The idea of overcoming one is not the same as the idea of overcoming the other because overcoming NDD might be an anthropocentric instrumentalist project that views 'nature' only as a means to human interests (in this case certain kinds of well-being). Moreover, the 'nature' involved is (relatively) nonhuman nature; and it is only with respect to *some* of nonhuman nature that an absence of exposure counts as a deficit to be associated with reduced well-being. It is only parts of nature involved in the biophilia hypothesis: the environment of our evolution and subsequent hunter-gatherer existence. 'High-quality green spaces' providing the kind of 'contact with nature' that significantly improves human well-being and reduces health-related economic costs do not include extremely arid deserts and the lava flows of erupting volcanoes, for example. We do not have to try to live in such 'hostile' environments in order to overcome participatory estrangement. But, as we have been understanding it, the latter does require us to refrain from misrecognizing them – from seeing them only as calling for denigration and our hostility. Concern for high-quality green spaces as a means of avoiding or curing NDD is consistent in principle with such misrecognition of what from the standpoint of this concern look like very low-quality nonhuman spaces.

of the natural world, and perhaps less appreciative of the continuity between those and the humanized parts, and consequently of the dependence of the latter on the former. Juniper suggests that overcoming this and 'reconnecting with the Earth' in this sense might be easier than it sounds: 'Perhaps the emerging science on how contact with nature benefits people could logically lead to equally important new laws, for example, in setting a minimum distance that homes should be from high-quality green space, and new standards for urban designs to better incorporate nature? Perhaps there should be official guidance to schools to require that children spend at least a couple of days a month undertaking activities in natural areas' (Juniper 2013, p. 265). The old laws to which these measures would be 'equally important' are the British 1851 Public Health and 1956 Clean Air acts that ensured clean drinking water and reduced emissions. These brought dramatic improvements in public health and 'were based on a growing understanding that how we treat the environment has consequences for people's well-being' (Juniper 2013, p. 269).

246   Entailments and entanglements

My point here, however, is that the distinctions between participatory and cognitive estrangement and between participatory estrangement and NDD are abstract distinctions. They relate to the fact that these are not the same *ideas*.[26] But this is consistent with it being the case that progress in overcoming one of these types of estrangement is a condition of overcoming the other type in our actual situation. Humanized landscapes and nonhuman nature are to a degree intertwined within the natural world, and so are cognitive and participatory types of estrangement from the natural world.

Thus ensuring the presence of significant nonhuman nature to avoid NDD in otherwise highly humanized landscapes *requires* refraining from blanket misrecognition of the nonhuman and from the self- (or purely human-) regarding drive to fully humanize our surroundings, overwrite them altogether with human agency or reduce them to commodities for short-term profit. Therefore it also requires that we live with some estrangement in the different sense of estrangement from nonhuman nature. This suggests an interesting twist to Evernden's view of humanity as a 'natural alien' species. If the NDD story is right then there is a (well-being-related) sense in which we are more 'at home' in the presence of at least some kinds of significantly nonhuman nature than we are in a more thoroughly humanized, artefactual environment. Yet the extent to which it is nonhuman is also the extent to which we are estranged from it in that it does not entirely reflect human purposes and designs or embody human labour.

Notice how important it remains to see this as a matter of degree. Obviously, parks, gardens, rural countryside and trees planted at the roadside embody human labour, designs and purposes. Again we need to avoid reification and the wrong sort of estrangement from our surroundings qua humanized landscape. But such things embody human labour, designs and purposes less than plastic trees, 'concrete jungles' and the interiors of space-shuttle cockpits and virtual warfare simulations. 'Contact' with them *as an antidote to NDD* must include a significant element of estrangement from the nonhuman in the sense discussed in Chapter 4. Indeed, I suggested in the previous chapter that exposure to 'nature' as an antidote to NDD is closer to the idea of estrangement from the nonhuman than it is to the idea of overcoming participatory estrangement. But that was in the context of trying to clarify the latter as a distinct idea of alienation from nature. Now that I am emphasizing the connections between these ideas of alienation from nature it is important

---

[26] Notice also then that the ideas of alienation from nature currently in play do not rely on the NDD story and the empirical claims specific to that.

Nature deficit

to emphasize that the element of estrangement from the nonhuman involved in the kind of 'encounter with nature' taken to be an antidote to NDD unavoidably delivers both a requirement to address participatory estrangement and a foothold for doing so. This is another case of the mutual entailment between overcoming that estrangement from the more than human natural world and living with some estrangement from nonhuman nature *in our actual problem situation.*

It should be clear also that there are important connections here with landscape estrangement. For example, I have argued that issues concerning the unjust distribution of environmental goods and bads fall under the heading of (pernicious) estrangement in the landscape context. Access to high-quality green space is an environmental good, the distribution of which raises questions of justice, no less than the distribution of other 'services' related to healthcare provision and well-being.[27] I have argued also that encounters with nonhuman nature in the form of green spaces of the sort to prevent NDD involve some acceptance of estrangement from nonhuman nature and a more adequate participation within the natural world. The distribution of opportunities to live with estrangement from the nonhuman and overcome participatory estrangement from the natural world is an issue of environmental justice too. Notice, for example, that the presence of significant local green space within otherwise highly humanized landscapes militates against the need, illustrated at the start of this chapter, to leave such landscapes to search out a more adequate participation in the 'wilderness'. In this way also the NDD story illustrates how a concern for environmental justice (for overcoming estrangement in *that* sense) raises further concerns, not just about cognitive estrangement from the natural world, but also about such estrangement in the more radical participatory sense.

[27] Compare Juniper (2013, pp. 248ff).

8   Concluding remarks

In the previous chapter I set out some of the ways in which the different senses of alienation from nature and the issues they encompass entail each other as components of the overall environmental crisis. I take that to complete and validate my overall argument for the utility of talk of alienation from nature. Despite the problems it raises, such talk can be justified, useful and important. It can help us to think through our environmental situation when understood in a nuanced, pluralistic way involving different interrelated senses of alienation from nature, *some of which are to be viewed positively, as something to be accepted or even encouraged, rather than avoided or overcome*. As I put the argument in the Introduction, this is because:

1. The different senses of alienation from nature entail each other, in that concern for one rationally requires concern for the others in our actual environmental crisis situation.

    Therefore,

2. Adopting a pluralistic approach involving these different senses of alienation from nature enables us to see important relationships between them.
3. The different senses of alienation from nature capture different specific environmental concerns, including both anthropocentric (for example, instrumental and constructionist) concerns and nonanthropocentric concerns (for example, respect for nonhuman nature and resistance to the domination of nature).

    Therefore,

4. Under the description of the associated senses of alienation from nature, these environmental concerns entail each other: in our actual environmental situation concern for one rationally requires concern for the others.

248

Concluding remarks

Therefore,

5. The pluralistic approach allows us to see important relations between different specific environmental concerns. Particularly important are relations of entailment rather than zero-sum opposition between various anthropocentric and nonanthropocentric concerns.

I will finish the book now by briefly summarizing some of the main points to take away from this. The pluralistic approach shows how we can usefully talk of our alienation from nature as something over and above the more common or garden problems and more easily stated environmental issues. We can do this without committing ourselves either to returning to the wilderness or transforming the world into a fully humanized home. It is possible to talk of alienation from nature without triviality and without losing all critical purchase when the focus is nonhuman nature. And it is possible to talk meaningfully of our alienation from nature when the focus is our inescapable location within the wider natural world.

I have argued that, in order for these things to be possible, a workable account of alienation from nature needs to draw upon and modify a range of intellectual tools in environmental philosophy and wider philosophy, encompassing anthropocentric and nonanthropocentric perspectives on our situation. Ecological ignorance and irrationality are parts of the resulting picture along with our inescapable presence in the wider natural world. But so is our inevitable difference to nonhuman nature, and the need to avoid a turbo-charged anthropocentric stance of domineering mastery over it. This means that a key component of the resulting account is that, in some important senses, alienation from nature is something we should welcome and live with, rather than seek to overcome entirely.

The resulting account speaks of the overall situation, the bigger picture. Indeed, talk of alienation from nature lends itself to the bigger picture, especially when the bigger picture is held to be one of environmental crisis. On the other hand, to be helpful, it needs to be nuanced and flexible to locate concrete problems within the overall situation and also show their relation to other problems. If it is true that *The Problem* is alienation from nature, it is not true that this is just one thing. The big picture is one of problems with our ways of coping with the continuity and difference, sameness and otherness in our surroundings, and in our relations to wider nature. Faced with this, a satisfactory account of alienation from nature (or any environmental philosophy) will help us to keep in touch with our need to be at home in our surroundings without allowing this human project to defeat itself by degenerating into one of

250   Concluding remarks

dominating the wider world in an attempt to make it homely without qualification. The intertwining of human and nonhuman within the natural world means that benign 'landscaping' concerns associated with making ourselves at home (including establishing environmental justice and satisfactory 'places') cannot be addressed adequately without limiting landscaping in certain ways to allow space for estrangement from the nonhuman and addressing concerns associated with *that*, such as ecological justice and respect for nature.

It is surely obvious that the environmental crisis has a number of different aspects, involving different environmental contexts and concerns. If the aim is to help illuminate some of these through the use of different ideas of alienation from nature, then none of these ideas should be taken to have an ultimate priority or permanent foundational status. These different ideas are not completely distinct ideas that are merely juxtaposed, however; like the environmental contexts they concern, they are connected rather than isolated. This picture of *interrelated* elements, contexts and concerns does involve a form of holism in that whichever idea of alienation from nature is taken as a starting point, the others appear more or less quickly as part of the overall scene. But the holism does not take an absolutist form that says the whole is ultimately more real than the parts or that the proper aim of thought, including environmental thought, is to establish some kind of communion with that ultimate reality. The picture is complex and nuanced then, with a lot of moving intertwining parts. It has to be given the complexity of the problem, which is obviously such that it can only be partly addressed in a book like this. But what I think is clear and what I want to emphasize here is that dealing with the environmental crisis requires progress on all the fronts encompassed by the pluralist account of alienation from nature, not just some entirely at the expense of the others.

Thus when people say that our situation is one of 'alienation from nature' this is best interpreted as invoking a multidimensional problem situation encompassing a plurality of intertwining environmental contexts and so also of problems and issues. Talk of our alienation from nature can address this situation if it is underpinned by a plurality of ideas of alienation from nature open to suggestions from a variety of traditions; and if, in some of its senses, the normative charge traditionally associated with alienation is reversed or qualified.

It is tempting to encapsulate this complex plurality of interrelated concerns and contexts, and the accompanying rejection of fixity, strict dichotomies and finished solutions, with Merleau-Ponty's metaphor of the intertwining of the flesh within primordial perception. This seems to me to be helpful. There is kinship between the touching and the touched;

Concluding remarks

251

they require each other and bring each other onto the scene. Yet they cannot be resolved into a finished unity or their relations simplified by reducing one side to the other. If something less 'touchy-feely' would be preferred here, something that looks more like a technological analogy, then I suggest that of a 'critical refractor'. The type of refractor I have in mind is the device used by optometrists to determine what kinds of lens combinations are required to improve a patient's vision. Patients look through the refractor at an initially blurry image and a variety of lenses are slotted in front of each eye to discover what combination delivers optimum clarity. The patient is not expected to put up with, or be helped by, whatever combination happens to be in place from the previous patient. The lenses will need adjusting, other combinations tried and ideally the optometrist would be able to modify the lenses themselves to maximize clarity of vision, at least for the time being.

The refractor analogy is a version of the tool analogy; it suggests a view of theories, ideas and assumptions as 'lenses' to assist in clarifying some situation or issue, here the environmental situation. Our initial, inchoate sense of crisis suggests that at least some traditional assumptions bearing upon the environmental situation are not to be trusted. So the analogy does need to be that of a *critical* refractor: we should not expect the view to be improved very much by simply applying the usual unadjusted lenses. To improve things we should consider changing the lenses, discarding some and adjusting others. We need to be careful, however: there are pitfalls to be avoided. For example, it would not be helpful to simply replace the view of the situation with one of *something else*, however pleasing in other respects (a picture of timeless epistemological or axiological security, say, or a vision of humanity as Lord of Creation). Nor would it be helpful to try out just one or two lenses regardless of how well they do or do not work in tandem or frustrate each other. I have taken and adjusted some lenses from the box labelled 'alienation' and some others from the box labelled 'nature'. In and of itself, the resulting combination does not exactly or mechanically *tell us what to do* in any detail in any specific context, of course. That it should would be an expectation no less absurd than that one's normal glasses should tell one what to do or where to go. They bring things into focus to inform us of our surroundings and allow us to see some possible ways of getting around in them. They do not constitute a *decision* machine, in the sense of a device one could simply switch on so that it would tell us exactly what to do and in that way make our decisions for us.

This shows that the refractor analogy is not perfect, however. Indeed it might suggest to some that the theory should be regarded as a kind of *precision* tool in some strong sense of 'precision'. The account of

252   Concluding remarks

alienation from nature offered here is not supposed to deliver absolute precision, at least not in the form of certainty and the total absence of fuzziness. I take it that fuzziness is a feature of the environmental situation, not just of the lenses from the alienation and nature boxes. A theory delivering absolute precision about a field of completely clear and distinct items in which logic and decision-making can operate in a way unfettered by ambiguities and fuzzy matters of degree would not be a theory about our actual environmental situation. The sensible aim to have is more clarity, not absolute clarity. I think that suitably adjusted and arranged in the ways I have suggested the alienation and nature lenses bestow more clarity on the overall environmental situation.

This is to reaffirm once again the pragmatic pluralism of the overall account of alienation offered in this book. Rather than aiming to deliver certainty or fix in place final truths about ourselves and our place in the world the philosophy is meant as a set of tools to assist with a problem situation – the environmental crisis. It is pluralist in its willingness to countenance a range of dimensions to the situation and to take seriously a range of philosophical traditions as potentially helpful, at least when appropriately adjusted. It aims to bring them into fruitful contact with each other rather than either leaving them in a state of zero-sum opposition or simply bracketing all their differences. This is a matter of putting the tools on the table for cooperative mutual adjustment rather than merely leaving them out of the picture for the sake of a shallow consensus on policy. The overall point, however, is that if what I have said in this book is right then the boxes labelled 'alienation' and 'nature' are sources of useful tools that, when suitably adjusted, help to structure deliberation about the environmental crisis in fruitful ways. At least provisionally: further deterioration, or improvement, in the situation might require further adjustments or entirely new lenses.

References

Abram, David 1996. *The Spell of the Sensuous*. New York: Vintage Books.
——2007. 'Earth in Eclipse', in Suzanne Cataldi and William S. Hamrick (eds.), *Merleau-Ponty and Environmental Philosophy: Dwelling in the Landscapes of Thought*. Albany: SUNY Press, pp. 149–76.
Athanasiou, Thomas and Baer, Paul 2002. *Dead Heat: Global Justice and Global Warming*. New York: Seven Stories Press.
Barry, Brian 1999. 'Sustainability and Intergenerational Justice', in Andrew Dobson (ed.), *Fairness and Futurity: Essays on Environmental Sustainability and Social Justice*. Oxford University Press, pp. 93–117.
Baxter, Brian 2005. *A Theory of Ecological Justice*. London: Routledge.
Bell, Derek 2008. 'Carbon Justice? The Case Against a Universal Right to Equal Carbon Emissions', in Sarah Wilks (ed.), *Seeking Environmental Justice*. Amsterdam: Rodopi, pp. 239–57.
——2011. 'Does Anthropogenic Climate Change Violate Human Rights?', *Critical Review of International Social and Political Philosophy* 14(2): 99–124.
Belsey, Andrew 1994. 'Chaos and Order, Environment and Anarchy', in Robin Attfield and Andrew Belsey (eds.), *Philosophy and the Natural Environment*. Cambridge University Press, pp. 157–67.
Bennett, Jane 2010. *Vibrant Matter: A Political Ecology of Things*. Duke University Press.
Benton, Ted 1992. 'Ecology, Socialism and the Mastery of Nature: A Reply to Reiner Grundmann', *New Left Review* 194(1): 55–74.
——(ed.) 1996. *The Greening of Marxism*. New York: Guilford Press.
——2001. 'Why Are Sociologists Naturephobes?' in Jose Lopez and Gary Potter (eds.), *After Postmodernism: An Introduction to Critical Realism*. London: Athlone, pp. 133–45.
Bernstein, Richard 2010. *The Pragmatic Turn*. Cambridge: Polity.
Biro, Andrew 2005. *Denaturalizing Ecological Politics: Alienation from Nature from Rousseau to the Frankfurt School and Beyond*. University of Toronto Press.
——2011. 'Introduction: The Paradoxes of Contemporary Environmental Crises and the Redemption of the Hopes of the Past', in Andrew Biro (ed.), *Critical Ecologies: The Frankfurt School and Contemporary Environmental Crises*. University of Toronto Press, pp. 3–19.
Brook, Isis 2005. 'Can Merleau-Ponty's Notion of "Flesh" Inform or even Transform Environmental Thinking?', *Environmental Values* 14(3): 353–62.

254   References

Brown, Charles S. and Toadvine, Ted 2003. 'Eco-phenomenology: An Introduction', in Charles S. Brown and Ted Toadvine (eds.), *Eco-Phenomenology: Back to the Earth Itself*. Albany: SUNY Press, pp. ix–xxi.

Brubaker, Elizabeth 1995. *Property Rights in the Defence of Nature*. London and Toronto: Earthscan.

Callicott, J. Baird 1986. 'The Metaphysical Implications of Ecology', *Environmental Ethics* 8(4): 301–16.

——2002. 'Environmental Philosophy Is Environmental Activism: The Most Radical and Effective Kind', in David Schmidtz and Elizabeth Willott (eds.), *Environmental Ethics: What Really Matters, What Really Works*. Oxford University Press, pp. 546–56.

Callicott, J. Baird, Grove-Fanning, William, Rowland, Jennifer, Baskind, Daniel, Heath French, Robert and Walker, Kerry 2011. 'Reply to Norton, re: Aldo Leopold and Pragmatism', *Environmental Values* 20(1): 17–22.

Caney, Simon 2009. 'Human Rights, Responsibilities and Climate Change', in Charles R. Beitz and Robert E. Goodin (eds.), *Global Basic Rights*. Oxford University Press, pp. 227–47.

Cannavò, Peter 2007. *The Working Landscape, Founding, Preservation and the Politics of Place*. Cambridge, MA: MIT Press.

Carter, Alan 1989. *The Philosophical Foundations of Property Rights*. Hemel Hempstead: Harvester Wheatsheaf.

Cataldi, Suzanne L. and Hamrick, William S. (eds.) 2007. *Merleau-Ponty and Environmental Philosophy: Dwelling in the Landscapes of Thought*. Albany: SUNY Press.

Cerbone, David R. 2008. 'Perception', in Rosalyn Diprose and Jack Reynalds (eds.), *Merleau-Ponty: Key Concepts*. Stocksfield: Acumen, pp. 121–31.

Challenger, Melanie 2011. *On Extinction: How We Became Estranged From Nature*. London: Granta Books.

Chenu, Marie-Dominque 1997. 'Nature and Man – the Renaissance of the Twelfth Century', in Lester K. Little (ed. and trans.) and Jerome Taylor (ed.), *Nature, Man and Society in the Twelfth Century*. Toronto University Press, pp. 1–48.

Clarke, Melissa 2002. 'Ontology, Ethics and Sentir: Properly Situating Merleau-Ponty', *Environmental Values* 11: 211–25.

Cook, Deborah 2011. *Adorno on Nature*. Durham: Acumen.

Costanza, Robert, d'Arge, Ralph, de Groot, Rudolf, Farber, Stephen, Grasso, Monica, Hannon, Bruce, Limburg, Karin, Naeem, Shahid, O'Neill, Robert V., Paruelo, Jose, Raskin, Robert G., Sutton, Paul and van den Belt, Marjan 1997. 'The Value of the World's Ecosystem Services and Natural Capital', *Nature* 387:253–60.

Cowen, Tyler 2003. 'Policing Nature', *Environmental Ethics* 25: 169–82.

Cripps, Elizabeth 2010. 'Saving the Polar Bear, Saving the World: Can the Capability Approach do Justice to Humans, Animals and Ecosystems?', *Res Publica* 16: 1–22.

Crist, Eileen 2004. 'Against the Social Construction of Nature and Wilderness', *Environmental Ethics* 26(1): 5–24.

Cronon, William 1995. 'The Trouble with Wilderness; or, Getting Back to the Wrong Nature', in William Cronon (ed.), *Uncommon Ground: Rethinking the Human Place in Nature*. New York: W.W. Norton & Co., pp. 69–90.

References 255

Crutzen, Paul 2002. 'Geology of Mankind', *Nature* 415: 3.

Davidson, Marc 2014. 'Rights to Ecosystem Services', *Environmental Values* 23(4): 335–52.

di Paola, Marcello 2013. 'Environmental Stewardship, Moral Psychology and Gardens', *Environmental Values* 22(4): 503–21.

Dennett, Daniel C. 1991. *Consciousness Explained*. London: Penguin.

Dewey, John 1929. *The Quest for Certainty*. London: Allen and Unwin.

——1958. *Experience and Nature*, 2nd edn. New York: Dover.

——2004. *Reconstruction in Philosophy*. Mineola, NY: Dover Press.

Diamond, Jared 1987. 'The Worst Mistake in Human History?', *Discover*, May: 64–6.

Dobson, Andrew 2003. *Citizenship and the Environment*. Oxford University Press.

Dreyfus, Hubert L. 2007. 'Response to McDowell', *Inquiry* 50(4): 371–7.

Dupré, John 2001. *Human Nature and the Limits of Science*. Oxford University Press.

Eckersley, Robyn 1992. *Environmentalism and Political Theory: Towards an Ecocentric Approach*. London: UCL Press.

Elliot, Robert 1992. 'Intrinsic Value, Environmental Obligation and Naturalness', *The Monist* 75(2): 138–60.

——(ed.) 1995. *Environmental Ethics*. Oxford University Press.

Ellis, Erle 2011. 'Anthropogenic Transformation of the Terrestrial Biosphere', *Philosophical Transactions of the Royal Society A: Mathematical, Physical and Engineering Sciences* 369: 1010–35.

Evanoff, Richard J. 2005. 'Reconciling Realism and Constuctivism in Environmental Ethics', *Environmental Values* 14: 61–81.

Evans, Fred 2008. 'Chiasm and Flesh', in Rosalyn Diprose and Jack Reynolds (eds.), *Merleau-Ponty: Key Concepts*. Stocksfield: Acumen, pp. 184–93.

Evernden, Neil 1992. *The Social Construction of Nature*. Johns Hopkins University Press.

——1993. *The Natural Alien: Humankind and Environment*, 2nd edn. University of Toronto Press.

Fanon, Frantz 2008. *Black Skin, White Masks*, Charles L. Markmann (trans.). London: Pluto Press.

Fraser, Nancy 1997. *Justice Interruptus: Critical Reflections on the 'Postsocialist' Condition*. New York: Routledge.

Gardiner, Stephen 2006. 'A Perfect Moral Storm: Intergenerational Ethics and the Problem of Moral Corruption', *Environmental Values* 15(3): 397–413.

Geras, Norman 1995. *Solidarity in the Conversation of Mankind: The Ungroundable Liberalism of Richard Rorty*. London: Verso.

Goodin, Robert, E 1992. *Green Political Theory*. Cambridge: Polity Press.

Gray, Kevin 1991. 'Property in Thin Air', *Cambridge Law Journal* 50(2): 252–307.

Green, Karen 1996. 'Two Distinctions in Environmental Goodness', *Environmental Values* 51(1): 31–46.

The Guardian 2011. 'People Out of Touch With Nature, Warns Sir David Attenborough', www.guardian.co.uk/tv-and-radio/2011/dec/01/nature-urbanisation-david-attenborough (accessed 10 September 2014).

Guha, Ramachandra 1989. 'Radical American Environmentalism and Wilderness Preservation: A Third World Critique', *Environmental Ethics* 11: 71–83.

256   References

Gunster, Shane 2011. 'Fear and the Unknown: Nature, Culture and the Limits of Reason', in Andrew Biro (ed.), *Critical Ecologies: The Frankfurt School and Contemporary Environmental Crises*. University of Toronto Press, pp. 206–28.

Habermas, Jürgen 1988. *The Philosophical Discourse of Modernity*. Cambridge: Polity.

——1999. 'From Kant to Hegel and Back Again: The Move Toward Detranscendentalization', *European Journal of Philosophy* 7(2): 129–57.

Hacking, Ian 1999. *The Social Construction of What?* Harvard University Press.

Hailwood, Simon 2004. *How to Be a Green Liberal: Nature, Value and Liberal Philosophy*. Chesham: Acumen.

——2012. 'Bewildering Nussbaum: Capability Justice and Predation', *The Journal of Political Philosophy* 20(3): 293–313.

Hayward, Tim 1998. *Political Theory and Ecological Values*. Cambridge: Polity Press.

Hegel, G.W.F. 1977. *Phenomenology of Spirit*, trans. A.V. Miller. Oxford University Press.

——1991. *Elements of the Philosophy of Right*, trans. H.B. Nesbitt, ed. A. Wood. Cambridge University Press.

Hettinger, Ned and Throop, William 1999. 'Refocusing Ecocentrism: De-emphasizing Stability and Defending Wildness', *Environmental Ethics* 21(1): 3–21.

Heyd, Thomas (ed.) 2005. *Recognizing the Autonomy of Nature: Theory and Practice*. Columbia University Press.

Honneth, Axel 1995. *The Stuggle for Recognition: The Moral Grammar of Social Conflicts*. Cambridge, MA: MIT Press.

——2008. *Reification: A New Look at an Old Idea, with Judith Butler, Raymond Geuss and Jonathan Lear*, ed. Martin Jay. Oxford University Press.

Hood, Robert 1998. 'Rorty and Postmodern Environmental Ethics: Recontextualising Narrative, Reason and Representation', *Environmental Ethics* 20(2): 183–93.

Hourdequin, Marion 2011. 'Climate Change and Individual Responsibility: A Reply to Johnson', *Environmental Values* 20(2): 157–62.

Hume, David 1969. *A Treatise of Human Nature*. Harmondsworth: Penguin.

James, Simon 2007. 'Merleau-Ponty, Metaphysical Realism and Nature', *International Journal of Philosophical Studies* 15(4): 501–19.

James, William 1912. *Essays in Radical Empiricism*. London: Longmans, Green & Co.

——1956. *The Will to Believe and Other Essays in Popular Philosophy*. New York: Dover Publications.

——1977. *A Pluralistic Universe*. Harvard University Press.

Jay, Martin 2008. 'Introduction', in Axel Honneth, *Reification: A New Look at an Old Idea, with Judith Butler, Raymond Geuss and Jonathan Lear*. Oxford University Press, pp. 3–16.

Johnson, Alan 1998. 'The Affinities of Richard Rorty and Edward Bellamy', *Radical Philosophy* 91: 33–6.

Johnson, Baylor 2011. 'The Possibility of a Joint Communiqué: My Response to Hourdequin', *Environmental Values* 20(2): 147–56.

References

257

Joye, Yannick and De Block, Andreas 2011. 'Nature and I Are Two: A Critical Examination of the Biophilia Hypothesis', *Environmental Values* 20(2): 189–215.

Juniper, Tony 2013. *What Has Nature Ever Done For Us? How Money Really Does Grow on Trees*. London: Profile Books.

Keeling, Paul 2008. 'Does the Idea of Wilderness Need a Defence?', *Environmental Values* 17(4): 505–19.

Kellert, Stephen R. and Wilson, Edward O. (eds.) 1993. *The Biophilia Hypothesis*. Washington, DC: Island Press.

Kirchhoff, Thomas and Vicenzotti, Vera 2014. 'A Historical and Systematic Survey of European Perceptions of Wilderness', *Environmental Values* 23(4): 443–64.

Kirkman, Robert 2007. 'A Little Knowledge of Dangerous Things: Human Vulnerability in a Changing Climate', in Suzanne Cataldi and William S. Hamrick (eds.), *Merleau-Ponty and Environmental Philosophy: Dwelling in the Landscapes of Thought*. Albany: SUNY Press, pp. 19–36.

Knight, Carl 2014. 'Moderate Emissions Grandfathering', *Environmental Values*.

Knowles, Dudley 2002. *Hegel and the Philosophy of Right*. London: Routledge.

Korsgaard, Christine 1983. 'Two Distinctions in Goodness', *The Philosophical Review* 92(2): 169–95.

Larmore, Charles 1987. *Patterns of Moral Complexity*. Cambridge University Press.

Lease, Gary 1995. 'Introduction: Nature Under Fire', in Michael E. Soulé and Gary Lease (eds.), *Reinventing Nature? Responses to Postmodern Deconstruction*. Washington, DC: Island Press, pp. 3–16.

Lee, Keekok 1994. 'Awe and Humility: Intrinsic Value in Nature. Beyond an Earthbound Environmental Ethics', in Robin Attfield and Andrew Belsey (eds.), *Philosophy and the Natural Environment*. Cambridge University Press, pp. 89–102.

Lewis, Clive S. 1967. *Studies in Words*, 2nd edn. Cambridge University Press.

Liberman, Kenneth 2007. 'An Inquiry into Intercorporeal Relations Between Humans and the Earth', in Suzanne Cataldi and William S. Hamrick (eds.), *Merleau-Ponty and Environmental Philosophy: Dwelling in the Landscapes of Thought*. Albany: SUNY Press, pp. 37–50.

Light, Andrew and Katz, Eric (eds.) 1996. *Environmental Pragmatism*. London: Routledge.

Llewelyn, John 2003. 'Prolegomena to Any Future Phenomenological Ecology', in Charles S. Brown and Ted Toadvine (eds.), *Eco-Phenomenology: Back to the Earth Itself*. Albany: SUNY Press, pp. 51–72.

Llinás, Rodolfo 1987. 'Mindedness as a Functional State of the Brain', in Colin Blakemore and Susan Greenfield (eds.), *Mindwaves: Thoughts on Intelligence, Identity and Consciousness*. Oxford: Basil Blackwell.

Locke, John 1960. *Two Treatises of Government*, ed. Peter Laslett. Cambridge University Press.

Lopez, Jose and Potter, Gary (eds.) 2001. *After Postmodernism: An Introduction to Critical Realism*. London: Athlone.

Louv, Richard 2010. *Last Child in the Woods: Saving Our Children from Nature-Deficit Disorder*. London: Atlantic Books.

258   References

Lukács, Georg 1971. 'Reification and the Consciousness of the Proletariat', in Georg Lukács (ed.), Rodney Livingstone (trans.), *History and Class Consciousness*, new edition. London: Merlin Press.

Malachowski, Alan 2002. *Richard Rorty*. Chesham: Acumen.

Martin, D. Bruce 2011. 'Sacred Identity and the Sacrificial Spirit: Mimesis and Radical Ecology', in Andrew Biro (ed.), *Critical Ecologies: The Frankfurt School and Contemporary Environmental Crises*. University of Toronto Press, pp. 111–38.

Markandya, Anil, Taylor, Tim, Longo, Alberto, Murty, M.N., Murty, S. and Dhavala, K. 2008. 'Counting the Cost of Vulture Decline – An Appraisal of the Human Health and Other Benefits of Vultures in India', *Ecological Economics* 67(2): 194–204.

Marx, Karl 2007. *Economic and Philosophic Manuscripts of 1844*, trans. and ed. Martin Milligan. New York: Dover.

Matthews, Eric 2002. *The Philosophy of Merleau-Ponty*. Chesham: Acumen.

McKibben, Bill 1990. *The End of Nature*. London: Viking.

McLellan, David (ed.) 2000. *Karl Marx: Selected Writings*, 2nd edn. Oxford University Press.

Merleau-Ponty, Maurice 1968. *The Visible and the Invisible, Followed by Working Notes*, ed. Claude Lefort, trans. Alphonso Lingis. Northwestern University Press.

——2002. *Phenomenology of Perception*, trans. Colin Smith. London: Routledge.

Mészáros, István 2005. *Marx's Theory of Alienation*, 5th edn. London: Merlin Press.

Midgley, Mary 1996a. 'Earth Matters', in Sarah Dunant and Roy Porter (eds.), *The Age of Anxiety*. London: Virago.

——1996b. *Utopias, Dolphins and Computers*. London: Routledge.

Mill, John Stuart 1904. 'On Nature', in *Nature, the Utility of Religion and Theism*. London: Rationalist Press, pp. 7–34.

——2004. *Principles of Political Economy*. Amherst: Prometheus Books.

Minteer, Ben A. 2012. *Refounding Environmental Ethics: Pragmatism, Principle and Practice*. Temple University Press.

Naess, Arne 1973. 'The Shallow and the Deep, Long Range Ecology Movement: A Summary', *Inquiry* 16: 95–100.

——1990. '"Man Apart" and Deep Ecology: A Reply to Peter Reed', *Environmental Ethics* 12: 185–92.

Nagel, Thomas 1991. *Equality and Partiality*. Oxford University Press.

Nolt, John 2013. 'Anthropocentrism and Egoism', *Environmental Values* 22(4): 441–59.

Norton, Bryan 1984. 'Environmental Ethics and Weak Anthropocentrism', *Environmental Ethics* 6(2): 131–48.

Norton, Bryan and Hannon, Bruce 1998. 'Democracy and Sense of Place Values', *Philosophy and Geography* 3: 119–46.

Nozick, Robert 1974. *Anarchy, State and Utopia*. Oxford: Basil Blackwell.

Nussbaum, Martha 2006. *Frontiers of Justice: Disability, Nationality, Species Membership*. Harvard University Press.

O'Neill, John 2012. 'Editorial: the Ethics of Engineering', *Environmental Values* 21(1): 1–4

Patten, Alan 1999. *Hegel's Idea of Freedom*. Oxford University Press.

References

259

Peterson, Anna 1999. 'Environmental Ethics and the Social Construction of Nature', *Environmental Ethics* 21(4): 339–57.

Plumwood, Val 1993. *Feminism and the Mastery of Nature*. London: Routledge.

——1995. 'Nature, Self and Gender: Feminism, Environmental Philosophy and the Critique of Rationalism', in Robert Elliot (ed.), *Environmental Ethics*. Oxford University Press, pp. 155–64.

——2002. *Environmental Culture: The Ecological Crisis of Reason*. London: Routledge.

——2006. 'The Concept of a Cultural Landscape: Nature, Culture and Agency in the Land', *Ethics & The Environment* 11(2): 115–50.

Rawls, John 1971. *A Theory of Justice*. Harvard University Press.

——1985. 'Justice as Fairness: Political Not Metaphysical', *Philosophy and Public Affairs* 14(3): 223–51.

——1996. *Political Liberalism*, 2nd edn. Columbia University Press.

——2001. *Justice as Fairness: A Restatement*. Harvard University Press.

Reed, Peter 1989. 'Man Apart: An Alternative to the Self-realisation Approach', *Environmental Ethics* 11: 53–69.

Regan, Tom 1983. *The Case for Animal Rights*. University of California Press.

Rolston, Holmes 1979. 'Can and Ought We to Follow Nature?', *Environmental Ethics* 1: 7–30.

——1995. 'Does Aesthetic Appreciation of Landscape Need to Be Science Based?', *British Journal of Aesthetics* 25(4): 374–86.

——1997. 'Nature for Real: Is Nature a Social Construct?', in Timothy Chappell (ed.), *The Philosophy of the Environment*. Edinburgh University Press, pp. 38–64.

Rorty, Richard 1980. *Philosophy and the Mirror of Nature*. Princeton University Press.

——1982. *Consequences of Pragmatism*. University of Minnesota Press.

——1989. *Contingency, Irony and Solidarity*. Cambridge University Press.

——1998. *Truth and Progress: Philosophical Papers III*. Cambridge University Press.

——1999. *Philosophy and Social Hope*. Harmondsworth: Penguin.

Rowlands, Mark 2000. *The Environmental Crisis: Understanding the Value of Nature*. Basingstoke: Macmillan.

Ryle, Gilbert 1971. 'On Forgetting the Difference Between Right and Wrong', in Gilbert Ryle (ed.), *Collected Papers Volume 2*. London: Hutchinson.

Sale, Kirkpatrick 1985. *Dwellers in the Land: The Bioregional Vision*. San Francisco: Sierra Book Club.

Schlosberg, David 2007. *Defining Environmental Justice: Theories, Movements and Nature*. Oxford University Press.

——2012. 'Climate Justice and Capabilities: a Framework for Adaptation', *Ethics & International Affairs* 26(4): 445–561.

Schmidtz, David and Willott, Elizabeth (eds.) 2002. *Environmental Ethics: What Really Matters, What Really Works*. Oxford University Press.

Shue, Henry 1998. 'Bequeathing Hazards: Security Rights and Property Rights of Future Generations', in Mohammed Dore and Timothy Mount (eds.), *Global Environmental Economics: Equity and the Limits of Markets*. Oxford: Wiley-Blackwell, pp. 38–53.

Singer, Peter 1979. *Practical Ethics*. Cambridge University Press.

——2004. *One World: The Ethics of Globalization*. Yale University Press.

260 References

Smith, Mick 2011. *Against Ecological Sovereignty: Ethics, Biopolitics and Saving the Natural World*. University of Minnesota Press.

Soper, Kate 1995. *What Is Nature?* Oxford: Blackwell.

Soulé, Michael E. and Lease, Gary (eds.) 1995. *Reinventing Nature? Responses to Postmodern Deconstruction*. Washington, DC: Island Press.

Steffen, Will, Crutzen, Paul and McNeill, John 2007. 'The Anthropocene: Are Humans Now Overwhelming the Great Forces of Nature?' *Ambio* 36(8): 614–21.

Stephens, Piers 2000. 'Nature, Purity and Ontology', *Environmental Values* 9(3): 267–94.

Stone, Alison 2005. *Petrified Intelligence: Nature in Hegel's Philosophy*. Albany: SUNY Press.

——2006. 'Adorno and the Disenchantment of Nature', *Philosophy and Social Criticism* 32(2): 231–53.

Taylor, Charles 2004. 'Merleau-Ponty and the Epistemological Picture', in Taylor Carman and Mark B.N. Hansen (eds.), *The Cambridge Companion to Merleau-Ponty*. Cambridge University Press, pp. 26–49.

Taylor, Paul 1986. *Respect for Nature: A Theory of Environmental Ethics*. Princeton University Press.

Toadvine, Ted 2009. *Merleau-Ponty's Philosophy of Nature*. Evanston: Northwestern University Press.

Vogel, Steven 1996. *Against Nature: The Concept of Nature in Critical Theory*. Albany: SUNY Press.

——2002. 'Environmental Philosophy after the End of Nature', *Environmental Ethics* 24(1): 23–39.

——2011. 'On Alienation and Nature', in Andrew Biro (ed.), *Critical Ecologies: The Frankfurt School and Contemporary Environmental Crises*. University of Toronto Press, pp. 187–205.

Waldron, Jeremy 1988. *The Right to Private Property*. Oxford University Press.

White, Lynn. 1967. 'The Historical Roots of Our Ecological Crisis', *Science* 155: 1203–7.

Williams, Bernard 1973. 'A Critique of Utilitarianism', in J. J. C. Smart and Bernard Williams, *Utilitarianism For and Against*. Cambridge University Press, pp. 77–150.

Williams, Raymond 1980. *Problems in Materialism and Culture*. London: NLB.

——1990. *Keywords, a Vocabulary of Culture and Society*, revised edition. London: Fontana.

Wissenburg, Marcel 2011. 'The Lion and the Lamb: Ecological Implications of Martha Nussbaum's Animal Ethics', *Environmental Politics* 20(3): 391–410.

Woodcock, George 1977. *The Anarchist Reader*. London: Harvest Press.

——2004. *Anarchism*. University of Toronto Press.

Young, Iris Marion 1989. 'Throwing Like a Girl', in Jeffner Allen and Iris M. Young (eds.), *The Thinking Muse: Feminism and Modern French Philosophy*, Indianapolis: Indiana University Press, pp. 51–70.

——1990. *Justice and the Politics of Difference*. Princeton University Press.

Zalasiewicz, Jan, Williams, M., Fortey, R., Smith, A., Barry, T., Coe, A., Bown, P., Rawson, P., Gale, A., Gibbard, P., Gregory, F.J., Hounslow, M., Kerr,

References

A., Pearson, P., Knox, R., Knox, Powell J. Waters, C., Marshall, J., Oates, M. and Stone, P. 2011. 'Stratigraphy of the Anthropocene', *Philosophical Transactions of the Royal Society A: Mathematical, Physical and Engineering Sciences* 369: 1036–55.

Zerzan, John 1994. *Future Primitive and Other Essays.* New York: Autonomedia.

Index

Abram, David, 198, 213–15, 219
Adorno, Theodor, 98, 130–6, 151, *see also*
    Vogel, Steven on Adorno
alienation
    different senses of, 12–13, 16, *see also*
        alienation from nature, estrangement,
        Hegel, G.W.F., and alienation,
        Marx, Karl, and alienation, property
        alienation, reification
alienation from nature
    and environmental crisis, 1–2, 4, 6,
        9–13, 24, 26, 29, 38, 50, 69, 71, 102,
        107, 177–8, 184–5, 189, 197, 210–11,
        227, 232, 234, 248–52
    problems with the idea, 4, 6–10, 17,
        126, 186
    relations between different senses,
        11–12, 15–21, 31, 33, 39, 47, 80, 86,
        140, 153, 155, 185, 220, 223, 228,
        230–7, 241–2, 248, 250
    see also estrangement, property
        alienation, reification, pluralism, Biro,
        Andrew and alienation from nature
        Evernden, Neil and alienation from
        nature, Vogel, Steven and alienation
        from nature, and alienation from
        something like nature
Anthropocene, 4–5, 139, 147–8, 152, 176,
    184, 260–1
anthropocentric instrumentalism, 21,
    24–5, 29, 41–2, 46–7, 51, 60, 62,
    64, 70–1, 75, 77–8, 81–2, 98, 125,
    127, 139, 141, 146, 153, 155, 158–60,
    162–4, 168–9, 172–3, 175, 179–80,
    182, 186–7, 192, 204–5, 215–18, 225,
    229, 231–2, 237, 239–40, 242, 245
anthropocentric/nonanthropocentric, 1, 6,
    11, 13–15, 18, 20–1, 24, 38, 50, 52,
    58–62, 70–1, 74, 77, 79–80, 82–4,
    86, 102, 124–5, 129, 136, 145–6,
    155, 157–8, 172, 182, 185–6, 191,
    196, 199, 204–5, 207, 216, 218,

223, 232–3, 236, 248–9, *see also*
    anthropocentric instrumentalism
applied philosophy, 12, 23–4
Attenborough, David, 2

Bell, Derek, 104–5
Benton, Ted, 38, 65, 130, 136–41, 182,
    231, *see also* labour, ecoregulatory
Bernstein, Richard, 52–3, 56
biophilia hypothesis, 3, 37, 216, 245
biopiracy, 100, 119, 229
Biro, Andrew
    and alienation from nature, 7, 26–7, 30,
        38, 132
    and basic and surplus alienation from
        nature, 27, 30, 49, 121, 127
    on Rousseau, 7, 27, 30
Brook, Isis, 198, 207–8, 210, 219, 222
Brown, Charles, 195

Callicott, J. Baird, 23, 59, 61–2
Cannavò, Peter
    and practice of place, 88,
        117–20, 125–6
    and working landscape, 122–3, 141
capitalism, 28, 32, 38, 55, 77, 86, 95, 120,
    130, 137, 144, 183, 196, 231, 241
cartesianism, 21, 29–30, 35, 49, 52, 54, 64,
    84, 98, 143–4, 146, 196, 211
climate change, 1, 13, 20, 23, 87, 92, 101,
    104, 108–15, 122, 129, 143, 163, 176,
    178, 219, 228
    and justice, 13, 20, 102, 104–5, 109–10,
        116, 119, 121–2, 143, 163, 219, 229
critical refractor, 251
Cronon, William, 5, 47, 100, 104, 106,
    121, 193, 227, 254
Crutzen, Paul, 5

Darwinism, 67, 69–70, 79
deep ecology, 2, 22–3, 25, 132, 149,
    151, 221

Index

democracy, 50, 56, 67, 76–8, 80, 116–17, 119, 122–3, 125–6, 148, 181, 183, 229
Dewey, John, 50, 58–60, 66–7, 75–6, 78–9, 95, 190, 214
and certainty, 12, 51, 53
and natural piety, 81–2
Dobson, Andrew, 101, 110–11, 116
domination, 10–11, 14–15, 18–19, 49, 78, 127, 129–34, 136, 139–43, 145, 147–8, 153, 155–8, 162, 164–5, 174, 177, 180, 183, 185, 188–9, 197, 210–11, 215, 219, 225–6, 228–30, 232–4, 239, 248, 250

Eckersley, Robyn, 130–1, 177
eco-phenomenology, 195–8, 206–7, 210, 226, 230, see also phenomenology
egoism, 24, 37, 83, 125, 178, 209, 217
environmental philosophy, 2, 12, 16, 21, 38, 52, 58–61, 74, 127, 130, 158, 172, 249
critical, 12, 14–15, 24, 29, 39, 46, 49, 58, 60, 84–5, 143, 185–6, 189, 191–2, 196–7, 206, 210, 215, 221, 228, 230, 239, 251
estrangement
cognitive, 15, 18–19, 188–9, 191–2, 197, 209, 230, 232, 234–7, 239, 241–7
encouraged, 14, 17–20, 26, 31, 38, 47, 49, 62, 70–1, 73, 75, 81, 86, 88, 91, 116, 120–3, 125, 127–8, 130, 134, 136, 139–43, 145–50, 152–3, 155–9, 163–4, 174, 177, 180, 182, 184–5, 188, 223, 228–30, 232–3, 236, 240, 242, 246–7
idea of, 16–17, 26, 30–1, 33, 126
and justice, 13, 20, 86–8, 90–2, 107–8, 110, 116, 119, 121–2, 142–3, 145–6, 152, 155, 157–8, 164, 218, 220, 229, 232–3, 239, 247, 250
from landscape, 13–15, 17–20, 32, 39, 56, 61, 71, 82, 86–8, 92, 102, 107–8, 110–11, 114–17, 119–22, 124, 140–2, 147, 150, 164, 180–1, 206, 217, 223, 227–36, 239, 246–7
from nonhuman nature, 14, 17–21, 31, 34, 36, 38, 40, 49, 62, 70–1, 73–5, 81, 86, 124–8, 130, 133–6, 139–50, 152–3, 155–9, 163–4, 174–5, 177, 180, 182–3, 185, 187–9, 192, 206, 214, 220–1, 223, 228–33, 236, 240–3, 246–7, 250
from the natural world, 14–15, 17–20, 29, 31, 96, 141, 144–5, 147, 149, 153, 185–95, 197–8, 205–6, 209–10,

212–13, 215–16, 218–21, 223–4, 226–8, 230–6, 241–7
participatory, 15, 19, 186–7, 194, 196, 199, 209–10, 213–16, 218, 220–4, 226–8, 230, 232, 234–6, 241–3, 245–7
see also alienation from nature, Marx, Karl, marxism, property alienation, reification, otherness
Evernden, Neil, 21–2, 26, 30, 35, 49, 98, 212
and constructionism, 29, 31, 35, 38, 83–4
and natural aliens, 28–31, 84, 124, 211–13, 246
extensionism, 14, 144–9, 152–3, 218, 220

flesh, the, 19, 186–7, 190, 194, 198–9, 201, 206–11, 213–15, 217–22, 224–7, 234, 250, see also Merleau-Ponty, Maurice, and the flesh
Foreman, Dave, 5, 193
forgetting, 95, 190–6
foxes, 135–6, 150–1
Frankfurt School, 27, 130–4, 136, 141, see also Biro, Andrew
Fraser, Nancy, 88–9, 142–3, 219

Gardiner, Stephen, 110
geo-engineering, 6, 140
Goodin, Robert, 47, 142, 216
gulls, 40, 127–9, 138, 168, 235, 241

Habermas, Jurgen, 108–9, 122, 131, 169–70, 174–5, 177
Hegel, G. W. F., 13, 19, 54, 56, 76, 87, 108, 111, 113, 117, 119, 122, 160, 191
and absolute spirit, 18, 55, 108, 174–7
and abstract right, 160, 172–3, 182
and alienation, 4, 26, 31, 55
and nature, 172–3, 176
and objective spirit, 109, 113, 115, 169–77, 180, 214
and property, 14, 55, 113, 155, 158, 167, 169–73, 175, 177, 179, 181–2, 226
Honneth, Axel
on Lukács, 93–5, 97, 190
and primordiality, 95–7, 187, 190, 194, 214
and recognition, 88–9, 96–7, 99, 108, 160, 187, 190–1, 195, 214, 224
and reification, 92–7, 99, 108, 119, 160, 187, 190, 195, 201, 206, 209, 214, 218, 220, 224, 232, 235, 237
and reification of nature, 87, 95–9, 108, 114, 131, 159–60, 182, 191, 198

264　Index

Hume, David, 54, 57, 167

intrinsic value, 38, 52, 58–61, 74–5, 78,
80, 82–3, 129, 142, 146, 172, 196

James, Simon, 198, 201, 205, 207–8, 210
James, William, 50, 176
Juniper, Tony, 3, 15
and NDD, 3, 8, 243–5, 247
on what nature does for us, 236–9,
241, 243–4
justice
capability, 90, 147–8, 153, 218, 221
distributive, 20, 89–92, 102–5, 107–8,
110–11, 122, 142, 157–8, 163, 165,
229, 247
ecological, 18–19, 111, 143–6, 152, 155,
159, 164–5, 218, 220, 229–30, 232–3,
241, 250
environmental, 1, 13, 15, 43, 87, 102–3,
105, 107–10, 116, 119, 121, 123–4,
142, 163, 216, 227, 229, 233–4, 239,
241, 243, 247, 250
and personhood, 88–91, 102, 108, 157,
217, 226, 228
recognitional, 13–14, 20, 87–91,
99–100, 102–9, 111, 120–2, 142,
144–6, 152, 159, 164–5, 218, 220,
229–30
see also climate change and justice,
estrangement and justice, property
alienation and justice, reification and
justice

Kant, Immanuel, 45, 54, 76, 88, 90, 167,
169–70, 173, 199, 207
Katz, Eric, 58–9, 74
Korsgaard, Christine, 74

labour, 2, 7, 12, 18, 27, 32–4, 37, 39–40,
43, 55, 70, 94, 96, 100, 107, 109, 113,
116, 119, 124, 131–2, 136–40, 147,
152, 155, 157, 162–3, 166–9, 179,
181–3, 214, 225, 227–8, 231, 237,
239–40, 243, 246
alienation of, 4, 10, 32, 37, 55–6, 77,
86, 88, 91, 94, 107, 119–20, 139, 141,
157, 179, 181–2, 225, 231
ecoregulatory, 34, 136–41, 147, 239–40
landscape
and climate change, 87, 102, 104–5,
109–10, 114, 163, 228–9
idea of, 16, 40–2, 46–7, 64, 67, 69–70,
82, 86, 96, 109
and justice, 13, 43, 87–8, 92, 102–8,
110, 116, 119, 144, 163–4, 183,

216–17, 229, 231, 233, 239,
247, 250
as matter of degree, 12, 45–9, 72, 81,
83–4, 124, 134, 146, 152, 177, 187,
229, 235
as practice, 41–3, 46–7, 62–4, 68, 71,
79, 81, 87, 99, 108, 113, 117, 120,
122, 135, 139, 143, 148, 153, 159–60,
163, 165, 167–9, 173, 178, 188,
205–6, 215, 217, 240, 242, 250
as vehicle of recognition, 13, 70, 86–8,
97–108, 114, 116, 121, 124, 228–9
see also constructionism, estrangement
from landscape, Hegel, G. W. F., and
objective spirit, place, Plumwood, Val
and landscape, property alienation
and landscape, reification and
landscape
Lease, Gary, 38, 42–3
Lewis, C. S., 44–6, 67
Liberman, Kenneth, 207, 211, 217, 226–7
Light, Andrew, 58, 74
Locke, John, 14, 43, 109, 155, 166–8, 179
Lukács, Georg, 93–5, 97, 132, 190

Marx, Karl, 4, 27, 33, 42, 54–6, 130
and alienation, 26, 31–2, 56, 132
and domination of nature, 14, 130–1,
136–7, 140–1
see also estrangement, labour, property
alienation, reification
Marxism, 12, 14, 18, 32, 37–8, 57, 77,
86, 88, 91–4, 107, 109, 117, 119–20,
130, 136, 139–41, 157, 164, 178,
180–2, 214, 225, 229, 231, see also
Marx, Karl
McKibben, Bill, 47
Merleau-Ponty, Maurice, 15, 190, 194,
207, 211, 226
and embodied perception, 198, 200–7
and the flesh, 19, 186–7, 198–9, 206–8,
217, 219, 222, 250
and hyper-reflection, 199, 227
and perceptual faith, 199, 209
and primordiality, 198–208, 250
see also eco-phenomenology, the flesh,
phenomenology
Midgley, Mary, 22–3, 52, 110
Mill, John Stuart, 34–7, 44, 146, 167
Minteer, Ben
and Dewey, 59–60, 75–6, 78, 81–2
and environmental ethics, 58–9, 61,
82, 129
and environmental pragmatism, 51, 58,
60–1, 72, 81–2
see also Dewey, John, pragmatism

Index

265

Naess, Arne, 14, 132, 149, 151–2
natural world
  idea of, 16, 33, 38–9, 44–6, 133, 198,
    209, 232
  see also estrangement from the natural
    world, property alienation and the
    natural world, the flesh
nature
  construction of, 12–13, 30, 38–40, 43,
    47, 52, 54, 57, 61–5, 68–71, 73, 75,
    79, 83–5, 95, 127, 199, 204, 229
  end of, 47, 152, 176, 184, 229, 235
  and essentialism, 36–8, 74–5
  following, 34–8, 81
  see also nonhuman nature, natural world,
    landscape
nature deficit disorder (NDD), 2–3, 8, 15,
  215–17, 243–6, *see also* Juniper, Tony,
  and NDD
nonhuman nature
  as matter of degree, 12, 17, 46–7, 49, 72,
    127, 129, 134, 146, 149, 229, 235–6,
    242, 246
  idea of, 16, 33, 38–9, 42, 44, 46, 63, 67,
    69–70, 75, 79, 83, 126, 133, 135, 146
  recognition of, 14, 64, 70, 78–81, 143–7,
    152, 155–7, 159, 164–5, 168, 174,
    191–2, 218–21, 229, 231, 241, 245
  respect for, 11, 14, 19, 21, 52, 75, 79,
    81, 125–6, 129–30, 134, 136, 139–41,
    148, 182–3, 185–6, 242, 248, 250
  see also domination, estrangement from
    nonhuman nature, otherness, property
    alienation and nonhuman nature
Norton, Bryan, 58, 81–2
Nussbaum, Martha, 90, 92–3, 145–8, 153,
  218, 221

otherness, 17, 36, 42, 46–7, 55, 80, 83–4,
  98–9, 121, 125–9, 131–4, 144–6,
  150–3, 159, 174–5, 187–8, 192, 205,
  228–9, 232, 241, 249

phenomenology, 19, 22, 28–9, 44, 83,
  95, 110, 117, 186, 188, 190, 194–5,
  198–9, 201, 203–4, 206, *see also*
  Merleau-Ponty, Maurice
place, 13, 15, 20, 28–31, 79, 87–8, 105,
  107, 111, 117–23, 125–6, 129,
  149–50, 156–7, 176, 178, 206, 226,
  228–9, 233–4, 250
Plumwood, Val, 14, 22, 43, 47, 100, 106,
  134, 146, 149, 152, 211
  and constructionism, 25, 43, 47–8
  and deep ecology, 132, 149–51
  and landscape, 41, 47

and otherness, 150, 152
and Reed, 151–2
pluralism, 10–12, 15–16, 19–20, 25, 51,
  58, 67, 69, 72, 76, 79, 88, 103, 118,
  125, 142, 175, 183, 192, 223, 241,
  248–50, 252
pragmatism, 38–9, 56, 58, 95, 183,
  190, 197
  and anthropocentrism, 58, 60–2, 76–7,
    79–81, 232
  and constructionism, 13, 39, 62, 64–5,
    68–71, 73, 75, 83, 85
  and matters of degree, 49, 134, 203
  re-described goal, 76–7, 242
  starting from a practical problem, 12,
    24, 49–50, 53, 69, 177, 214, 252
  theories as tools, 12–13, 51–3, 62, 70,
    84, 252
  see also Dewey, John, Minteer, Ben,
    Norton, Bryan, Rorty, Richard,
    pluralism, quest for certainty
primitivism, 2, 5, 7, 22, 192–3
property, 15, 87, 125, 155–6, 158, 160,
  165, 169, 177–8, 229, 232
  collective, 14, 122, 161, 163,
    177, 180–3
  common, 14, 122, 156, 161, 163, 177,
    180, 183
  concept of, 160–4, 171, 175, 179–81
  private, 14, 27, 31–3, 77, 88, 91, 113,
    122, 139, 141, 156, 160–8, 170–2,
    177, 179–81, 183
  see also anthropocentric instrumentalism,
    Hegel, G. W. F. and property, Locke,
    John, justice and property, property
    alienation
property alienation
  encouraged, 14, 17–18, 20, 25, 33, 38,
    49, 62, 70–1, 75, 125, 155–8, 164–5,
    168, 174, 177–8, 180, 182–3, 185,
    187, 223, 229–30, 232
  idea of, 16, 25, 31–2, 155, 229
  and justice, 13, 87, 91–2, 119–20, 155,
    157–8, 162, 164, 229, 231, 233
  and landscape, 15, 17, 71, 82, 86–7, 92,
    114, 142, 154, 158, 162, 187, 217,
    223, 225, 227, 229, 231–3
  and nonhuman nature, 14, 17–18,
    20, 33, 40, 49, 62, 70–1, 75,
    125, 154–8, 164–5, 168, 174–5,
    177–8, 180, 182–3, 185, 187, 223,
    229–30, 232
  and the natural world, 17, 230, 232
  see also alienation from nature, Hegel,
    G. W. F. and property, Marx, Karl,
    marxism, property

266   Index

quest for certainty, 51–4, 56, 58–9, 61–2,
    114, 134–6, 197, 209, 214, 252,
    see also Dewey, John, pragmatism

Rawls, John, 72, 89–90, 122, 175
Reed, Peter, 14, 132, 149, 151–3
Regan, Tom, 146
reification
    idea of, 16, 32–3, 36, 38–9, 55, 79, 96,
        98–9, 162, 228
    and justice, 87–8, 90–3, 102, 104–8,
        110, 116, 119, 124, 142, 158, 183,
        217, 229
    and landscape, 13, 15, 17, 32, 43, 69,
        71, 82, 86–7, 96–102, 104–8, 110,
        115–19, 124–5, 142, 154, 162, 164,
        166, 181, 187, 191, 223, 227, 229–30,
        232–3, 237, 246
    see also alienation from nature,
        constructionism, Honneth, Axel,
        Marx, Karl, Marxism, Vogel, Steven
        and alienation from something
        like nature
Rolston, Holmes, 35–6, 38, 41, 44,
    59, 65, 69
Rorty, Richard, 39, 51, 74, 76–8
    and anthropocentric instrumentalism,
        70–1, 73, 76–9
    and constructionism, 66–71
    and neopragmatism, 65–9, 78, 80, 85
    and platonism, 66, 68–70, 72, 77–8,
        80, 83
    see also Dewey, John, pragmatism
Rousseau, Jean-Jacques, 1, 7, 22, 26–7,
    30–1, *see also* Biro, Andrew on
    Rousseau
Ryle, Gilbert, 193

savannah hypothesis, 3, 8, 37, 216
Schlosberg, David, 87, 148

and ecological justice, 143, 145, 218–19
and environmental justice, 101, 103
and recognition of nature, 89, 142–3,
    145, 152, 219–20
and recognitional justice, 89, 103,
    105, 220
sea squirts, 53, 57, 59, 61–2, 134–6, 142,
    176, 197
Singer, Peter, 79, 104
Smith, Adam, 27, 33, 37
Smith, Mick, 1, 22, 26, 35, 127, 144, 146,
    193, 198
Soper, Kate, 38, 43–4
sprawl, 20, 118–20, 124, 229
Stone, Alison, 133, 172–4

Taylor, Paul, 146
Toadvine, Ted, 195, 198, 207, 210, 222

Vogel, Steven, 194
    and Adorno, 131–4
    and alienation from nature, 7–10, 17,
        30, 126, 132–4, 186
    and alienation from something like
        nature, 10, 33, 54, 56, 113, 127, 133
    and constructionism, 12, 38, 40, 54, 56,
        61, 63, 114
    and Hegel and Marx, 55–6
vultures, 237–8, 240–1, 243

Waldron, Jeremy, 160–3, 171, 181, 183
White Jr, Lynn, 22
wilderness, 2, 5, 42–3, 47, 70, 83, 100,
    104, 106, 108, 117–19, 121, 124, 129,
    148, 152, 166, 183, 224, 226–8, 233,
    247, 249
Williams, Bernard, 112
Williams, Raymond, 25–6, 31–2, 43, 110

Young, Iris Marion, 88, 117, 120, 204

Printed in the United States
By Bookmasters